# Rethinking Orphanages for the 21st Century

# Rethinking
# Orphanages
## for the 21st
# Century

Edited by
## Richard B. McKenzie

**SAGE Publications**
*International Educational and Professional Publisher*
Thousand Oaks   London   New Delhi

*For information:*

SAGE Publications, Inc.
2455 Teller Road
Thousand Oaks, California 91320
E-mail: order@sagepub.com

SAGE Publications Ltd.
6 Bonhill Street
London EC2A 4PU
United Kingdom

SAGE Publications India Pvt. Ltd.
M-32 Market
Greater Kailash I
New Delhi 110 048 India

Printed in the United States of America

*Library of Congress Cataloging-in-Publication Data*

Main entry under title:

Rethinking orphanages for the 21st century/edited by Richard B. McKenzie.
    p.  cm.
    Includes bibliographical references and index.
    ISBN 0-7619-1443-9 (cloth: acid-free paper)
    ISBN 0-7619-1444-7 (pbk.: acid-free paper)
    1. Orphanages—United States—History.  2. Orphanages—Government policy—United States.  3. Foster home care—United States.  I. McKenzie, Richard B.  II. Title: Rethinking orphanages for the twenty-first century.
    HV983 .R48  1998
    362.73'2—ddc21                      98-19673

99  00  01  02  03  04  10  9  8  7  6  5  4  3  2

| | |
|---|---|
| *Acquiring Editor:* | Margaret Zusky |
| *Editorial Assistant:* | Corinne Pierce |
| *Production Editor:* | Wendy Westgate |
| *Production Assistant:* | Nevair Kabakian |
| *Typesetter/Designer:* | Marion S. Warren |
| *Cover Designer:* | Candice Harman |

# Contents

# Foreword

An enthusiastic "Y'know what I'm gonna be?!" is a frequent comment I hear from young people living in "orphanages," "children's homes," "residential boarding schools," and "youth villages" in the United States and in other countries. The excitement of so many of these children about their promising futures is the strongest impression remaining from my visits to more than 30 programs. Almost without exception, however, these young people are from economically and socially disadvantaged backgrounds. Only the students in "prep" schools come from "advantaged" backgrounds. Most had entered their residential programs with little self-esteem and few prospects for a productive future.

Why, then, are long-term residential environments for at-risk children and youth so poorly viewed by people in the United States? Why is it considered acceptable, if not attractive, to send a young person from a supportive, affluent family away to a residential boarding school, whereas it is considered destructive to send a young person from an unsafe, unhealthy home environment to a nurturing, educational, residential setting? Because of popular imagery of past orphanage life, now well out of date, many residential education programs have folded during the past four or five decades. There are now few education-focused, residential settings available for young people, especially adolescents, who have neither homes that can support them nor schools that can effectively teach them. There are, however, tens of thousands of children who could benefit from such care.

*Rethinking Orphanages for the 21st Century* provides the foundation for a real national policy debate. The short-lived, sound-bite-based national policy debate on orphanage care that took place in late 1994 was, regrettably, founded on old orphanage stereotypes. House Speaker Newt Gingrich extolled the 1930s movie *Boys Town*, whereas his critics in the Clinton administration countered with visions of orphanages in London in the late 1800s, as depicted in Charles Dickens's novel *Oliver Twist*. Major newsmagazines supported these popular stereotypes with turn-of-the-century pictures of pathetic orphanage residents on their covers. The debate lasted only a few months. The critics claimed victory once again, and nothing was done.

This edited volume is the first attempt to rethink critical issues relating to the long-term residential education of at-risk, disadvantaged young people. One contributor evaluates the current dreadful state of care for many American children. Another contributor evaluates the scholarly literature relating to orphanage care and finds much of it wanting. Yet another contributor does what the critics have not done—surveys orphanage alumni about how they have done in life and how they look back on their experiences. The orphanage critics will be surprised with what this author found: The orphanage alumni have done quite well! Other contributors assess the obstacles to bringing back some modern form of permanent residential education for children. Unfortunately, the reality of residential education settings—as distinct from carefully crafted Washington-based and Hollywood-based portrayals of them—has never been described in the depth presented here.

In the United States, residential possibilities for disadvantaged young people include the following:

- Treatment centers for emotionally troubled children
- Juvenile detention facilities
- Foster care

These options are suitable and beneficial for some young people, and they are available in most communities. What are all too often missing in the list are residential settings that prevent further serious emotional deterioration and self-destructive behavior. What are also missing are healthy, structured, affordable settings in which young people can live for periods longer than a few months and can begin to believe that they "belong" and matter to a community. The name we give these settings—orphanages, children's homes, children's villages, or residential schools—is unimportant. What is important is that the settings allow the children in their care to develop for long stretches of time away from their otherwise corrosive neighborhoods and dysfunctional families.

Residential education settings also tend to be more affordable than detention facilities, treatment centers, and some types of foster care largely because they do not use and do not need a plethora of expensive, highly trained psychiatrists and social workers. They can also be effective because the children are in residence for long stretches of time and do not have to endure repeated cycles of multiple placements in the foster-care system. Make no mistake about it: There is a crying need in the United States for settings that can offer many disadvantaged children a sense of permanence, stability, and security. What residential education programs currently exist in the United States? There are two state-run programs, in Indiana and Pennsylvania, for children of military veterans. The only federal programs for at-risk children and youth under the age of 16 are the network of residential schools for Native Americans, now largely run by Native Americans themselves, and the National Guard's Challenge Program. The federal government's Job Corps Program is for low-income, 16- to 24-year-olds. There is a smattering of privately funded programs—the Milton Hershey School and Girard College in Pennsylvania, the Connie Maxwell Home for Children in South Carolina, Boys Home in Virginia, and Girls and Boys Country in Texas; a few African American boarding schools; and a handful of settings begun as orphanages that have survived and kept their missions intact. These are few and far between, given the magnitude of the need.

New residential education programs are beginning to open throughout the country. Some homes are privately funded. For example, in 1993, the American Honda Education Corporation opened the Eagle Rock School in Colorado. SOS Children's Villages, Incorporated has opened homes in Florida and Illinois. Public and private home partnerships have merged: The Boston University Residential Charter School opened in September 1997. New residential charter schools are opening in New Jersey and the District of Columbia. As of this writing (fall 1997), the Pennsylvania legislature was considering passage of the Residential Education Act of the Commonwealth of Pennsylvania, under which three new residential schools would be developed. In addition, a few private, nonprofit organizations have been formed by citizens committed to opening new residential schools in urban areas. A few sectarian groups, which have traditionally supported orphanages, are considering reopening or converting treatment centers to orphanages. For example, the Lutheran Church of California in 1997 was plotting the organization of a home-for-children project called "20/20/20"—20 homes in 20 cities in 20 years. These local efforts continue despite the lack of national policy support for the residential option for children and youth. The lack of support is largely due to popular, misguided myths about residential education that are based on a lack of knowledge about the realities of past settings. In fact, national policies and practices have actually obstructed the emergence of more residential care options. They have, as a consequence, caused many American kids to suffer poor care or to receive no care at all.

*Rethinking Orphanages for the 21st Century* highlights issues that need further review by those policymakers and laypeople who wish to seriously consider a return of residential education for at-risk, disadvantaged young people. Accordingly, the book reviews the unmet needs of the foster care and family-preservation systems, child labor practices, government regulations that increase costs, critics' hostility to the residential care option, and quality and cost trade-offs. It identifies elements in the children's homes that are vital to the development of the many young people for whom the residential education option, which will always be one of a continuum of care options for young people, is most appropriate. These elements necessarily include safety, permanence, positive role models, supportive peers, structure, work ethic, community service, and responsibility. The book is enriched by the wide variety of disciplines and professions from which contributors are drawn.

Prevailing myths and other harmful attitudes about long-term residential settings are debunked with facts. One common myth is that children are placed in residential schools after being ripped from the arms of loving parents and guardians by welfare authorities. This may have been the practice in the 1920s, but it is not the practice today. In a national study of American residential education programs completed 2 years ago by the International Center for Residential Education, it was found that the vast majority of young people in the programs were sent by parents who wanted something better for their children. Almost all schools also have some students known as "pilgrims." These are students who somehow manage to walk to the doors of the schools, satchels in hand, and say in so many words, "Please take me in!"

First Lady Hillary Rodham Clinton has maintained in her widely read book published in 1996 that "It takes a village" to properly rear children. Richard McKenzie, this book's editor, writes in his memoir of growing up in an orphanage, "For many children, orphanages were nothing short of 'visible extensions' of families. They were, in effect, villages that arose in response to community needs." McKenzie asks in the introduction to this volume, "Might it not be that any reinvigorated orphanage system developed in the 21st century could be far superior than what existed 100 or more years before?"

For those who refuse to accept the labeling of tens of thousands of at-risk young people as "throwaway children," I urge you to read this book and then reengage the national debate over rethinking the orphanage option. The debate starts here. Expanded opportunities for children await the outcome of the debate.

HEIDI GOLDSMITH
International Center for Residential Education
Washington, D.C.

# Acknowledgments

Anyone who has edited a collection of articles understands that the process is more taxing than it might seem. Nevertheless, this project was eased for me by a number of key people, including many of the contributors who made a special effort to submit their chapters in a timely manner. I am confident of the quality of the contributions to this book because of the willingness of the researchers and child welfare practitioners who participated in a 1997 symposium (which was organized around the chapters in this book) to read, critique, and make suggestions for improvement of the chapters. These symposium participants, who are listed in the appendix of Chapter 16, were also instrumental in the development of recommended policy reforms that are outlined in Chapter 16.

I am also indebted to my colleague in child development. Professor Wendy Goldberg carefully read all contributions to the book and offered many valuable suggestions for improvement. Karen McKenzie provided many editorial improvements to the manuscript, as did Margaret Zusky and Dan Hays at Sage. I am thankful to my student research assistant Anita Rowhani, who greatly facilitated the editing process in a multitude of ways. Finally, this project would not have been possible without the support of Michael Joyce, Hillel Fradkin, and Diane Sehler at the Lynde and Harry Bradley Foundation in Milwaukee, which provided funding for the project.

# CHAPTER 1

# Rethinking Orphanages
## An Introduction

RICHARD B. MCKENZIE

Hundreds of thousands of the nation's children are at risk of growing up in unfortunate, if not dire, circumstances. Most will miss one or both parents in their homes, and even many parents who are present will not give their children the supervision and direction they need. A large number of the children at risk will be neglected and abused by their parents or caregivers.

Unfortunately, many children will also find little real help from the current child welfare system that relies extensively on state and federal funds and on some variant of foster parenting to deliver what care is received. Indeed, many of the more than half a million children in the contemporary government-supported child welfare system will be harmed by the system itself, given that all too often the children in the system will have to cope with the profound insecurity that comes from being shipped from one set of foster parents to another, sometimes dozens of times.

The designers of the contemporary child welfare system proposed that the permanent care of children in institutions be replaced with temporary care in foster homes. That was an untested dream decades ago. Regrettably, for far too many children, the dream has become a nightmare. For many children, foster care has become the worst of all forms of care—permanent temporary care.

Far too many children must endure the life that "Suzi" endured. She went to her first foster home at age 6 mainly because her mother was allegedly a crack addict and her father allegedly abused her (Zamichow, 1997). She thought that her stay would be no more than a week or so. Instead, she was bounced from one foster placement to another and then back to her parents (with her father teaching her how to roll marijuana joints and sip hard drinks by age 9), only to be bounced back into foster care. Suzi's fate was particularly sad, given that she was deaf and found that few people in the system were prepared to communicate with her or to help her learn sign language. When she arrived at a Los Angeles-based treatment center for severely troubled children at age 13 (after threatening to kill one of her foster parents), she had the signing vocabulary of a 4-year-old. Her therapist noted that she had been "severely neglected, severely abused and severely deprived of communication. The deprivation of communication was probably the worst abuse Suzi suffered" (Zamichow, 1997, p. A12). Understandably, at age 17 and after 10 foster placements, plus stays in mental hospitals, she lamented, "No one told me it would be forever" (p. A12).

Predictably, too many disadvantaged children in the United States will grow up only to perpetuate the cycles of poverty, abuse, and neglect with their own children. Why? Partly because the children are being held hostage by abusive biological parents who are unloving and irresponsible or by a child welfare bureaucracy that too often uses the count of children in care as a measure of how much is accomplished.

Doubt such claims? Consider Conna Craig and Derek Herbert's assessment in Chapter 2 of this book of "The State of Child Welfare" in the United States. Craig, who heads the Institute for Children, provides some dreary numbers on the sorry state of the current child welfare system, but she also brings her numbers to life with real accounts of abused children. Hear the cries of "Catrina," who, according to Craig, was removed from her biological mother more times than she should have been able to count at her young age, only to be returned again and again. The last time she was returned, she was burned numerous times with the butt of her mother's cigarettes. Catrina, who was wise beyond her 10 years, lamented, "I understand the first nine times, the judge was trying to give my mom a fair chance" (p. 24).

Consider the view of the child welfare system from the federal bench provided by Estella Moriarty, a federal judge, in Chapter 3. Judge Moriarty laments the lack of child care options available to her colleagues on the bench who must deal daily with real-life cases of child abuse, endangerment, and neglect. She repeats a comment of another judge who was bedeviled with a decision judges have to make regularly, albeit tragically, for the child's sake:

> I'm not going to take a child from his home to be put in a foster home where he will be abused. If he is going to be abused, let him be abused by people who love him instead of being abused by strangers. (p. 42)

Next, consider Richard Gelles's account in Chapter 4 of how current child welfare policy, which is heavily focused on family preservation and reunification at virtually all costs, is doing bodily harm to children and showing few, if any, positive results for the families that are the object of the preservation and reunification efforts. Gelles, who directs the Family Violence Research Program at the University of Rhode Island, concludes,

> For there to be an intelligent and useful discussion of the value and limitations of congregate care, we need to throw out all the assumptions and myths about orphanages and focus on safety and permanence. The key assumption that "children always do best when cared for by their biological parents" must be revealed as a canard. Children need, first and foremost, safety and protection from harm and permanence. Permanence means that children must have caretakers who are there for them in an unconditional relationship. Moving back and forth between abusive and neglecting caretakers and foster care is not safe nor is it permanent. Moving from foster home to foster home is not permanent. Waiting in a foster home while maltreating caretakers are given one more chance to rid themselves of abusive partners or drug and alcohol problems is no permanence. Also, waiting years for a parent to learn how to be a nurturant and caring caretaker is not permanence. (p. 60)

A better way must be found. Reforms of the child welfare system are needed, and all chapters in this book point to a set of reasonable reforms discussed in Chapter 16 that, if adopted, would enable private charitable groups to become more involved at lower cost in the care of children in more permanent and stable residential settings. The work of Craig and Herbert, Gelles, and Moriarty suggests that the emphasis on family preservation and reunification must be reevaluated with an open mind and with an eye toward more quickly terminating parental rights in serious cases of abuse and neglect. We must realize that the repeated efforts of the child welfare system to rehabilitate and reunify children with their biological parents over an extended period of time imposes emotional and physical costs on the children and, because the children age in the process, makes them less adoptable. The legal system needs additional options for care that do not necessarily solve the entire child welfare problem the country faces but can contribute, albeit in minor ways, to the solution.

In the United States, we have idealized the "family," assuming that all families are like those that are portrayed on television by the likes of Ozzie and Harriett in the 1950s—warm places that invariably provide a bountiful measure of security and nurturing for children. We easily forget that with all the talk of "family values," many families value very little, especially the little ones in their midst. Many parents could not care less about their children and provide even less care, adequate security, and nurturing. People who work in today's crisis management centers for seriously troubled children understand all too well that a sizable share (possibly one third to one half) of the children they see should never go home and would be better served by never having to go back into the foster care system. Nevertheless, the system requires that the children be moved again after only a short respite.

Orphanages (or institutions that provide long-term care for disadvantaged children) have never been perfect substitutes for loving families. They cannot be. At the same time, the central issue at stake in the current debate over what to do about the growing numbers of disadvantaged children in the United States is not whether a perfect child welfare system can be found but whether significant improvements in the nation's multifaceted child welfare system can be devised. The issue is whether or not orphanages can be—will be—part of the solution for some children.

Granted, as recounted in several of the chapters that follow, many child welfare professionals dismiss orphanages, which were common in the United States before the 1950s, for damaging children in almost all regards—intellectually, emotionally, and economically.[1] They charge that "child welfare experts recognize that orphanages are the wrong place for children who (a) have a loving parent capable of caring for them and (b) have no need for residential care and treatment" (Child Welfare League of America, 1994). Such a position is on its face syllogistic, if not downright silly.

Of course, orphanages are the wrong place for children who "have no need for residential care." No one would ever be interested in proposing the institutionalization of children who "have a loving parent capable of caring for them." That oft-stated reframe of child welfare professionals does nothing other than obfuscate the real concern in the current child welfare debate: What should we do—can we do—with children whose parents are unloving, are incapable of providing reasonable care, are unwilling to do so, or all three?

According to the prevailing wisdom in the child welfare profession, the verdict on orphanages has been in for some time: "Examination of the historical record of orphanages of the 19th and early decades of the 20th century reveals characteristics that would make the creation of a new system of orphanages expensive and highly unfeasible" (Smith, 1995, p. 115). Is that really true? Certainly, many people seem to think so. Might it not be that any reinvigorated orphanage system developed in the 21st century could be far superior than what existed 100 or more years before, especially because incomes are higher and our knowledge of group care should be superior? Might not the debate be rigged by constantly dredging up images of group care (which may not themselves be accurate characterizations) from "the 19th and early decades of the 20th century"? In Chapter 6, Ross London, a criminologist, chronicles the answers and counteranswers to some of the critical questions that were tendered in the short-lived orphanage debate that was sparked in late 1994 by House Speaker Newt Gingrich's comments that many welfare children might be better served in orphanages.

This book was conceived from several questions—Did orphanages work? Can they work again? and How might they be a more prominent part of the solution to the problems children face?—as open issues, worthy of reconsideration by professionals not only in child care but also in other disciplines that could have much to contribute to the debate, such as history, economics, business, law, and political science. Interestingly, the answers to the questions are far more complex than policy proponents have suggested. As readers will find in Chapter 5, Marvin Olasky, a professor at the University of Texas at Austin who is widely known for his book *The Tragedy of American Compassion,* presents a far more positive history of orphanages in the United States than is commonly presented. Olasky stresses that orphanages spread in the 19th century to meet real and abiding needs and, from most accounts, worked remarkably well. His analysis is supported by the work that historians Cmiel (1995), Goldstein (1996), and Zmora (1994) have performed on orphanages that arose in Baltimore and Chicago. Cmiel and Zmora found that problems abounded in the group homes they studied, but many of the problems were endemic to the era in which the homes arose and were often related to the prevailing standard of living and understanding of diets and medical care of the time.

Does the child welfare literature support the sweeping claims of the experts on what orphanages did not accomplish? Surprisingly, given the strength of the often repeated, unqualified claims of unmitigated harm, the child care literature is very weak, if not misleading, regarding the central issues in the debate. John McCall, a professor of psychology (emeritus) at the University of Southern Illinois, reports in Chapter 8 on his examination of a sizable share of the child welfare literature relating to institutional care. He found most of the widely cited studies to be seriously flawed. The studies often covered few children (as few as 10), and several included children who may have been clinical referrals (not randomly drawn samples from the orphanage population) and who may have received care in a variety of "institutions," including mental hospitals, nurseries, and juvenile detention centers. From his survey of the literature, McCall draws the following important conclusions:

> 1. Theories about the detrimental effects of maternal deprivation receive highly tenuous, indirect support at best from orphanage research. Where psychological deterioration in infants was found, it is not clear whether the mother's absence or simple physical and social neglect was the essential cause. Neither was there any evidence that such neglect was a widespread practice.
> 2. Some teenagers and young adults with orphanage experience show deficits in language development, intellect, personality, or social skills. It is far from clear, however, that these were caused by their orphanage care. Orphanage care, per se, was almost never directly observed or explicitly manipulated in this research.
> 3. Most of the research suffers from the overuse of small, opportunistic samples, and there is a general failure to describe population sources and methods of selection. These limitations make it impossible to generalize findings based on isolated samples to all orphans or orphanages.
> 4. Most orphanage research is limited to a narrowly focused, clinical search for psychological damage. Very little of it deals with the effects of age at placement. None of it deals with the role of sibling support, the effects of age or gender groupings, the role of work, moral training, and a host of other practical issues in orphanage care.
> 5. Critics of orphanage care seem overzealous to produce negative evidence and then generalize their findings to all orphans or orphanages. More consideration should be given to positive orphanage experiences and ways of assessing their effects. Besides the controlled experiments with infants using social stimulation, there was only one developmental study that directly measured change. More developmental research is needed. (p. 147)

In Chapter 7, McKenzie does what child welfare experts have heretofore failed to do—evaluate the orphanage experience by asking middle-aged and older alumni from nine orphanages in the South and Midwest how they have done in life and how they evaluate their experiences from the perspective of many years of hindsight. The general conclusion is stark and stands in sharp contrast to conventional child welfare wisdom: As a group, the alumni have outpaced their counterparts in the general population by significant margins on practically all measures, not the least of which are education, income, and attitude toward life. Practically all the alumni look back on their orphanage experiences favorably, and they attribute their success to critical attributes of orphanage life: a better than average education; insistence on personal, moral, and religious values; and the inculcation of a work ethic.

An indication of the impact of orphanages can be made by assessing the extent to which the substitution of foster care for orphanage care affected the adoption of children. If orphanages were having the negative impacts widely claimed and if foster care could be expected to live up to the policy promises, then adoptions should have risen because of the substitution of foster care for orphanage care. In a cross-state analysis of the changing adoption rates in the late 1950s discussed in Chapter 9, however, William Shughart and William Chappell, economics professors at the University of Mississippi, found that adoption rates decreased with the spread of foster care (after considering changes in a number of other relevant factors). They conclude that foster care made children less adoptable, perhaps because the children aged and became more troubled as they were shuttled in and out of foster care placements.

Why did so many orphanages fold after World War II? The contributors to this book offer a variety of answers. Without much doubt, advances in medical care that lowered death rates of parents decreased the need for orphanages as did the upward trend in family income. As the country's poverty rate fell throughout the 1940s, 1950s, and 1960s, there was less of a need for homes for disadvantaged children because there were gradually fewer children whose parents could not afford to care for them. It is also probably true that reports of abuse and inadequate care in some orphanages sullied the reputation of all orphanages, fortified the growing conviction that any conceivable form of family-type care must be superior to existing forms of institutional care, and gave rise to calls for more direct financial aid to parents through government programs such as Aid to Families With Dependent Children.

The debate, however, may have been biased from the start. In the first third of this century, orphanage care had been found to be imperfect. Foster care had not been attempted extensively, meaning its potential flaws were not so obvious. Foster care expanded because it was presumed to be more like warm and personal family care and not like orphanage care that was imagined to be (and depicted as) cold and impersonal "institutional" care. The movie *Oliver Twist,* with the unforgettable scene of Oliver pleading for more "gruel," probably convinced many moviegoers, including policymakers and potential orphanage benefactors, that orphanage life was dreadful and to be avoided at virtually all costs.

The contributors to this book, however, bring to light additional explanations for the demise of orphanages that have not been widely discussed. Karol and Donald Boudreaux, law and economics experts at Clemson University, explain in Chapter 10 the demise of orphanages partially in terms of old-fashioned interest group politics:

> Changing patterns of federal funding under the Social Security Act of 1935, in combination with the historic professional biases of social workers, arguably are a major factor explaining the movement of orphans from private institutions into foster care homes. Not only would such a move require a higher ratio of social workers to orphans (because each orphan in a foster home requires monitoring by a social worker, whereas a number of orphans in an institution can be monitored by fewer caregivers) but also such a move would capture greater amounts of federal funding, as a result of both Title V grants and the 1961 amendments to the Social Security Act of 1935. Thus, we suggest that the dramatic mid-20th-century decline in the use of orphanages is explained at least in part by the self-interested lobbying of social workers to promote greater reliance on public foster care over institutional care. (p. 189)

Similarly, University of Georgia economist Dwight Lee suggests in Chapter 11 that politics will inevitably hinder the reemergence of orphanages:

> Orphanages provided much more than material assistance to young people in need. They also provided companionship, love, instruction, responsibility, and a sense of permanence and place for children who otherwise would have lacked these important ingredients in growing up. Orphanages are not institutions that can be effectively run from afar, subject to standardized rules and procedures formulated by remote authorities. They are local institutions best run by people who possess the local information of time and place. They may be primarily private or primarily public, but they are almost by necessity local.
> The local nature of orphanages is an important element in understanding why they have declined in importance and why this decline has corresponded closely with the increased centralization of government efforts to fight poverty. Political forces behind the centralization of government poverty programs, and behind government centralization in general, have resulted in spending more money in the name of helping the poor, particularly poor children, but have also resulted in less being done to actually help. The poor have become treated less as people in need of our responsible compassion and more as pawns in a competition for government largess. This is not a

political environment in which orphanages can expect to thrive. For the very reasons that orphanages are better (not perfect) than centralized transfer programs for delivering responsible compassion to children most in need, they no longer play the important role in social welfare they once did. (pp. 193-194)

Like it or not, any careful examination of the country's child welfare policies is likely to reveal that established policies are often the product of pressing political forces pushing their own private agendas, including the well-being not so much of children as that of the people who work in the system. The work of the Boudreauxs and Lee suggests that in searching for a new direction for national and state child welfare policies, the United States' political leaders must critically reevaluate the extent to which the personal interests of the system's workers have unduly dictated policy and driven up the cost of institutional care that people in the system then decry.

Privately funded and operated orphanages may be a potential alternative to the publicly funded and directed child welfare system mainly because their operations can, to a degree, escape the constraints on the type and direction of child care imposed by special interest groups through the political process. The ability of private orphanages to emerge and sustain the care of children, however, will be affected by the cost of care, which in turn can be substantially driven by government regulations that are supported by political interest groups that benefit from them.

Indeed, the considerable rise in the cost of institutional care after the 1930s may explain the substitutions of parental, kinship, and foster care for orphanage care of children. Orphanage care gradually became uncompetitive as the costs of care in orphanages escalated, causing many homes for children to close their doors or convert to crises management centers for severely troubled children and their dysfunctional families.

In Chapter 15, Del Bradshaw and Donald Wyant, certified public accountants from the accounting firm of Bradshaw, Gordon, and Clinkscale (Greenville, South Carolina), with the assistance of Richard McKenzie report their audit of the accounting records of two homes for children in North and South Carolina. They found that the cost of basic care per child (not including depreciation of the buildings and equipment) for one institution (A) when it operated as an orphanage or home for disadvantaged children rose from just under $4,000 a year in 1935 to $7,100 in 1950 (an 18% increase over the cost in 1935 in constant 1996 dollars) and then jumped to over $17,000 a year in 1965 (a 140% real increase over the cost in 1950 and a 333% real increase over the cost in 1935), at which time the institution began a conversion to a crisis management center for severely troubled children. As a crisis management center, the cost of care at this institution began to mount until the cost per child reached $63,500 per year in 1995 (an increase of 269% over the cost in 1965 and nearly 1,500% higher than the cost in 1935). In the other institution studied (B), which continued to serve mainly disadvantaged children throughout the study period, the average cost rose from $7,500 per year in 1950 (the earliest year of available data) to $9,800 in 1965 (an increase of 32%) and over $32,000 in 1995 (an additional increase of 227% over the cost in 1965), but in 1995 the average cost at Institution B was only half the average cost of care at Institution A.

Bradshaw, Wyant, and McKenzie show that the cost of care at both institutions rose in every category (clothing, food, medical, supplies, and recreation) but mainly in the salaries and benefits paid to a growing number of staff for each child in care. At Institution A, there were three or four children per staff member in 1950, under 2.5 children per staff member in 1965, and 0.75 of a child per staff member (or 1.5 staff members per child) in 1995. At Institution B, there were approximately 5 children per staff member in 1950, 3.5 children per staff member in 1965, and 1.25 children per staff member in 1995. Obviously, in comparing the accounting records at the two institutions, much of the increase in the cost of care in Institution A is related to the growing severity of the problems the children in care faced. As evident in the more than fourfold increase in the annual cost per child for Institution B, however, other forces were clearly at work.

Several contributors to this book offer explanations for why the cost of institutional care might have risen. Margaret MacFarlane Wright, an Irvine, California, attorney specializing in labor issues, reviewed the evolution of child labor law over the past half-century in several states. She notes that children in orphanages in the 1950s and before performed a considerable variety of chores on their homes' farms and in their shops. Indeed, the children often supplied a significant portion of the food served in the dining halls and covered a substantial share of the costs of maintenance of the grounds and buildings. Wright also found, however, that child labor laws have gradually become more limiting in the work children younger than age 18 can legally undertake. She asks in the title of Chapter 12, "Who Will Mow the Lawn at Boys Town?" (with Boys Town referring to the Nebraska home for difficult children made famous in a film by the same name) because asking institutionalized children to do work on the grounds is now problematic, given the variety of state regulations that limit the power equipment, including lawn mowers, that institutionalized children can operate. Parents can ask their children to use any size riding lawn mower, but institutions are far more restrictive.

Even when identified chores assigned to children might be legal, today homes might not make the work assignments because of concerns over whether or not the institutions can or will assume the financial burden associated with the accompanying liability for any harm that might come to the children while working. The problem is especially acute with regard to operating cars and trucks, given that institutionalized children often have problems getting driver licenses. It is also questionable whether or not homes do not have to pay the children minimum wage for their hours of work on many assigned chores for which children decades ago did not receive compensation. Wright's analysis leads to the conclusion that the changes in child labor laws have definitely raised the cost of institutional care by increasing the maintenance work that must be done by staff members and by increasing the reliance on markets for the food that children eat. Understandably, Bradshaw, Wyant, and McKenzie found that at Institution A the cost of food per child rose sixfold in real terms and the maintenance expenditures doubled in real terms in the 1935 to 1965 period.

Wright's analysis also suggests that the cost of institutional care might be moderated by clarifying the issues of liability and by expanding the scope of legally permissible chores that children can undertake. Given that many alumni reported in McKenzie's survey that their unpaid work experience at their orphanages was important to their long-term success, consideration should be given to exempting child care centers from state and federal wage minimums. After all, families are not required to pay their children the minimum wage for work around the home or farm. The reasoning is basic: Children should be asked to contribute to the welfare of the family, and the work should be viewed as an obligation and is often good training.

Michael DeBow, a law professor at Samford University, shows in Chapter 13 that a major contributing factor to the rise in costs of institutional care has been the growth in state regulations. From an examination of the child care laws in six states, DeBow found that institutions must now operate under myriad rules that not only specify the maximum number of children per institutional staff member but also dictate the exact credentials of many members of the staff. State regulations can also limit the work of volunteers (as well as making the act of volunteering an ordeal, given that volunteers can be subjected to fingerprinting and extensive background checks, as if they are criminals) and can require the institutions to limit the number of children per bedroom and to have a specified amount of square feet of housing space per child. Agencies that accredit homes impose additional requirements, a fact that is often limiting because the homes often need accreditation to be approved for government funding. DeBow stresses the obvious point: Regulations, although often well intended, can unnecessarily add to the cost of institutional care, thus limiting the number of children who can be served. The cost concern is real, especially with regard to staffing requirements.

In their study, Bradshaw, Wyant, and McKenzie found that at Institution A, salaries and fringe benefits per child per year increased fivefold in real terms between 1935 and 1965. By 1995, the salaries and benefits per child per year were ninefold what they were in 1965 and nearly 42 times what they were in 1935.[2] In 1935, staff salaries and benefits represented one fifth of the daily cost of care per child. By 1965, such costs had risen to only one fourth of total daily costs. By 1995, salaries and benefits had risen to nearly three fifths of the daily cost of care. The rise in the ratio of salaries and fringes to total cost followed much the same pattern for Institution B.

DeBow suggests that to increase the number of children who can receive care, states with the most restrictive and most costly regulations should at least consider substituting more lenient, less costly regulations that work well in other states. Obviously, special attention should be given to the requirements relating to the number of staff members and their credentials. McKenzie's positive survey findings of alumni, most of whom were in orphanages before many of the staffing and credential requirements were put in place, should cause policymakers to pause and ask if the requirements have produced benefits that are in line with the costs imposed. At the very least, DeBow stresses, child care institutions should be granted greater flexibility in the use of volunteers.

When private homes for children accept public funding for their programs, they must expect that the government agencies will restrict how the funding is used. They should also expect less freedom in developing their programs, especially those relating to religious and value-based instruction. Joseph Maxwell, who has spent years working for the Palmer House, a strictly private home for disadvantaged children in Columbia, Mississippi, in Chapter 14 explores the various ways the goals of private homes can conflict with the goals of public-funding agencies. He writes,

> The glut of government-funded child care facilities in America has created numerous unfortunate side effects; one of those not often considered is the cookie-cutter effect such funding promotes. To get funds, a home must comply with so many government regulations that when all is said and done,

> all the homes end up practicing the same type of child care philosophy with little room for innovation and positive experimentation. (p. 263)

Maxwell concludes that not taking public funding can provide homes for children with more flexibility in the creation of new programs and, at the same time, help keep costs under control.

Maxwell makes a point that should not go unnoticed by policymakers: One of the obvious problems with the gradual but persistent state and federal takeover of child care—including the substitution of foster care for orphanage care—has been the considerable reduction in the variety of approaches to helping children. The country may have lost the benefits that could have come with the experimentation that could have spawned improvements over the years with the continuation of a healthy private institutional-based child care system. Any call for a revival of institutional care is necessarily a call for more private groups becoming involved in the never-ending search for "what works." The call is also founded on the presumption that there is no one way to help children. Indeed, there must be many ways of helping children with different backgrounds and different needs.

Admittedly, the themes developed in this book run counter to the prevailing wisdom in the established child welfare industry. Perhaps that is what makes the contributions valuable: They challenge readers to set aside preconceived impressions of orphanage life and be open to the prospects that past images, carefully cultivated by many child care professionals, may be far off the mark of what orphanage life was really like. We need to rethink orphanages for a simple reason: The lives of children are at stake. Again, orphanages might never be a major part of the solution for problems that so many children face, but they might be a minor yet important part—as they were in the past. Orphanages, however, must first be viewed as they actually were and not as the novels and movies have portrayed them. They need to be seen for the considerable good that they did for many children and not just for their failings, which they no doubt had.

What were orphanages really like? Why were many of them as successful as they were? Admittedly, I have answers that connect both professional and personal interests, given that I grew up in an orphanage in the 1950s.[3] The development of easily understood answers to the previous questions comes from an unexpected source, however—the writings of someone who has been an avowed opponent of bringing back orphanages.

First Lady Hillary Rodham Clinton argued forcefully in her 1996 book that it takes not only a family but also a "village"—what she calls "visible extensions" of families—to rear children successfully. At the same time, in the middle of the short-lived orphanage debate of late 1994, initiated by off-the-cuff comments by House Speaker Newt Gingrich, the first lady also denounced as "unbelievable and absurd" all proposals to bring back orphanages.

If Ms. Clinton knew as much about orphanages as the tens of thousands of Americans who grew up in them, she might recognize that many orphanages had all the markings of the village she admires. Indeed, many of the private orphanages that in a bygone era dotted the welfare landscape were, indeed, "children's villages," which may explain some of their success.

The alumni who grew up in orphanages decades ago understand the extent to which their orphanages were villages. At the same time, they and I realize that most orphanages were imperfect and often lacked some amenities, not the least of which are the daily hugs taken for granted by many children who grow up in loving families. Orphanages did not always have the type of caring and responsible surrogate parents around to play with the children in the evenings or who "dressed up in sheets and told ghost stories," as Ms. Clinton recalls so eloquently about the parents in her neighborhood. Many orphanages, however, such as Barium Springs Home for Children (my home), had other important characteristics of small villages. The Home, which is what the middle-aged and older alumni continue to call it (with a capital "T" and "H" to indicate that it was, in some ways, self-contained), was set apart from the world on a campus in rural North Carolina, 5 miles from the nearest sizable town. As seen from the highway that runs through it, The Home could easily be mistaken for a small college. More than 200 boys and girls, ages 2 to 18, resided at Barium Springs Home for Children in the early 1950s (and as many as 350 children were there in the 1930s).

Like so many orphanages portrayed in films, the children had several large, turn-of-the-century cottages, each housing 20 to 30 young children, many of whom went to bed on unheated sleeping porches. Unlike the orphanages in the films *Annie, Oliver Twist,* or *Boys Town,* however, The Home also had cottages for older children that were boarding school quality, with 2 kids to a room, 16 to a cottage, and these cottages had living and television rooms (as well as small apartments for the house mothers). Meals, however, were served in the main dining hall, which was central to village life not only because it sat squarely in the middle of campus but also because it was the focus of much of the social life for the children, staff, and visitors, all of whom could find seats around the 40 or more tables. The bell in the dining hall tower set the pace for the day, rousing the children from sleep and beckoning them to meals, to school, or to work.

Many of The Home's 1,500 acres covered a vast track of unspoiled woods in which the children spent much of their free time exploring, building forts, damming streams, and taming pets. There were also many acres of pastures for the 60 milking cows that the older boys milked and for the 200 head of beef cattle, 100 head of sheep, 100 head of hogs, and 500 laying hens they tended. Along with hired hands, many of whom lived on or around the edges of the campus, the children of The Home worked extensively (for as many as 50 unpaid hours a week during the summers and for as many as 20 hours per week after school and on the weekends) on the hundreds of acres of fields of corn and alfalfa, table crops, and fruit trees.

At The Home, the children were constantly made aware that work was important not only to put food on the table and to keep the cost of the care in line but also because work was believed to be good for their souls—a theme that Ms. Clinton, no doubt, would laud. Like so many villages of the 1950s and before, The Home had its own slaughtering plant, print shop, cannery, carpenter and plumbing shops, and chicken coops. For most of the 1950s, the children had their own on-campus elementary and high schools (which were generally better than the schools in the surrounding county). Their varsity teams played against city schools that were 20 times the size of their own student body (but teams from The Home won more often than not—with the support of the surrounding community!). Moreover, the children had their own swimming pool (in addition to the swimming holes hidden in the woods), tennis courts, football field, and horseshoe pits. They even had their own village church and gymnasium, with the latter used for basketball games, roller-skating, and dances.

The campus was set apart from much of the rest of the world, and some of the alumni consequently had problems adjusting to the "real world" on their departure, but their difficulties probably were much like those faced by other kids from isolated farms and communities when they moved to much larger cities. Orphanage critics, however, may have exaggerated the problems associated with the isolation of rural homes for children. Many of the children, especially the older boys, went to the nearby towns practically every weekend. Given that they had their own on-campus schools (until the last half of the 1950s), children from the surrounding communities went to school, sporting events, and dances with the children of The Home. Of course, the children became more integrated into the surrounding communities when they started attending public schools after the mid-1950s. They dated girls and boys from other communities, who visited the campus and the cottages. There was always a flow of people in and out of The Home, just as there would likely be in any village Ms. Clinton might imagine.

Ms. Clinton writes warmly about how villages are mutually supporting networks of people. Clearly, The Home could not provide the individualized nurturing that loving and responsible families can provide (after all, the number of children per adults was higher than is the case in most families), but neither did The Home environment duplicate the deplorable family circumstances in far-removed villages from which so many of the children had come and to which so many children today are condemned for the duration of their childhoods. The children of The Home did not always get affection, but, at the very least, they got supervision, which many children today lack completely or get rarely, before or after school.

As Ms. Clinton found among the adults in her community, many of the kids of The Home found worthy mentors among staff members who considered their work more a mission (most were highly religious) than a profession (few had formal training in child care). Many alumni who were in The Home before the 1950s remember fondly the care and concern (as well as the discipline) of Mr. J. B. Johnston, who, like Father Flanagan in the movie *Boys Town,* headed The Home but knew the name of every child during his tenure as head of The Home and was renowned for taking groups of children for nature walks on Sunday afternoons. The children of the 1950s found a worthy example in Reverend Albert McClure, who demanded that the children heed every commandment but who also insisted that work and education would permit them to rise above their circumstances. Also, there is not a child who went through The Home from the 1930s until the 1970s who does not remember fondly Ms. Rebekah Carpenter, the caseworker who always had a bright smile and a word of encouragement. She never married, but she "mothered" hundreds.

Although the housemothers were not always warm and affectionate, neither did they descend to the abuse levels of the boozing Ms. Hannigan in the movie *Annie,* nor did the meanest of the mean houseparents (and there were a couple of very difficult adults) match the cruelty of the headmaster in *Oliver Twist,* who refused Oliver's pleas for more gruel. Regarding the food, it resembled the food served in most college cafeterias in the 1950s, generally well balanced, if not always inspired (and the food was generally far better than what many of the children had to eat prior to attending The Home). Perhaps the orphanage's food and heavy reliance on work and sports explain why, during World War II, only 1.4% of the boys from The Home were turned down for military service, whereas nearly 40% of the boys from the general population flunked the physicals for military enlistment or draft.

Critics of orphanage villages often point to what the children in them did not have, but many alumni often press a different perspective for evaluating their orphanage experience: They compare what they had in their villages with what they would have had in the dysfunctional families and communities they left behind.

Was the record of The Home all positive? The answer is clearly "No." A few kids longed to return to their families; some did return, both by the parents reclaiming their children and by the children running away. No doubt, some alumni remain distraught by the separation from their parents and by the regiment of institutional life. At the same time, readers should keep in mind that such claims could also be made about life in normal families and in foster families. All villages harm some of the people in them. The relevant question is what has been the "batting average"—the ratio of successes and failures—of alumni who had good experiences to those who had bad ones and of alumni who did well and look back fondly to those who did not do well and who look back with some bitterness. Reports in this book suggest that the ratio is far more positive than has been widely believed. The fact that three and four decades after their homes closed or changed missions tens of thousands of alumni from numerous orphanages still gather each year for homecoming to reflect on and celebrate must indicate something about the unheralded value of the orphanages to many of the children who grew up in them.

I close this chapter with a personal note. In late 1994, just after the Republicans won a landslide victory in the midterm election and their leaders began to hint that they might propose to bring back orphanages as a part of their welfare reform package, I wrote an article for the *Wall Street Journal* (McKenzie, 1994) in which I tried to relate a simple sentiment—that orphanages are a pretty good idea for some (but hardly all) children. During the intervening years, I have been stunned by the depth of emotion the publication of that column and subsequently my memoir (McKenzie, 1996) have touched, as judged by the response, mainly from orphans who have come out of the woodwork from around the country to say, in so many words, "Right on!" They not only confessed to having had a great life as children in orphanages but also an unbelievable number, like I did, called their home "The Home." These orphans attest that the way they grew up was important to their successes. Clearly, my story is the tale of many.

Why have so many orphans from so many homes done so well and look back with appreciation? If conventional wisdom about orphanages is accepted, it is a mystery. Any positive claims to the contrary must be treated with suspicion. The alumni, however, often point to an answer that is obvious to them but is least likely to be accepted by the critics: These orphanages did not live down to the carefully crafted dreadful stereotypes. In general, they were reasonably good, cost-effective private solutions to a social problem. For many children, orphanages were nothing short of "visible extensions" of families. They were, in effect, villages that arose in response to community needs. Almost all were a functioning part of larger religious and charitable communities that had a stake in the success of the children in their care.

When critics judge institutional care, they often cite the regimentation, the absence of "bonding," and the lack of toys. When asked what they believe to be the advantages of their homes, the orphans point to specific factors either ignored or cited critically by child care critics: the sense of responsibility, discipline, work ethic, and religious and moral values instilled in them during their stays in these institutions. What seems to be an unexpected but important finding from the survey reported later in this book is the value of permanence: The longer the orphans stayed in their orphanage, the happier they currently appear to be and the more favorably they look back on their orphanage experiences. Is it not possible that the absence of hugs in institutions was and remains overrated, especially given that so many children never experience what it is like to be loved by their parents who are close at hand?

If the nation had few problems with its current child welfare system, if all families matched the mold set by *Ozzie and Harriet,* no one would want to reconsider bringing back orphanages. The fact remains, however, that the country's child welfare problems are grave and getting worse. We have a child care system that is, in many cases, heaping abuse on children. Far too many disadvantaged children today have to endure multiple foster care placements before reaching high school age. Many wonderful foster parents are graciously giving their time and energies—their lives—to the care of disadvantaged children. An untold number of foster parents, however, often treat their foster children as second-class family members and can, and often do, discard the children in their care with the advent of the slightest behavioral problems or even because of no problem at all. Foster parents can literally dump their problem children on someone else. The one unheralded advantage a home for children had was that the children knew that it was there and would always be there.

Given the absence of truly permanent placements for many children, should we wonder why so many disadvantaged children today wind up in a mental or emotional rehabilitation program or incarcerated as a "child predator"? Doesn't anyone (other than the orphanage alumni) understand the value of permanence and stability to children?

As stressed in this chapter and elsewhere in this book, our child welfare system is guided by a two-word mindless ideology: "family preservation." Before taking children from unfit parents, we wait until the children have been gravely and repeatedly neglected and abused. Then, after a short respite during which we seem to expect magical reforms on the part of the parents, we return the children to once again be neglected and abused by their parents and their environment. Doesn't anyone understand that some families are the problem, at least partially, and that institutions are not always worse for children than families? Doesn't anyone realize the value of children being catapulted once and for all away from bad family circumstances into totally different environments, albeit imperfect orphanages?

We must reconsider orphanages for a simple reason: In the past, many of them worked reasonably well for large populations of children. For many of today's disadvantaged children—the ones who have never known loving and responsible parents—orphanages might be a substantial improvement over being destroyed by the current child care system.

## ▓ Notes

1. These private orphanages were founded by every conceivable religious and community group (e.g., Catholics, Jews, every Protestant denomination, Odd Fellows, and Masons) and by individual benefactors.

2. The annual salary and fringe benefits per child increased in real terms by more than 15-fold between 1965 and 1995 at Institution A. This was a period during which the average real incomes of the nation's production workers was approximately the same in 1995 as it was in 1965.

3. See my memoir (McKenzie, 1996) of growing up in an orphanage.

## ▓ References

Child Welfare League of America. (1994, December 14). *Welfare reform: Facts on orphanages.* Washington, DC: Author.

Clinton, H. R. (1996). *It takes a village, and other lessons children teach us.* New York: Simon & Schuster.

Cmiel, K. (1995). *A home of another kind: One Chicago orphanage and the tangle of child welfare.* Chicago: University of Chicago Press.

Goldstein, H. (1996). *The home on Gorham Street and the voices of its children.* Tuscaloosa: University of Alabama Press.

McKenzie, R. B. (1994, November 29). An orphan on orphanages. *Wall Street Journal,* p. A24.

McKenzie, R. (1996). *The Home: A memoir of growing up in an orphanage.* New York: Basic Books.

Smith, E. P. (1995, January/February). Bring back orphanages? What policymakers of today can
    learn from the past. *Child Welfare, 74,* 115-138.
Zamichow, N. (1997, March 3). No longer a prisoner of silence. *Los Angeles Times,* pp. A1, A12.
Zmora, N. (1994). *Orphanages reconsidered: Child care institutions in Progressive Era Baltimore.*
    Philadelphia: Temple University Press.

# PART I

## child CARE
## IN THE UNITED STATES

# CHAPTER 2

# The State of Child Welfare

CONNA CRAIG
DEREK HERBERT

T he future of America's most vulnerable citizens is on the line. On any given day in this country, more than half a million children are in the care of a government-run system so bureaucratically complex that it often harms the very children whom it was designed to protect. Its aggregate outcomes affect not only the lives of needy children but also the stability of our communities. Government-run substitute care—"the system"— is a social policy disaster in process. Tens, if not hundreds, of thousands of children are being abused twice over (a) by their biological parents who neglect or injure them and (b) by the public child welfare system in which they are trapped.

We need not give up on these youngsters. Research indicates that even children who have endured extreme suffering can grow up to be productive, well-adjusted, and healthy adults. A major study identified "resiliency-building factors," including parental watchfulness, strong peer relationships, and mentoring, that contribute to a child's potential to overcome early trauma.[1] These conditions—elements necessary to repair and rebuild the life of a child who has been harmed—are not guaranteed by today's child welfare system; indeed, it could be argued that they could not possibly be provided by government.

The guidance and nourishment that all children need are best provided by a family. When a child's biological family (family of origin) is permanently unable or unwilling to rear the child responsibly, adoption is by far the best

choice. There are times, however, when a child in the system is not yet freed
for adoption. Today, those children linger in the uncertainty of foster home,
group home, and shelter settings. The state of child welfare is reviewed with
some urgency and with orphanages in mind for this reason: By providing
stability and continuity, modern orphanages harbor the prospects of helping
children who might otherwise continue to be abused if they remained stranded
in the clutches of the system as it is now constituted.

## ▓ The Case of Catrina

Catrina is 12 years old. She has spent most of her life in state-run, government-funded substitute care.[2] When asked, "What's it like?" she responds
matter-of-factly that by the time she was 2 years old, she had been taken away
from and returned to her biological mother 10 times. Catrina explains, "I
understand the first nine times, the judge was trying to give my mom a fair
chance." On the tenth time, however, then 2-year-old Catrina was found with
48 cigarette burns on her head. Although Catrina's biological mother admitted
to burning the child, the judge in the case did not see such behavior as grounds
for terminating parental rights and once again sent Catrina "home." A few
months later, she was back in foster care—this time for the rest of her
childhood.

At age 12, Catrina states that what she wants, more than anything, is to
be adopted. She is not legally free for adoption, however, and she has thus
spent more than 10 years being "bounced"—moved, sometimes without
warning—from state-run foster homes to group homes to shelters.[3] She
qualifies for a panoply of federal-, state-, and county-run programs, but she
has no permanent home. When asked about her life, she replies, "Everywhere
I go, somebody gets money to keep me from having a mom and dad."

Catrina is one of more than 700,000 American children who will spend
all or part of this year in state-run substitute care, including foster family
homes, group homes or orphanages, children's shelters, and other state-run
facilities.[4] She is among what has been labeled a "lost tribe" (ABC News,
1994)—hundreds of thousands of "system kids," as they often refer to themselves—that is growing at a rate 33 times greater than the U.S. child population in general (Tatara, 1993a, p. 23). By the end of the decade, more than half
a million more children will enter the system. Every year, more children enter
than exit (Tatara, 1993b, p. 5).

As Catrina grows from toddler to young adult, she is kept in limbo. Although it may seem that Catrina has been forgotten, the system that holds her hostage is the center of a great deal of attention. For each of the many reasons that children enter substitute care, researchers and advocates have produced tomes of policy guidelines and recommendations. Every step of Catrina's trek through the system is regulated by federal policies and state laws. Armies of "experts" will discuss and review her case on an individual level and as part of aggregate data. Catrina, however, in her innocence already has her finger on the pulse of the system: Everywhere she goes, somebody indeed "gets money" to maintain her status as a child without a permanent, loving home. Child welfare today is a system based on reverse incentives. Federal funding to the states for substitute care is allocated on a per-day, per-child basis: Funding is not based on how well children are cared for but on the number of children who enter and remain in substitute care.

The odds are against Catrina and her peers in the system. There are some kids who make it out and are able to live productive, healthy adult lives, but statistics reveal that for many others, prospects are dim. Every year, 15,000 foster children "graduate" from the system—that is, they are discharged from the system by turning 18 years old or some other age set by the state.[5] They are rootless, they are effectively parentless, and they are left to navigate early adulthood on their own. In one year, New York City discharges approximately 4,000 foster care graduates out of the system when they reach the age of majority (P. O'Brien, personal communication, February 12, 1996). Westat, Incorporated (1991) of Rockville, Maryland, studied youth who had left foster care 2.5 to 4 years earlier and found that "46% had not completed high school, 38% had not held a job for more than 1 year, 25% had been homeless for at least one night, and 60% of young women had given birth to a child. Forty percent had been on public assistance, incarcerated, or a cost to the community in some other way" ("A National Evaluation," 1991, as cited in U.S. General Accounting Office, 1995, pp. 14-15).[6] In New York City alone, more than 60% of the homeless population in municipal shelters are former foster children (Coalition for the Homeless, 1989, p. 101). A Bureau of Justice statistics study of a nationally representative sample of inmates in local jails found that 17% were once in substitute care (Craig, 1995a, p. 123).

System kids are brought up in a world that treats them as cases and not as human beings. The system is designed to facilitate their survival but not to meet their needs or show them love. Children in substitute care are denied meaningful interpersonal relationships because foster parents are instructed not to bond with the children in their care. In some states, it is against policy to hug a child in a state-run group home. Instead of being given the promise that comes with commitment to a child's well-being, system kids are offered programs. These programs attempt to expand their life experiences, but often they are misdirected: Abused children are offered art classes, but they are not offered permanent homes. For teens in foster care, the federal government funds the $70 million per year Independent Living Program, which is designed to prepare foster teens for adult life. In one California county, the first day's lesson is to show foster teens all the local homeless shelters (M. Lynch, personal communication, July 3, 1996).

This is the state of child welfare today: Government-run attempts are driven by reverse incentives that perpetuate the system's size and scope but do little to remedy loss in the lives of children. The public child welfare industry has become program oriented rather than child oriented. Its own outcome measurements are indicative of the problem: Success is defined by the growth of programs and the steady increase of funding and not by data on child well-being or longitudinal studies of the effects of the state's involvement. Observations of the system's failure are not limited to the pens of newspaper columnists or political pundits. The following damning statement is from a textbook on social work (Pecora, Whittaker, & Maluccio, 1992, p. 434): "Many child welfare agencies as currently organized are not outcome-focused, are not client-centered in terms of involving clients meaningfully, and are not implementing what the empirical literature has documented as effective."

The cost of failure is high and takes many forms. According to the American Civil Liberties Union, a year in foster care costs $17,500, including per-child payments to foster families and administrative costs of child welfare agencies. This does not include counseling and treatment programs for biological parents or foster parent recruitment and training (American Civil Liberties Union Foundation, 1995, p. 1). State-run group home care can exceed $50,000 per year per child (for a nonhandicapped teen!). Consider also the long-term social costs, such as the economic impact of a former foster child being nearly 30 times more likely to be incarcerated than a person who never spent time in foster care. The biggest costs, the ones that can never be adequately tallied and that are impossible to recompense, are the human costs: months or years spent waiting for the chance to grow up in a permanent family.

It seems that the child welfare system has given up on children. The literature is replete with references to children who are too troubled, too "damaged" by the system itself, to be saved. Child advocates continue to call for more funding and more programs, which is like adding water to a sinking ship. Blue-ribbon commissions and expensive government-funded studies underscore the failures of today's child welfare system but do little in the way of making a difference in the life of a single child. What is needed is a shift in thinking about how to meet the needs of parentless children. The first step must be to revitalize the private, charitable sector's involvement in child welfare. For most of America's history, child welfare was largely a private endeavor. Private groups—driven by mission and by the marketplace—had to evidence their ability to meet the needs of children. By contrast, government programs are not good at self-examination, and they are even worse at strategic reform. The mechanisms of bureaucracy are not designed to allow reflexivity; in the scope of child welfare, the cost of such rigidity can be the loss of a childhood.

For the sake of Catrina and others like her, it is imperative to understand the major contributors to the failure of public child welfare today: a reverse incentive funding scheme that drives the system, program orientation rather than child orientation, and the outgrowth of these two elements combined—a system that, as it has become more entrenched rather than more effective, has given up on the children.

## ▓ Funding for Failure

For years, the rallying cry of many children's activists has been "More money!" The call for increased funding is rooted in the notion that government funding is a panacea for family disintegration. Some child advocates seem convinced that the perpetuation of federal funding will safeguard the future of America's children. In early 1996, the Coalition for America's Children, made up of 300 national organizations including the Children's Defense Fund, joined forces to support "These Children Have Faces." This effort, launched by a woman "who was concerned and angry about proposed budget cuts of the 104th Congress," encouraged citizens to send a picture of a child (and $1 or more) to its headquarters; the pictures would be forwarded to members of Congress as a reminder that budget decisions affect real children (Children Now, 1996). The assumption, it seems, is that budget increases will be beneficial; the incentive structure of federal funding in child welfare rewards any program growth, however, even for programs with poor outcomes.

Americans are spending $12 billion annually on public agency substitute care (Lipner & Goertz, 1990, p. 3; U.S. House of Representatives, 1996, p. 695). The legal mandates attached to this funding require states to invest in programs that sometimes place children in jeopardy. To secure funds for foster care, states are required to meet "reasonable efforts" to return children to their biological parents, even in cases of extreme abuse or neglect. Until 1997, nowhere did the federal government define reasonable efforts, and few states defined it in statute; this decision was left to the discretion of individual judges. The disposition of federal funds, which have for nearly two decades been directed largely by the Adoption Assistance and Child Welfare Act of 1980 (Public Law 96-272), required that states place primary emphasis on reunification and family preservation. In 1997, the Adoption and Safe Families Act attempted to clarify reasonable efforts but left open a very large loophole, excusing states from many levels of accountability when states choose to place children with relatives in state-funded kinship foster care. The Child Welfare League of America (CWLA) (1991) endorses the position, stating that "No one can truly substitute for the family of origin" (p. 6).

On the surface, family reunification appears to be a worthwhile goal. In practice, however, it often has tragic consequences: When a girl named Halie was just 2 years old, her biological mother and her mother's boyfriend tied Halie, face forward, to an electric heater and left her there for hours.[7] Little Halie's face and chest were completely disfigured. After weeks of hospitalization, Halie entered foster care. For 10 years, caseworkers helped Halie's mother maintain her legal rights to the child. When Halie was 12 years old, her caseworkers and a judge began planning for Halie to return to her biological mother. Although Halie's mother refused to relinquish her parental rights, she did not want to raise Halie. Halie spent years in group homes and foster homes. She turned 18 in foster care (Craig, 1995b, p. 46). Nationwide, nearly two thirds of foster children are reunited with their biological parents. The federal government, however, admits that one in three of the children who return home eventually reenters the system (as reported in the *Federal Register* in 1987 and cited in Hess, Folaron, & Jefferson, 1992).

For some children adrift in substitute care, family reunification is ruled out when their biological parents' rights are terminated. This does not guarantee a timely move to the permanency of adoption, however. At the start of fiscal 1997, more than 53,000 foster children were legally free to be adopted but languished in the uncertainty of state-run substitute care (Craig & Herbert, 1997, p. 9). Meanwhile, qualified families wait to adopt children of all ages, all racial and ethnic backgrounds, and with every type of disability. Although some states go so far as to label children "unadoptable," private agencies are finding families that states say do not exist (Craig, 1996). The Children with AIDS Project of America, a private group in Phoenix, has recruited more than

1,000 families to adopt HIV-positive children and AIDS orphans. In New York City, an all-volunteer group called You Gotta Believe! is finding families for foster teens.

Few would call public-agency foster care a success story, but even admissions of program failure point the blame at deficient funding. Pecora et al. (1992) state,

> Part of the problem—besides poor program design—is inadequate funding. . . . The nation's social services and public assistance programs have been battered by federal, state, and local budget cuts, while there have been increases in real need on the part of families and children. We have a rising rate of foster care placement in this country, a rate that is not entirely due to rising rates of drug abuse and homelessness, but caused in part by the lack of service alternatives and the resources to support creative interventions to meet the unique needs of individual families. (pp. 27-28)

What is ignored in statements such as these are the resources available in the private, charitable sector.

Some child advocates say that it is poverty in general that has led child welfare to its current state. The National Commission on Family Foster Care, convened by the CWLA, claims that the foster care crisis is "the logical result of two decades of national neglect in providing funding and services for children, youths, and their families" (CWLA, 1991, p. 3). Following this logic, it is suggested by some that one method of reducing the burden on government child welfare agencies is simply to increase income support to families. Pecora et al. (1992) state,

> Raising family income, then, might be an effective way to reduce some of the problems that child welfare workers face and to reduce the budgetary pressures on agencies that deliver child welfare services. To improve children's lives, an "incomes" strategy supplements the "services" strategy that social workers are more familiar with. (p. 59)

Children from low-income homes are more likely to be victims of child abuse (Pecora et al., 1992, pp. 66-67). Antecedent characteristics that lead to poverty may also lead to a greater likelihood of neglecting or abusing one's child (consider drug use as a predictor). Multigenerational dependence on welfare offers some evidence that provision of funds does not erase character deficits. Other evidence, more specific to child welfare, can be found in the case records of tens of thousands of children whose biological parents—despite

the best and most expensive rehabilitation programs and parenting classes that
state money can buy—repeatedly failed to prove their fitness.

Inherent in the failure of child welfare is the reality that government
agencies are not mission driven, rather they are funding driven. Title IV-E
funds flow to the states for the adoption of "special needs" foster children. It
may come as no surprise, then, that several states categorize 100% foster child
adoptions as special needs (Curtis, Boyd, Liepold, & Petit, 1995, pp. 90-91).
Today, nearly two thirds of all foster children qualify as special needs. In 1993,
all but 3 states used "race" or "race plus age" as a trigger for special needs
categorization, and 20 used "emotional ties to foster parents" (Curtis et al.,
1995, pp. 86-87). In some states, this categorization could mean that a child
has a sibling, is of an ethnic minority, is an older child, or has been in foster
care for longer than 18 months. There are many consequences to this practice—special needs children are wrongly viewed as less desirable, sometimes
even called "unadoptable"; the needs of truly vulnerable children are downplayed because a severely handicapped child is included in the same category
as a child who is biracial. This misrepresentation is neither just nor beneficial
to children (Craig, 1995b, p. 42).

Public agency child welfare today is by its very nature missionless. Most
government-run child welfare agencies have a mission statement that defines
the goals of the agency in such sweeping terms as "work for the best interests
of children." Even people within the system, however, admit that the lack of
true mission is a big problem. Pecora et al. (1992) noted,

> One of the dysfunctional phenomena that we are seeing in some child welfare
> organizations across the country is administrator avoidance of a well-articu-
> lated vision or clear agenda for action. This approach is used as a power
> retention device by limiting organizational communication, fragmenting
> program units, and maintaining institutional confusion. (p. 433)

In stark contrast are the incentives at work in the private charitable sector.
Privately funded charities of all types must define and adhere to their mission
to maintain their livelihood. The head of a private charity must be able to say
to funders "The mission of this organization is to do X" and then do it. Often,
there is a personal relationship between the charity and its funders, and nearly
always the charity is held accountable for meeting its mission. How many
funders would invest in a children's charity that consistently failed to help its
wards? Could a private funder be convinced to give money to a child welfare
entity that based its work on the notion that some children are hopeless and

that—no matter what efforts are made—some children are doomed to fail? A privately funded child welfare agency would go bankrupt if it subscribed to such a bleak philosophy of pessimism.

There are private programs working successfully throughout the country. In Glendale, California, Child SHARE (Shelter Homes: A Rescue Effort) is a private charity that for 10 years has worked with the church community to recruit and support foster and adoptive families. Children in Child SHARE homes experience fewer placements and are more likely to be adopted than children in state-run foster care. Such private-sector response captures the essence of an observation by the Urban Institute (Reed, 1996):

> Through their small scale, nonbureaucratic nature, local knowledge and personal relationships, neighborhoods, families, churches, and voluntary associations can respond rapidly, accurately, and in a more acceptable manner to local and individual needs in ways that large, formal institutions such as government agencies cannot. (p. 41)

The major difference between government-run programs and private businesses or charities is accountability. The market mechanism in place in the private sector demands that private groups prove their effectiveness at solving the problems that they are set up to address. The benefits of this efficiency have the potential to meet the dire needs of parentless children.

## ▓ Programs Before Promise

Federal funding for public child welfare in essence rewards states for failing to secure safe, permanent homes for children. Children are shuffled from one federally funded program to another, some to emerge at age 18 after having been foster children, then "special needs" children as they qualified by age or length of time in the system, then group home kids or wards of shelters or detention centers, then participants in the federal Independent Living Program. These programs were no doubt designed with good intentions, but as Richard Weaver (1948) wrote, "Good intention is primary, but it is not enough: That is the lesson of the experiment of romanticism" (p. 25).

Foster care is the largest program within the system of substitute care. Some researchers have romanticized foster care, claiming that it is not deleterious to later life. A study of 277 foster care graduates from New York

City (Festinger, 1983, as cited in Fein, Maluccio, & Kluger, 1990) found that former foster children

> were not so different from others their age in what they were doing, in the feelings they expressed, and in their hopes about the future.
>
> The assumptions and expectations that abound concerning the dire fate of foster care children seem to have little validity. The products of foster care—the young adults whom we followed in this study—did not measure down to such dire predictions. They were not what might be described as problem ridden when they were discharged nor did they become so in subsequent years; there was no support for the generational repetition of foster care; there was no evidence of undue economic dependence on public support; and their records of arrest were not excessive. (pp. 8-9)

These "findings" serve only to underscore the limits of the study's scope. Unfortunately, its results are belied by national data, as indicated by the Westat (1991) findings cited previously.

In government-run substitute care, the emphasis on programs can sometimes override a concern for protection. Practitioners talk about "serving" families with programs such as family preservation, even in cases that would seem precarious: "[A]lleged child abuse or neglect is not sufficient reason for placement since many children who have been abused or neglected can be served and protected in their own homes" (Pelton, 1990, p. 20). For nearly two decades, the mandate of Public Law 96-272 was to make family preservation and reunification the first goal of public child welfare agencies. This goal does not always protect the well-being of children. Richard Gelles, one of the leading experts on child welfare in the country, stated that it is not possible to balance family preservation and child safety (Capital Research Center, 1996, p. 6).

For children in state-run substitute care, the fastest-growing program is kinship foster care or placement with a biological relative of a child. In New York City, for example, the number of children in kinship foster care placements grew from 1,000 in 1986 to 24,000 in 1992 (CWLA, 1994, p. 16). The CWLA rates kinship foster care the second best option after reunification; both are seen by the group as preferable to adoption by a nonrelative. A promising finding of kinship foster care in California is that children experienced fewer placements (moves to different homes) than children in nonrelative foster care. The findings of several small-scale studies, however, reveal that children in kinship foster care placements stay in foster care longer, and kinship foster caregivers are less likely to have a high school education and five times more likely to be recipients of Temporary Aid to Needy Families

(TANF; foster care payments are not applicable against TANF benefits). Even without measurements of the long-term effects of kinship foster care, child advocates present it as preferable to adoption.

The system remains program oriented as children get closer to leaving it, either through emancipation or adoption. One proposal to ensure that young adults leaving foster care have some stability in their lives is to pay foster families to be available to foster care graduates. Proponents freely admit the program's dual goal of serving children and also providing income for foster families (Fein et al., 1990): "Because of the poor economic situation of many foster families of adolescents, some form of continued financial support to the foster parents would reinforce the importance and extent of their commitment to the youth" (pp. 44-45). The system remains program oriented even after adoption. A CWLA committee recommends that, when reunification and permanency with a kinship family is not appropriate, agencies should "provide a range of postplacement and postadoption supports, subsidies, and services for families who adopt to maintain the child's well-being and family stability" (CWLA, 1994, p. 71).

Because there are no market mechanisms in place to punish failure or reward success of public child welfare programs, examination of their efficacy is left to researchers—usually, studies are conducted or at least funded by the government itself. The research tends to focus on process and short-term effects, whereas studies of outcomes are decried as superfluous (Pecora et al., 1992):

> Because many of the studies of residential child care are outcome studies— often conducted by outside researchers—many practitioners doubt the value of the research enterprise and feel that its findings are of little use in shaping day-to-day practice. Almost by definition, outcome research cannot be directly useful, since it does not focus on the treatment process as it is occurring but on a "payoff" that occurs, if at all, long after children have left care. (p. 412)

What such an approach overlooks is the danger of perpetuating flawed programs.

## ▓ Giving Up on Children

The following description of children is from *The ABCs of Casework With Children* (Zwerdling, 1974): They are "basically narcissistic" and "demand to be the center of attention and are impulsive and self-gratifying" (p. 2). This handbook for social workers advises that even though it is hard to tolerate rejection of a child, "as social workers we have to identify with parents and other significant adults in the child's life and know the reasons for the rejection if we are to help them" (p. 19). This sentiment is representative of the manner in which child welfare today has all but given up on children. Instead of recognizing how a safe and permanent environment can nurture even the most abused or neglected child back to emotional and physical health, the system categorizes some children as hopeless or unlovable. One study of foster teens who had experienced a number of placements found that "they were a group of 'difficult' children" (Fein et al., 1990, p. 72). Another study found that a barrier to permanency for children in group homes is that child care workers considered the children "unadoptable" (Cole, 1989, p. 96).

The importance of permanency in a child's life is understood intuitively and has been well documented: Stable and continuous caregiving is important to child development, children need parents who are committed to them, having a permanent family leads to predictability and security for children, and "children are better raised by autonomous families than by the state" (National Legal Resource Center for Child Advocacy and Protection, 1989, pp. 9-10). Researchers, however, claim that permanency is not really an option for hundreds of thousands of foster kids. Fanshel, Finch, and Grundy (1989) note,

> A scrutiny of the national data suggests that more than a quarter of the children in foster care in the United States have had such unstable life histories that the assumptions underlying permanency planning, as envisioned in the Adoption Assistance and Child Welfare Act of 1980, are not particularly applicable. (p. 61)

What, then, is the alternative? It is hoped that program designers can see the paradox and danger of long-term "temporary" care.

Maybe the child welfare field has also given up on itself. Overwhelming caseloads, "skyrocketing" rates of child abuse and neglect, and an increase in the number of babies who are born drug affected are oft-cited factors that hinder the system's ability to meet the needs of families and children today. To that list are added unemployment, underemployment, "family breakup through divorce or desertion," and the "imbalance of power between men and women" (Abramovitz, 1991; Miller, 1991). Societal problems, however, cannot receive the sole blame for child welfare's failure to create better, workable solutions (Horn, 1994, p. 165). If we are to save the children, then we must go beyond blame and look for answers that truly address the immediate and long-term personal needs of our nation's most vulnerable children.

As national attention is paid to considering the efficacy of the orphanage, it is imperative to keep the following in mind: incentives drive programs, success must be determined by long-term outcomes for the clients of programs and not by the growth of programs per se, and, most important, no child is beyond hope.

## ▓ Notes

1. The Search Institute in Minneapolis has pioneered research on resiliency factors.
2. Catrina's story is true; her name has been changed here.
3. For a brief commentary on the deleterious nature of bouncing, see Benoit (1994, p. 246).
4. "Substitute care" is out-of-home placement under the supervision of a public child welfare agency. In this chapter, the term *foster care* is used as an umbrella term for out-of-home, government-run substitute care, encompassing care in foster families (including kinship care foster families), group homes, and other institutions. The term does not refer to children who are receiving family preservation services in their biological family homes. The American Public Welfare Association reported that at the end of fiscal year 1990, 74% of children in substitute care were in foster homes, 3% were in nonfinalized adoptive homes (i.e., they were already with their adoptive families but the formal process was not yet complete), 16% were in group homes or emergency care, <1% were living independently, and 6% were in "other" living arrangements (Tatara, 1993a, p. 95). This finding is based on 28 states reporting and accounts for 276,355 children, about 68% of the total substitute care population at the end of the fiscal year 1990.
5. This finding is based on 24 states reporting, accounting for 106,713 children, approximately 53% of the total estimated number of children exiting substitute care during fiscal year 1990 (Tatara, 1993a, pp. 71-72, 1993b, p. 10).
6. For more details on the state of foster care, see Craig and Herbert (1997).
7. Halie's story is true; her name has been changed.

## ▓ References

*A national evaluation of Title IV-E Foster Care Independent Living Program for Youth: Phase II final report* (Vols. I and II). (1991). Rockville, MD: Westat.

ABC News. (1994, December 21). The Charlotte Lopez story. *Turning point.* New York: American Broadcast Companies, Incorporated.

Abramovitz, M. (1991). Putting an end to doublespeak about race, gender, and poverty: An annotated glossary for social workers. *Social Work, 36*(5), 369-464.

Adoption Assistance and Child Welfare Act, Pub. L. No. 96-272 (1980).

American Civil Liberties Union Foundation. (1995). *Children's rights fact sheet.* New York: Author.

Benoit, M. B. (1994). The quality—not the category—of care. In D. J. Besharov (Ed.), *When drug addicts have children* (pp. 239-248). Washington, DC: Child Welfare League of America.

Capital Research Center. (1996). Children, abortion, and art: Why the Robert Sterling Clark Foundation wants to "fight the right." *Foundation Watch, 1*(3), 1-8.

Child Welfare League of America. (1991). *A blueprint for fostering infants, children, and youths in the 1990s.* Washington, DC: Author.

Child Welfare League of America. (1994). *Kinship care: A natural bridge.* Washington, DC: Author.

Children Now. (1996, May 28). *Internet update.*

Coalition for the Homeless. (1989). Blueprint for solving New York's homeless crisis (Report to Mayor D. Dinkins, p. 101). In P. O'Brien (Ed.), *Youth homelessness and the lack of relational planning for older foster children* (p. 1). New York: You Gotta Believe!

Cole, E. S. (1989). Permanency planning and residential care. In E. A. Balcerzak (Ed.), *Group care of children: Transitions toward the Year 2000* (pp. 91-99). Washington, DC: Child Welfare League of America.

Craig, C. (1995a, November). What I need is a mom. *Reader's Digest,* 122-126.

Craig, C. (1995b, Summer). "What I need is a mom": The welfare state denies homes to thousands of foster children. *Policy Review,* 41-49.

Craig, C. (1996, March 14). Adoptable kids go wanting. *USA Today,* p. 12A.

Craig, C., & Herbert, D. (1997). *The state of the children: An examination of government-run foster care.* Dallas: National Center for Policy Analysis.

Curtis, P. A., Boyd, J. D., Liepold, M., & Petit, M. (1995). *Child abuse and neglect: A look at the states.* Washington, DC: Child Welfare League of America.

Fanshel, D., Finch, S. J., & Grundy, J. F. (1989). Group care in the lives of children in long-term foster care: The Casey family program experience. In E. A. Balcerzak (Ed.), *Group care of children: Transitions toward the Year 2000* (pp. 37-65). Washington, DC: Child Welfare League of America.

Fein, E., Maluccio, A. N., & Kluger, M. P. (Eds.). (1990). *No more partings: An examination of long-term foster family care.* Washington, DC: Child Welfare League of America.

Festinger, T. (1983). *No one ever asked us. . . . A postscript to foster care.* New York: Columbia University Press.

Hess, P. M., Folaron, G., & Jefferson, A. B. (1992, July). Effectiveness of family reunification services: An innovative evaluative model. *Social Work, 37*(4), 304-311.

Horn, W. F. (1994). Implications for policy making. In D. J. Besharov (Ed.), *When drug addicts have children* (pp. 165-174). Washington, DC: Child Welfare League of America.

Lipner, R., & Goertz, B. (1990). Child welfare priorities and expenditures, W-Memo (Vol. 2, No. 8, pp. 3-13). Washington, DC: American Public Welfare Association.

Miller, J. (1991). Child welfare and the role of women: A feminist perspective. *American Journal of Orthopsychiatry, 61*(4), 592-598.

National Legal Resource Center for Child Advocacy and Protection. (1989). *Court rules to achieve permanency for foster children: Sample rules and commentary.* Washington, DC: American Bar Association.

Pecora, P. J., Whittaker, J. K., & Maluccio, A. N. (1992). *The child welfare challenge.* Hawthorn, NY: Aldine.

Pelton, L. H. (1990). Resolving the crisis in child welfare: Simply expanding the present system is not enough. *Public Welfare, 48*(4), 19-25, 45.

Reed, L. W. (Ed.). (1996). *Private cures for public ills.* Irvington-on-Hudson, NY: Foundation for Economic Education.

Tatara, T. (1993a). *Characteristics of children in substitute and adoptive care.* Washington, DC: American Public Welfare Association.

Tatara, T. (1993b, August). *U.S. child substitute care flow data for FY 92 and current trends in the state child substitute care populations* (VCIS Research Notes, No. 9, pp. 1-11). Washington, DC: American Public Welfare Association.

U.S. General Accounting Office. (1995, September). *Child welfare: Complex needs strain capacity to provide services* (GAO/HEHS-95-208). Washington, DC: U.S. Government Printing Office.

U.S. House of Representatives, Committee on Ways and Means. (1996). *1996 Green Book.* Washington, DC: U.S. Government Printing Office.

Weaver, R. M. (1948). *Ideas have consequences.* Chicago: University of Chicago Press.

Westat, Incorporated. (1991). *A national evaluation of Title IV-E foster care independent living program for youth: Phase II final report* (Vols. I and II). Rockville, MD: Author.

Zwerdling, E. (1974). *The ABCs of casework with children: A social work teacher's notebook.* Washington, DC: Child Welfare League of America.

# Chapter 3

# The Nation's Child Welfare Problems as Viewed From the Bench

ESTELLA MAY MORIARTY

F ew judges in recent times have removed children from their homes solely for economic reasons. Children are removed because they have been abused, abandoned, or neglected while in the custody of their families.

When parents sexually abuse their children, leave them alone for days at a time at a young age, beat them, burn them, sell them for sexual purposes, involve them with drugs, or abuse them in any of the sad litany of ways that children suffer, there is no choice—the children must be removed.

In all too many cases, parents are not good prospects for rehabilitation. The discussion of maternal deprivation or of reunification becomes moot. The real challenge is to find the best alternative placement. Judges have few choices in the placement of children after they are removed from their homes. The state child welfare system takes over, and usually the judge can do little more than suggest or lecture. The alternatives are limited to placement with extended family, adoption, or family foster care. Permanent care in a group setting or "orphanage," such as that provided by the Milton Hershey School or by SOS Children's Villages, should be an additional option for children when these placements are unsuitable and reunification is not possible.

Since time immemorial, extended families have stepped in to provide substitute care when parents died or were unable to care for their children. Extended families, however, may be unable or unwilling to provide constant care.

I remember the case of the three little Watkins girls (all names have been changed). The school nurse reported that they had symptoms of gonorrhea, which was confirmed. The father was charged with sexual assault. The mother refused to believe it, so the girls were placed with the grandmother, who gave them her only bed and sat up in a chair all night. When the father bailed out of jail and started dropping by her home, the grandmother asked to have the little girls placed elsewhere. Placed in foster care, the oldest (only 8 years old) was molested by the foster father. The social worker said there was no other foster home available and asked to place them back with the grandmother, who felt unable to protect them. I agreed with the grandmother and told the state worker to find another placement. The following Monday, I learned that the children had in fact been returned to the grandmother and the father had molested one of them again. For many weeks thereafter, I visited foster and shelter homes to see if "my" kids were safe.

Adoption is a wonderful alternative for the very young child who is abandoned. If, however, the child remains in an abusive home throughout the early years or remains in the limbo of the courts too long, not only do prospective adoptive parents become scarce but also the child begins to accumulate emotional scars and behavior patterns that make it less likely that the child will fit successfully into an adoptive home. Adoptive homes may be unavailable for sibling groups that wish to remain together.

No adoptive home has been found for the Stevens brothers, all seven of them, ages 3 to 13. They were abandoned by their mother 3 years ago. They are extremely dependent on each other, and the court wants to keep them together; no foster home, however, would take all seven. They have been separated and have been in at least four different homes. Three of the middle children have become so angry and depressed that they are now on the waiting list for therapeutic treatment centers.

Adoption did not work for Donny. Donny has been in foster care since he was 6 years old. He is now 14 years old. After many foster homes, many hearings, and a therapeutic treatment center, he was finally placed in an adoptive home with a middle-class family. He was so filled with anger, so far behind academically, and so unable to adjust, however, that the adoptive placement failed. Donny is now back in foster care.

Usually, the only remaining alternative is family foster care. Family foster care is best suited and is designed to be temporary care until a child is placed with nuclear or extended family or placed with adoptive parents. For thousands of children, however, it becomes a permanent situation. Florida legislatively determined that 7 of 10 children placed in foster care do not return to their biological families after the first year (Florida Statute 39.45). Family foster care is not a happy permanent solution. Most women of child-raising age are now employed outside the home. The pool of available foster parents has shrunk accordingly. It is not unusual to find 8, 10, or even more children placed in one foster home.

Foster families also undergo their own stresses: For example, marriages break up, family members change employment or become ill, deaths may occur, and children may be born. Behavior problems of the foster child may frustrate the foster care parent. Struggles among foster children striving for recognition within a large group may exacerbate the frustration. The result is an appalling lack of stability of placement in any particular home.

The social worker comes to the home, often with no notice to the child, and packs the child's meager belongings into a plastic bag, and then they are off to the next placement. The child becomes a member of the plastic bag brigade—a sad progression of homeless children, displaced refugees, shuttled from foster home to foster home, each carrying their small possessions in plastic garbage bags.

Statistically, in Florida, 29% of the children in foster care as of May 1996 have been in five or more placements. It is not unusual to see children who have been placed in 10 to 15 different homes. Each move is another loss—of friends, school, and surroundings—and another rejection for the child. All too often, the child blames himself or herself for the perceived rejection and becomes convinced of his or her unworthiness.

Each move makes it a little harder to trust the next adult and a little harder to bond. Each change of school impairs scholastic success. In Broward County, Florida, of 1,451 children in foster shelter care, 220 were ages 16 to 18, but only 6 graduated from high school in 1991. Moreover, the child who has so little connection with school becomes disruptive and is often suspended or expelled. Truancy is common, and runaways are frequent.

Without consistent moral guidance, without consistent discipline, without a positive self-image, and with no cause for hope, the child becomes a fertile soil for delinquent behavior and for drug involvement. Children become depressed, and some become suicidal. Some become violent and angry, and many become mentally ill, sociopathic, or psychotic.

Dolly is 13 years old. She and her three younger siblings came into foster care 2 years ago. Dolly had been sexually abused by two uncles and a neighbor. She had been kept out of school for a year because she was the principal caretaker of the younger children. On occasion, she had to beg food from neighbors to feed the family. Her mother is borderline retarded. Since she has been in foster care, Dolly has shown severe depression and has been hospitalized following a suicide attempt. She has been in shelter care and two foster homes. The siblings are separated from each other.

Joanne is 9 years old. She has been in foster care for 3 years. Her mother, a drug addict, left Joanne with anyone who would watch her, and in 1991 she did not return at all. Joanne was sexually abused in the last house in which she lived. In the past 18 months, she has been in four different foster homes. She is frightened, depressed, and filled with anger.

Who will adopt these children? Who can meet their needs? They are permanent marchers in the plastic bag brigade. They are disadvantaged almost as much by the deprivation of their homes as by the circumstances that led to their removal. They lose their bedrooms, their school, their neighborhood friends, and often their siblings.

What is a judge to do when faced with a choice of leaving a child in an abusive home or placing a child in overcrowded foster care knowing the emotional and sometimes physical abuse that is likely to follow? One frustrated judge (A. Hastings, personal communication, 1993) declared at a hearing,

> I'm not going to take a child from his home to be put in a foster home where he will be abused. If he is going to be abused, let him be abused by people who love him instead of being abused by strangers.

The saddest part of a juvenile judge's job is watching the progress of a tiny victim of adult crime as he or she is molded by the system into a delinquent and eventually a criminal. The Dade County, Florida, grand jury (fall term, 1995) found that of children entering foster care who were age 8 or over, 40% had criminal cases pending within 5 years of entrance.

One such child is Tom. Tom came into my court when he was 12 years old. His parents were divorced. His father, who had custody, had remarried a woman with two children who did not want Tom. The father called the state welfare office after putting Tom on the plane for Florida. The mother's new lover did not want him either. Both parents were physically as well as emotionally abusive. Tom was placed in foster care, where he was sexually abused by the foster parent. He ran away and lived on the streets for nearly 6 months. The next foster parent was hastily recruited after calling in response to a newspaper story. Tom lived with her until Christmas. She then called me, frantically stating that Tom was sniffing gasoline while she was at work and was doing so while smoking the cigarettes his mother had given him, which were her only Christmas gift. Tom was placed in a shelter, which he vandalized in an emotional outburst and was subsequently hospitalized. He stayed with his attorney, guardian *ad litem,* until the attorney's wife gave birth to twins. He was placed with a lady from the church and then ran away. Finally, Tom became an adult. A year or 2 later, he killed a man in a fight and was sent to prison for 4 years. After release, he married a woman who also had grown up in the foster care system. They have two children who are now also in state custody. Thus, the cycle repeats itself.

An "orphanage" that consisted of small group homes with residential house parents would provide stability where it is otherwise unattainable. In such a case, even if the house parent left, the child could keep his or her school, friends, and home. Administrative staff would be able to maintain continuity of psychological or other counseling.

SOS Children's Villages, established in 1949 in postwar Europe, now care for children in 104 countries, providing single-family homes presided over by an employee "parent" in a village setting. An SOS Children's Village opened in Florida in 1992, and another opened in Illinois in 1993. Children in SOS Children's Villages both in the United States and abroad live much as their middle-class neighbors: attending public schools, sharing household chores, learning to live with the siblings in the home, biological or otherwise, and forming emotional bonds with the parent who lives with them. The parent makes a commitment to remain with the children in that house until they reach majority.

The Carter girls, four sisters ages 6 to 11, were the first children admitted to the SOS Children's Village in Coconut Creek, near Fort Lauderdale, Florida. Tanya, the eldest, said to her sisters, "We can live here until we are 55." Perhaps that is longer than necessary, but at least there are no more plastic bags in their future.

There is another category of children who need the stability of an orphanage. These are the children whose parents can best be described as marginal: parents who are in and out of jail for crimes unrelated to child abuse, parents who are mentally ill, parents who hook up with one unsuitable partner after another, or parents who battle addiction problems. These parents may love their children and attempt to comply with rehabilitative efforts offered to them. The children may have strong bonds with these parents. The parents may pull themselves together for a time, the children do fairly well, and then the next crisis occurs and the children are back in the system. They become a part of the same plastic bag brigade as the abused child.

Wealthy parents have long solved such problems with boarding schools. Although literature is full of tales of problems in boarding schools and scars inflicted by them, nevertheless thousands of productive people have been educated in such institutions and look back fondly on their experience in such places.

Orphanages such as the Milton Hershey School in Pennsylvania provide stability, friends, education, and guidance without removing the child from the love of his birth family. Children could be placed in such residences by their parents without going through the humiliation and delay of court proceedings. The courts could use them as an alternative when severing parental rights is not warranted but reunification must be deferred frequently or for long periods.

The movement toward deinstitutionalization that prevailed in the 1970s and 1980s has permeated the thinking of social workers and state agencies, and it is reflected in the law. The Federal Adoption Assistance and Child Welfare Act provides that foster care maintenance payments may be made only to a child in a foster family home or in a child care institution that accommodates no more than 25 children (42 U.S.C. 672(c)). States are required to maintain detailed records of the number of children in foster care and the length of their stay, with no distinction made for children in long-term agency care.

State laws implement the federal laws and add their own restrictions. Florida Administrative Code 10M-6.127 provides that a foster family home rather than group care is the placement used for all children under 6 years of age and for the majority of children from 6 to 12 years in middle childhood, excluding those with problems requiring specialized care.

The constant emphasis on returning children to the biological families or placing them for adoption is reflected in the attitudes of social workers, who fear damaging children by "institutionalizing" them. The fear of causing maternal deprivation by placing children in "institutions" results in so many foster placements that some children will call every woman "mother" but be unable to bond with any of them.

The word orphanage connotes many things. No one would return to the world of Oliver Twist, in which an orphanage was a warehouse for unwanted children administered by cruel and uncaring adults. It is time to examine the realities facing children, however. It is time to develop multiple solutions that will meet their diverse needs. It is time to recognize that the belief that every family can be rehabilitated or at least that there is an adoptive family for each and every child is a fairy tale.

The foster care system not only fails to prevent maternal deprivation but also fails to provide the stability of place, friends, school, and discipline that can be provided by an appropriate orphanage. We have thrown the baby out with the bath water, and the baby is out in the cold.

# CHAPTER 4

# Family Preservation and Child Maltreatment

RICHARD J. GELLES

O n an oppressively hot summer evening in the Southeast section of Washington, D.C., 22-year-old Lenora Price[1] sweltered in her one-bedroom apartment, only a dozen or so blocks from the Capitol building. Lenora was hot, tired, and hungry. Her 6-week-old daughter Leticia was also hot, tired, and hungry and wailed inconsolably. One-year-old Cornell slept fitfully in his bed in the room he shared with his mother and new sister. Shortly before midnight, unable to get Leticia to stop crying, Lenora suffocated her. Lenora then left the apartment to meet her boyfriend for a drink—leaving behind her sleeping son and the corpse of her infant daughter. The next morning, Lenora called the police to report that she had killed her daughter.

Cornell was initially placed in a foster home and was subsequently moved to two additional foster homes. Cornell's maternal grandmother could not care for him because she was already caring for Cornell's half brother. Lenora's parental rights had been terminated on her oldest child, Leon, for reasons of neglect.

Four years after she had killed her daughter, Lenora gave birth to another child—a son, Dayton. She had completed her high school equivalency and secured a position with a manpower-training program. She also had been arrested for credit card fraud. Cornell was in his third foster home. He had spent three fourths of his young life in foster care. His mother had given birth to four children fathered by four different men. Although she made some progress in organizing her life, her arrest for credit card fraud was about to result in her being incarcerated for a period of no less than 1 year.

While Lenora's case wound its complicated and complex way though the legal and child welfare system, the plan for Cornell was "reunification" with his mother—the caretaker with whom he had lived 1 year; the caretaker who killed his sister, perhaps while he was awake in the next room; the caretaker who already had her parental rights terminated on another of Cornell's half siblings.

The Department of Social Services caseworkers were frustrated. Although Lenora had made some progress, she had not made sufficient progress to convince the caseworkers that Cornell would be safe if he was returned to his mother. Lenora had been provided with the latest and most comprehensive services in the child welfare field—intensive family preservation services. The time period for the services had ended, and yet the caseworkers were still not convinced Lenora was capable of caring for both Cornell and her newborn son. The caseworkers' frustration was exacerbated because they had not yet found a suitable foster home for Cornell: He would soon have to be moved to his fourth foster home because his foster mother was not interested in a long-term placement. There were no relatives who were ready and willing to care for Cornell. Even though Lenora had shown no real signs of change or parental competence—her arrest for credit card fraud and impending jailing were hardly encouraging signs—the caseworkers continued to recommend reunification in part because they knew of no viable and cost-effective permanent placement for Cornell.

Forty or 50 years ago, the caseworkers and those involved with Lenora, Cornell, and the other siblings and family members would not have had such a dilemma or been so frustrated. Forty or 50 years ago, Cornell would likely have been placed in what was then called an orphanage. No doubt caseworkers would have tried to counsel Lenora, work with her, and provide her services. No doubt the caseworkers would have had reunification as their goal. Whether they could have helped Lenora or not, we cannot know. Irrespective of how Lenora might have responded, Cornell would have had a permanent home and would likely not have been moved four times in 4 years.

Why are there so few permanent placements for children like Cornell? Why are orphanages or what are now called "congregate care" facilities not generally found on the menu of services and resources available to children served by the child welfare system? Why are children like Cornell either returned to caretakers who are likely to reabuse them or are left in limbo in a series of moves in and out of foster care and kin care (foster care provided by relatives)? First, the answer is somewhat complicated and involves the evolution of a cultural ideology that claims that children always do better when cared for by their biological parents. Second, the answer can be found in a well-intended federal law that was supposed to provide children permanence but actually ended up denying permanence and placing thousands, if not hundreds of thousands, of children at heightened risk of maltreatment. Third, the answer involves a nearly missionary marketing of the virtues of intensive family preservation services. Last, to justify efforts to reunify children with maltreating parents, we have demonized, without adequate evidence, congregate care (orphanages) and foster care.

## ▓ Family Preservation and Reunification as National Policy

### *The Modern Evolution of Family Preservation as Social Policy*

Child abuse and neglect have, for more than a century, been conceptualized as a child welfare problem that is best responded to by the social service or child welfare system. Because child maltreatment is viewed as a child welfare matter, the basic assumption that guides intervention is that social and clinical interventions are more effective in protecting children and preventing the reoccurrence of abuse and neglect than arrest, prosecution, or other legal interventions. Because the essential philosophy of the child welfare system is compassion and not control (Rosenfeld & Newberger, 1977), the preferred response is to provide support for families as a means of protecting children.

At the core of the compassionate approach is the belief that children do best when cared for and raised by their biological caretakers. The theoretical and empirical work on attachment (Bowlby, 1958, 1969; Harlow, 1958, 1961; Lindsey, 1994) has been used to support this assumption, but even professionals and policymakers who are unfamiliar with research on attachment endorse the assumption that the preferred method of intervening in cases of child maltreatment is to preserve the family, so long as the safety of the child can be ensured.

Family preservation and reunification programs are not new. They date at least to the turn of the century, with the settlement house movement, Hull House, and Jane Addams. Family preservation services are designed to help children and families, including extended and adoptive families, that are at risk of abuse or delinquency or are in crisis.

The main exception to the practice of family preservation occurred in the wake of the rediscovery of child abuse in the 1960s. When Kempe, Silverman, Steele, Droegemueller, and Silver published their seminal paper, "The Battered Child Syndrome" in 1962, they focused almost exclusively on serious and life-threatening acts of physical violence directed at young and mostly defenseless children. Kempe et al. and the medical community advocated the enactment of mandatory reporting laws for child abuse so that serious injuries to children were not deliberately or inadvertently overlooked and untreated by professionals.

Mandatory reporting, combined with public awareness campaigns and technological developments such as toll-free lines (800 numbers) and pagers, resulted in extraordinary increases in reports of child abuse and neglect. At the same time, because the medical and psychiatric community was at the forefront of the campaign to identify child abuse as a serious social problem, the prevailing causal model was a medical/psychiatric/psychopathology model that explained abuse as a function of the psychopathology of the caretaker. Because the cause of abuse was thought to be a character or personality defect of the parents or caretakers, for almost a decade, separating children from abusive parents became an important initial and long-term intervention. Even during this period, however, it was rare that more than half of validated cases of abuse and neglect resulted in an out-of-home placement.

By 1978, there were slightly less than 1 million reports of child maltreatment in the United States each year and approximately 500,000 children in foster care in the United States (Pelton, 1989; Tatara, 1993). The combination of increased reports, increased numbers of children in out-of-home placements, and the cost of such placements raised concerns throughout the child welfare system. At the same time as these concerns were raised, there was a shift in the explanation of child abuse and neglect. The shift changed the model from a medical and psychiatric model, which focused on character disorders, personality disorders, and psychiatric problems, to a social and social psychological model that focused on poverty, social isolation, social learning that resulted in the intergenerational transmission of violence and abuse, and cultural attitudes about children and physical punishment (Gelles, 1973; Gil, 1970; Parke & Collmer, 1975).

The shift had a gradual but major impact on child welfare interventions and policy. Abusive parents, rather than being thought of as characterologically disordered and different, were now viewed as being at one end of a continuum of parenting. Their abusive and neglectful behavior was not considered the sole result of a personality or psychiatric disorder but rather the result of a surplus of stressors and a deficit of resources. Anyone, this model proposed, could abuse or neglect a child given certain social and economic circumstances. Even if there were clinical signs of psychiatric disorder, these too were thought to arise from social and environmental conditions (Gelles, 1973; Lindsey, 1994). This being the case, the major task of child welfare agencies became case management that assisted families in coping with stressors and providing personal, social, and economic assistance.

By the late 1970s the new model explaining child abuse and neglect was well integrated in the scholarly and professional literature. At the same time, as noted previously, out-of-home placements had reached 500,000 (Pelton, 1989; Tatara, 1993). In addition, news reports more frequently described situations in which children were harmed or even killed in foster care placements. In Rhode Island, for example, a youngster named Keith Chisolm was removed from his mother by the Department of Social and Rehabilitative Services. The boy had not been physically or sexually abused; rather, he was the victim of neglect. Keith was later beaten to death by his foster father, a man who had previously been arrested for assault and battery. Cases such as this made child protective workers in Rhode Island reluctant to remove any but the most grievously injured children from their biological parents. Cases such as this cause what Lindsey (1994) refers to as the "child welfare pendulum" to swing from the side of focusing on child protection to the other side that focuses on family preservation.

## The Adoption Assistance and
## Child Welfare Act of 1980

The child protection and family preservation policy that emerged in the late 1970s was crystallized by the federal Adoption Assistance and Child Welfare Act of 1980 (Public Law 96-272), which experts and advocates generally consider the most significant legislation in the history of child welfare. The two major child welfare provisions of the act were on permanency planning and "reasonable efforts." Permanency planning was a response to concerns over what child welfare experts had labeled "foster care drift." Although data on foster care were scarce and often incomplete at that time, researchers and practitioners generally believed that too many children were going into foster care each year and too few children were leaving the foster care system. Permanency planning mandated that states develop permanency plans for children—either that they be returned to their birth parents or placed for adoption—within 18 months of entrance into the child welfare system. The second child welfare provision of the legislation was embodied in the two words, reasonable efforts. Again, aimed at reducing foster care drift and inappropriate out-of-home placement, the policy of reasonable efforts was stated in a brief, but important section of the legislation (§ 471 a 15):

> In each case, reasonable efforts will be made (A) prior to the placement of a child in foster care, to prevent or eliminate the need for removal of a child from his home, and (B) to make it possible for the child to return to his home. (p. 503)

States had to demonstrate that they made reasonable efforts and that they were in compliance with the permanency planning provision of the law to qualify for federal funding for adoption and foster care.

It appeared that the Adoption Assistance and Child Welfare Act of 1980 had the desired effect. Data on foster care placements indicated that out-of-home placements declined to under 300,000 per year by the mid-1980s (Pelton, 1989; Tatara, 1993). The reduction, however, did not continue, and by the mid-1990s foster care placements approached 600,000 per year (Tatara, 1993).

Despite the good intentions behind the law and likely initial success in reducing foster care placements, the Adoption Assistance and Child Welfare Act of 1980 had some unintended consequences. One problem was the ambiguity regarding the very concept of reasonable efforts. Nowhere in the federal legislation or ensuing legal decisions in state courts was the concept reasonable efforts ever clearly defined. As a result, child protection workers, administrators, legal staff, and judges had no guidelines for how much or how long they had to make efforts at reunification before moving to permanent out-of-home placement for abused and neglected children. A second problem was the actual implementation of the law. Because there were no specific definitions or guidelines for what constituted reasonable or what constituted efforts, and because family preservation was a long-held bedrock value of the child welfare system, child welfare workers and administrators often interpreted reasonable efforts to mean that they should make "every possible effort" to keep children with, or reunite them with, the birth parents.

### Intensive Family Preservation Services

Intensive family preservation services are an alternative to the "business-as-usual" family preservation and family reunification child welfare casework used by child welfare agencies. The intensive family preservation services movement began in Tacoma, Washington, in 1974. Child psychologists David Haapala and Jill Kinney developed a program they called "Homebuilders" with a grant from the National Institute of Mental Health. The goal of the program was to work intensively with families before a child is removed. There are now many variations of intensive family preservation services in use throughout the country. The core goal of such programs is to maintain children safely in the home or to facilitate a safe and lasting reunification. Intensive family preservation services programs were designed for families that have a serious crisis threatening the stability of the family and the safety of the family members.

Although, as noted previously, there are many variations of intensive family preservation services programs, the essential feature is that such programs are short-term crisis intervention. Services are meant to be provided in the client's home. The length of the sessions is variable. Unlike traditional family preservation services, intensive family preservation services are available 7 days a week, 24 hours a day. Perhaps the most important feature of intensive family preservation services is that caseloads are small—caseworkers may have only two or three cases. In addition, the length of time is brief and fixed at a specific number of weeks. Both hard and soft services are provided. Hard services include food stamps, housing, and homemaker services; soft services include parent education classes and individual or family counseling or both.

## ■ Are Intensive Family Preservation Services Effective?

The initial reports regarding the effectiveness of intensive family preservation services were uniformly enthusiastic. The programs were claimed to have reduced the placement of children, reduced the cost of out-of-home placement, and, at the same time, ensured the safety of children. Foundation program officers and program administrators claimed that families involved in intensive family preservation services had low rates of placement and "100% safety records" (Barthel, 1991; Forsythe, 1992). Program administrators also claimed success in reducing placement and ensuring safety. Susan Kelley, director of the Division of Family Preservation Services, Office of Children and Youth Services for the state of Michigan, testified before

Congress that of 2,505 families that participated in Michigan's Families First program in the first year, one incident of abuse was reported (Barthel, 1991).

There were, however, major methodological and design limitations of the early evaluations of intensive family preservation services. The vast majority of the evaluations of intensive family preservation services either employed no control group or used a comparison group that was not an appropriate match for the group receiving treatment. Moreover, there were questions raised about whether "placement avoidance" was the appropriate outcome measure for the evaluations. Peter Rossi (1992) cautioned that placement avoidance was not a proper outcome variable because placement avoidance was itself the treatment. In his 1992 review, Rossi concluded that the evaluation studies did not convincingly demonstrate that intensive family preservation services reduced placement or reduced child welfare costs. The claim that children were safe was never actually evaluated.

To date, there have been at least 46 evaluations of intensive family preservation services of one form or another (Heneghan, Horwitz, & Leventhal, 1996; Lindsey, 1994). Of these 46 evaluations and of nearly 850 published articles on intensive family preservation, only 10 studies actually evaluated intensive family preservation services, included outcome data in the report, and used a control group of some kind. In California, New Jersey, and Illinois, the evaluations used randomly assigned control groups, included outcome data, and had large enough samples to allow for rigorous evaluation. In all three studies, there were either small or insignificant differences between the group receiving intensive family preservation services and the control group receiving traditional casework services. Even in terms of placement avoidance, there was no difference between the two groups, thus suggesting that earlier claims that intensive family preservation services were successful in reducing placement obtained those results because of the low overall rate of placement in child welfare agencies. These results also point to how difficult it is for child welfare caseworkers to accurately classify a family as "high risk" for being placed because 80 to 90% of the children in the control group were not placed, even though these children were theoretically selected for the study because they were at high risk of being placed.

As noted previously, the outcome measures of most evaluations do not include data specifically designed to measure child outcome. Thus, it is also impossible to verify the claim of the safety record of intensive family preservation services. Critics of intensive family preservation services programs argue that children are injured or even killed when they are inappropriately returned to their abusive caretakers (Gelles, 1996). Indeed, there is considerable anecdotal evidence that such children are injured and killed when left with or returned to abusive parents. There are no data, however, on whether children involved in intensive family preservation services have higher rates of reinjury or fatalities compared with children served by traditional child welfare casework.

Thus, the empirical case for intensive family preservation has yet to be made. Amid the claims and counterclaims on intensive family preservation and following the funding of the Family Preservation and Support Act of 1993, the Department of Health and Human Services funded a national evaluation of family preservation and support services. This evaluation, conducted by Westat, The Chain Hall Center for Children, and James Bell Associates, is examining a full range of family preservation and support programs at a number of sites throughout the country. The study is using a randomized trial design with a variety of outcome measures, including placement, cost, and family functioning.

Given that the claims for the effectiveness of intensive family preservation have not been supported by scientific evidence, there is concern for the widespread adoption of intensive family preservation services. Peter Rossi (as quoted in MacDonald, 1994) criticized the states and the federal government for running "pell mell into family preservation without considering the evidence for it" (p. 53).

## ▓ The Current Crisis in Child Welfare

It is fair to say that most people who know about the child welfare and child protective system in the United States know that the system is in crisis. The crisis is more than simply a failure of one part of the system. As the U.S. Advisory Board on Child Abuse and Neglect (1990) concluded 6 years ago, this is not a failure of a single element of the system but a chronic and critical multiple-organ failure.

The failure is not the result of an enormous increase in the number of reported cases of child maltreatment (National Center of Child Abuse and Neglect, 1996). This is not a crisis caused solely by too few child protective workers responding to an increased number of reports. This is not a failure caused solely by having too few resources available to public and private child welfare agencies.

The current crisis of the child welfare and child protective system and our inability to help get vulnerable children out of harm's way and provide them with permanent caretaking is the result of the following:

1. The overselling of intensive family preservation services as a cost-effective and safe means of protecting children: Although intensive family preservation services might be effective for some families under certain conditions, the case cannot be made for its overall effectiveness. The inability to find evidence for the effectiveness of intensive family preservation services would not be so problematic if foundations, agency directors, child advocacy groups, and even administrators in the Department of Health and Human Services were not effusively touting the successes of intensive family preservation services.

2. The inappropriate implementation of the Adoption Assistance and Child Welfare Act of 1980: After 16 years of experience with this law, it is quite clear that child protective workers often misunderstand and misapply the law. As noted earlier, many caseworkers, lawyers, and judges state very clearly that their mandate is to make every possible effort to keep children with their biological caretakers.

3. The belief that children always do best when raised by their biological caregivers: Recently, an administrator from the Missouri Department of Social Services cited research that said that children do best when left with their biological caretakers (Bradley, 1996). Indeed, this is true as long as their caretakers do not abuse and maltreat them. Children who are abused and neglected, however, do not do best when they are left with or are reunited with the caretakers who maltreated them. In fact, compared to children left with caretakers who maltreat them, children placed into foster care, children who are adopted, and even children raised in orphanages generally do better (Benson, Shorma, & Roehlkepartain, 1994; Bolton, Laner, & Gai, 1981; Fanshel & Shinn, 1978; McKenzie, 1996; Wald, Carlsmith, & Leiderman, 1988).

4. The belief in the fiction that one can actually balance family preservation and child safety: Such a balancing act almost inevitably ends up tilting in favor of parents and places many children at risk. More than 1,200 children are killed by their parents or caretakers each year in the United States, and nearly half of these children are killed after they or their parents have come to the attention of child welfare agencies (Gelles, 1996). Tens of thousands, if not hundreds of thousands, of children are reabused each year after they or their parents have been identified by child welfare agencies.

5. The belief that it is easy to change parents who maltreat their children: Child protective agencies often confuse compliance with change and fail to recognize the process by which people change. Just because parents or caretakers are reported for abuse and are threatened with the loss of their children does not mean they will change their behavior. Also, just because

people are provided with state-of-the-art interventions and services does not mean they will change their behavior. Behavior change is thought by many in the child welfare system to be a one-step process—one simply changes from one form of behavior to another. For example, if someone is an alcohol or substance abuser, then change involves stopping using alcohol or drugs. If the person stops but then begins again, then the change has not successfully occurred. A second assumption is that maltreating parents or caretakers all want to change—either to avoid legal and social sanctions or because they have an intrinsic motivation to be caring parents. As a result, those who design and implement child abuse and neglect interventions assume that all, or at least most, parents, caretakers, and families are ready and able to change their maltreating behavior. Research on behavior change, however, clearly demonstrates that change is not a one-step process. Rather, changing behavior is a dynamic process and one progresses through a number of stages in trying to modify behavior. It also assumes that there are cognitive aspects to behavior change that can be measured (Prochaska & DiClemente, 1982, 1983, 1984; Prochaska, Norcross, & DiClemente, 1994).

One of the reasons why child welfare interventions in general, and intensive family preservation programs in particular, may have such modest success rates is that most interventions are "action" programs often provided to individuals and families in what Prochaska and colleagues call the precontemplator or contemplation stage of change—what others may refer to as denial or ambivalence about the need for change.

## ■ Family Preservation, Child Placements, and Orphanages

Irrespective of how professionals in the field of child maltreatment feel about intensive family preservation services, the effectiveness of the Adoption Assistance and Child Welfare Act of 1980, and other aspects of the child welfare system, nearly all professionals agree that children need permanent caretaking. Second, nearly every professional in the field views the lack of suitable placements for children at risk as a major constraint that must be overcome if the crisis in the child welfare system is to be resolved. There are more than 3 million reports of child abuse in the United States each year, the number of children in foster care each year is approaching 600,000, and there is evidence that children are entering foster care at younger ages and are staying longer than they have in the past (Barth, Courtney, Berrick, & Albert,

1994). Any attempt to reform the child welfare system inevitably confronts the question, "Where will all the children who need protection be placed?"

For a time, it appeared that intensive family preservation services would solve this problem: Children could remain with their own parents assuming that the parents would be helped by intensive family preservation services. This option, however, appears less viable as more research fails to find that intensive family preservation services is a widely effective intervention.

A second option is kin placement, or placement with relatives. A major provision of the Adoption Assistance and Child Welfare Act of 1980 was that in instances in which maltreated children have to be placed outside of the home, the placement must be the least restrictive option. Placement with relatives is considered to be the least restrictive of all placement options. In addition, states can and sometimes do pay lower rates for kin placements compared to nonkin foster care. Unfortunately, kin placement is not often a viable option. First, as in the case of Lenora, relatives may not be able to take any or all the children who need placement. Second, relatives may be inappropriate as placements. Given the fact that there is an intergenerational transmission of child maltreatment, estimated to be about 30% (Kaufman & Zigler, 1987), a significant proportion of relatives may be child maltreators themselves.

A third option is adoption. There are a substantial number of families and individuals who wish to adopt children. The majority of potential adoptive parents, however, prefer to adopt children under 1 year of age and to adopt children without significant medical, social, or emotional problems. Because states are under a federal mandate to make reasonable efforts to keep or reunite children with their biological parents, states rarely terminate parental rights until a considerable amount of time, effort, and legal reviews have taken place. This means that by the time they are actually freed for adoption, maltreated children are often either too old or too badly harmed (physically and emotionally) to be likely to be placed for adoption.

A fourth option is congregate care or orphanages. Others have provided a more detailed history of the rise and fall of orphanages in the United States (Olasky, 1996; Smith, 1995; Spar, 1994). Although the term itself has not been used in quite some time, perhaps because of the decline in the number of actual orphans who needed placement, the facilities, what we now call congregate care or "group care," still exist. In fact, although the number of children living in group facilities has decreased in recent years, the actual number of group care facilities has grown (Spar, 1994). Contemporary group homes are smaller and care for fewer children than orphanages or group homes of the past.

Orphanages became a contemporary issue early in 1994 when the Republican majority in Congress began to draft welfare reform legislation that would have, and ultimately did, change welfare from an open-ended entitlement to block grants to the states. The block grants came with mandates for having welfare recipients work, time limits for welfare benefits, and removal of immigrants, both legal and illegal, from cash benefit eligibility. After the midterm 1994 elections, Speaker of the House Newt Gingrich suggested that welfare reform also include orphanages for children whose parents (mostly mothers) could not rid themselves of drug problems, find jobs, and get off welfare rolls within 2 years.

Speaker Gingrich's suggestion set off a rapid and emotional response. The orphanage debate resurfaced images out of *Oliver Twist*—of long, dark hallways, cavernous dormitories, gruel, and poor children either emotionally abandoned or physically and sexually victimized. Orphanages are believed to be harmful to children and undesirable placement for children at risk.

Of course, today's congregate care and group care facilities hardly resemble the physically and emotionally barren places portrayed by Dickens and conjured up by opponents of orphanages. They also rarely resemble, however, the warm and nurturous *Boys Town* of Mickey Rooney and Spencer Tracy fame—pointed to by Speaker Gingrich. Today's orphanages are expensive. Spar (1994) estimated that the annual per cost of a child in group care under the auspices of the child welfare system ranged from $8,700 to $50,400, with an average annual cost per child of almost $35,000.

Unfortunately, the emotional public debate over orphanages, laden with images drawn from movie portrayals, has diverted attention from a more clear-headed analysis of the place of congregate care in the child welfare system. Moreover, even before the public debate erupted after Speaker Gingrich's comments, orphanages were rarely part of the child welfare discourse. The emphasis on efforts to preserve families where maltreatment has occurred, combined with the federal mandates of reasonable efforts and least restrictive placements, resulted in congregate care being considered an absolutely last resort on the menu of child welfare services. The annual per child cost of congregate care also pushed congregate care to the last resort far end of the continuum of services.

It is both unfortunate and inappropriate that congregate care facilities are seen as a last resort. Cost per child not withstanding, congregate care facilities, such as Boys Town in Nebraska and the Milton Hershey School in Pennsylvania, are plausible and cost-effective placements for abused and battered children, although they are probably not appropriate for children under 3 years of age.

For there to be an intelligent and useful discussion of the value and limitations of congregate care, we need to throw out all the assumptions and myths about orphanages and focus on safety and permanence. The key assumption that "children always do best when cared for by their biological parents" must be revealed as a canard. Children need, first and foremost, safety and protection from harm and permanence. Permanence means that children must have caretakers who are there for them in an unconditional relationship. Moving back and forth between abusive and neglecting caretakers and foster care is not safe nor is it permanent. Moving from foster home to foster home is not permanent. Waiting in a foster home while maltreating caretakers are given one more chance to rid themselves of abusive partners or drug and alcohol problems is no permanence. Also, waiting years for a parent to learn how to be a nurturant and caring caretaker is not permanence.

Orphanages or congregate care facilities are not the solution to the crisis of the child welfare system. Orphanages and congregate care, however, are an appropriate and underused component of a child welfare system—especially a system that should place safety and permanence as the main goals of child welfare.

## ■ Note

1. This case study is based on an actual case. The names and some of the facts of the case have been altered to protect the identity of those involved.

## ■ References

Adoption Assistance and Child Welfare Act, Pub. L. No. 96-272 (1980).

Barth, R. P., Courtney, M., Berrick, J. D., & Albert, V. (1994). *From child abuse to permanency planning: Child welfare services pathways and placements.* New York: Aldine.

Barthel, J. (1991). *For children's sake: The promise of family preservation.* New York: Edna McConnell Clark Foundation.

Benson, P., Shorma, A. R., & Roehlkepartain, E. C. (1994). *Growing up adopted—A portrait of adolescents and their families.* Minneapolis, MN: Search Institute.

Bolton, F. G., Laner, R., & Gai, D. (1981). For better or worse? Foster parents and foster children in an officially reported child maltreatment population. *Children and Youth Services Review, 3,* 37-53.

Bowlby, J. (1958). The nature of the child's tie to his mother. *International Journal of Psychoanalysis, 39,* 350-373.

Bowlby, J. (1969). *Attachment and loss. Vol. 1: Attachment.* New York: Basic Books.

Bradley, D. (1996, October 13). New group hopes to change way Kansas handles child abuse reports. *Kansas City Star,* p. 54.

Fanshel, D., & Shinn, E. (1978). *Children in foster care: A longitudinal investigation.* New York: Columbia University Press.

Forsythe, P. (1992). Homebuilders and family preservation. *Children and Youth Services Review, 14,* 37-47.

Gelles, R. (1973). Child abuse as psychopathology: A sociological critique and reformulation. *American Journal of Orthopsychiatry, 43,* 611-621.

Gelles, R. J. (1996). *The book of David: How preserving families can cost children's lives.* New York: Basic Books.

Gil, D. (1970). *Violence against children: Physical child abuse in the United States.* Cambridge, MA: Harvard University Press.

Harlow, H. (1958). The nature of love. *American Psychologist, 13,* 673-685.

Harlow, H. (1961). The development of affection patterns in infant monkeys. In B. M. Foss (Ed.), *Determinants of infant behavior* (Vol. 1). London: Methuen.

Heneghan, A. M., Horwitz, S. M., & Leventhal, J. M. (1996). Evaluating intensive family preservation programs: A methodological review. *Pediatrics, 97,* 535-542.

Kaufman, J., & Zigler, E. (1987). Do abused children become abusive parents? *American Journal of Orthopsychiatry, 57,* 186-192.

Kempe, C. H., Silverman, F. N., Steele, B. F., Droegemueller, W., & Silver, H. K. (1962). The battered child syndrome. *Journal of the American Medical Association, 181,* 107-112.

Lindsey, D. (1994). *The welfare of children.* New York: Oxford University Press.

MacDonald, H. (1994). The ideology of "family preservation." *The Public Interest, 115,* 45-60.

McKenzie, R. B. (1996, Spring). Orphanages: The real story. *The Public Interest, 123,* 100-104.

National Center of Child Abuse and Neglect. (1996). *Study findings: Study of national incidence and prevalence of child abuse and neglect: 1993.* Washington, DC: U.S. Department of Health and Human Services.

Olasky, M. (1996, May). American orphanages: How we used to care for children. *Philanthropy, Culture and Society,* 1-6.

Parke, R. D., & Collmer, C. W. (1975). Child abuse: An interdisciplinary analysis. In M. Hetherington (Ed.), *Review of child development research* (Vol. 5, p. 102). Chicago: University of Chicago Press.

Pelton, L. (1989). *For reasons of poverty: A critical analysis of the public child welfare system in the United States.* New York: Praeger.

Prochaska, J. O., & DiClemente, C. C. (1982). Toward a more integrative model of change. *Psychotherapy: Theory, Research and Practice, 19,* 276-288.

Prochaska, J. O., & DiClemente, C. C. (1983). Stages and processes of self-change in smoking: Toward an integrative model of change. *Journal of Consulting and Clinical Psychology, 5,* 390-395.

Prochaska, J. O., & DiClemente, C. C. (1984). *The transtheoretical approach: Crossing traditional boundaries of change.* Homewood, IL: Dow Jones/Irwin.

Prochaska, J. O., Norcross, J. C., & DiClemente, C. C. (1994). *Changing for good.* New York: William Morrow.

Rosenfeld, A., & Newberger, E. H. (1977). Compassion vs. control: Conceptual and practical pitfalls in the broadened definition of child abuse. *Journal of the American Medical Association, 237,* 2086-2088.

Rossi, P. (1992). Assessing family preservation programs. *Child and Youth Services Review, 14,* 77-97.

Smith, E. (1995). Bring back the orphanages: What policymakers of today can learn from the past. *Child Welfare, 74,* 115-142.

Spar, K. (1994). *Orphanages: A new issue on welfare reform* (Report No. 94-986 EPW, CRS report for Congress, Congressional Research Service). Washington, DC: Library of Congress.

Tatara, T. (1993). *Characteristics of children in substitute and adoptive care.* Washington, DC: American Public Welfare Association, Voluntary Cooperative Information System.

U.S. Advisory Board on Child Abuse and Neglect. (1990). *Child abuse and neglect: First steps in response to a national emergency.* Washington, DC: U.S. Department of Health and Human Services.

Wald, M. S., Carlsmith, J. M., & Leiderman, P. H. (1988). *Protecting abused and neglected children.* Stanford, CA: Stanford University Press.

# PART II

## THE HISTORY AND IMPACT OF ORPHANAGES

# Chapter 5

# The Rise and Fall of American Orphanages

MARVIN OLASKY

O rphanage! The word connotes bleakness; Charles Dickens's British vision has become our own, with some Faulkneresque grotesque added in. The conventional history of American orphanages is a tale of sound and fury directed against the helpless, with the absence of close government oversight leading to unmitigated child abuse. The real story, however, is richer; it shows how good orphanages combated both material and spiritual poverty among children who would otherwise have been the truly wretched of the earth. Oversimplifications have consequences, and our bias toward accentuating the negative in the history of orphanages has often led us to eliminate the positive. This chapter surveys the history and does not merely major in malice.

## ▓ Initial Efforts

The first orphanage in what is now the United States opened in 1729 in New Orleans. The second, the Bethesda Orphan House, emerged in Georgia a dozen years later through the ardent fund-raising of famed evangelist George Whitefield. Such early efforts were rare; not until the 19th century did homes specifically devoted to orphaned or abandoned children become common in a land in which families were big and extra water for an orphan was often thrown into the soup. In the colonial era, small children without parents were taken in by relatives or cared for by neighbors; older children were indentured to a master, who would teach them a trade. Apprenticeship bore no stigma because it was common to send a child at approximately age 13 into another person's home for training or education; all who had hands capable of work were expected to use them at an early age.

The growth of towns and the disruption that the Revolutionary War created in some of them led to a more structured approach to orphans at the end of the century. As a result of the British seizure of Charleston, South Carolina, in 1780, not only buildings but also families were destroyed; when the tide of independence washed out the occupying forces after Yorktown, some orphans remained, and the Charleston city council appointed commissioners to gather up parentless children and lodge them in private homes, with the government paying room and board. A few years later, the commissioners appealed to the public for contributions to build an orphanage, and—according to a mid-19th century account (a speech given by DeSaussure in 1855)—"All classes of citizens vied with each other in the grateful work of contributions in money, labor, material, and services" (DeSaussure, 1891, p. 29). The Charleston orphanage was completed in 1794 and occupied by 115 children.

By 1800, there were five to seven orphanages in the United States; sources vary as to the exact number (Friedman, 1994; Smith, 1995, p. 118). Local governments promoted the efforts by urging citizens to contribute to them, with members of legislatures sometimes offering part of their salaries (Vedder, 1891, p. 29). Typically, a "society of citizens" would take the initiative; in New York City, the New York Orphan Asylum Society in 1806 rented a two-story frame house in Greenwich Village, hired a "pious and respectable man and his wife" as superintendent and matron, and mandated that "The orphans shall be educated, fed, and clothed at the expense of the Society and at the Asylum. They must have religious instruction, moral example, and habits of industry inculcated on their minds" (Schneider, 1969, p. 189). The asylum—"asylum" at that time meant merely a place of security—opened with 12 orphans in 1806 and soon expanded into a facility housing 200 orphans.

Orphanages typically showed a strong religious commitment, but during those years shortly after passage of the First Amendment the concerns about separation of church and state voiced privately by Thomas Jefferson were not in public evidence. The Charleston city council in 1801 proposed a contributions drive to erect a building for religious services on orphanage land, with provision that the building "be open to the clergy of all denominations"

(Vedder, 1891, p. 29). After a few years, the New York Orphan Asylum Society received a state subsidy for its care of orphans, but the emphasis on religious instruction remained. Americans understood in the 19th century that government was not to establish any particular denomination as a state church, but that government should not try to banish God.

The number of orphanages grew throughout the first half of the 19th century largely in connection with an outpouring of evangelical benevolence, with women often in the forefront. In Petersburg, Virginia, females in 1812 petitioned the legislature for authorization to set up an orphan asylum because they were "deeply impressed with the forlorn and helpless Situation of poor Orphan female Children . . . and wish to snatch [them] from ignorance and ruin" (Lebsock, 1984, p. 202). Every epidemic, such as the cholera disaster of 1832, created orphans and new orphanage efforts; by 1850, there were between 71 and 77 orphanages. Individual and church contributions paid most of the cost, but it was not unusual for municipalities to pay up to a third and for expenses to be held down through some work by the orphans themselves: Boys learned manual skills while making repairs, and girls, under the instruction of a sewing teacher, often made clothes for all the residents.

By midcentury, orphanages often were impressive buildings; the orphan house in Charleston, after undergoing remodeling and enlargement from 1853 to 1855, was longer than a football field and five stories high. The first floor contained 3 dining rooms, 3 play rooms, and 10 other rooms, including a kitchen, pantry, and laundry room. The second story included classrooms, parlor and reception rooms, and other rooms for sewing and office space. Three upper stories were largely bedroom space, with steam heat throughout. Architects reported that the building contained 2,355,000 bricks, 222 doors, 298 windows, and 39,000 feet of piping (DeSaussure, 1891, pp. 79-80).

## ▨ A Massive Network

The Civil War greatly expanded demand for orphanages, and the supply skyrocketed to over 600 by 1880. Character as well as quantity changed; early in the century, a "half-orphan" was supposed to live with a surviving parent, but in the late 1800s children of destitute single parents increasingly found their way to orphanages. The Protestant monopoly also disappeared as Catholic and Jewish child care institutions proliferated. The New York Catholic Protectory, established in 1862, became the largest children's institution in the United States (Folks, 1907, p. 63). Jewish organizations dated from shortly before the war—both the Jewish Foster Home of Philadelphia and the Association for the Relief of Jewish Widows and Orphans in New Orleans were founded in 1855—but uncivil deaths plus massive immigration led to a massive network of institutions that reached its peak between 1880 and 1920. Most orphanages were segregated by race, with institutions such as the Colored Orphan Asylum in New York City becoming predominant.

The most comprehensive report about orphanages during this period resulted from investigations in 1875 by William P. Letchworth, commissioner of the New York State Board of Charities. Letchworth visited approximately 130 institutions for children and had positive impressions concerning nutritious food, safe living conditions, and factors such as "a high standard of personal cleanliness" (Letchworth, 1876/1974, p. 20). Letchworth also emphasized religious and moral training, which he thought a matter for the public interest because good citizenship arose only when a child learned his "obligations to the Deity" and was "taught the importance of living an upright life" (Letchworth, 1876/1974, p. 20).

Letchworth's (1876/1974) 470 pages of detailed notes on his site visits to the institutions throughout the United States are valuable not only for his physical descriptions but also for his reporting of how orphanage managers viewed their work. He quoted Mrs. Helen Mercy Woods, the very trustworthy matron of the Onondaga County Orphan Asylum in Syracuse, New York, as stating (contrary to current stereotypes),

> I do not believe in shutting children up, frightening them, or making them go without their meals. . . . I try to impress upon them, especially upon the boys, that it is not what people do for them that is going to avail, but what they do for themselves. I endeavor to convince the boys that they can be any thing they please if they will only try for it. I do not see why they should not fill positions of respectability as well as others. (p. 456)[1]

Orphanage directors during the second half of the 19th century, particularly when they dealt with children of immigrants, viewed their mission as not merely furnishing basic material needs but also creating model American citizens. They tried to instill virtues such as thrift, self-reliance, and sobriety and to create a capacity for hard work; they believed in busy daily routines and strict discipline. The morning schedule at the Philadelphia Orphan Asylum featured children rising at daybreak, attending a chapel service 30 minutes later, and then marching quietly—two by two and holding hands—to large dining halls with long tables; there, they were segregated by sex, and anyone wishing an extra helping had to raise his or her hand.

Similar schedules were followed throughout the country. Mrs. F. B. Tufts, matron of the Utica (New York) Orphan Asylum, was proud of the routine her charges had in 1875. She stated (as quoted in Letchworth, 1876/1974),

> The children rise at six o'clock, dress and wash, after which prayers are said in the sitting room. After breakfast the older children go to their work. The boys clear off the table, sweep the dining room, and the girls make their own beds with the assistance of the superintendent. All assemble in the school at nine o'clock and remain there until twelve, with the exception of an intermission of fifteen minutes. Dinner is served at twelve, after which there is recreation until half-past one, when they enter the school-room again and remain till half-past four. After school they have recreation till five o'clock. Supper is served at five. In winter they have supper very soon after school. The little girls set the tables and assist in light branches of housework. After supper the children play till bedtime. In winter the younger children go to bed about seven, but the older ones are permitted to stay up a little later. Prayers are said before retiring. Sometimes the children sing; sometimes they repeat psalms. The exercise is varied. (p. 494)

Observers at the time generally considered such disciplined activity to be benign, but some critics of orphanages over the years have muttered about regimentation and mean-spirited harshness (Rothman, 1971). From 1850 on, records show an increase in questioning as to whether orphanage life was best for children in distress.

## ■ The Alternative to Orphanages

A positive type of questioning underlay the efforts of Charles Brace, a writer and missionary who felt called to gain firsthand knowledge of how the orphaned or abandoned lived. Settling in New York City at midcentury, Brace visited "centres of crime and misery" and was then able to describe how "the street-boys were trained by older pickpockets and burglars for their nefarious callings" and how "little girls who flitted about with baskets and wrapped in old shawls became familiar with vice before they were out of childhood" (Brace, 1880, pp. 93-94). Brace soon set up six homes for orphans and abandoned children that provided not only shelter but also classes in reading and industrial arts, along with Bible lessons; the largest of the lodging houses served approximately 90,000 children from 1854 to 1872.

Brace emphasized rules that would "discourage pauperism" and show the rewards of honest work. Instead of handing out clothes upon request, Brace preferred to "give the garments as rewards for good conduct, punctuality, and industry." Once they came to know the children, housekeepers who saw cases of immediate, dire want could relieve them with less likelihood of deception and without harm to the character-building process. The best way to turn often-troubled children into good citizens, he knew, was to give them the security of adoption by a family: There were not enough willing families in New York City, and Brace agonized over questions such as "How were places to be found? . . . And when the children were placed, how were their interests to be watched over, and acts of oppression or hard dealing prevented or punished?" (Brace, 1880, pp. 226-227).

Brace hit upon the idea of allowing adults who took in children to do good and do well at the same time. He decided to try sending children (aged 7 to 17) to farmers' homes, where—in return for room, board, education, and personal attention—the children would work part-time. Brace (1937) began by sending out to fellow evangelicals a circular that proposed the economic arrangement but also stressed the theological reasons for personal involvement:

> Something must be done to meet the increasing crime and poverty among the destitute children of New York. As Christian men, we cannot look upon this great multitude of unhappy, deserted, and degraded boys and girls without feeling our responsibility to God for them. . . . We bear in mind the One died for them, even as for the children of the rich and happy. (pp. 132-134)

Response was enormous; Brace (1880, p. 227) wrote, "Hundreds of applications poured in at once from the farmers and mechanics all through the Union." Brace and associates then relied on volunteer committees in towns in upstate New York and throughout the Midwest—a committee usually included the mayor, a minister, a newspaper editor, a banker, and a storekeeper—to each assume responsibility for the placing of several dozen New York City boys in local families. When a committee contacted Brace and told him it had publicized the need through newspaper articles and preaching, and made plans for temporary housing and feeding of the children, Brace would send a carload of children on what became known as an "orphan train" (pp. 227-232).

When the children arrived, the committee attempted to make sure, in Brace's (1880, p. 223) words, that the children would "find themselves in comfortable and kind homes, with all the boundless advantages and opportunities of the Western farmer's life about them." That sounds too good to be true, but it generally was true for the more than 91,000 children placed by Brace between 1853 and 1893 for several reasons. First, in small-town and rural areas, committee members had personal knowledge of applicants, and perversities were hard to keep secret. Second, as Brace wrote, the process of placing the children "is carried on so publicly . . . that any case of positive abuse would at once be known and corrected by the community itself" (p. 240). Third, an agent visited newly placed children within a few months and checked for either pampering or overwork, both of which were seen as pernicious. In a culture that preached compassion and practiced neighborly surveillance, it appears that cases of neglect or abuse were rare (Hart, 1885, pp. 144-145; Letchworth, 1876/1974, p. 240).

Brace's New York Children's Aid Society did prosecute two cases of child abuse and occasionally removed children, generally when parents reneged on their agreement to provide education. Records show occasional cases of farmers working children too long and of a few even evicting children when the demands of the harvest were past. Some children were placed several times before a good match was made. Even critics of the program admitted, however, that the typical result was portrayed in one report of an inspection tour (Brace, 1880):

> Wherever we went we found the children sitting at the same table with the families, going to the school with the children, and every way treated as well as any other children. Some whom we had seen once in the most extreme misery, we beheld sitting, clothed and clean . . . and gaining a good name for themselves in their village. (p. 240)

One reason for success probably was the willingness of Brace and others to use economic incentives. Because extra hands were so useful on farms, some observers worried that the "farmer, while he appeared to be influenced by high motives, might be thinking too much of the economic gains he would secure through the children placed in his home" (O'Grady, 1930, p. 99). Brace, however, argued that taking in a child from the slums was often an emotionally draining activity that should not be economically draining as well. In an agricultural economy, Brace suggested, child placement could be advantageous for both child and farmer. His message was clear: It is much better to get orphans into fresh air and a fresh life than to keep them cooped up in an institution!

Journalistic support, for which Brace worked hard, helped to spread that message. Brace (1880) noted,

> I made it a point to keep our movements, and the evils we sought to cure, continually before the public in the columns of the daily journals. Articles describing the habits and trials of the poor; editorials urging the community to work in these directions [made the public] thoroughly imbued with our ideas and a sense of the evils which we sought to reform. (p. 282)

Brace's Children's Aid Society was flattered by widespread imitation of its methods. The New York Foundling Hospital began sending some young children to the New England and mid-Atlantic states. The Chicago Orphan Asylum sent its charges to downstate farms, with farmers agreeing to clothe and feed children, treat them kindly, and provide religious instruction.

## ▓ The Late 19th-Century Mainstream

The number of children in orphanages continued to grow during the late 19th century from 74,000 in 1880 to close to 90,000 in 1900 and 110,000 in 1910. The word orphanage became a misnomer because children of parents who were still living but had problems with finances or alcohol found the institutions safer and better than life at home. Backers of orphanages near the turn of the century still viewed their work as good. Charleston Mayor George S. Bryan wrote in 1891, on the 100th anniversary of his local orphan house, that "I have lived long, and have witnessed many anniversaries in Charleston, but none ever gave me such unalloyed and absolute satisfaction." Bryan praised "the discipline which has molded this matchless institution, and which has harmonized all its details, and combined them into a perfect and symmetrical whole" (DeSaussure, 1891, pp. 45-46).

Praise for orphanages did not come only from politicians; journalists and the children themselves noted the close relationship between resident children and the superintendents who developed a long-term relationship with their charges. Some 1960s-style historians sniffing for oppression have scorned reports and records that show positive interactions of most children and most supervisors, but Nurith Zmora, in her excellent recently published history of Baltimore orphanages, provides specific detail of compassion at work. One orphanage principal, she notes, "was everywhere, watching carefully every detail of the girls' education, discussing their future vocations with them, and encouraging them to excel. She knew when to be soft and kind and when to be tough and strict" (Zmora, 1994, p. 142). Another superintendent "knew each child's tendency, talents, and weaknesses and was there to encourage and develop the talents or correct the mistakes" (p. 137).

Some late 19th- and early 20th-century orphanages did provide fodder for stereotypes, but many others displayed patterns of discipline combined with love. When a pastor from Vicksburg journeyed to the Palmer Home for Children in Columbus, Mississippi, to drop off four children, he stayed 2 days, and on his return wrote to the superintendent (as cited in Maxwell, 1995),

> I have never seen a healthier or happier looking lot of children. . . . What pleased me most was the family atmosphere of it. . . . I noticed that the children ran over to your house whenever they felt like it with the same confidence that any little child runs to its father's house. (p. 33)

Some orphanages battled not only the devils within but also the patterns of segregation that dominated American society. When Father Edward J. Flanigan opened his Boys Home in Omaha, Nebraska, which soon became the famed Boys Town, he made it officially color-blind and stuck to his policy of integration even when townspeople protested the "mingling of races" ("Boys Town," n.d., p. 7).

## ▓ Growth of an Antiorphanage Spirit

Even as the numbers and the anniversary rhetoric swelled and as the quality of care was evident to observers, however, questioning of orphanages started to turn negative in tone. Much of the criticism had an ideological tinge, with what had seemed to be the virtuous solution to children's needs at the start of the 19th century beginning to be portrayed as materially satisfactory but psychologically inhumane. In 1893, 2 years after the Charleston celebration, Chicago orator Jenkin Lloyd Jones (1893) praised with faint damn the 11 homes for children within the windy city: "It is not that these massive buildings with their 'modern improvements,' well-heated and well-ventilated, and in the main well managed, are not much better than something worse." He noted that orphanages had trained many children in "habits of usefulness, making of them self-reliant and self-supporting men and women."

This was not enough, according to Jones (1893). He exulted,

> I believe there is a more excellent way. I know not which to pity the more, the boy who knows not where his tomorrow's dinner is to come from, or that other boy, dressed in uniform, at least when he goes to meeting, who is scrubbed by rule, fed from a printed bill of fare, who always knows on what days bean or potato soup is to be expected; who knows which are pie and which are pudding days; the boy who is marched to the table, marched to his playground, marched to his bed.

Then Jones made it clear that he most pitied the child in that "unnatural classification" known as an orphanage because the child was being forced to abandon his or her old, free nature and take on a new style of thinking and living.

The positive example of what Charles Brace and others had accomplished along with the negative reputation orphanages were beginning to have among those who thought that an emphasis on religion and discipline sucked the natural goodness out of children combined to push orphanages down a slippery slope of early-1900s social unpopularity. The White House Conference on the Care of Dependent Children in 1909, and a second one in 1919, bent in an antiorphanage direction: Single mothers were to receive financial aid so that children could stay at home, and orphans or those completely abandoned should be placed in foster care. The 1919 conference specified that, "The carefully selected foster home is for the normal child the best substitute for the natural home" (Smith, 1995, p. 134). Orphanages were places where matrons suppressed that "old, free nature" of children.

Washington-centric social workers tended to overlook the ways in which orphanages were functioning as a decent fallback for many children who would otherwise have had miserable lives. On the eve of World War I, large cities had an amazing variety of orphanages: Baltimore had 28, including 12 Catholic, 2 Jewish, 7 declared Protestant, and 7 labeled private but organized and run by Protestant philanthropists. (There were also race and ethnic divides: 6 were for blacks, 3 for Germans, 2 for the Irish, and 1 for Russian Jews [Smith, 1995, p. 19].) As Nurith Zmora (1994) notes, some of today's historians would call the typical Baltimore orphanage "a jail-like institution; they would assume that it was depressing in appearance and oppressive in its overreliance on harsh discipline, rigid routine, and lack of respect for the individual" (p. 2). Orphans themselves, however, interviewed later, tended to attribute their "success in life to the upper-middle-class education and culture provided by the charitable institutions." (p. 2).

The number of children in orphanages peaked in the 1920s, with the census bureau recording 143,000 residents in 1923. Most were small, with one fourth holding fewer than 30 children and 65% housing fewer than 80 (U.S. Department of Commerce, 1927, as cited in Smith, 1995, p. 118). Anti-institutionalism, however, was flourishing in the Roaring Twenties—one founder of a family care agency, Dr. Henry Dwight Chapin, argued in 1926 that the United States was an "institution-ridden country"—and orphanages of all sizes were tarred with that brush. Furthermore, as more children of living parents who were troubled or temporarily impoverished entered orphanages, the children frequently became short timers and one of the pro-orphanage arguments—the stability that they could bring to the lives of confused children—became less salient.

The Brace concept of emphasizing homes rather than institutions for orphans triumphed finally in the 1930s but with a twist. As early as the 1880s and 1890s, a few agencies, convinced ideologically that labor was not good for children, had begun paying foster parents for boarding children so that the children would not have to work.[2] By the 1930s, however, there was little choice in the matter; industrialization and urbanization had so transformed the American landscape that open-armed farm families were no longer available in great abundance. Brace had done wonderful work in his time, and most of the charitable procedures he fought for in the 19th century were still usable in the 20th century, but this one was not. When families that housed children would no longer be financially recompensed by added success in the market-place, they had to look to government for their monthly bread, and that government was heading toward bloated bureaucracy.

## ▓ Oversimplifications Have Consequences

Other problems with the new conventional wisdom soon emerged. Institutions were bad and homes were good, but most of the children who needed help had a surviving parent or parents who had not freed children for adoption. Therefore, the homes for many children would be temporary, and yanked-around children would end up with less stability than the orphanages had provided. Homes were good, but nonfarm parents would have to be paid to provide temporary shelter; such responsibility in the New Deal era was of course seen as governmental, so states started to pay for foster care. Government bureaucrats who supervised foster placement developed an empire-building economic incentive to keep children in foster care rather than placing them in permanent adoptive homes.

Even in the 1920s, there were wrenching scenes at the Hebrew Orphan Asylum in Baltimore as children were selected for foster families; many did not want to leave behind orphanage friends and siblings, but they had to go (Zmora, 1994, p. 187). By the late 1940s, it was clear that foster care was not a panacea; Michael Sharlitt, who grew up in an orphanage and later ran one, noted at that time the problem of children becoming disoriented as they went through a succession of foster homes (Zmora, 1994, p. 188). Nevertheless, federal funding emerged for urban-area foster care in 1951 and became large by 1961; the increase in available dollars, along with a rash of journalistic articles about child abuse during the 1960s, led to a dramatic increase in foster care. Orphanages, however, were largely forgotten in the popular press until Newt Gingrich brought up the subject late in 1994 and gave journalists an opportunity to clank the chains of Christmases past.

## ▨ Notes

1. Mrs. Woods's statement should be taken as accurate description because she was not a person disposed to dissemble; she went on to manage for two decades a refuge in Chicago for pregnant, unmarried women. In researching one of my books, I became familiar with her work there, which stands as a testimony to perseverance in doing good.

2. Tim Hacsi (1995, p. 17) notes board payments by the Post Temporary Home for the Destitute and the State Primary School of Massachusetts.

## ▨ References

Boys Town. (n.d.). *Boys Town: Memories and dreams* [Booklet]. Omaha, NE: Author.

Brace, C. L. (1880). *The dangerous classes of New York and twenty years' work among them.* New York: Wynkoop & Hallenbeck.

Brace, C. L. (1937). First circular of the Children's Aid Society. In E. Abbott (Ed.), *Some American pioneers in social welfare.* Chicago: University of Chicago Press.

DeSaussure, H. A. (1891). In *Charleston orphan house centennial celebration.* Charleston, SC: Walker, Evans, & Cogswell.

Folks, H. (1907). *The care of destitute, neglected and delinquent children.* New York: Macmillan.

Friedman, R. S. (1994). *These are our children.* Hanover, NH: University Press of New England.

Hacsi, T. (1995, January/February). From indenture to family foster care. *Child Welfare.*

Hart, H. (1885). Placing out children in the West. In *Proceedings of the National Conference of Charities and Correction.* Boston: George H. Ellis.

Jones, J. L. (1893). *Not institutions but homes* [Speech]. Chicago: All Souls Church.

Lebsock, S. (1984). *The free women of Petersburg.* New York: Norton.

Letchworth, W. P. (1974). *Homes of homeless children.* New York: Arno. (Original report transmitted to the New York State Legislature 1876)

Maxwell, J. (1995). *Palmer Home for Children: A century of hope, a passion to care.* Columbus, OH: Palmer House.

O'Grady, J. (1930). *Catholic charities in the United States.* Washington, DC: National Conference of Catholic Charities.

Rothman, D. J. (1971). *The discovery of the asylum.* Boston: Little Brown.

Schneider, D. M. (1969). *The history of public welfare in New York State, 1609-1866.* Montclair, NJ: Patterson Smith.

Smith, E. P. (1995, January/February). Bring back the orphanages? What policymakers of today can learn from the past. *Child Welfare, 74,* 115-138.

U.S. Department of Commerce, Bureau of the Census. (1927). *Children under institutional care, 1923.* Washington, DC: U.S. Government Printing Office.

Vedder, C. S. (1891). In *Charleston orphan house centennial celebration.* Charleston, SC: Walker, Evans, & Cogswell.

Zmora, N. (1994). *Orphanages reconsidered: Child care institutions in progressive Baltimore.* Philadelphia: Temple University Press.

# CHAPTER 6

# The 1994 Orphanage Debate
## A Study in the Politics of Annihilation

ROSS D. LONDON

P oliticians and social scientists make strange bedfellows. Ideally, politicians rely on social research to explain important societal problems and trends and to propose innovative solutions. Social scientists, in turn, rely on politicians to implement their ideas in the real world. It can be a marriage made in heaven, but often it is a marriage made in hell. This is the story of one such hellish encounter—the "orphanage" controversy initiated by Republican Newt Gingrich in 1994.

## ■ Delinquency: Causes and Prevention Strategies

Among criminal justice researchers during the past several decades, the concept of residential treatment as a crime prevention measure has steadily gained wider acceptance as the linkages between social deviance and parental neglect have become more apparent and as a number of early childhood intervention programs have proven their effectiveness over time.

Of all the factors found to contribute to delinquency (Binder, Geis, & Bruce, 1988; Farrington, Loeber, Elliot, & Hawkins, 1990; Hirschi, 1969), the clearest and most exhaustive evidence concerns the adequacy of parenting

(Loeber & Stouthamer-Loeber, 1986). Parents who are incompetent, abusive, or rejecting (Besharov, 1987; Loeber & Dishion, 1983; Wright & Wright, 1994), parents who fail to maintain adequate supervision over their children, and parents who, indeed, are little more than children themselves have direct effects on the antisocial behavior of their children (Cohen & Brook, 1987; Laub & Samson, 1988). Inadequacy of parenting cannot be viewed in isolation as the sole "cause" of delinquency. Its association with other factors, however, is critical in predicting future delinquency (Loury, 1987). Research gathered over the past several decades indicates that most prisoners come from single-parent families, more than one fourth have parents who abuse drugs or alcohol, and nearly one third have a brother with a jail or prison record (DiIulio, 1994).

In conjunction with significant efforts to identify the most significant risk factors that determine delinquency (criminality and drug abuse of parents, prenatal deficiency, lack of education, poor supervision, and inadequate disciplinary measures; Farrington, 1987), researchers and planners have begun to construct and evaluate programs that attempt to counteract these factors. Chief among the factors indicative of later serious delinquency is the age at onset of significant misbehavior: The earlier the child is found to have committed a youthful offense, the more likely it will be that such delinquency will continue and worsen over time (West & Farrington, 1977; Wolfgang, Figlio, & Sellin, 1972). Researchers have found that intervention must be performed at the earliest possible opportunity if it is to have any lasting effect. Indeed, some criminologists have explained the failure of many programs directed toward adolescent rehabilitation by noting that, by the age of adolescence, the interventions have come too late to be effective (Wilson & Loury, 1987). There is widespread agreement among child-development professionals that by far the most critical years for social development are birth to 6 years old (Rose, Rose, & Feldman, 1989).

Because of the centrality of parenting as a factor contributing to delinquency and because of the critical importance of early manifestation of misconduct in predicting future criminality, leading criminologists have looked to early childhood intervention as the most promising societal response to delinquency thus devised (Zigler, 1992). This research, coupled with mounting evidence that the number of children born into "dysfunctional" families is far beyond the capacities of our existing institutions, has led some intrepid souls to raise the possibility of resurrecting an old and somewhat discredited form of residential placement—the orphanage.

## ■ Orphanages Reconsidered

The rearing of children in "orphanages" is primarily a 19th-century phenomenon that was largely phased out during the second half of the 20th century. Prior to 1800, most children without parents were cared for informally by family members or through the apprenticeship system. As of 1800, there were only seven orphanages in America. During the 19th century, the number of orphanages grew as religious institutions took over the cause. In addition, as a result of epidemics, war, and the social dislocation from the conversion of a rural to an urban and industrialized economy, the number of orphanages grew considerably by midcentury. At the same time, the mission of orphanages changed from addressing the needs of truly parentless children to addressing the needs of impoverished parents and children of neglectful or alcoholic parents. Furthermore, the goal of orphanages was transformed from merely providing the necessities of life to unfortunately deprived children to the remolding of their character. Olasky (1996) noted,

> Orphanage directors during the second half of the 19th century saw their mission as not merely furnishing basic material needs but creating model American Citizens. . . . They try to instill virtues such as thrift, self-reliance, and sobriety and to create a capacity for hard work; they believe in busy daily routines and strict disciplines. (p. 1)

By the turn of the 20th century, orphanage populations grew to 100,000. Considerable debate had arisen, however, as to the desirability of institutionalizing children instead of promoting efforts to preserve the family. Following a series of criticisms of practices within orphanages, White House conferences on the care of dependent children in 1909 and 1919 strongly favored the goal of family preservation over institutionalization. The 1919 conference concluded that "the carefully selected foster home is for the normal child the best substitute for the natural home." Criticisms of institutional care have continued throughout the 20th century. In support of the deinstitutionalization process, a number of social science researchers noted that many children raised in institutions tended to exhibit difficulties maintaining relationships, psychological disorders, and difficulties parenting their own children (Ford & Kroll, 1995).

The preference for family preservation over institutionalization was highlighted by the adoption of the Aid to Families With Dependent Children (AFDC) program, which began as part of the 1934 Social Security Act. As the

scope of AFDC expanded radically over the next several decades, the number
of institutionalized children dropped precipitously. By the early 1970s, most
orphanages were closed or converted to mental health facilities (Smith, 1995).

In the late 1980s, a number of voices were raised contesting the "conventional wisdom" that parental care is always preferable to institutional care. In
1988, Lois Forer, a retired Philadelphia juvenile court judge, was moved to
write of her experiences with abused and neglected children:

> Deaths and abuses in children occur not because social workers are uncaring
> (although some are) and not because judges fail to treat child abuse as a
> serious crime (although some do), but because there are no places for these
> children to live. For at least 25 years, Americans have been captivated by two
> concepts that have become accepted public policy: deinstitutionalization and
> preservation of family. Both are worthy goals pursued to unworthy extremes.
> I suggest that it is time for us to demand that government provide permanent,
> well-run orphanages for the more than two million abused children who are
> "de facto" orphans. (p. 18)

In 1989, Joyce Ladner, an African American sociologist, wrote,

> Our current child welfare system is in a state of crisis. Its policies are woefully
> out-of-touch with the sorry realities that now confront many children. So
> harsh are those realities that I believe it's time to reintroduce in the new, more
> humane form an institution many had hoped would never be needed again:
> the orphanage.
>     What these children need is permanency but the chances are that it will
> continue to be difficult to find adoptive families for these so-called high-risk
> youngsters. I advocate that we bring back the orphanage—not the huge
> depersonalized warehouses of old, but the small scale caring institutions that
> can offer children, and their siblings, a place that they can count on to nurture
> them. (p. B1)

The negative connotations of the word orphanages were known at the
outset. As one African American journalist who favored orphanages stated,
"If the label offends, call them permanent residences or community group
homes, or child care villages. But create a form of placement that will allow
children to get off the foster care roll-a-coaster before they break their necks"
(Jefferson, 1994, p. F1).

While the orphanage concept was slowly gaining respectability among
certain child welfare advocates, the idea was taken up with a passion by
conservative theorists as well. In October 1993, Charles Murray, a conserva-

tive researcher associated with the American Enterprise Institute, wrote an op-ed article in the *Wall Street Journal* titled "The Coming White Underclass" (1993b) that laid the blame for a variety of inner-city travails on illegitimacy. He wrote,

> My proposition is that illegitimacy is the single most important social problem of our time—more important than crime, drugs, poverty, illiteracy, welfare, or homelessness because it drives everything else. Doing something about it is not just one more item on the American political agenda, but should be at the top. (p. A14)

Murray (1993b) had no hesitance in proposing a solution to the problem: the wholesale elimination of economic support for unwed mothers:

> The AFDC payment goes to zero. Single mothers are not eligible for subsidized housing or for food stamps . . . bringing a child into the world when one is not emotionally or financially prepared to be a parent is wrong. The child deserves society's support. The parent does not. (p. A14)

Murray (1993b) recognized that when the checks stop coming in, there will be untold thousands of unwed mothers and children who are affected. What do we do for the mothers? Nothing. They must "get support from someone, anyone, other than from the government." As for the children, he contemplated an increase in adoption for most, and for the rest,

> For them, the government should spend lavishly on orphanages. I am not recommending Dickensian barracks. In 1993 we know a lot about how to provide a warm nurturing environment for children and getting rid of the welfare system frees up lots of money to do it. Those who find the word "orphanages" objectionable may consider them as 24-hour a day pre-schools. (p. A14)

Murray was certainly not the first commentator to consider the possibility of bringing back orphanages, but he was by far the most influential. More than anyone else, Murray had resurrected not only an idea but also an emotionally charged word that had all but been dismissed from our natural psyche as an unpleasant memory from a bygone age.

Although many in the child care community continued to philosophically oppose the concept of any form of institutionalized care, the idea of providing residential care for neglected children was still thought by many liberals to be worthy of serious consideration. Early proponents included a number of Democrats as well as Republicans. Democrat Susan Gerard, the main proponent of an orphanage bill in Arizona, stated (as quoted in Winton, 1994, p. A1), "Maybe we would be better off with the orphanages because what's most important is stability." Also intrigued by the idea was Scott Salmon, a Republican from Massachusetts, who said (as quoted in Winton, 1994, p. A1), "With foster care, kids have to be moved over and over." In Illinois, where orphanage proponents included Governor Jim Edgar, the supervising judge of the Cook County Juvenile Court, and the county's public guardian (Walsh, 1994), a task force was created to study the feasibility of establishing orphanages. Milwaukee Mayor John Nordquist, a liberal Democrat, also supported the idea: "You need to have a place to put children who are in an irresponsible home" (Walsh, 1994, p. A9).

With interest expressed by conservative Republicans and liberal Democrats, the possibility arose for bipartisan support for a new humane version of residential care for the most neglected children.


## ▓ The "O" Word Goes Public

Hopes for nonpartisan support for residential child care were promptly dashed when Murray's (1993b) orphanage proposal caught the attention of a distinctively partisan politician, Republican Newt Gingrich of Georgia. In 1994, Gingrich emerged as the political and ideological spearhead of a movement he proudly characterized as the "Republican Revolution." For Gingrich, the 1994 congressional election was not merely a matter of rebounding from the 1992 presidential defeat suffered at the hands of Bill Clinton. Gingrich (as quoted in Gillespie & Schellhas, 1994, p. 182) stated, "What is at issue is literally not a Republican or Democrat or liberal or conservative, but the question of whether or not our civilization will survive."

Although Clinton had promised to "end welfare as we know it," the Republicans in their "Contract with America" promised to go much further. Gillespie and Schellhas (1994) stated,

> The Great Society has had the unintended consequences of snaring millions of Americans into the welfare trap. Government programs designed to give a helping hand to the neediest of Americans have instead bred illegitimacy, crime, illiteracy, and more poverty. Our Contract with America will change this destructive social behavior by requiring welfare recipients to take personal responsibility for the decisions they make. Our contract will achieve

what some thirty years of massive welfare spending has not been able to accomplish: reduce illegitimacy, require work, and save taxpayers money. (p. 65)

Central to the Republican proposal to overhaul welfare was the Personal Responsibility Act of 1995, the goals of which were to discourage illegitimacy and teen pregnancy by prohibiting AFDC support for teenage mothers, to deny increased AFDC for additional children while on welfare, and to enact a "two-year in-and-out provision with work requirements to promote individual responsibility" (Gillespie & Schellhas, 1994, p. 10). The act also had several suggestions for ways in which savings from AFDC cutbacks could be used, including the building of orphanages: "The States may use the funds . . . to reduce out-of-wedlock pregnancies, to promote adoption, to establish and operate orphanages; to establish and operate residential group homes for unwed mothers, or for any purpose the State deems appropriate" (Personal Responsibility Act of 1995, § 441, p. H159).

The Republican proposals struck a responsive chord with voters. The November 1994 elections were a stunning victory for conservative Republicans, who regained control of both houses, and for Gingrich personally, who fulfilled his long-sought ambition of becoming Speaker of the House.

Just as suddenly, the political fortunes of President Clinton went into a steep decline. Having gained the Democratic nomination in 1991 largely by positioning himself as a moderate, a number of politically costly defeats, including his on-again, off-again embrace of gay rights in the military and the national health care fiasco, coupled with withering personal attacks by Gingrich and other ideological conservatives finally took its toll. The 1994 Republican victory was widely attributed to resentment of "angry white males" to Clinton's perceived liberal agenda. Clinton's only hope for political survival was to recapture the political center. To accomplish this task, Clinton and his advisers saw their opportunity in the incendiary pronouncements of Gingrich. After huddling with his top political advisers, Clinton returned to Washington with "a broad outline of a strategy to resurrect his presidency based in part on hopes that the Republicans will look so radical they will scare America away" (Devroy, 1994, p. A12).

In the summer of 1994, Representative Gingrich, in discussing the proposed Republican overhaul of the welfare system, sent the following message to "welfare mothers": We will help you with foster care, we will help you with orphanages, we will help you with adoption—but not with the cash subsidies (Van Biena, 1994). Gingrich's remarks were largely unreported in the press.

Following the 1994 elections, however, Gingrich's political stock had risen to astronomical levels (Kurtz, 1995):

> With remarkable swiftness, the Georgia college professor who once gave hour-long speeches to an empty house chamber began to be treated like a newly elected president. His every utterance was analyzed, his advisers and gurus scrutinized, his past scandals exhumed as journalists immersed themselves in all-things Newtonian. Bill Clinton was blown off the radar screen. (p. 8)

Appearing on a Sunday morning TV interview shortly after the election, Gingrich expounded on the Contract With America proposals. Without mentioning the orphanage proposal specifically, Gingrich made it clear that upon the adoption of the contract, able-bodied parents who could not support their children by their own efforts could no longer look to government to do so (American Broadcasting Companies, 1994):

**Newt Gingrich:** I think people ought to have to do something for any resources they get if they're able-bodied under the age of retirement.

**Sam Donaldson:** And if they don't, then what?

**Newt Gingrich:** Then they had better go find a way to do something. I'm willing to expand . . .

**Sam Donaldson:** You're not for a safety net for the children?

**Newt Gingrich:** I am very much for a tax credit for people to give to private charities. I'm very much . . .

**Sam Donaldson:** We're talking about welfare reform Mr. Gingrich.

**Newt Gingrich:** That's right, and I'm saying to you that I'd rather have the Salvation Army than local government . . .

**Sam Donaldson:** I understand sir, but I'm asking for those who don't find a job, what is your prescription?

**Newt Gingrich:** I think I would like to expand private charities.

**Sam Donaldson:** And that would be their recourse?

**Newt Gingrich:** That would be their recourse.

On the same day that Gingrich pronounced his views on welfare reform on TV, the *New York Times* featured a front-page article on the Republican attack on welfare, which, for the first time, highlighted the orphanage proposal contained in the Contract With America (DeParle, 1994). Significantly, the article, which was nationally syndicated through the *Times*'s news service, identified Newt Gingrich as the architect and chief proponent of orphanages for children cut off from welfare support. The article stated,

> He would allow states to end assistance to large numbers of AFDC recipients, whether or not they are willing to join a work program. He would use some of the money to build orphanages or group homes for the children of those families rendered destitute. (p. A1)

With the media now riveted on Gingrich's every word, the resurrection of the "o" word triggered an immediate wave of controversy:

> To hear Newt Gingrich tell it, we are going to be taking young, unmarried mothers off of welfare and building orphanages for their children. Do you think that's what American people want to see? (Marchini, 1994)
>
> Gingrich is a walking, one-man intellectual gridlock. He espouses family values but would put the children of unemployed, unwed mothers into orphanages. (Nelson, 1994a, p. A6)
>
> The Gingrich faction, borrowing heavily from the agenda of sociologists Charles Murray of *The Bell Curve* fame, wants to turn the poor over to orphanages and private charities and get government out of the business of helping people helping themselves. (Editorial, 1994, B2)
>
> Alarms are being raised by another Gingrich succession from removing children from parents who are on long-term welfare and putting them into state orphanages. (Brody, 1994, p. 1)
>
> It would be hard imagining sending little Lamara, Vincent, or Clyde to an orphanage merely because their mom had received government assistance. Yes, that is actually one of Gingrich's proposals, as insane as that might seem to anyone whoever had a mother. (Morse, 1994a, p. A3)
>
> Mr. Gingrich apparently thinks that throwing children into orphanages would be good for them and would avoid creating a welfare dependent underclass. What this policy risks is a class of emotionally damaged children. (Gainer, 1994, p. 15)
>
> Is this how we build family values? Is this what our country is about? This is what Gingrich is proposing. No more safety net at all—just prisons and orphanages. (Estrich, 1994, p. A15)
>
> The GOP may talk family values, but many of its leaders don't raise valued families. Gingrich proposing pushing poor kids on welfare into orphanages like rag-a muffins in Oliver Twist. (Reynolds, 1994, p. A13)

The clergy entered the controversy at an early stage. At a meeting of Catholic bishops, Gingrich's proposals to limit welfare support and to rely more heavily on private charity were strongly criticized. The Reverend

Richard H. Ricard, Bishop of Baltimore, stated (as quoted in Goodstein, 1994, p. A3), "The state has an obligation to take care of those who cannot take care of themselves. Children will be adversely affected by policies such as these. . . . America should be a caring community, a caring society."

A number of child welfare groups joined the attack on the orphanage proposal, reemphasizing the primacy of family preservation over institutionalization. In a *New York Times* op-ed piece, Ronald Feldman (1994), Dean of the Columbia University School of Social Work, stated,

> Children raised in residential homes are more likely to have serious problems adjusting to society when they leave. Children raised in supportive, family-like environments will become better adults, parents, and taxpayers—all things that Mr. Gingrich says he wants. (p. A29)

A position paper of the North American Council on Adoptable Children concluded that "fifty years of research reconfirms the same findings: Long-term institutionalization in childhood leads to recurrent problems in inter-personal relationships, a higher rate of personality disorders, and severe parenting difficulties late in life" (Ford & Kroll, 1995). The Child Welfare League of America (1994) maintained that "children experience a great deal of stress and trauma when they are forced to leave their birth parents. Severe emotional, psychological, and behavioral problems result" (p. 3). According to one New York State official who was involved in the closing of orphanages during the 1960s and 1970s, "They are not appropriate places for children to develop properly. The evidence was so blatant, we assumed we'd never revisit the issue" (Shogren & Mehren, 1994, p. 1). The executive director of the Federation of Protestant Welfare Agencies, Incorporated (as quoted in McLaughlin, 1995) concluded that "historical evidence shows that institutionalizing children did not solve the problems of poor families in the past and will not do so today" (p. 61).

During the month of November, public criticism against the Republican welfare proposal and of Gingrich continued unabated:

> He's like a 19th century nightmare. Dickens couldn't create a Scrooge like this. (Roth, 1994, p. 15)
>
> In these parts, we don't have much use for such ideas as taking children away from young unwed mothers and putting them in orphanages. Come to think of it, "Newt Gingrich" could be the name of a villain in a Dickens novel. (Morse, 1994b, p. A3)

The Dickensian theme was taken up by major news magazines such as *Newsweek*'s "The Gingrich That Stole Christmas" and *Time*'s "Uncle Scrooge." Sam Donaldson told Gingrich on *This Week With David Brinkley* (American Broadcasting Companies, 1994), "A lot of people are afraid of you. They think you are a bomb thrower. Worse, you are an intolerant bigot. Speak to them."

The tumultuous response to Gingrich's rhetoric was a cause for celebration in the White House. One commentator observed (Devroy, 1994), "Aides reacted this week not with dismay but almost glee as new Republican leaders unleashed a string of conservative rhetoric from which they hope the country will recoil" (p. A12). Democrats quickly seized the opportunity to skewer Gingrich as a radical. Democratic Whip David Bonior (as quoted in Phillips, 1994) stated that his party would fight welfare cuts and Gingrich's proposed reliance on orphanages: "We are not about tearing away babies from their mothers" (p. A10). Bonior (as quoted in Kiely, 1994) stated that the Republican's proposals were "out of touch, including most recently his suggestion that children on welfare might be better in orphanages. This is an extreme agenda . . . basically they just want to rewrite the Constitution" (p. A1).

The onslaught caused a number of leading Republicans to withdraw. Bob Dole early on expressed misgivings about orphanages (Frank, 1994). According to Republican Congressman Clay Shaw of Florida, many Republicans thought that Gingrich's plan to substitute orphanages for welfare checks could prove "unduly harsh" (DeParle, 1994). Representative Marge Roukema, Republican of New Jersey, made it known to the press that she had warned Gingrich not to press the idea of orphanages but to no avail (Nelson, 1994b). Even Republican James Talent, one of the original sponsors of the orphanage proposal for the Contract With America, was dismayed at the public's reaction. He stated (as quoted in Shirk, 1994), "I'll pull out of the proposal if it continues to get all the attention" (p. B1). Regarding Gingrich's embrace of the issue, Talent added, "He's really the only one who keeps talking about it. And I think he's really just using it to highlight how bad the existing system is" (p. B1).

On November 30, the controversy was escalated by an explicit attack on Gingrich's proposal by First Lady Hillary Clinton. In a speech before the New York Women's Agenda, a nonpartisan coalition of women's groups, Mrs. Clinton stated (as quoted in "First Lady," 1994), "Unless we want to see literally thousands and thousands of people on our streets, seeing the unbelievable and absurd idea of putting children into orphanages because their mothers couldn't find jobs." (p. A28).

The first lady's ridicule of the GOP plan, and Gingrich's orphanage proposal in particular, ignited a new storm of controversy. Hundreds of newspaper editorials throughout the country were openly critical of Gingrich's proposal. In the words of one op-ed writer (Ivins, 1994, p. A27), "If Representative Newt Gingrich is for orphanages for kids on welfare, let us support concentration camps." Former presidential contender Jesse Jackson (as quoted in Foskett, 1994, p. A9) declared, "You can't say while our heads are bowed, let's separate mothers from babies and put them in state orphanages."

President Clinton, without specifically mentioning Gingrich, took the opportunity to turn the ideological tables on his Republican adversary. Although liberal Democrats have long been criticized for their reliance on "big government" and their lack of emphasis on "family values," Clinton characterized Gingrich's proposal as a Republican effort to replace child rearing by families with child rearing by institutions. Clinton (as quoted in Jehl, 1994) stated,

> There are some people out there who argue that we should let some sort of big, new institution take a parent's place, that we should even take children away from parents as we cut off welfare, even if they are doing a good job as parents. . . . Well those people are dead wrong . . . Governments don't raise children, parents do. (p. A6)

Gingrich, rather than distancing himself from the orphanage controversy, eagerly entered the fray, calling the attacks by the media and by the White House "a grotesque distortion" of his proposal (Wines, 1994). In defending himself against charges from the White House that the government should leave the task of raising children to families, Gingrich stated (National Broadcasting Company, 1994),

> I don't understand liberals who live in enclaves of safety who say "Oh, this would be a terrible thing. Look at the Norman Rockwell family that would break up." The fact is we are allowing a brutalization and a degradation of children in this country, a destructiveness. We say to a 13-year-old drug addict who is pregnant, you know, "Put your baby in a dumpster, that's OK, but we're not going to give you a boarding school, we're not going to give you a place for that child to grow up."

When asked about Hillary Clinton's characterization of the orphanage proposal as "unbelievable and absurd," Gingrich responded (National Broadcasting Company, 1994), "I'd ask her to go to Blockbuster and rent the Mickey Rooney movie about Boys Town." Later that month, Gingrich went on to host a TV showing of the 1940s melodrama on New Year's Eve.

The administration continued its attacks on Gingrich's proposal by concentrating on its cost. On December 29, 1994, Secretary of Health and Human Services Donna Shalala denounced the Republican bill as a "cruel hoax," saying it would consign many thousands to orphanages without giving states enough money to pay for care of these institutions. While conceding the necessity for residential placement for certain children, she added (as quoted in Pear, 1994, p. A22) that orphanages were "big, impersonal, bureaucratic warehouses, not the friendly homes portrayed by Mr. Gingrich."

Indeed, the revelation of the high cost of orphanages became a significant turning point in the debate. Boys Town, the home for troubled teens extolled by Gingrich, was found to cost $40,000 to $48,000 per year per child. The Republicans did not deny the White House's claim that of the 9.7 million children on AFDC support, 5.3 million would eventually be denied benefits under the Republican proposals (Pear, 1994). At a cost of approximately $100 per day, Shalala claimed, the cost of providing orphanage space for even 20% of those affected would be approximately $36 billion yearly versus an average of $2,644 for a family with one child receiving AFDC benefits and food stamps and $4,800 for foster care. Shalala, in her statement to Congress, claimed that the Republican proposal would pay for only approximately 9,000 orphanage slots for the entire nation and asked "what would happen to the other 5 million children?" (p. A22)

A statement in response from the Republican Ways and Means Committee chairman made no attempt to refute Shalala's data but sought to minimize the probability of orphanages being chosen by parents who were no longer eligible for welfare (as quoted in Pear, 1994):

> Why does Secretary Shalala assume that any children will go into orphanages as a result of Republican policy? She apparently assumes that if children lose part of their government benefits, they would immediately run to the nearest orphanages and surrender their children. (p. A22)

In fact, the statement predicted, "Adults on welfare will protect their children by working or getting married" (p. A22).

Despite the efforts of Republican leaders to explain the orphanage proposal as only one among many suggested means for states to use their federal
funding, the cost issue did not go away. It became apparent to many that, rather
than raising funds necessary to spend "lavishly" on orphanages, as Charles
Murray originally proposed, the Republican solution of permitting states to
use savings in AFDC cutbacks for the creation of orphanages was woefully
insufficient even for the most basic form of institutional care. Gary Stangler,
Human Services Director of the American Public Welfare Association, stated
(as quoted in Shogren & Mehren, 1994), "I have calculated I'd have to take
10 families off welfare to fund one child in the lowest costing institution. We
decided some years ago what we really have to talk about is strengthening
families. It's so much cheaper" (p. 1). Indeed, even the possibility that states
would voluntarily create orphanages from the savings from AFDC was seen
by leading Republicans as unlikely. Republican James N. Talent from Missouri, who drafted several sections of the GOP plan for welfare reform, stated
"I think the states aren't going to go that route" (p. 1).

With the growing understanding that orphanages or group homes are
much more costly per child than welfare costs (McDonald, 1994), fewer
Republicans declared public support for the orphanage concept. Nor was the
public enamored with the concept. In a December 1994 poll, only 17% of
those polled expressed interest in adopting Gingrich's orphanages concept
(Muzzio & Behn, 1995). In Illinois, the task force created to study the
possibility of building orphanages for neglected children dismissed the orphanage concept as "absolutely wrong-headed" (Kuczka, 1995, p. 12).

By early February 1995, it had become clear to Republican pollsters that
the orphanage concept was no longer politically viable. In a strategy memorandum prepared by Republican pollster Frank Luntz, Luntz warned Republican readers to be careful of their language. He stated (as quoted in Barabak,
1995), "In one sense, this memorandum is about taking back our language.
. . . Don't talk about cutting programs that have popular support . . . and
please, when it comes to welfare reform, any word is better than orphanage."
(p. A3).

From that time forth, Gingrich stopped using the term orphanage (Drew,
1996). In fact, the term orphanage was withdrawn from the Republican
Contract With America, although the original contract, rather than mandating
orphanages, only cited orphanages as one of several possible alternatives that
the states could use with savings from AFDC cutbacks. It was clear by January
1995, however, that the term orphanage, even in the context of a suggestion,

was political poison, and the term was deleted from the text. The national controversy on orphanages had effectively ended.


## ▓ Political Aftermath

By the summer of 1995, the orphanage controversy was little more than an unpleasant memory. One women's magazine writer (Bennett, 1995, p. 158) asked, "Remember Speaker Newt Gingrich's suggestion that poor children should be taken away from their mothers and be placed in orphanages?" The Democrats's goal of regaining the center by depicting their adversaries as unfeeling radicals appeared to be succeeding. The Democrats's exploitation of the "Scrooge" theme in relation to Gingrich's orphanage proposal was the first to draw blood after Gingrich's November 1994 triumph. Greenberg (1995, p. 1037) stated, "Under an avalanche of shocked outcries and barbed cartoons, he quickly dropped the subject, from which little has been heard in recent months." Following a number of other political miscalculations and retractions, by the end of 1995 Gingrich appeared to have exhausted his political capital and was now being described as bombastic and reckless. No longer captivated by Gingrich's verbal daring, political pundits now opined that "recklessness is not a quality that the public wants in a national leader" (Schneider, 1995, p. 126).

In 1996, Gingrich came to be viewed as a liability to the Republican party and a chief contributing factor in their loss to Clinton. Representative Peter King of New York considered Gingrich to be "damaged goods. He should step aside for the good of the country, for the good of the party" (as quoted in Dorning, 1996, p. 3). Many Republicans blamed Gingrich for 13 freshmen defeats and Bob Dole's lackluster performance in the presidential contest. Running against an unknown professor who accused her of "protecting Newt," Representative Nancy Johnson, Republican of Connecticut and the Ethics Panel chairman, barely escaped defeat, winning by approximately 2000 votes. Representative Chris Shays, Republican of Connecticut, bluntly stated (as quoted in Grady, 1996, p. 8), "People hate Newt Gingrich. . . . In truth, Gingrich's clout has been diminished. . . . No more blabber about orphanages. Newt vows to throttle his motor mouth."

For the Clintons, the orphanage debate was a significant victory in a policy dispute in which political expedience outweighed intellectual consistency. Hillary Clinton regained her fighting form after having been temporarily silenced in the aftermath of the aborted national health care proposal. After publicly chiding Gingrich for failing to recognize that "children are best left with their families" (Clinton, 1995, p. 22), Mrs. Clinton wrote that "it takes a village" to properly rear children and not merely an individual family. President Clinton was remarkably successful in regaining the political center that he had sought all along. Democratic strategists in early 1995 recognized that "welfare reform represents Bill Clinton's best political opportunity to reanimate his presidency" (Secrest & Walker, 1995, p. 47). Clinton maintained his distance from any form of orphanage or "child treatment proposal," and in 1996 he endorsed a welfare reform package that was regarded by many liberals as unduly punitive to the poor. In words reminiscent of Clinton's attacks on Gingrich the previous year, Clinton's critics on the left complained (Scheer, 1996),

> Clinton is buying into the conservative principal that welfare helped to destroy families by offering perverse economic incentives to young women giving birth to babies out of wedlock. (Peels, 1995, p. 40)
>
> Clinton knows the nuances of the welfare debate as well as anyone and he knows this bill is a disaster in the making. It is nothing to do with serious reform of welfare and everything to do with the random brutal assault on the poor, most of whom are children. (Scheer, 1996, p. B7)

Clinton, however, was no longer as concerned about his approval rating among liberals and minorities because his aim was to regain a more moderate constituency—especially those "angry white men" whose defection proved so costly in 1994. In the end, Clinton had accomplished all his goals: He regained the political center, he regained the momentum of his administration, and he regained the presidency.

## ▓ Back to Zero

The resurrection of the orphanage concept began in the late 1980s as an anguished attempt to answer the question of placement for the thousands of abused and neglected children for whom the existing system of subsidies and foster care was failing. The cause was taken up both by liberal Democrats, who envisioned comprehensive child treatment, and by conservatives, who sought an alternative to welfare subsidies. After several months of furious debate in the fall and winter of 1994, however, the orphanage concept virtually disappeared from the national agenda. What went wrong?

### A Victim of Rhetoric

The proponents of the orphanage concept understood the emotionally laden connotation of the term *orphanage* and repeatedly advised against its use. James Q. Wilson, an early advocate of residential alternatives, said the term orphanage reverberates "like a hand grenade at a dinner party." The use of a more neutral term, such as group home or residential care facility, would undoubtedly have moved the discussion to a higher level. Even in the midst of the debate, both Gingrich and the Democrats recognized the need for intelligent discussion but could not restrain themselves from rhetorical excesses to punish their adversaries. The Democrats, who had suffered blistering verbal assaults from Gingrich, appeared to take delight in branding his ideas as absurd, unbelievable, and a cruel hoax and depicting Gingrich as a latter-day Scrooge. Clinton's political adviser George Stephanopoulos exulted (as quoted in Morganthau, 1994, p. 38), "We'll mail all the Republicans and members of Congress a copy of *Oliver Twist.*" Gingrich contributed little more than rhetoric in support of the concept—claiming orphanages to be a preferable alternative to "dumpsters" for children of unwed mothers and hosting a TV screening of *Boys Town* as a way of justifying his proposal.

The frenzied political battle of loaded images and inflammatory rhetoric ran its course over several months, and despite the commonality of interest on both sides of the political spectrum, no conclusion or common ground was achieved. Criminologist John DiIulio (1995) reacted with disgust:

> Hey kids knock it off! Apparently they still haven't gotten the message. The American people want Washington to deal with pressing national concerns in a frank forthright creative and conscientious way. . . . Policies that forbid the creative, community center development of orphanages or like institutions must be counted among the real root causes of our welfare and crime problems. (p. C1)

By early 1995, however, the damage had been done. On the basis of a strong recommendation of their polling advisers, Republicans removed the term orphanage from their vocabulary and removed references to its possible use in all future additions of their Contract With America.

Did Gingrich know what he was doing in using this loaded term? Many commentators at the time believed that Gingrich was simply "thinking out loud," and that his words were deliberately misconstrued by the media and Democrats anxious to depict him as an extremist.

It appears, however, that his use of the loaded term *orphanage* was intentional. Gingrich had publicly referred to the orphanage option in speeches announcing the Republican welfare plan 5 months before his postelection TV interviews that ignited the orphanage controversy. Although the use of the term *orphanage* could only have the effect of rendering the concept politically unviable, there is good reason to believe that Gingrich was more interested in the shock value of the term than the possibility of its implementation. According to journalist Elizabeth Drew (1996, p. 46), "Gingrich had a very deliberate purpose: to smash the current welfare system." In her book on Gingrich and the "Republican Revolution," Drew describes a meeting between Gingrich and conservative adviser William Bennett the day before a December 1994 *Meet the Press* interview, by which time the orphanage controversy was in full cry. In the meeting, Gingrich considered the use of the term *orphanage* not as a realistic policy alternative for children but as a device "to illuminate his rejection of the existing welfare system" (Drew, 1996, p. 46). Bennett tried to get Gingrich to shift away from the negative connotations of orphanages by referring to Boy's Town as a more appealing model. Gingrich agreed, but, in the TV appearance, he could not restrain himself from characterizing orphanages as his alternative to dumpsters. According to Gingrich's Press Secretary Tony Blankley (as quoted in Drew, 1996),

> The orphanage issue is fairly typical of the way Newt operates. He drew the contrast between a dumpster and Boys Town. "Orphanages" is a term that communicates very well. Over time we win the larger policy debate on welfare; it sharpens the focus on the existing program. It puts our opponents in an untenable position. (p. 46)

### A Victim of Economics

The cost of implementing a large-scale program of residential care was cited by numerous commentators as the primary reason for the failure of Gingrich's orphanages proposal. The proposal, in fact, did not require any additional expenditure of funds but relied on anticipated savings from AFDC cutbacks. Indeed, during the course of the debate, Gingrich complained that he was not calling for the erection of new orphanages by government but insisted instead that the matter should be primarily the concern of private charities.

Certainly, given the number of children who would eventually be affected by the proposed cutbacks in welfare support (by most estimates, approximately 5 million), and given the enormous cost of residential care per child, with estimates ranging up to $100 per day, the creation of new orphanages by private means was manifestly unfeasible. Although there is good reason to believe that the widely cited figure of $36,500 per child estimated by the Child Welfare League of America (Van Biena, 1994) is only applicable to residential care for seriously troubled youth, there was no significant effort on the part of Republican leaders to dispute the high costs cited by their Democrat opponents. Nor was any attempt made to explain how private charities would be able to absorb any additional costs because the bulk of their funding for group homes, shelters, and residential treatment centers is paid for by government (Collins, 1994). Therefore, whether or not the enormous costs cited by the Democrats and child welfare advocates were inflated, under the Republican plan to shift the burden of residential care to private charities the goal of establishing and maintaining well-staffed and well-equipped residences for neglected children was never an economically viable option.

## A Victim of Politics

If the plan was so clearly unworkable, what purpose did Gingrich have in proposing it? The dilemma of eliminating welfare support for illegitimate children without creating a massive government program for their residential care existed since the beginning of the orphanage discussion initiated by Charles Murray. Unlike the work of child care advocates who called for the resurrection of orphanages as a humane and well-equipped placement alternative for neglected children, Murray viewed orphanages primarily in the context of the battle against illegitimacy. Although Murray advocated lavish spending on orphanages, he proposed no plan to finance them. When pressed by *Crossfire* moderator Michael Kinsley as to the realistic placement alternatives available to mothers when AFDC support is discontinued, Murray's reply was most telling:

> **Kinsley:** [A]s a realistic matter, are the kids who are brought into this world going to end up in your luxurious, non-Dickensian orphanages? Are they going to end up . . .
>
> **Mr. Murray:** They are going to end up adopted. They are going to end up adopted.

Murray, however, had failed to remember that in his seminal *Wall Street Journal* article (1993b) on welfare reform, he had proposed orphanages precisely for those children for whom adoption was not a feasible option: "Some small proportion of infants and a larger proportion of older children will not be adopted. For them, the government should spend lavishly on orphanages" (p. A14).

The Republicans who accepted Murray's (1993b) orphanage concept clearly did so in the context of illegitimacy control rather than as a child welfare reform. The language of the proposed Personal Responsibility Act, the only component in the Contract With America that refers to the possibility of orphanages, explicitly states its intended goal: "The Personal Responsibility Act is designed to diminish the number of teenage pregnancies and illegitimate births" (Gillespie & Schellhas, 1994, p. 70). Because funding for orphanages was proposed to be derived from savings realized from AFDC cutbacks and because, by most estimates, the cost of institutional care is at least four times the cost of AFDC support, there would be no possibility of residential placement under the proposal for the vast majority of children cut from AFDC enrollment, even in states that opted to use their block grants to establish orphanages. Republican James Talent, a drafter of the Republican welfare policy, conceded (as quoted in Shirk, 1994, p. 1B), "I never intended to suggest [orphanages] as a feasible alternative for taking care of a large number of children."

Gingrich's use of the manifestly offensive label *orphanage* and the clear economic unfeasibility of his orphanage proposal is puzzling only if it is assumed that he was seriously interested in promoting orphanages as a significant child care measure. This does not appear to be the case, however. The reemergence of orphanages in the 1994 public debate was not about child protection but about ways to stop illegitimacy and welfare dependency. Raising the specter of orphanages was viewed as a means to persuade unmarried and welfare-dependent women on welfare into controlling their reproduction. As one political observer noted (Pollitt, 1995, p. 192), "It's about re-stigmatizing illegitimacy, i.e. making out-of-wedlock motherhood so painful that young women will eschew it, thus saving Western civilization." It was not for nothing that Murray's groundbreaking 1993 article was syndicated under the title "The Time Has Come to Put a Stigma Back on Illegitimacy " (Murray, 1993a).

Although the nation reacted with disdain at Gingrich's handling of the orphanage issue, the question that began the refocus on orphanages in the

1980s remained: What should we do with America's abused and neglected children? Even in the heat of the orphanage debate, administration officials, including Mrs. Clinton and Donna Shalala, admitted the need for residential placement as a "last resort" (Clinton, 1995; Roman, 1995). At the outset of the debate, there was a possibility of support from both ends of the political spectrum. Even Senator Ted Kennedy expressed interest in Gingrich's orphanage proposal—before the issue became politically untouchable. After meeting with Philadelphia Mayor Ed Rendell, who expressed the need for orphanages to address the needs of neglected children, Kennedy (as quoted in Lehigh, 1994, p. 62) said, "building more orphanages is something we ought to give additional thought to."

Following the short-lived and unseemly orphanage debate, however, there was little if any "additional thought" given by politicians to residential placement of any kind, even though both sides ultimately cooperated in passing a major welfare reform bill in 1996. In the bill, there were no funds directed toward the construction of residential treatment facilities, and, as expected, there was no mention of the word *orphanage*.

The task of finding suitable homes for neglected children—a task in which, by universal agreement, we are already failing—is, in fact, compounded by the 1996 Welfare Reform Act, which mandates extensive cutbacks in all forms of public assistance.

A superb opportunity to achieve bipartisan support to responsibly address a critical issue was thus squandered in the fury of political battle. In the current political climate, the reresurrection of the concept of residential care for neglected children as a politically viable option is a formidable challenge to conscientious political leaders and social scientists alike.

The political annihilation of this important issue is a cautionary lesson in the political misuse of social science—a lesson we cannot afford to repeat.

## ▓ References

(1993, December 2). *Crossfire* (Transcript No. 977).

(1994, December 30). *New York Times*, p. 1.

American Broadcasting Companies. (1994, November 13). *This week with David Brinkley* (Transcript No. 681). New York: Author.

Barabak, M. (1995, February 11). GOP pollster image maker takes language to cynical new lows. *San Diego Union Tribune*, p. A3.

Bennett, L. (1995, August). Working moms shouldn't lose their kids. *Parents Magazine,* 158.

Besharov, D. J. (1987). Giving the juvenile court a pre-school education. In J. Q. Wilson & G. C. Loury (Eds.), *From children to citizens: Vol. 3, families, schools and delinquency prevention*. New York: Springer-Verlag.

Binder, A., Geis, G., & Bruce, D. (1988). *Juvenile delinquency: Historical, cultural and legal perspectives*. New York: Macmillan.

Brody, I. (1994, November 16). Gingrich leads crusade for restoration of school prayers. *Times of London*, p. 1.

Child Welfare League of America. (1994, December 14). *Welfare reform: Facts on orphanages*. Washington, DC: Author.

Clinton, H. R. (1995, January 16). Welfare: Lets move to discussion of what is best for the children that is open, honest and fair. *Newsweek*, p. 22.

Cohen, P., & Brook, J. (1987). Family factors related to the persistence of psycho-pathology in childhood and adolescence. *Psychiatry, 50,* 332-345.

Collins, S. (1994, December 19). There are no free lunches: Newt Gingrich's plan to put welfare children in orphanages appears to make little economic sense. *U.S. News and World Report, 117*(24), 55.

DeParle, J. (1994, November 13). The 1994 election: Momentum builds for cutting back welfare system. *New York Times*, p. 1.

Devroy, A. (1994, November 20). President plots a course toward the political mainstream. *The Washington Post*, p. A12.

DiIulio, J. J., Jr. (1994, September). The question of black crime. *The Public Interest, 117,* 3.

DiIulio, J. J., Jr. (1995, January 15). The plain ugly truth about welfare; Getting kids out of bad homes is the key to lasting reform. *The Washington Post*, p. C1.

Dorning, M. (1996, November 12). *Chicago Tribune*, p. 3.

Drew, E. (1996). *Showdown: The battle between the Gingrich Congress and the Clinton White House*. New York: Simon & Schuster.

Editorial. (1994, November 15). *Buffalo News*, p. B2.

Estrich, S. (1994, November 17). Newt's mean-spirited edge. *USA Today*, p. A15.

Farrington, D. P. (1987). Early precursors of frequent offending. In J. Q. Wilson & G. C. Loury (Eds.), *From children to citizens: Vol. 3, families, schools and delinquency prevention* (pp. 27-50). New York: Springer-Verlag.

Farrington, D. P., Loeber, R., Elliot, D. S., & Hawkins, J. D. (1990). Advancing knowledge about the onset of delinquency in crime. *Advances in Clinical Psychology, 13,* 283-342.

Feldman, R. (1994, December 13). *New York Times*, p. A29.

First lady assails orphanage plans. (1994, December 1). *New York Times*, p. A28.

Ford, M., & Kroll, J. (1995, March). *There is a better way: Family based alternatives to institutional care* (Research Brief No. 3). Washington, DC: North American Counsel on Adoptable Children.

Forer, L. (1988, April 20). Bring back the orphanage: An answer for today's abused children. *Washington Monthly Magazine*, 17-22.

Foskett, K. (1994, November 30). 'The alternative to welfare is jobs' Jackson says. *Atlanta Journal Constitution*, p. A9.

Frank, B. N. (1994, November 14). GOP leaders in Congress plan staff cuts, welfare reform. *CNN News* [Broadcast]. Atlanta: Cable News Network.

Gainer, L. (1994, November 16). Editorial. *Daily Telegraph*, p. 15.

Gillespie, E., & Schellhas, B. (Eds.). (1994). *Contract with America*. New York: Times Books.

Goodstein, L. (1994, November 15). Bishops critical of Gingrich on welfare cutback. *The Washington Post*, p. A3.

Grady, S. (1996, November 18). What if we didn't have Newt to kick around? *Milwaukee Journal Sentinel*, p. 8.

Greenberg, D. (1995, April 22). After the Republicans' first 100 days. *Lancet, 345,* 1037.

Hirschi, T. (1969). *The causes of delinquency.* Berkeley: University of California Press.

Ivins, M. (1994, November 30). The Newt's politics is to go further than opponent's. *Houston Post,* p. A27.

Jefferson, S. (1994, June 19). Should we bring back the orphanage? *Palm Beach Post,* p. F1.

Jehl, D. (1994, December 11). Clinton says orphanages can't replace strong parents. *New York Times,* p. A6.

Kiely, K. (1994, November 18). Democrats go back on a fence. *The Washington Post,* p. A1.

Kuczka, S. (1995, January 12). Task force dismisses plan for orphanages. *Chicago Tribune,* p. 12.

Kurtz, H. (1995, February 26). Spin cycles, a guide to media behavior in the age of Newt. *Washington Post Magazine,* p. 8.

Ladner, J. (1989, October 29). Bring back the orphanages, they're better for children than addicted parents and heartless foster care. *The Washington Post,* p. B1.

Laub, J. H., & Samson, R. J. (1988). Unraveling families in delinquency; Of the analysis of the Glueck's data. *Criminology, 26,* 355-380.

Lehigh, S. (1994, November 24). Sen. Kennedy expresses doubts about working with some in GOP. *Boston Globe,* p. 62.

Loeber, R., & Dishion, T. J. (1983). The early predictors of male delinquency. *Psychological Bulletin, 94,* 1968-1969.

Loeber, R., & Stouthamer-Loeber, M. (1986). Family factors as correlates and predictors of juvenile conduct problems and delinquency. In M. Tonry & N. Morris (Eds.), *Crime and justice; An annual review of research* (Vol. 7, pp. 29-150). Chicago: University of Chicago Press.

Loury, G. (1987). The family as context for delinquency prevention: Demographic trends and political realities. In J. Q. Wilson & G. C. Loury (Eds.), *From children to citizens: Vol. 3, families, schools and delinquency prevention.* New York: Springer-Verlag.

Marchini, D. (1994, November 14). *CNN News* [Broadcast]. Atlanta: Cable News Network.

McDonald, J. (1994, December 8). Reforms of welfare debated; Orphanages plan shapes discussion. *Hartford Current,* p. A1.

McLaughlin, M. (1995, November 1). Orphanages are not the solution. *USA Today,* p. 61.

Morganthau, T. (1994, December 12). The orphanage. *Newsweek,* p. 38.

Morse, R. (1994a, November 16). Newt: The cauldron's nastiest ingredient. *San Francisco Examiner,* p. A3.

Morse, R. (1994b, November 20). A reading from the Newt testament. *San Francisco Examiner,* p. A3.

Murray, C. (1993a, November 7). The time has come to put a stigma back on illegitimacy. *Sacramento Bee,* p. F1.

Murray, C. (1993b, October 29). The coming white underclass. *Wall Street Journal,* p. A14.

Muzzio, D., & Behn, R. (1995, February). Thinking about welfare, a view from New York. *Public Perspective, 6*(2), 35.

National Broadcasting Company. (1994, December 4). *Meet the Press* [Transcript]. New York: Author.

Nelson, L.-E. (1994a, November 15). Newt reaps fruit of white-mans anger. *Newsday,* p. A6.

Nelson, L.-E. (1994b, November 22). Hint to Democrats: Let the GOP govern. *Denver Post.*

Olasky, M. (1996, May). The real history of orphanages. *Philanthropy, Culture and Society,* 3.

Pear, R. (1994, December 30). White House says young will suffer under GOP plan. *New York Times,* p. A1.

Peels, S. (1995, January 23). Cut through the white lies about black families in welfare. *Washington Times,* p. 40.

Personal Responsibility Act of 1995, § 441 Cong. Rec. Vol. 141(5), p. H.159 (1995).

Phillips, L. (1994, November 18). The road to welfare reform strewn with pitfalls. *USA Today,* p. A10.

Pollitt, K. (1995, February 13). Subject to debate: Politics and orphanages. *The Nation, 260,* 192.

Reynolds, B. (1994, November 18). These political Christians neither religious nor right. *USA Today,* p. A13.

Roman, N. (1995, January 11). Orphanages fit into Clinton's welfare reform: Archer forces concession by Shalala. *Washington Times,* p. A1.

Rose, S. L., Rose, S. A., & Feldman, R. (1989). Stability of behavior problems in very young children. *Development and Psychopathology, 1,* 5-19.

Roth, B. (1994, November 19). Officials map dem comeback. *Houston Chronicle,* p. 15.

Scheer, R. (1996, July 30). Terrorism in the guise of reform. *Los Angeles Times,* B7.

Schneider, W. (1995, December 16). Running against Newt: Will it work? *National Journal,* p. 126.

Secrest, N., & Walker, D. (1995, April). The politics of welfare reform: The Democratic perspective. *National Journal,* 47.

Shirk, M. (1994, December 18). An orphan of an idea: The Republican's welfare alternative would cost lots more than welfare. *St. Louis Post-Dispatch,* p. B1.

Shogren, E., & Mehren, E. (1994, December 26). Close look suggests role for orphanage a complex one. *Los Angeles Times,* Part 8, p. 1.

Smith, E. P. (1995, January). Bring back the orphanages? What policy makers of today can learn from the past. *Child Welfare, 74,* 1.

Van Biena, D. (1994, December 12). The storm over orphanages. *Time,* p. 58.

Walsh, E. (1994, March 1). As at-risk children overwhelm foster care, Illinois considers orphanages. *The Washington Post,* p. A9.

West, D. J., & Farrington, D. P. (1977). *The delinquent way of life.* New York: Crane Russak.

Wilson, J. Q., & Loury, G. C. (Eds.). (1987). *From children to citizens: Vol. 3, families, schools and delinquency prevention.* New York: Springer-Verlag.

Wines, M. (1994, December 7). Team in place, Gingrich comes out swinging. *New York Times,* p. B11.

Winton, B. (1994, April 8). Foster care problems raising new interest in orphanages. *Phoenix Gazette,* p. A1.

Wolfgang, M. E., Figlio, R. M., & Sellin, T. (1972). *Delinquency in a birth cohort.* Chicago: University of Chicago Press.

Wright, J., & Wright, S. (1994). A policy maker's guide to controlling delinquency through family intervention. *Justice Quarterly, 112,* 193.

Zigler, E. (1992). Early childhood intervention: A promising alternative for juvenile delinquency. *American Psychologist, 47,* 997-1065.

# CHAPTER 7

# Orphanage Alumni

*How They Have Done and How*
*They Evaluate Their Experience*

RICHARD B. McKENZIE

A lthough orphanages have been widely and soundly criticized in the scholarly child care literature, this chapter revisits the orphanage issue by reporting the results of the only known extensive survey of the alumni of orphanages. When policy critics of long-term institutional care for disadvantaged or dependent children (as distinct from delinquent or severely troubled minors) capsule the prevailing view among scholars, the claims tend to be strongly critical and sweeping. Writing for the North American Council on Adoptable Children, Ford and Kroll (1995) maintain that "fifty years of research reconfirms the same findings: Long-term institutionalization in childhoods leads to recurrent problems in interpersonal relationships, a higher rate of personality disorders, and severe parenting difficulties late in life" (p. 5).

The Child Welfare League of America (CWLA, 1994) is equally adamant in its appraisal of the scholarly findings: "Children experience a great deal of stress and trauma when they are forced to leave their birth parents. Severe emotional, psychological, and behavioral problems result." Moreover, the CWLA avers that "child welfare experts recognize that orphanages are the wrong place for children who (a) have a loving parent capable of caring for them and (b) have no need for residential care and treatment." Finally, an editor of the policy journal *Child Welfare* (Smith, 1995) maintains that orphanages should not be brought back because

> Examination of the historical record of orphanages of the nineteenth and early decades of the twentieth century reveals characteristics that would make the creation of a new system of orphanages expensive and highly unfeasible. Proponents of new orphanages would also have the burden of disproving past criticism by professionals, based on the perceived harm done to children by institutional care. (p. 115)

Of course, such policy-level denunciations of orphanage care are founded on the equally harsh assessments of established scholars. Goldfarb (1947) concludes,

> Privation effects are permanent in institution children. . . . The permanence of institutional effects and the homogeneity of the institution group respecting the resultant character trends have contributed to a keen sense of professional discouragement. . . . Our studies and clinical experience showed that maladjustment was by far the outstanding trend in institution children after they had left the infant's home and were in foster homes. (p. 450)

In this chapter, I offer new evidence on what orphanages may or may not have accomplished: I asked orphans, all of whom are now middle aged or older, how they have done in life and how they feel about their orphanage experience. Because of limitations of the survey methods, which are detailed later, conclusions drawn are in no way intended to be definitive. The survey response rate, however, was remarkably high, making the findings worthy of consideration. Moreover, the performance of the orphans in their adult lives, as measured by a number of social and economic variables, plus the orphans' generally positive assessments of their orphanage life stand in sharp contrast to the expectations that might be drawn from a review of the scholarly assessments of orphanages. Clearly, the findings suggest that scholars of institutional care from the past several decades, who have been serious critics of orphanages, may not have considered some consequences of long-term institutional care that the orphans found beneficial.

## ■ The Child Care Literature

Concern with the impact of institutional care on children began in the early part of this century (Zmora, 1994), but the issue was not seriously and extensively investigated until World War II, when many English children were separated from their parents and sent to "residential nurseries" in rural areas away from the bombings in the cities. Freud, Solnit, and Goldstein (1973) determined that despite relatively good living conditions, the separated children suffered from feelings of not being wanted and from being deprived of maternal affection. Spitz (1945) agreed with Freud et al. that children institutionalized in foundling homes for periods extending beyond 6 weeks were bound to develop a syndrome of emotional and psychological disorders, which he named "hospitalism."

In a series of studies of a small group of children from a New York City orphanage, Goldfarb (1943, 1945a, 1945b, 1947, 1949) found evidence from projective, personality, and ability tests that the orphans showed deficiencies in speech, intelligence, personality, and social development. Drawing on the work of others, Bowlby (1951) identified "maternal deprivation" as the factor he believed to be the cause of the psychological damage found by others. Bowlby argued that children are seriously damaged emotionally when deprived early in life of maternal contact and affection. Institutionalization necessarily breaks the mother-child bond that is needed for a child's healthy psychological development. Institutions not only deprive children of maternal care but also are bound to aggravate the emotional problems of children because of the high turnover rates of caregivers in institutions (Freud et al., 1973). Other researchers have argued that orphanage experiences have led to a relatively high rate of admissions of problem children in at least one mental institution (Bender, 1945), impaired children's language development (Provence, 1989), raised children's "neuroticism" scores (Brown, 1937), increased the likelihood that the children will become involved in criminal activity (Bowlby, 1944; Rutter, Quinton, & Hill, 1990), diminished the children's ability to enter the labor force (Bodman, McKinlay, & Sykes, 1950), and undercut the children's social and parenting skills (Quinton, Rutter, & Liddle, 1984).

These and other child care studies appear to constitute a strong case against care of disadvantaged children in orphanages. Appearances can be misleading, however. In his evaluation of the studies cited and of many others covered in substantial detail in this book, psychology professor John McCall identifies several strong criticisms that can be marshaled against much of the research on institutional care. Briefly, McCall concludes that the samples of orphanage children covered in the studies are often small, rarely including more than 100 and often involving 15 or fewer institutional-reared children.[1] Moreover, the researchers often fail to explain how their samples were selected.[2] The studies tend to be one-time appraisals of the children, with no follow-up evaluations; when follow-up studies have been conducted, the follow-up evaluations have been made within relatively short periods of time after the initial evaluations, from 14 years at most to as short as 8 months. The studies also tend to be short term in terms of both the length of the children's orphanage stays and the period of time the children are evaluated.[3] A number of the studies base their conclusions on nothing more than the impressions of the researchers or caregivers, many of whom may have been predisposed to find fault with orphanages (Bender, 1945; Bowlby, 1944, 1951; Goldfarb, 1949). The studies that found problems with children from institutions do not consider the fact that the identified problems may have been caused by the children's experiences prior to their institutionalization. Although orphanage critics are quick to cite negative findings, they often overlook or ignore research evidence that does not show negative effects of institutionalization.[4] Given the decline in orphanages in recent decades, researchers have extended their criticisms of orphanage care based on outcomes of severely troubled youth placed in group homes, detention centers, and mental hospitals (Shealy, 1995). Given that orphanage care for disadvantaged children several decades ago was substantially different from the care of severely troubled children today, the conclusions of the previously discussed studies may not apply.

■ **The Survey:**
**Methods and Respondents**

To provide additional data on the truly long-term impact—measured in decades—of institutional child care, surveys were sent to 4,500 people on the mailing lists of the alumni associations of nine homes (or group care centers or, as many of the institutions were known in the 1960s and before, "orphanages") for disadvantaged children.[5] Many of the people on the mailing lists, however, were either deceased alumni or not alumni (many were former staff members and the children and spouses of deceased alumni). Probably fewer than 4,000 names and addresses were actually those for living alumni (an unknown number of the alumni were in the homes or institutions after they converted to serving severely troubled youth). Slightly more than 1,800 alumni returned the eight-page questionnaire, implying a response rate of approximately, if not more than, 50%.

## ▨ The Nature of the Included Orphanages

The nine orphanages covered in the survey were in the South and Midwest (Illinois, one; Ohio, two; North Carolina, three; South Carolina, one; Florida, one; and Texas, one).[6] Private religious and charitable groups (Presbyterians, Methodists, Baptists, Jews, Odd Fellows, and Masons) sponsored eight of the orphanages; a state government ran only one of the orphanages. All cared exclusively for white children, and all but one were in rural or small-town environments.[7] During the period the respondents were in residence, all the orphanages were set up to provide long-term residential care for between 100 and 500 children. All homes had extensive work requirements in shops or farms, and most had on-campus schooling at one time or another during their histories.

When the respondents were in residence, all the orphanages served exclusively disadvantaged or dependent children (as distinguished from severely troubled or delinquent children). By the late 1960s, seven of the nine homes had closed or had substantially changed their missions to serve severely troubled or delinquent children or both. Only two of the orphanages remain in operation today as homes for disadvantaged children.

## ▨ The Respondents

Given the changes in most of the homes since the late 1960s, this report focuses on the 1,589 respondents (of the 1,806 total respondents) who had left their orphanages prior to 1967. All had arrived at their homes between 1901 and 1961 (mean year of their arrival, 1936). At the time of their arrival, they were between 0 (just after birth) and 16 years of age (mean age of arrival, just under 8 years of age). The respondents left their homes between the ages of 2 and 23 (mean age at departure, 17 years of age or, generally, upon high school graduation). At the time of the survey, all respondents were 45 years of age or older (maximum age, 101; mean age, 67), with 51% male and 49% female.

When asked why they had been sent to their orphanages, the respondents gave the following reasons in descending order of frequency cited (the percentages total more than 100% because the respondents could check more than one category):

| Reason | % |
|---|---|
| One parent dead | 60 |
| Lack of support | 34 |
| Broken homes | 18 |
| Other reasons | 17 |
| Both parents dead | 15 |

The respondents had stayed in their orphanages from 1 to 17 years (mean stay, 9 years). On average, 1.9 siblings went with the respondents to their orphanages. Families were often split in the process, however, given that the respondents report a mean of 1.6 siblings staying behind with living parents or relatives. The respondents report the following forms of abuse encountered before going to the orphanages (they could choose more than one category):

| Abuse | % |
|---|---|
| Physical | 10 |
| Mental | 9 |
| Sexual | 5 |
| Other forms | 3 |

The definitions of the various forms of abuse were very "loose," although some guidance was provided on the survey instrument.[8] Of course, the respondents may be reporting forms of physical and mental treatment that are considered "abuse" today but were not considered abuse three or more decades ago.

A mother's education is understandably a strong predictor of how her children will do in terms of education and income (Hess & Holloway, 1984). Unfortunately, less than half the respondents were able to provide the educational attainment of their parents. For those who knew their mother's educational attainment, however, the mean highest grade attained was ninth grade.

The survey methods have definite limitations, harboring the potential for upward biases in the findings. The alumni who have been more successful and who look back with greater fondness on their orphanage experience may be disproportionately represented on the alumni mailing lists, given that those on the mailing lists must maintain their membership in the alumni associations. The alumni who responded to the survey may have been disproportionately more successful and may look back with greater fondness on their orphanage experience than those alumni who did not respond.

There was no way to check on the first potential upward bias—that members of the alumni association are more successful and favorable about their experience than those who are not members.[9] Most of the homes have closed or have radically changed their mission. None have maintained mailing lists of all alumni. Using the mailing lists of the alumni associations was the only practical, cost-effective way to obtain the responses of a very large number of alumni.[10]

To assess the second potential bias, the names of 100 alumni were randomly drawn from the mailing list of one orphanage (containing a total of 576 names). These 100 alumni were polled by phone. In the telephone interviews, the alumni were asked two questions. First, they were asked, "Did you complete and return your survey?" Second, they were asked the following question drawn from the survey:

Overall, how would you evaluate your experience at [name of orphanage]?

_____ Very favorable

_____ Somewhat favorable

_____ Mixed; both favorable and unfavorable

_____ Somewhat unfavorable

_____ Very unfavorable

This telephone poll found that a slightly higher percentage of the nonrespondents (vs. the respondents) chose "very favorable" and "somewhat favorable."

At the same time, factors that might bias the findings downward should also be recognized. All the respondents had spent a significant amount of time in an orphanage. Half of the respondents had spent 9 or more years in their orphanages, and only 1.6% had spent 2 years or less.[11] Also, a substantial majority of the alumni had entered their orphanages as a result of disadvantaged or abusive family circumstances. It is expected that if the criticisms of long-term orphanages noted earlier are correct, both the respondents' family backgrounds and their orphanage experiences should be expected to have held the alumni back in life. Even with the potential upward biases in the survey methods, it might still be expected that the respondents, as a group, would have fared less well in life than their counterparts in the general population.

## ▓ Survey Findings

Many of the questions on the survey distributed to the orphans were taken directly from the survey instrument used for the 1990 census. Use of Census Bureau questions permits comparisons between the respondents and the general population. Because all the respondents are white, however, their responses must be set in contrast with statistics for the general white population in the United States. Overall, the findings tend to support a strong general conclusion that is at odds with conventional arguments: As a group, the respondents have outpaced their counterparts of the same racial and age group in the general population by wide margins on practically all measures, not the least of which are education, income, and attitude toward life. The only social measure on which the respondents fell comparatively short is their relatively higher divorce rate.

### Education Attainment

As shown in Table 7.1, the respondents have a high school graduation rate of 88%, which is 17% higher than the 75% graduation rate for whites in the general population who are 45 years of age or older. It should be noted, however, that the graduation rate for the older respondents is lower than that for the younger respondents. At the same time, the older respondents have relatively higher graduation rates than their counterparts in the general white population. Over the decades covered by the survey, the graduation rate for the general white population climbed more rapidly than that for the respondents. The respondents also have relatively higher rates of college degrees and advanced degrees. Only 25% of the respondents have college degrees, but this is 39% higher than the college graduation rate of their white counterparts. Moreover, the respondents have more than two times the percentage of master's degrees and a 17% higher rate of doctorates. The respondents in only one age group, 50 to 59 years old, have a relatively lower number of doctorate degrees.

### Median Incomes

The 1994 median household incomes by age groups for the general white population and for the respondents are reported in Table 7.2. (The focus is on median household incomes, not mean incomes, because one alumnus reported an income of $50 million for 1994, which greatly distorts the mean calculations.)[12] The respondents' relative income statistics, however, appear to be in

**TABLE 7.1** Education of White Population and Orphanage Respondents

| Education | % of White Population, 1994 (1) | % of Respondents, 1995 (2) | % Difference [(2)/(1) – 1] |
|---|---|---|---|
| High school diploma, all ages | 75 | 88 | 17 |
| 50-59 Years old | 86 | 94 | 9 |
| 60-64 Years old | 78 | 91 | 17 |
| 65 Years old or older | 67 | 86 | 28 |
| College degree, all ages | 18 | 25 | 39 |
| 50-59 Years old | 24 | 31 | 29 |
| 60-64 Years old | 19 | 28 | 47 |
| 65 Years old or older | 13 | 22 | 69 |
| Master's degree, all ages | 5 | 6 | 20 |
| 50-59 Years old | 7 | 9 | 29 |
| 60-64 Years old | 5 | 7 | 40 |
| 65 Years old or older | 3 | 5 | 67 |
| Professional degree, all ages | 1.3 | 4.5 | 246 |
| 50-59 Years old | 1.5 | 4.1 | 173 |
| 60-64 Years old | 1.5 | 5.3 | 253 |
| 65 Years old or older | 1.1 | 4.4 | 300 |
| Doctorate degree, all ages | 1.2 | 1.4 | 17 |
| 50-59 Years old | 1.6 | 1.3 | –19 |
| 60-64 Years old | 1.3 | 1.3 | 0 |
| 65 Years old or older | 0.8 | 1.5 | 88 |

line with their relative achievements in education. The median household income for respondents 45 to 54 years old ($55,000) is 10% higher than that of their white counterparts of the same age in the general population. The median income of respondents 55 to 64 years old ($50,000) is 36% higher and the median income for those respondents 65 years of age or older ($30,000) is 61% higher than those of their white counterparts.

In evaluating the income statistics, it should be noted that less than three fourths of the respondents (1,129) reported their household incomes for 1994. If those respondents who did not report their incomes have distorted the median income upward, then the upward distortion appears most likely to be concentrated in the elderly age group.[13]

## Attitude Toward Life

Assessing the emotional impact of orphanages on children is difficult in the best of circumstances. The emotional impact of separation from parents and family members can be substantial in the short term, given that children must make major adjustments, all of which cannot be anticipated. Over the long term, however, the impact need not be so great, given that children who are familiar with deprivation usually can find ways of coping. In addition, indirect measures of emotional impact must be used, especially when the orphans are far removed in time from their stays in their homes, and their behaviors and attitudes cannot be observed directly. From the findings of this study, all that can be said on the issue is that the respondents profess to be "happier" than other Americans.

The National Opinion Research Center (NORC) at the University of Chicago has assessed people's "happiness" for nearly 40 years with one question: "All things considered, how would you say things are going these days?" The respondents are given three choices for answers: "very happy," "somewhat happy," and "not too happy."[14] Twenty-nine percent of Americans in NORC's 1994 poll answered very happy. More than twice that percentage (61%) of the orphanage respondents chose very happy. Twelve percent of those people polled by NORC chose not too happy, whereas less than half that percentage (5%) of the orphanage respondents chose this response.[15]

The orphans were also asked if they had ever suffered from a mental or emotional problem that was serious enough to require the services of a psychologist or psychiatrist. Just 13% of the respondents reported they had. (The only remotely comparable statistics for Americans in general are from studies reporting that at any point in time 20-28% of all Americans suffer from a diagnosable psychiatric or addictive disorder [as reported in Sykes, 1992, p. 13; see also U.S. Department of Health and Human Services, n.d., Chapter 3].) Only 2.5% of the respondents (or one fifth of those who had sought psychiatric or psychological care) reported the problems for which they had sought counseling were related to their orphanage experience. The overwhelming majority of these respondents indicated their emotional or mental problems had developed after they left their orphanages (e.g., because of divorce or the death of a spouse or child).

### Other Social and Economic Measures

Table 7.3 provides several other measures of the relative "success" of the orphanage alumni compared to the general white population. The only measure on which the orphans appear disadvantaged is in divorce rate. In 1990 (the latest year for available data), in the general white population, people 45 to 49 years of age and 50 to 54 years of age (the oldest age group for which data were available) had divorce rates of 34% and 27%, respectively. Respon-

**TABLE 7.2**  Median Household Incomes of General White Population and
Orphanage Respondents, 1994

| Age of Householder | White Population ($) (1) | Respondents[a] ($) (2) | % Difference [(2)/(1) – 1] |
|---|---|---|---|
| 45-54 Years old | 50,019 | 55,000 | 10 |
| 55-64 Years old | 36,817 | 50,000 | 36 |
| 65 Years old or older | 18,670 | 30,000 | 61 |

a. Seventy-two percent of orphans reported their household incomes.

dents in both age groups had divorce rates of 44%. This means that the
respondents' divorce rates were 29% and 63% higher than those of their
respective age groups in the general population.

For all respondents who were not retired (one third of all respondents),
the unemployment rate was 1% in 1995—one fourth the unemployment rate
for white workers 45 years of age or older. The poverty rate for the respondents
was at least 30% lower than the poverty rate for their counterparts in the
general population.[16] In 1993, 21% of American households (of all races) were
receiving at least one noncash benefit (other than Social Security and Medicare).[17] In 1995, only 2.1% of the respondents reported being on any form of
public assistance (other than Social Security and Medicare). Only 3.8% of the
respondents reported ever having been on any form of public assistance (other
than Social Security and Medicare).

Two percent of the respondents reported having spent time in a city or
county jail, state prison, or federal prison. More than half of the respondents'
incarcerations were for a few days (presumably for relatively minor offenses).
Only 0.8% of the respondents spent more than 4 days incarcerated in any
facility. Only 0.3% (5 of the 1,589 respondents) spent 1 year or more
incarcerated. Strictly comparable statistics are not available for the general
white population. The Justice Department, however, estimates that a white
American has a 1.6% chance of spending time in a state prison at some point
in his or her life (unpublished data provided by the U.S. Justice Department);
thus, the probability for being incarcerated in any jail, state prison, or federal
prison undoubtedly is significantly higher for the general white population.[18]

## Political Affiliation and Participation

Table 7.4 indicates that there are more Democrats (47%) than Republicans (43%) in the general population. The respondents, however, are divided

**TABLE 7.3**  Other Characteristics of General White Population and
Orphanage Respondents

| Characteristic | % of White Population (1) | % of Respondents (2) | % Difference [(2)/(1) – 1] |
|---|---|---|---|
| Divorce rate[a] | 1990 | 1995 | |
| 45-49 Years old | 34 | 44 | 29 |
| 50-54 Years old | 27 | 44 | 63 |
| Unemployment rate | 1994 | 1995 | |
| 45 Years old or older | 4.0 | 1.0 | –75 |
| 45-64 Years old | 4.0 | 1.6 | –60 |
| 65 Years old or older | 4.0 | 0.5 | –88 |
| Poverty rate[b] | 1993 | 1995 | |
| 45 Years old or older | 8.9 | 6.3 | –30 |
| 45-54 Years old | 7.0 | 2.9 | –59 |
| 55-59 Years old | 8.0 | 1.4 | –83 |
| 60-64 Years old | 9.7 | 2.1 | –78 |
| 65 Years old or older | 10.7 | 8.8 | –18 |
| Rate of public assistance | 1993 | 1995 | |
| Households receiving at least one noncash benefit | 21 | | |
| Currently on any form of public assistance other than Social Security and Medicare | | 2.1 | |
| Ever received any form of public assistance other than Social Security and Medicare | | 3.8 | |
| Incarceration rate | 1995 | 1995 | |
| Likelihood that a white American will spend time in a state prison during his or her life | 1.6 | | |
| Orphans who have spent time in a jail or state or federal prison | | | |
| Any time at all | 2.0 | | |
| More than 4 days | 0.8 | | |
| One year or more | 0.3 | | |

a. The divorce rate for the general white population is the percentage of people divorced after the first marriage. The divorce rate for orphans is the percentage ever divorced.
b. Poverty rate for orphans is calculated based on the poverty income threshold for a nonfarm family of four, which in 1993 was $14,763. This means that the poverty for orphans is very likely overstated, given that many of the low incomes reported were for households and families with fewer than four people.

**TABLE 7.4**  Political Affiliation and Voting Records of General Population
and Orphanage Respondents

| *Political Affiliation and Voting Records* | *% of General Population, All Races (1)* | *% of Respondents (2)* | *% Difference [(2)/(1) – 1]* |
|---|---|---|---|
| Political affiliation | 1994 | 1995 | |
|   Democrats | 47[a] | 39[d] | –17 |
|   Republicans | 43[b] | 39[d] | –9 |
|   Independents | 10[c] | 17[d] | 70 |
|   Other | 1[c] | 3[d] | 200 |
| Citizens 45 years old or older who voted in the 1992 presidential election | 72 | 88 | 22 |
| Presidential vote in 1992 | | | |
|   Bill Clinton | 43[c] | 41[d] | –5 |
|   George Bush | 37[c] | 45[d] | 22 |
|   Ross Perot | 19[c] | 11[d] | –42 |
|   Other | <1[c] | 3[d] | 200 |

a. All ages. The category of Democrats includes people who view themselves as "strong," "weak," and "independent" Democrats.
b. The category of Republicans includes people who view themselves as strong, weak, and independent Republicans.
c. All ages.
d. Forty-five years old or older.

evenly, with 39% belonging to each major party. Nearly twice as many of the respondents, compared to the general population, claim to be political independents or members of political groups other than the major parties.

The turnout in the 1992 presidential election among the respondents (88%) was more than one fifth higher than the turnout for all Americans 45 or older (72%). Bill Clinton beat George Bush in this election by a margin of 43% to 37%. Among the respondents, Bush beat Clinton by a margin of 45% to 41% (although it should be noted that the candidate receiving the most votes differed among the alumni from the different homes). Ross Perot received 19% of all votes cast in the election but 11% of the respondents' votes.

## *Preference for Adoption, Own Families, and Foster Care*

The respondents were asked to appraise their orphanage stays in several ways, not the least of which was in terms of the amount of abuse encountered.

As indicated in Table 7.5, 13% of the respondents reported being abused in some way (physical, mental, sexual, or other) during their stay at orphanages. Of the respondents, 10% reported physical abuse, 7% reported mental abuse, 2% reported sexual abuse, and 1% reported some other form of abuse. These percentages are similar to the percentages of respondents who reported forms of abuse (physical, mental, sexual, or other) prior to their orphanage stays.

A total of 338 respondents, or 21% of all respondents, indicated they had been abused in one of the several listed ways prior to or during their orphanage stays or both. Forty-two percent of these 338 abused respondents (and 9% of all respondents) indicated they had been abused in some way before their orphanage stays but not during their orphanage stays, 21% of the abused respondents (and 4% of all respondents) said they had been abused in some way before and during their orphanage stays, and 37% of the abused respondents (and 8% of all respondents) indicated they had been abused during their orphanage stays but not before.

The alumni were asked if they had ever, while at their orphanages, wanted to be adopted. In contrast to the widely held presumption that children in orphanages prefer adoption to continued stays in their orphanages, 86% of the respondents indicated that they either "never" or "rarely" wanted to be adopted. Only 3% indicated that they "frequently" or "constantly" preferred adoption to continued stays in orphanages. Much higher percentages of the respondents indicated an interest in returning to their families. It should be noted, however, that only 16% indicated they frequently or constantly wanted to do so. Nearly half (46%) said they never or rarely wanted to return to their families.

The respondents' preference for their orphanage care is supported by the statistics in Table 7.6. The alumni were asked to indicate whether they preferred growing up in their orphanages or with available members of their own families. Sixteen percent of the respondents indicated a preference for their own families, whereas 72% indicated a preference for their orphanage. Nine percent indicated they were uncertain, and the remaining respondents did not answer the question.

Table 7.6 also reveals that an overwhelming majority of all respondents (89%) indicated a preference for orphanage care over foster family care. No doubt, many of the respondents based their relative assessments of orphanage and foster care on limited information about the foster care system. A sizable number of the respondents (almost 300), however, had actually spent time in foster care before or after going to their orphanages or had worked in professions (social work, education, medicine, or law enforcement) that

**TABLE 7.5**  Overall Assessments of Orphanage Stays and Percentage of Orphanage Respondents

| Assessment | % |
|---|---|
| Forms of abuse encountered at orphanage | |
| Any form of abuse | 13 |
| Physical | 10 |
| Mental | 7 |
| Sexual | 2 |
| Other | 1 |
| No abuse reported | 87 |
| Wanted to be adopted | |
| Never | 81 |
| Rarely | 5 |
| Sometimes | 9 |
| Frequently | 2 |
| Constantly | 1 |
| No answer | 2 |
| Wanted to return to family | |
| Never | 31 |
| Rarely | 15 |
| Sometimes | 30 |
| Frequently | 10 |
| Constantly | 6 |
| No answer | 8 |

allowed them to report having "a great deal" or "some" knowledge of the foster care system. These groups indicated an overwhelming preference (90-92%) for orphanage care over foster care.

### Respondents' Overall Assessments of Orphanage Stays

The alumni were also asked to provide overall assessments of their orphanage stays. As indicated in Table 7.7, 76% of all respondents gave their orphanages a "very favorable" rating. Another 8% gave a "somewhat favorable" rating. As is obvious in Table 7.7, the percentages for very favorable and somewhat favorable ratings increase with the age of the respondents. For example, 62% of the respondents 45 to 54 years old gave their orphanages very favorable ratings, whereas 80% of the respondents 65 years old or older gave the same rating.

**TABLE 7.6**  Preference for Way of Growing Up and Percentage of
Orphanage Respondents

| Preference | % |
| --- | --- |
| Orphanage versus own family, all respondents | |
|    Staying at the orphanage | 72 |
|    Going with members of own family | 16 |
|    Uncertain | 9 |
| Orphanage versus foster care, all respondents | |
|    Staying at the orphanage | 89 |
|    Going in foster care | 2 |
|    Uncertain | 8 |
| Orphanage versus foster care | |
| Respondents who said they knew "a great | |
| deal" about the foster care system | |
|    Staying at the orphanage | 90 |
|    Going in foster care | 3 |
|    Uncertain | 5 |
| Respondents who said they had "some" knowl- | |
| edge of the foster care system | |
|    Staying at the orphanage | 92 |
|    Going in foster care | 1 |
|    Uncertain | 6 |

Slightly more than 2% of the respondents gave their orphanages "some-what unfavorable" (0.7%) and "very unfavorable" (1.4%) ratings. The unfavorable ratings decrease with the age of the respondents. For example, 3.4% of the respondents 45 to 54 years of age gave their orphanages very unfavorable ratings, whereas only 0.7% of the respondents 65 years old or older gave their orphanages that rating.[19]

## ■ Positive and Negative Attributes of Orphanage Care

The alumni were asked to provide three "positive" and three "negative" attributes of their orphanage stays. (There were no suggested positive or negative attributes; the respondents could write anything they wished in the space provided.) Tables 7.8 and 7.9 summarize the respondents' answers. More than half of the respondents indicated, in some way, that their orphan-

**TABLE 7.7**  Overall Evaluation of Orphanage Experience and Percentage of Orphanage Respondents

| Evaluation | % |
|---|---|
| Very favorable rating, all respondents | 76 |
| 45-54 Years old | 62 |
| 55-64 Years old | 75 |
| 65 Years old or older | 80 |
| Somewhat favorable rating, all respondents | 8 |
| 45-54 Years old | 12 |
| 55-64 Years old | 8 |
| 65 Years old or older | 6 |
| Mixed rating, both favorable and unfavorable, all respondents | 13 |
| 45-54 Years old | 22 |
| 55-64 Years old | 14 |
| 65 Years old or older | 11 |
| Somewhat unfavorable rating, all respondents | 0.7 |
| 45-54 Years old | 1.3 |
| 55-64 Years old | 0.3 |
| 65 Years old or older | 0.7 |
| Very unfavorable rating, all respondents | 1.4 |
| 45-54 Years old | 3.4 |
| 55-64 Years old | 1.8 |
| 65 Years old or older | 0.7 |

**TABLE 7.8**  Positive Attributes Cited and Percentage of Orphanage Respondents

| Positive Attribute | % |
|---|---|
| Personal values and direction<br>Responsibility, discipline, work ethics, family values, and honesty/trust/integrity | 60 |
| Sense of self-worth<br>Belonging, self-esteem, confidence, encouragement, and love | 59 |
| Basic amenities<br>Food, housing, medical care, recreation, and sports | 50 |
| Education, skills development, and guidance | 49 |
| Friendships and close sibling ties | 38 |
| Religious and spiritual values | 29 |
| Sense of stability and permanence | 13 |
| All positives<br>Specific claims that everything was positive | 1 |

**TABLE 7.9**  Negative Attributes Cited and Percentage of Orphanage
Respondents

| Negative Attribute | % |
|---|---|
| Separation from immediate families and siblings<br>  Lack of loving family, no family support, lack of visitations<br>  with siblings, and homesickness | 34 |
| Lack of love and emotional support from institution and staff<br>  Lack of attention, little effort to instill self-esteem, lack of<br>  guidance, unconcerned staff, and no sense of belonging | 31 |
| Lack of education, skill development, and guidance<br>  Poor education, no career guidance, no skills training, no<br>  preparation for the real world, and no counseling | 27 |
| Lack of freedom<br>  Too little freedom, too much routine, no independence, and<br>  no privacy | 15 |
| Excessive punishment<br>  Excessive and abusive punishment, threats of punishment and<br>  expulsion, and concentration on negatives | 12 |
| Excessive work demands<br>  Too many hours of and demands at work, too few hours of<br>  leisure, and harsh work environment | 6 |
| Lack of amenities<br>  Lack of food, clothing, shelter, or overcrowding or poor<br>  equipment | 6 |
| Poorly trained, underpaid, and unmotivated staff<br>  Uneducated and untrained staff; abusive, inattentive, and<br>  unconcerned staff; and few role models | 6 |
| No negatives<br>  Specific claims that there were no problems | 20 |

NOTE: There were no respondents who claimed everything or almost everything was negative.

ages provided personal values and direction (60%), contributed to their sense
of self-worth (59%), and provided basic amenities (50%). Education, skill
development, and guidance were positive attributes mentioned by 49% of the
respondents, whereas 38% mentioned friendship and close sibling ties as
positive attributes. Religious and spiritual values were mentioned by 29% of
the respondents, and 13% indicated their orphanages provided a sense of
stability and permanence. One percent of the respondents indicated, in various
ways, that everything about their orphanage was positive.

Separation from family and siblings was the most frequently cited negative attribute (34%). Lack of love or emotional support from the institution or its staff members was cited by 31% of the respondents, whereas 27% cited inadequate education, skill development, and guidance. Lack of freedom was cited by 15%, and excessive punishment was cited by 12%. Other negatives, each cited by 6% of the respondents, were excessive work demands, lack of amenities, and poorly trained, underpaid, and unmotivated staff. Interestingly, one fifth of the respondents indicated in various ways that there were no negatives to their experience.

Not all respondents gave negative and positive attributes. More respondents cited positives than negatives, however. All together, the respondents identified almost 80% more distinctly different positive attributes (3,976) than negative attributes (2,212).

## ■ Concluding Comments

Surveys have definite limitations, and this survey of orphanage alumni is no exception. Certainly, the "entire population" of orphans cannot be surveyed in its entirety or even by random selection. This survey had to rely on the mailing lists of nine orphanages for disadvantaged children.

By the same token, the findings can also be assessed by the claims and limitations of past scholarly work on the impact of institutionalization on children. As noted, Goldfarb (among others) has made strong negative assessments (e.g., "Privation effects are permanent in institution children" [1947, p. 450]) based on studies that also have serious built-in limitations, not the least of which is the small number of children from selected homes studied who are compared with an equally small number of children in traditional family settings or in foster care. As noted, past studies involving follow-up evaluations have been performed for relatively short periods of time and have focused on a limited number of variables—for example, IQ scores or a short identified list of behavioral disorders. Performance in life over long stretches of time is clearly a function of numerous variables. The highly favorable findings from this survey, which appear to stand in sharp contrast with what might have been expected given strong and widely held professional criticisms of orphanages, may be attributable to the inherent biases in the survey methods. The favorable findings, however, may also be due to the fact that the orphanages studied did not impose the disadvantages other researchers found in the institutions they studied. Moreover, the orphanages studied may have offered many advantages that have gone unnoticed and unassessed by other researchers.[20]

Clearly, the respondents in this survey report that they have done better on a variety of economic and social measures than might have been expected, given the sweeping criticisms of institutional care. The findings should, at the least, cause some critics to reexamine their conclusions and to extend their research. Certainly, not all orphans were helped by their orphanage experience. No doubt, some orphans were actually "damaged" in one way or another. Very unfavorable assessments were given by slightly more than 1% of the respondents. At the same time, one conclusion stands out: For a high percentage of the respondents, orphanage care seemed to "work." This conclusion is supported by the high percentage of respondents who attest that they have done well in life and who here and elsewhere attribute at least some of their success to their orphanage experience (Bogen, 1992; Chandler, 1990; McKenzie, 1996; Seita, Mitchell, & Tobin, 1996). It is also supported by what appears to be a growing number of volumes detailing the histories of various orphanages, most notably by Cmiel (1995) and Zmora (1994).

## ▓ Notes

1. For example, Spitz (1945) compared the behavior of only 69 infants whose mothers were in prison with 61 infants in a foundling home whose mothers were absent. In his series of studies, Goldfarb (1943, 1945a, 1945b, 1947, 1949) compared as few as 15 orphans with foster care children, and all the orphans appear to have been from the same orphanage. Provence (1989) compared 75 1-year-olds from an orphanage with 75 1-year-olds in foster care.

2. For example, whether the individuals included in the study were selected randomly or by clinical referrals. There is simply no way to judge the representativeness of the samples.

3. Quinton et al. (1984) and Rutter et al. (1990) undertook follow-up studies 14 and 10 years, respectively, after the initial evaluations. For all other studies, however, follow-ups were done after much shorter periods of time after the initial evaluations. Hodges and Tizard's studies (1989a, 1989b) used 8-year follow-up periods. Other studies, however, involved no follow-up or had follow-up periods that were no more than a few months (Goldfarb, 1945a, 1945b; Spitz, 1945). Although 8 years may be "long," given professional standards, it may not be sufficiently long for the advantages or disadvantages of institutional care to appear in outcome variables.

4. For example, although Goldfarb's 1943 study of 30 12-year-old foster care children found that those 15 children with orphanage experience scored relatively lower on IQ tests, Trotzkey (1930) found in a much larger study of over 2,000 children that the orphanage and foster care children had normal IQ scores. Orphanage critics seem convinced that any amount of maternal deprivation by way of stays in orphanages is harmful to children. The evidence on maternal deprivation, however, has also been significantly criticized by researchers (Langmeier & Matejcek, 1975; O'Connor, 1956; Orlansky, 1949; Stone, 1954). Pinneau (1955) criticized Spitz's (1945) work for being defective on a number of grounds, not the least of which was the lack of adequate

descriptions of the children in the sample and the testing procedures and the fact that the Hetzer-Wolf Baby Tests that Spitz used in his evaluations had been poorly standardized. When these problems were corrected and the developmental quotient (DQ) scores were recalculated, it was shown that the DQ scores had declined sharply previous to the mothers' abandonment. Prugh and Harlow (1962) stressed that many children must endure "masked deprivation" in dysfunctional families. Other researchers have found that changes in substitute mothers do not always have the presumed negative consequences that advocates of maternal deprivation are convinced occur (Kagan, 1984; Mead, 1962).

5. The words "homes" and "orphanages" are used interchangeably in this article primarily because the alumni often cite their long-term care institutions as their homes. Although these institutions cared mainly for disadvantaged children with living parents, as the evidence from the survey indicates, the institutions were still widely called orphanages.

6. The only criteria for the homes to be included in the study is that they must have been in existence prior to the mid-1960s serving primarily disadvantaged (as distinguished from severely troubled) children. The first 10 homes for which an alumni list could be obtained were included in the study. One home was subsequently dropped from the study on the grounds that it became clear that the people on the submitted list had been screened by one or more administrators at the home.

7. For reasons of guaranteed confidentiality, the names of the orphanages cannot be given.

8. The forms of abuse were defined on the survey instrument as follows: physical abuse, "excessive use of force and corporal punishment"; mental abuse, "serious emotional deprivation or depreciation of your worth"; sexual abuse, "from fondling to intercourse"; other forms of abuse, left unspecified (but with space for the respondents to define what they meant by other forms of abuse).

9. An effort was made to conduct a national telephone survey by a national polling organization, but such a poll is not practical because polling organizations require an expected incidence of the targeted group (alumni of orphanages) of at least 15%, which is a multiple of the expected incidence of orphans in the population.

10. It is worth noting, however, that I estimate that at least 75% of all living alumni from my orphanage are on the mailing list of the alumni association.

11. The mean number of years the respondents spent in their orphanages is 8.8 years (standard deviation, 3.4 years), the median is 9 years, and the mode is 10 years.

12. For all respondents 45 years old or older, the mean income is just under $96,000.

13. The nonreporters of household incomes are disproportionately elderly, given that 60% of the respondents are 65 years old or older, but 78% of those who did not report their incomes are 65 years old or older (indicating that 22 percentage points of the 28% who did not report their incomes are elderly). The nonreporters of household income with at least an undergraduate college degree represent 25% of all respondents and 26% of the respondents who did not report their household incomes. Those with a high school diploma or more education represent 88% of all respondents but 82% of those who did not report their incomes. If there is a potential upward bias in the median income data based on age and education considerations alone, it may be due to the disproportionate number of nonreporters among those alumni who did not graduate from high school. The respondents who did not graduate from high school represent 12% of all respondents. Eighteen percent of those who did not report their incomes, however, did not graduate from high school.

14. This question is rather crude, but researchers at NORC have determined that it works as well in assessing people's happiness as 16 more detailed questions (Thomas Smith, General Social Survey, National Opinion Research Center, Chicago, personal communication, May 9, 1995).

15. During the period from 1957 to 1994, the high for the very happy category is 38%, obtained in 1964 and 1974; the low for this category was 22%, obtained in 1972. The lowest percentage

for the not too happy category for the general population is 7%, recorded in 1978. The high for this category is 20%, obtained in 1974 (for the years 1957-1988, see Niemi, Mueller, & Smith, 1989, p. 290; for the years 1989-1994 [except 1992], Thomas Smith, General Social Survey, National Opinion Research Center, Chicago, personal communication, May 9, 1995).

16. The rate of poverty calculated here for the respondents is probably higher than the actual poverty rate because the poverty rate for the respondents was based on the number of respondents whose households had less than the poverty threshold incomes for a family of four, which in 1993 was $14,763. Also, the poverty threshold income for an elderly person to be in poverty is lower than that for younger people. No doubt, a number of the respondents were elderly living in households with fewer than four people.

17. As reported by the U.S. Department of Commerce (1995, Table 590). "Noncash benefits" include food stamps, free or reduced-price school lunches, public or subsidized housing, and Medicaid. The Census Bureau notes a trend toward underestimation of noncash beneficiaries.

18. It should be noted that the incarceration rate for the respondents' full lifetimes may be higher than indicated, given that respondents could still spend time in a jail or prison before they die.

19. How the respondents have done in life or how they looked back on their orphanage experience at the time of the survey has, no doubt, been influenced by a host of factors. The survey was not originally designed to undertake detailed statistical analysis of the various causal factors affecting the "outcomes." The study, however, does cover three well-defined "outcome variables": (a) the respondent's gross household income for 1994; (b) the respondent's "happiness" in 1994 as measured by the "happiness index" (with the answers—not too happy, somewhat happy, and very happy—given scores of 1, 2, and 3, respectively); and (c) the respondent's overall appraisal of the orphanage experience (or the respondent's choice of alternative responses—very unfavorable, somewhat unfavorable, mixed reaction, somewhat favorable, and very favorable—given scores of 1, 2, 3, 4, and 5, respectively). Ordinary least squares regression equations were run with each of the outcome (or dependent) variables, including variables that appear to be potential predictors: year of arrival at the orphanage, years of stay in the orphanages, age, gender, and dummy variables for gender, high school diplomas, divorce, abuse encountered at the orphanage, and stays at different homes. A variety of combinations of these and other independent variables were attempted in many equations that are not reported here. Most of these trials proved unproductive. The regression results from the best equations that could be generated are available from my homepage (*http://www.gsm.uci.edu/mckenzie*). In general (and as expected for a study covering such a long time period), the equations reveal little about the determinants of the respondents' incomes and happiness. The respondents' overall assessments of their orphanage experience, however, appear to be explained, to a statistically significant degree, by all but one of the independent variables. Only the education (or high school diploma) variable is not statistically significant at the 10% level. All the coefficients of all variables other than education—arrival year, years of stay, age, gender, ever divorced, abuse encountered, and orphanage 1 and 2—are statistically significant at the 5% level (or much lower). If anything can be said about the determinants of the respondents' happiness at the time of the survey, it is that that outcome variable does not appear to have been depressed (or enhanced) by the length of orphanage stays. This tentative conclusion is complemented by the finding that the length of the respondents' stays at orphanages tended to have a statistically significant positive impact on their overall appraisals. This finding may be important because of the widespread presumption that longer stays in orphanages adversely affected the children. Although this may have been the case for short-term evaluations by some measures used in other studies, it does not appear to hold true for the very long term covered by this study. Indeed, the length of stay appears to positively impact the respondents' overall assessments of their stays. It must be kept in mind, however, that none of the equations run had an $R$-squared of more than 15%.

20. For example, the orphanages studied may or may not have lowered the IQ scores of the children in their charge. Even if the orphanages did lower the children's IQs (and these orphanages could have increased them), they may have instilled in many alumni advantages—for example, work experience, moral values, and work ethic—that may have more than compensated for the disadvantages.

# ■ References

Bender, L. (1945). Infants reared in institutions permanently handicapped. *Bulletin of the Child Welfare League of America, 24,* 1-4.

Bodman, F., McKinlay, M., & Sykes, K. (1950). The social adaptation of institutional children. *Lancet, 258,* 173-176.

Bogen, H. (1992). *The luckiest orphans: A history of the Hebrew orphan asylum of New York.* Urbana: University of Illinois Press.

Bowlby, J. (1944). Forty-four juvenile thieves. *International Journal of Psychoanalysis, 25,* 19-53, 107-128.

Bowlby, J. (1951). *Maternal care and mental health.* Geneva: World Health Organization.

Brown, F. (1937). Neuroticism of institution vs non-institution children. *Journal of Applied Psychology, 21,* 379-381.

Chandler, T. E. (1990). *HiTough mercy: Lost in despair, we found ourselves at the orphanage.* Thomasville: Baptist Children's Homes of North Carolina.

Child Welfare League of America. (1994, December 14). *Welfare reform: Facts on orphanages.* Washington, DC: Author.

Cmiel, K. (1995). *A home of another kind: One Chicago orphanage and the tangle of child welfare.* Chicago: University of Chicago Press.

Ford, M., & Kroll, J. (1995, March). *There is a better way: Family-based alternatives to institutional care* (Research Brief No. 3). Washington, DC: North American Council on Adoptable Children.

Freud, A., Solnit, A., & Goldstein, H. (1973). *Beyond the best interests of the child.* London: Andre Deutsch.

Goldfarb, W. (1943). The effects of early institutional care on adolescent personality. *Journal of Experimental Education, 12,* 106-129.

Goldfarb, W. (1945a). The effects of early institutional care on adolescent personality. *American Journal of Orthopsychiatry, 14,* 441-447.

Goldfarb, W. (1945b). Effects of psychological deprivation in infancy and subsequent stimulation, Rorschach data. *American Journal of Psychiatry, 102,* 18-33.

Goldfarb, W. (1947). Variations in adolescent adjustment of institutional-reared children. *American Journal of Orthopsychiatry, 17,* 449-457.

Goldfarb, W. (1949). Rorschach test differences between family-reared, institution-reared, and schizophrenic children. *American Journal of Orthopsychiatry, 19,* 624-633.

Hess, R. D., & Holloway, S. D. (1984). Family and school as educational institutions. In R. D. Parke (Ed.), *Review of child development research* (Vol. 7, pp. 179-222). Chicago: University of Chicago Press.

Hodges, J., & Tizard, B. (1989a). Social and family relationships of ex-institutional adolescents. *Journal of Child Psychology and Psychiatry, 30,* 77-97.

Hodges, J., & Tizard, B. (1989b). IQ and behavioral adjustment of ex-institutional adolescents. *Journal of Child Psychology and Psychiatry, 30*(1), 53-75.

Kagan, J. (1984). *The nature of the child.* New York: Basic Books.

Langmeier, J., & Matejcek, Z. (1975). *Psychological deprivation in childhood* (3rd ed.). New York: John Wiley.

McKenzie, R. (1996). *The Home: A memoir of growing up in an orphanage.* New York: Basic Books.

Mead, M. (1962). A cultural anthropologist's approach to maternal deprivation. In M. D. Ainsworth (Ed.), *Deprivation of maternal care: A reassessment of its effects* (No. 14). Geneva: World Health Organization.

Niemi, R. G., Mueller, J., & Smith, T. W. (1989). *Trends in public opinion.* New York: Greenwood.

O'Connor, N. (1956). The evidence for the permanently disturbing effects of mother-child separation. *Acta Psychologica, 12,* 174-191.

Orlansky, H. (1949). Infant care and personality. *Psychological Bulletin, 46,* 1-48.

Pinneau, S. R. (1955). The infantile disorders of hospitalism and anaclitic deprivation. *Psychological Bulletin, 52*(5), 429-462.

Provence, S. (1989). Infants in institutions revisited. *Zero to Three, 9*(3), 1-4.

Prugh, D., & Harlow, R. (1962). Masked deprivation in infants and young children. In M. Ainsworth (Ed.), *Deprivation of maternal care: A reassessment of its effects.* Geneva: World Health Organization.

Quinton, D., Rutter, M., & Liddle, C. (1984). Institutional rearing, parenting difficulties, and marital support. *Psychological Medicine, 14,* 107-124.

Rutter, M., Quinton, D., & Hill, J. (1990). Adult outcomes of institution-reared children: Males and females compared. In L. N. Robbins (Ed.), *Straight and devious pathways from childhood to adult life.* Cambridge, UK: Cambridge University Press.

Seita, J., Mitchell, M., & Tobin, C. (1996). *In whose best interest?: One child's odyssey, a nation's responsibility.* Elizabethtown, PA: Continental.

Shealy, C. N. (1995, August). From Boys Town to Oliver Twist: Separating fact from fiction in welfare reform and out-of-home placement of children and youth. *American Psychologist, 50*(8), 565-580.

Smith, E. P. (1995, January/February). Bring back orphanages? What policymakers of today can learn from the past. *Child Welfare, 74,* 115-138.

Spitz, R. A. (1945). Hospitalism: An inquiry into the genesis of psychiatric conditions in early childhood. *Psychoanalytic Studies of the Child, 1,* 53-74; *2,* 113-117.

Stone, L. J. (1954). A critique of studies of infant isolation. *Child Development, 25*(1), 9-20.

Sykes, C. J. (1992). *A nation of victims: The decay of the American character.* New York: St. Martin's.

Trotzkey, E. (1930). *Institutional care and placing-out.* Chicago: Marks Nathan Jewish Orphan Home.

U.S. Department of Commerce, Bureau of the Census. (1995). *Statistical abstract of the United States: 1995.* Washington, DC: U.S. Government Printing Office.

U.S. Department of Health and Human Services, Center for Mental Health Services. (n.d.). *Mental health, United States: 1994.* Washington, DC: U.S. Government Printing Office.

Zmora, N. (1994). *Orphanages reconsidered: Child care institutions in the Progressive Era.* Philadelphia: Temple University Press.

# CHAPTER 8

# Research on the Psychological Effects of Orphanage Care
## A Critical Review

JOHN N. McCALL

M any child care professionals still believe that orphanages are bad for children. Supposedly, young children fail to develop as they should, socially and psychologically. The prospective harm is even more certain if children are admitted as infants and remain for several years. Supposedly, this bad reputation is based on careful research, not *Oliver Twist* stories of gross maltreatment.

In this review, I attempt to answer two questions: How adequate is the research on orphanage care and are the criticisms of orphanages justified? Several criteria guide the review: (a) Were appropriate questions asked about orphanage care? (b) Were the research methods suited to the questions asked? (c) Do the conclusions correctly follow from the methods used and the data collected? and (d) How widely may we generalize the findings?

Many journals and books, dating back to the 1930s, were searched for relevant material. These were published by professionals in the fields of psychiatry, social work, and psychology. Some professionals worked directly with children, but most served as consultants to child care workers or as teachers and researchers. Autobiographical accounts, which can provide insights into orphanage care, were not considered pertinent to this review. The term *orphanage* is used by these researchers quite broadly. Sometimes, it refers to hospital wards, nurseries, or foundling homes, whereas at other times it refers to boarding homes and other forms of group care. Despite the general lack of detail on how children were treated, we can assume that all these institutions dealt with children who lacked easy access to their parents.

## ■ Perspectives on the Study of Orphanage Effects

Early in the 20th century, leaders in child care expressed the view that family care was preferable to orphanage care of needy children. This view seemed to be based on personal preference rather than careful comparison of their relative merits. The available reports were mostly anecdotal or isolated case studies. By 1930, trained social workers helped place children in orphanages or foster care, but they seldom evaluated general outcomes. Psychologists had already standardized ways to measure individual intelligence or social maturity, but these tools were seldom used outside of schools and clinics. Some clinical psychologists and psychiatrists evaluated selected orphanage children on an individual basis. These did not, however, constitute evaluations of orphanage programs as such. One important exception is the large-scale survey conducted in approximately 1929 (Trotzkey, 1930). Clinical psychologists compared individual intelligence for several thousand orphaned children and home-raised children, and comparable results were obtained for both groups of children. The former, however, showed greater gains in body weight than the home-raised children. No study of this magnitude has been conducted since that time!

Psychological theories about child development and ways to handle children had only a slight, indirect bearing on orphanage practice. For example, so-called behaviorists during the 1920s studied the emotional development of children. Their limited findings encouraged regular, somewhat rigid, eating and sleeping schedules. No systematic studies on the validity of these teachings were conducted in the orphanage setting. Freudian theories had some impact on child-rearing methods after the 1930s, when child-centered theories became popular. Psychiatrists with Freudian views recommended self-demand schedules plus liberal weaning and toilet-training methods. The aim was to prevent frustration, which might cause neurotic habits. Again, these suggestions were derived mostly from case studies of adult neurotics rather than from systematic study of orphanage youth.

About 1940, wartime conditions in Great Britain brought attention to the plight of children separated from their families. Authorities, who hoped to reduce casualties from the bombing of large cities, removed children from their families and placed them in special "residential nurseries." These group homes were located in isolated rural communities. Several psychiatrists warned of the risks (Langmeier & Matejcek, 1975; Spitz, 1945). Among these was Anna Freud, who had escaped to England with her father, Sigmund Freud. She was trained in psychoanalysis and committed to the study of child development. Invited by authorities to study the problem of child separation, she concluded from several case studies (Freud & Burlingham, 1944) that institutionalized children are doomed to fail psychologically because of maternal deprivation, despite good physical and social care.

This grave warning became widely accepted gospel in the postwar work of John Bowlby, a psychoanalytically trained psychiatrist from the Tavistock Clinic in London. He was commissioned by the World Health Organization to study maternal deprivation and recommend solutions. Limiting himself to European and U.S. findings, he concluded that institutional child care was in a terrible state. In too many cases, the physical care of children was inadequate. Even more serious was the psychological damage that many institutional children suffered despite good physical care. The cause, he assumed, was disruption of the special mother-child bond needed for healthy psychological development. His 1951 report, *Maternal Care and Mental Health,* was translated into several languages and circulated worldwide. Because his warning served the child care professionals' desire to replace orphanages with home care, the issue of "maternal deprivation" became a central concern for child care workers.

Another psychiatrist, Rene Spitz (1945), provided timely publicity. He reported on the emotional and physical regression of infants in a foundling home that he believed resulted from maternal separation. His film on the subject, *Grief* ("Milk and Love," 1952), further mobilized professional opinion against institutional care. Empirical support came from the clinical studies of William Goldfarb (1943, 1945, 1947, 1949), who tested small groups of adolescents from one New York City orphanage. His reports of serious deficiencies with speech, intellect, personality, and social development were widely circulated among social work professionals. Other scholars in England and the United States began to report similar problems.

A bleak view of orphanage care developed within the professional child care ranks. It was based more on selected clinical studies than on systematic evaluations or comparisons. In brief, it claimed the following: Any amount of orphanage experience is harmful. The damage is greatest during the first years of life and increases dramatically with length of stay in an institution. In addition to being irreversible, the resulting damage affects a wide range of psychological and social traits. Supporting popular opinion is illustrated in the extreme views of New York City's Mayor La Guardia, who exclaimed (as quoted in Goodwin, 1994, p. 416), "The worst mother is better than the best institution."

By 1960, child development researchers (Langmeier & Matejcek, 1975; O'Connor, 1956; Orlansky, 1949; Stone, 1954) wondered just what maternal deprivation really meant and was the evidence for its effects valid? New research on child development included both human and animal studies, and it partially discounted strong claims about the bad effects of maternal deprivation.

The demise of most orphanages by the 1980s limited further research with orphanage subjects. A few studies continue to be reported outside of England and the United States in Third World countries, where physical and social facilities are limited. Many of the orphanages that remain in the West have changed to treatment centers for special needs children who are delinquent or emotionally disturbed.

By and large, the child welfare profession and much of the general public are opposed to any child care option that is not family centered. For example, Ford and Kroll (1995), who are active in adoption work, state that "fifty years of research reconfirms the same findings: Long-term institutionalization in childhood leads to recurrent problems in interpersonal relationships, a higher rate of personality disorders, and severe parenting difficulties later in life" (p. 5).

## ■ How Crucial Is Maternal Deprivation?

Because the concept of maternal deprivation is central to arguments against orphanage care, it deserves careful study. Its theoretical importance stems, of course, from basic assumptions about the needs of developing children. It is agreed that growing children need strong, interactive relationships with responsible adults. Besides providing emotional and physical security, such ties help the child grow and learn to cope with an ever-changing world. In most societies, the child's parents are considered the optimal social arrangement for child care, and mothers are expected to play the central role.

What are the risks when a child is separated from its family for whatever reason? Can the mother's role be supplanted to a reasonable degree? Freudian theorists think not. Like Anna Freud (Freud, Solnit, & Goldstein, 1973), they believe the absence of a close, continuous relationship with a caring mother, or surrogate, spells doom for the psychological well-being of the infant. In layman's terms, these theorists argue that "mother-child bonding" is a necessary step toward developing a sense of trust in others, self-confidence, and a sense of right and wrong. This bonding process is assumed to overlay unconscious ego and superego developments, necessary for later psychological health. Such imagery appeals to family-centered professionals who want the authority of scientific theory. Unfortunately, several questions remain unanswered. Precisely what transpires during this bonding process? How well can surrogate mothers substitute for biological mothers? What is the evidence that shows group homes cannot meet this need?

Because the claimed unconscious processes are inferred and never directly observed, their validity remains in doubt. Romantic images of the mother and child looking happily to each other do not themselves discount the possibility that other mothering persons can replace the natural mother. One critic (Orlansky, 1949) notes that most psychoanalytic theories about personality development and its disorders were derived from conversations with adult neurotics. Sears's (1943) classic book reviewed studies designed to test psychoanalytic theory and concluded that no investigator prior to his review actually concentrated on infant behaviors and their relation to personality development. Generally, it is not the style of investigators to conduct systematic surveys of large samples in a range of conditions. Rather, they generalize from a small number of selected case studies.

What seems to be an exception to this reliance on isolated clinical cases is Rene Spitz's study (1945; Spitz & Wolf, 1946) of approximately 60 infants in a foundling home. He presents a so-called longitudinal study lasting 8 months in which he followed up infants who were admitted soon after birth. Their mothers, who could not care for them independently, nursed them for several weeks or months and then left their care to others. In addition to clinical observations of the infants' emotional and physical conditions, Spitz and staff used the Hetzer-Wolf Baby Tests to monitor their physical and social development while the mothers were present and then absent.

Spitz's (1945) graph of average developmental quotients (DQs) shows a dramatic decline that coincides with the departure of mothers. From these data and clinical observations, he concluded that infants separated from their mothers for more than 6 weeks develop a syndrome of disorders, which he calls "hospitalism." It is marked by tears, staring eyes, and other morbid signs of depression, plus a significant drop in DQ. Worse, 30% of these infants died during their first year! Spitz contrasted this image of wasted children with the more positive picture of infants in a prison nursery who thrived on the care of their inmate mothers. This appealing contrast continues to be cited in the child care literature.

A devastating criticism of Spitz's work appeared in a prestigious psychology journal (Pinneau, 1955). One problem is Spitz's confusing description of his infant subjects and the testing procedures. It is not clear how many infants were observed at different stages, what the family backgrounds were, what their conditions upon admission were like, and so on. Apparently, the foundling home was located in Latin America, where cultural attitudes about children of deprived or unwed mothers might have differed from North American attitudes in the 1940s.

After piecing together numbers from several different reports, Pinneau (1955) concluded that Spitz's study was not truly longitudinal. The graph that appears to show a decline in average DQs for the same infants at different months of age is actually based on overlapping groups of babies at different ages. The Hetzer-Wolf Baby Tests for measuring DQs were found by other critics to be poorly standardized. For example, these particular tests continue to give lower DQs with successive months of age. Thus, it is not surprising that Spitz's infants showed a lower DQ at a later age. Even more telling are Pinneau's recalculations, which show that average DQs declined sharply before the mothers departed! These facts discount Spitz's reported drop in DQs with months of separation. Pinneau concludes, despite his personal preference for mother care over institutional care, that there is no convincing evidence that mother separation rather than social deprivation causes psychological deterioration.

It has also been argued (Ribble, 1944) that emotional bonding during the first weeks of life is absolutely essential if underlying brain cell connections are to be completed, along with other physiological developments. Failures to bond interrupt these changes and causes serious physical damage. Pinneau (1950) demolishes much of this particular argument with convincing accounts of the neonate's physical development. Also, he reports that few infants reliably recognize their mothers before 3 months of age. Other child psychiatrists believe emotional bonding occurs at 6 to 9 months, when overt recognition is obvious.

The concept of maternal deprivation is often used inconsistently. Yarrow (1961) notes that it might be equated with orphanage placement, mother neglect at home, or the change in caregivers within the same home. Such variable usage ignores important qualitative differences and contributes to the tendency to not describe orphanage care in detail. Rheingold's (1960) time samples of mothering behavior in family homes and institutions illustrate the kind of careful observation that is needed. She found that home children had contact with more material objects than did orphanage children, but the activity levels of both were equal. Prugh and Harlow (1962) draw attention to patterns of "masked deprivation" within family homes in which parents have dysfunctional ties with their children. Parenting styles also vary radically with different socioeconomic groups. An example is the wealthy child who is placed in boarding schools at an early age. Even middle-class parents may change parenting styles, perhaps due to full-time employment of both. Long hours in a day care setting might also constitute maternal deprivation for some children.

Several authors (Bowlby, 1951, 1958; Freud et al., 1973) view staff turnovers in institutional practice as a serious risk to children because bonding with a single adult is difficult. It is tempting to subscribe to this argument, but hard, systematic data are lacking. Anthropologists report frequent use of multiple-mothering in other cultures. Margaret Mead (1962), for example, suggests this provides healthy continuity of care and a hedge against separation trauma. Kagan (1984) describes a nomadic tribe in Africa that believes the infant is better off if nursed by someone other than his or her mother. Later, the infant is cared for by different persons in the tribe. Of course, more clear information about the effectiveness of these different child-rearing patterns is needed, but they do indicate the importance of consistent mothering or social support, not biological mothers, per se.

The Israeli kibbutz has received consistent study. Here, infant mothering is shared by the actual mother and a paid child care worker. The former gives emotional support, whereas the latter attends to physical and personal education through most of the day. Rabin's (1957, 1958) studies of kibbutz children found some slowness in personal and social development for one group compared with nonkibbutz children. Another study showed that 9- to 11-year-old kibbutz children were more mature than the comparison group. Thus, local circumstances rather than universal effects of shared mothering seem to explain development outcomes.

An extreme example of multiple-mothering is the "home management house." These occur in educational settings in which women students learn infant care under the supervision of one adult. Although research is limited, one study (Gardner & Swiger, 1958) reported no differences between a sample of babies used in one house and regular home babies on measures of physical growth and the Gesell Scales for behavioral and social development.

I conclude that proponents of mother deprivation theory have an appealing theory but few supporting facts. Although emotional and physical deterioration surely occurred in some clinical studies, there is insufficient evidence to rule out physical and social neglect as essential causes. Thus, it is far from proven that simply losing one's mother or being placed in an institution by itself leads to psychological decline. Even if one accepts the role of maternal deprivation in the case of tiny infants, there is much less evidence that the same argument applies to older children who are admitted to orphanages.

## ▓ Reported Psychological Effects of Orphanage Care

In this section, I evaluate reports on the psychological development of children with orphanage experience. Table 8.1 lists many of the studies cited by child care professionals. For convenience, the studies are grouped into those published before 1951, the year of Bowlby's major review, and those published after 1951. Several studies that dealt with infants less than 1 year old are omitted because psychological evaluations at this age are difficult or unreliable. Also, this listing is far from complete, but it includes most of those studies cited by critics of orphanage care.

The studies within Table 8.1 are alphabetically arranged by author. The underlying research design and sample descriptions are also reported, along with major results. Most of the designs are direct correlation studies, wherein measures such as IQ scores are compared for a group of orphans and a group of family-raised children, perhaps matched by age and gender. Several designs amount to impressions, case studies, or retrospective reports. The several "follow-up" studies listed here should not be confused with genuine longitudinal studies that measure change over time. These follow-ups simply identify orphans at one stage of development and evaluate them at a later point in time. A small number of these studies are true experiments wherein a treatment variable is directly manipulated by the investigator. Here, subjects are randomly assigned to treatment and control group to ensure greater equivalence.

It is necessary to point out that although much of this research is designed to evaluate the psychological effects of orphanage experience, almost none of it deals with orphanage experience directly. Thus, what should be the primary independent or causal variable, the effects of which we are concerned about, is ignored until the studies state conclusions. In many cases, orphanage experience is assumed, without evidence, to be sterile or unchallenging. In contrast, home care is assumed to be universally warm and stimulating. Unlike Bowlby (1951), who forgave procedural faults when reviewing many of these same reports, I consider the effect that these slip-ups have on the scientific credibility of results.

## ▓ How Do Orphans Compare With Other Children?

Almost all research on orphanage children amounts to clinical evaluations of opportunistic samples. Because the method of selecting these children is seldom explained, it is unknown how representative they are of a particular orphanage or orphanage children in general. Typical studies assess one or two traits, such as intelligence, personality, language skills, or social maturity, usually with the help of trained examiners who use standardized tests.

The following is the most frequently posed question in these studies: How does the psychological development of children with orphanage experience compare with that of other children? The comparisons might be made with general population norms, selected foster children, or children raised by relatives. A glance at the results in Table 8.1 shows that the vast majority of these are negative. That is, when groups of children with orphanage experience are compared with other children, the average development for orphans is lower on measures of general intelligence, personality, language, or social skills. There are wide individual differences within some groups of children, but the overall trend is negative for orphaned subjects.

The research methods used partly explain this negative trend. For example, some of the findings amount to impressions or simple anecdotes and not objective evidence. Such reports are prone to reflect personal bias. Bender (1945) recalls how 10% to 20% of the problem children referred to the Bellevue Hospital in New York had orphanage backgrounds. This impression might have prompted further research to verify her suspicions, but we are not told of that. Neither are we told of base rate norms for admission to this hospital. We might suppose that needy children from socially and economically depressed homes are the rule. Thus, it is no surprise if a portion of these children had been placed in orphanages. Verry's (1939) anecdotal report describes one single graduate from an orphanage school who was unprepared to handle money, job demands, or the requirements for dating girls. Had the author never met an immature youth from a normal home? Although she

**TABLE 8.1** Reported Psychological Effects of Orphanage Experience

| Study | Design | Sample | Results |
|---|---|---|---|
| Studies before 1951 | | | |
| Bender (1945) | Impressions | Hundreds of problem children referrals to hospital | Recalled 5-10% had institutional background |
| Bodman, McKinlay, & Sykes (1950) | Direct correlation | 51 young adults with orphanage backgrounds, 52 from families, same age | Some orphans less sociable or mature, poor work adjustment |
| Bowlby (1944) | Retrospective | 44 teenage thieves | A large proportion had orphanage backgrounds |
| Bowlby et al. (1956) | Follow-up | 60 7- to 14-year-olds hospitalized as infants, 180 classmates | The previously hospitalized differed some in IQ, behavior adjustments |
| Goldfarb (1943) | Direct correlation | 15 12-year-olds, orphanaged, and fostered; 15 fostered only | Orphaned group lower on personality and intelligence tests |
| Goldfarb (1944) | Direct correlation | 15 12-year-olds, orphanaged, and fostered; 15 fostered only | Less emotional-perceptual maturity in responses to inkblots for orphans |
| Goldfarb (1945) | 9-Month follow-up | 15 orphans under 4 years; 15 fostered under 4 years | Orphans rated lower on a wide range of personality and ability tests |
| Goldfarb (1947) | Retrospective study | 15 well adjusted and 15 poorly adjusted with orphanage experience | Poorly adjusted were placed in home sooner and stayed longer |
| Goldfarb (1949) | Direct correlation | 15 orphans, 15 fosters, 15 schizoid: all 12 years old | Inkblot responses show immaturity for orphans and schizoid |
| Lowrey (1940) | Case study | 28 boarding home children with 3 years in orphanage | Showed isolation-type personality (self-centered, hostile, insensitive) |
| Skeels & Dye (1939) | Follow-up | 13 selected orphan infants; remaining infants stayed | 13 placed with feebleminded women gained in IQ; the others decreased |
| Skeels et al. (1938) | Controlled experiment | Matched pairs of orphan children put into experimental and control groups | Experimentals who got preschool training gained dramatically in IQ |
| Spitz (1945) | 8-Month follow-up | 69 infants, prison nursery; 61 infants, founding home | Development quotients increased for prison and decreased for foundling babies |
| Trotzkey (1930) | Developmental and correlation | 2,523 children in orphanage care; 1,214 foster care; New York City school | Physical health and IQs equal or better than Chicago or New York City school norms |

| Study | Design | Sample | Results |
|---|---|---|---|
| Studies since 1951 | | | |
| Hodges & Tizard (1989a) | 8-Year follow-up | All orphanage experience; 5 stay, 23 adopted, 11 returned | Behavioral and social adjustment the same for adopted and returned; those placed early had more problems |
| Hodges & Tizard (1989b) | 8-Year follow-up | All orphanage experience; some stay, others adopted, some returned to families | Those restored to families less adjusted than adopted, less parental skills |
| Pringle & Bossio (1960) | Direct correlation | 11 maladjusted and 5 rated stable with orphanage experience; 142 from family homes | Those with orphanage experience had less language skill; social maturity was same; maladjustment problems not serious |
| Provence (1989) | 8-Month follow-up | 75 1-year-olds from orphanage; 75 1-year-olds fostered | Orphaned slower to develop social, language, and intellectual skills |
| Quinton, Rutter, & Liddle (1984) | 14-Year follow-up | 81 female orphan adults; 51 matched controls | Orphaned showed more problems with social interaction, parenting |
| Rutter, Quinton, & Hill (1990) | Approximately 10-year follow-up | 120 with orphanage experience; 58 same age controls | Ratings show more personality and behavioral problems for some orphanage experienced; associated with parents' problems |
| Tizard (1979) | 6-Year follow-up | 20 orphanaged, then adopted; 10 orphanaged, returned parents | Adopted adjusted better than the returned; latter had family problems |
| Tizard & Hodges (1978) | 3.5-Year follow-up | 51 orphanaged (25 later adopted, 13 returned); 29 controls | Teachers saw more problems than did parents with orphaned children |
| Tizard & Joseph (1970) | Direct correlation | 30 nursery 2-year-olds and 30 2-year-olds from city | Nursery kids less well-developed language and mental skills, more fearful |
| Tizard & Rees (1975) | Direct correlation | All with orphanage background, age 4.5; 26 stay, 24 adopted, and 15 returned to family | The orphanage remainers had more problems than adopted and less attached to adults; all had same IQ = 100 |
| Wolkind & Rutter (1973) | Retrospective study | All 10 or 11 years old; 458 with behavioral problems, 100 with psychiatric problems, 172 controls | More behavioral-problem youth had orphanage background plus prior family disturbances |

137

suggests that sheltered conditions in the orphanage caused this unprepared-
ness, she gives no hard facts. These two reports are frequently cited in child
care journals. We need more systematic data to draw serious conclusions about
the social maturity of orphanage graduates.

Intelligence or related cognitive skills are widely reported to suffer from
orphanage experience. One of the most substantial studies (Trotzkey, 1930)
to discount this claim is seldom mentioned, perhaps because it was published
privately. It compared orphanage and foster care children in Jewish-sponsored
programs in Chicago, New York, and Cleveland with public school children.
More than 3,700 Jewish care children were involved, including 2,523 from
orphanages and 1,214 from foster homes. Data on IQ scores, using either
group tests or the individually administered Stanford-Binet, showed the
Chicago orphanage samples scored in the average range, as did children in
New York City elementary schools. The New York City orphanage samples
scored slightly lower than the comparison groups but scored well in the
average range. The borderline or retarded child was not eliminated from these
orphanage samples, as was usually the case in public schools. The slight
advantage that orphanage children had over foster children was suggested to
be the result of better education programs for the orphanage children. The
study also showed that orphanage children, despite being somewhat more
underweight upon admission, gained more weight than foster care children.
Both groups averaged slightly better weight gains than public school children
during the study period.

Goldfarb's work with small samples from a single New York City orphanage is widely cited by orphanage critics. One study (Goldfarb, 1943) included
IQ test results with tests for speech, educational achievement, and personality.
He compared 15 12-year-old orphans, who were later moved into foster care,
with 15 foster care-only youth. The former scored well below average on a
standardized intelligence test, whereas the latter scored close to average, or
about 100. Only 3 of 15 orphans showed average language skills, whereas
most of the foster youth had average language skills. Educational achievement, ratings for social maturity, and other measures showed the orphan
sample to be immature and underachieving.

A serious problem with this finding is the uncertain method of selecting
orphans for study. This, in addition to the small samples sizes, raises doubts
about how representative his subjects were of New York City Jewish orphans.
Trotzkey's (1930) results, which showed normal IQs, were based on 2,212
orphanage and foster care children in that same city.

Bowlby, Ainsworth, Boston, and Rosenbluth (1956) studied former hospital patients who were believed to suffer maternal deprivation during their 1- or 2-year stay in a tuberculosis sanitarium before age 4. They compared the 60 former patients, who were ages 7 to 14 at the time of the study, with schoolmates on measures of intelligence, ratings for school behavior, and rated performance while taking the intelligence tests. Average Stanford-Binet IQs for the two groups were found not to differ statistically. An examination of just part of the data, however, showed that patients admitted before 2 years of age more often scored in the lower-average range than patients admitted between 2 and 4 years. The hypothesis that the former patients would score lower received indirect support.

Somewhat questionable is Bowlby et al.'s (1956) treatment of the teacher ratings for school behavior. They found no significant differences in the average ratings for the hospitalized and control groups on each of the 28 rating items. The investigators, however, searched through the teacher ratings and threw out those data judged to show inconsistencies. That is, if a teacher rated a given student as "friendly" on one item and "has few friends" on another, these data, along with those for matched controls, were eliminated. For the much reduced sample, 11 of the 28 rating items showed significant differences in the desired direction. Besides other questionable manipulations, the authors equivocated about another finding that displeased them. The teachers happened to rate the former patients as adequate in regard to making close friendships. Having predicted a low ability to make friends, the authors concluded that either their rating items had been too crude to show deficient social skills or the subjects had covered up by making superficial friendships. This is a damned-if-you-do and damned-if-you-don't interpretation. The authors' discussion of results suggests an overzealous attempt to fault the previously hospitalized sample, who were long ago restored to their families.

Several investigators (e.g., Goldfarb, 1943) report problems with language skills. It is usually assumed, without direct evidence, that the orphanage offers inadequate adult models for speech. Neither is there evidence to show what is the minimally sufficient speech contact with adults. Evidence of speech development in these studies came from standardized tests or from informal observations. Pringle and Bossio (1960) evaluated a teenage sample from England that had orphanage experience and found below-average language and reading skills for those rated "stable" or "maladjusted" by teachers. Because most were currently in foster care, more information about the social status of their host families was needed to rule out explanations other than orphanage background. Some investigators (Goldfarb, 1943; Provence, 1989) report lower language development scores and impressions of poor language during testing for other skills. Although the testing and observation procedures seem adequate, we seldom learn if the orphanage sample under study comes from socioeconomic groups with characteristically poor language skills.

Studies of personality used standardized self-reports, ratings by classroom teachers, and subjectively interpreted inkblot responses. Brown's (1937) larger scale study tested more than 200 teenage boys and girls from one Philadelphia orphanage. He compared "neuroticism" scores for these orphans with the scores for a sample of boys from poor homes and a sample of youth from more advantaged city homes. The orphanage subjects, especially girls, were more neurotic than the city youth, but they differed little from boys in lower-class homes. He suggested the orphan youth might have come from a lower economic class.

Two studies by Goldfarb (1944, 1949) used Rorschach inkblots to assess personality. Comparing 15 teenagers in foster care who had orphanage backgrounds with 15 foster care-only subjects, he found that the former were much less mature emotionally. They were also not much different from a small sample of schizophrenic children. He concludes that foster care for these children did not help them overcome their orphanage experience. Without better evidence of the foster care conditions and the children's personality before admission to the orphanage, this conclusion is tenuous. He gives some details on the socioeconomic status of the foster care families, but there is no explanation of how the samples were chosen or how representative they were.

Goldfarb (1949) also notes that there are risks in using subjective interpretations of inkblot responses. Many clinicians prefer to use such inkblots only for impressionistic and not psychometric comparisons. This is partly due to the unreliability of percentage data for numeric comparisons. Except for reporting the use of independent test examiners in his work, Goldfarb does not convince readers that he copes well with his own personal bias.

Several studies focus on social adjustment and related behaviors. For example, Bowlby (1944) found that several individuals in his sample of teenage thieves had orphanage experience. This retrospective study, which imputes a causal connection between orphanage experience and criminal behavior, fails to rule out alternative explanations. Thus, the conclusion is poorly justified by the evidence. I wonder how Bowlby came to choose this sample? What unreported details about family conditions might explain either their orphanage placement or their criminal behavior?

Other studies of social and behavioral adjustment of orphans offer more details to explain background influences. Bodman, McKinlay, and Sykes (1950) compared occupational adjustment and other behaviors for 51 young adults and 52 controls, all from England. During the first year of work, 14% of the orphans failed on the job and returned to the orphanage compared with none of the controls. Fewer of the orphans participated in social clubs or had boy- or girlfriends. A 14-year follow-up (Quinton et al., 1984) of young adult females found that orphan subjects had fewer social and parenting skills than matched controls. Tizard's (1979) 6-year follow-up of younger orphans found that they adjusted better socially than others from the same institutions who were returned to their families. This atypical trend was explained by the latter group's home situation, in which family conflict prevailed. Rutter, Quinton, and Hill (1990) also showed some excess of personality disorders and criminal behaviors in young adults with orphanage backgrounds. As youths, they were placed there because of parental problems with drugs, alcohol, and mental illness. These authors stress that some of these children turned out satisfactorily and that later life conditions were correlated with these personality or behavior problems.

The procedures for these recent studies on social adjustment seem fairly adequate. Without definite knowledge of the validity and reliability of the instruments used, we have to accept the results at face value. What is seriously missing in these studies is an adequate accounting of the sample selection methods. The resulting inability to know which population groups are actually represented weakens confidence in the findings.

### *Does Early Placement Affect Development More?*

What are the effects of early placement or prolonged stay in orphanages? The available data on these two topics are extremely sparse. A retrospective study by Goldfarb (1947) compares two groups of 15 teenagers each, both with orphanage experience. One was rated as "poorly adjusted" and the other "well adjusted" by classroom teachers. More individuals in the former group were placed in the nearby orphanage before 6 months of age; individuals in the latter group were placed closer to 1 year of age. The poorly adjusted also stayed at the orphanage for about 3 years compared to 2 years for the well adjusted.

This retrospective study, which suggests a causal connection, gives very weak support for this explanation. It lacks controls for alternative causes such as early family discord that might have led both to orphanage placement and to behavior disorder. Such correlation data are best used to design future studies that carefully test for causal relationships.

In the absence of systematic data on the effects of age at first placement and on the effects of prolonged stay in orphanages, it is premature to draw serious conclusions. Clearly, we need far more careful comparisons of children admitted to different institutions at different ages and data on length of stay and the interaction of age at placement and length of stay. Also related to these issues is the matter of sibling support. Keeping brothers and sisters together might ameliorate several adjustment problems.

### Can Special "Mothering" or Social Stimulation Improve Individual Development?

This research question considers ways to accelerate individual development beyond the expected rate. It suggests the need for a controlled experiment that would provide the proposed stimulation to some individuals and not to others.

Some investigators report quasi-experiments that seem to test hypotheses about the treatment variable. For example, a widely quoted study by Skeels and Dye (1939) described how 13 infants were moved from an orphanage to a home for feeble-minded women. Measured intelligence in these infants increased dramatically compared with those infants who remained in the orphanage. The latter group's intelligence actually declined.

The study by Spitz (1945) also compared infants raised by their prison mothers with infants in a foundling home, in which direct mothering was inconsistent. The prison babies thrived under the spoiled attention they received compared with the deprived babies. This difference was measured by their DQs. Spitz realistically notes that the prison babies would likely suffer in later years from the undisciplined, spoiled attention. Neither study previously discussed was a true experiment because the investigators did not assign infants to treatment groups nor control the amount of mothering received. This leaves doubt about the precise role of mothering, which varies in extent and quality.

Finally, the Iowa Child Welfare group reported several studies in the 1930s that asked the following: Can a special preschool program increase the intelligence quotient for orphanage children?

Wellman and Pegham (1944) report on one of these studies. A controlled experiment gave preschool training to one group, whereas the matched control group remained in a less stimulating cottage program. The first group's mean

IQ increased from below average to average; the other group's below-average IQ declined even further. Another report on the same series of studies (Skeels, Updegraff, Wellman, & Williams, 1938) describes the living quarters of this orphanage in some detail. It is an extreme picture of rigid behavior controls and cramped space, with few amenities. Such conditions are not fairly ascribed to all orphanages.

A national expert in research design and psychometrics (McNemar, 1940) took Wellman and others in the Iowa Child Welfare group to task. He charged them with mishandling statistical analyses and with possible bias when testing children. Generally, psychometric professionals doubt that IQs can be increased as much as 15 points with enrichment. The exception might be acutely deprived children who are brought up to their potential under ideal conditions. This latter point could explain the Iowa group's reported success, and it further testifies to the extreme degree of repression in that particular orphanage.

## General Criticisms

There is no denying the negative picture portrayed by many of the published reports. Should we accept them at face value and assume it is a scientific fact that orphanages are not good for children? Before answering, we should consider several points.

### Were the Research Questions Appropriate?

Most of the research centers on a single issue: How do orphan children compare with other children psychologically? Although this is a legitimate outcome question, it does not deal directly with orphanage experience or the root causes of psychological development within the institution. Almost never are direct, systematic observations made of the quality of orphanage care or the kinds of social experience provided. We learn nothing about the sleeping, eating, and moral habits of orphanage children. Are these habits different, better, or worse because of the regular schedules and predictable rules that characterize many institutions?

The orphanage setting offered potentially rich opportunities to study child development, but this was rarely considered. Other questions might have focused on the advantages or disadvantages of large peer groups, associated with the segregation of similar age children and genders within one group cottage. What are the positive or negative effects of living with large peer groups? How did the required work—making beds, cleaning cottages, mowing lawns, preparing food, and so on—affect individual character or personal habits?

Assessments of outcome could be broadened to include surveys of achievement after leaving the orphanage. Two unpublished studies illustrate this point. One reported that the World War II nonorphan draftees in North Carolina showed a rejection rate of about 20% for physical fitness compared with 2% for draftees from orphanages in that state. A second study (McCall, 1951) reported that the occupational achievements for graduates from one particular large orphanage followed the same distribution as census norms for occupational levels in the United States. That is, there were equal proportions of professionals, skilled workers, unskilled, and so on.

### Were the Research Designs Appropriate?

Several professional journals in the child care field report anecdotal or retrospective findings that are frequently cited by others as evidence of psychological effects from orphanage care. Such data might be justified as background work, aiming toward hypothesis development, but they should not be taken as conclusive evidence.

This field of research leans too much on correlational designs to test hypotheses about causal relationships. For example, questions about IQ differences between orphans and other children are answered by comparing two groups of children at one point in time. Insufficient attention is paid to background differences other than orphanage experience. The results might give slight support to causal predictions, but they never give satisfactory proof. There is always the possibility that some unidentified cause explains score differences. For example, if more orphanage children come from lower socioeconomic classes in which intelligence scores are lower, we might expect lower IQ scores for these children. (We must not overlook the wide range of differences within each group and their overlap.)

Some of the most polished work was in the form of controlled experiments (Rheingold, 1956) that demonstrated that enriched social stimulation can enhance social responsiveness in infants. Much more work of this rigor is needed to test causal hypotheses about features of child care work.

There is too much reliance on extremely small samples. This is especially risky in correlational designs, in which numeric results are sensitive to uncontrolled or hidden factors. Because most psychometric instruments are subject to errors of measurement, large samples are needed to ensure more valid comparisons. Curiously, the single large-scale study of IQ scores in this survey of the literature (Trotzkey, 1930) gave a favorable impression of orphanage care.

Finally, the subject matter demands true developmental research. This is the method of measuring changes for the same children over time. Almost none of the research reviewed is developmental, although much of it was described as "follow-up" research. It simply identified children at one stage, and then evaluated them at a later stage. No actual changes were recorded. Again, the exception was Trotzkey's (1930) report of physical weight gains for several thousand children from Jewish orphanages. His results showed that children were underweight for their age when first admitted. Later, the majority were average or better for their age group. Other questions, such as the optimal age for placing children in orphanage care, could be much better answered by systematic developmental studies based on samples involving many institutions.

### Do Conclusions Properly Follow From the Procedures Used?

Often, the conclusions did not seem justified by the procedures. The primary reason for doubts about internal validity was faulty sample selection. Convenience or opportunistic samples were the rule. Almost never were the chosen samples shown to be representative of some given orphanage group. Needless to say, they were not shown to be representative of orphans in general. Very broad generalizations, however, were made about orphanage care.

An example of this problem is the postwar evaluation of young adults who were separated from their parents to escape bombing. Maas (1963) described a sample that adjusted rather well, but Bowlby (1951) cited a study that showed one group suffered psychiatric problems. Neither study makes a good case for representative samples.

Another complication is the fact that the subjects for study came from widely different institutions. Some were hospital patients, some were infants in foundling homes, and some were in foster care; these are in addition to the more conventional institutions in which children are cared for in large groups. All these children might be separated from their own families, but this is about the only characteristic that they shared.

There was a general tendency to conclude that orphanage care was the cause of reported psychological defects. Mere membership in the orphanage population, however, was the only way that orphanage care was indicated. Actual treatment conditions were often assumed but seldom observed. The majority of such studies used no control for length of stay or other descriptions to show the quality or amount of care received.

The credibility of certain results was diminished by claims that cross-age samples provided developmental data. At best, the design reported by Spitz (1945) is a confusing mixture of cross-age and longitudinal sampling. There also appears to be some lack of restraint in twisting results to make them suit predictions. This is obvious in Bowlby et al.'s (1956) follow-up study of previous hospital patients in which some teachers' ratings were omitted that appeared unreliable. Other studies had skimpy descriptions of sample selection and testing procedures and failed to show how investigator bias was controlled.

### Why So Many Negative Outcomes?

We might accept some of this research at face value. Where there is obvious failure to provide for the emotional or social needs of children, we should expect psychological deficits. This concession is far from granting that neglect was a common or general practice.

It is fair to say that bias against the orphanage care option dominates the child care profession. Thus, it is not surprising that most reports are "politically correct." We might also expect editors to be more lenient with borderline research designs or methods. To some extent, we are dealing with so-called "applied" research that is characteristically less rigorous about rules of procedure. This point is illustrated by Bowlby's (1951) frank recognition that the evidence is largely clinical and not systematic or statistically controlled. He concluded that the persistent negative trend had more scientific importance than procedural rules.

Another selection factor is the tendency for editors in most fields to reject studies that show no difference for the comparison groups. For example, it is hard to be sure why a sample of orphans have the same average intelligence as a sample of home care children. There might be no true difference, chance errors might have made it appear so, or mistakes by the investigator might have obscured true differences. Also, because most editors expect orphanage samples to show less intelligence, they are skeptical of exceptions.

## ▨ Conclusions

The following conclusions may be derived from this critical review:

1. Theories about the detrimental effects of maternal deprivation receive highly tenuous, indirect support at best from orphanage research. Where psychological deterioration in infants was found, it is not clear whether the mother's absence or simple physical and social neglect was the essential cause. Neither was there any evidence that such neglect was a widespread practice.

2. Some teenagers and young adults with orphanage experience show deficits in language development, intellect, personality, or social skills. It is far from clear, however, that these were caused by their orphanage care. Orphanage care, per se, was almost never directly observed or explicitly manipulated in this research.

3. Most of the research suffers from the overuse of small, opportunistic samples, and there is a general failure to describe population sources and methods of selection. These limitations make it impossible to generalize findings based on isolated samples to all orphans or orphanages.

4. Most orphanage research is limited to a narrowly focused, clinical search for psychological damage. Very little of it deals with the effects of age at placement. None of it deals with the role of sibling support, the effects of age or gender groupings, the role of work, moral training, and a host of other practical issues in orphanage care.

5. Critics of orphanage care seem overzealous to produce negative evidence and then generalize their findings to all orphans or orphanages. More consideration should be given to positive orphanage experiences and ways of assessing their effects. Besides the controlled experiments with infants using social stimulation, there was only one developmental study that directly measured change. More developmental research is needed.

## ▨ References

Bender, L. (1945). Infants reared in institutions permanently handicapped. *Bulletin of the Child Welfare League of America, 24,* 1-4.

Bodman, F., McKinlay, M., & Sykes, K. (1950). The social adaptation of institutional children. *Lancet, 258,* 173-176.

Bowlby, J. (1944). Forty-four juvenile thieves. *International Journal of Psychoanalysis, 25,* 19-53, 107-128.

Bowlby, J. (1951). *Maternal care and mental health.* Geneva: World Health Organization.

Bowlby, J. (1958). The nature of the child's tie to the mother. *International Journal of Psycho-analysis, 39,* 1-24.

Bowlby, J., Ainsworth, M., Boston, M., & Rosenbluth, D. (1956). The effects of mother-child separation: A follow-up study. *British Journal of Medical Psychology, 29,* 211-247.

Brown, F. (1937). Neuroticism of institution vs. non-institution children. *Journal of Applied Psychology, 21,* 379-381.

Ford, M., & Kroll, J. (1995, March). *There is a better way: Family-based alternatives to institutional care* (Research Brief No. 3). Washington, DC: North American Council on Adoptable Children.

Freud, A., & Burlingham, D. (1944). *Infants without families.* New York: International University Press.

Freud, A., Solnit, A., & Goldstein, H. (1973). *Beyond the best interests of the child.* London: Andre Deutsch.

Gardner, D. B., & Swiger, M. K. (1958). Developmental status of two groups of infants released for adoption. *Child Development, 29,* 521-530.

Goldfarb, W. (1943). The effects of early institutional care on adolescent personality. *Journal of Experimental Education, 12,* 106-129.

Goldfarb, W. (1944). Effects of early institutional care on adolescent personality: Rorschach data. *American Journal of Orthopsychiatry, 14,* 441-447.

Goldfarb, W. (1945). Effects of psychological deprivation in infancy and subsequent stimulation, Rorschach data. *American Journal of Psychiatry, 102,* 18-33.

Goldfarb, W. (1947). Variations in adolescent adjustment of institutionally reared children. *American Journal of Orthopsychiatry, 17,* 449-457.

Goldfarb, W. (1949). Rorschach test differences between family-reared, institution-reared, and schizophrenic children. *American Journal of Orthopsychiatry, 19,* 624-633.

Goodwin, D. K. (1994). *No ordinary time* (p. 416). New York: Simon & Schuster.

Hodges, J., & Tizard, B. (1989a). Social and family relationships of ex-institutional adolescents. *Journal of Child Psychology and Psychiatry, 30,* 77-97.

Hodges, J., & Tizard, B. (1989b). IQ and behavioral adjustment of ex-institutional adolescents. *Journal of Child Psychology and Psychiatry, 30,* 53-75.

Kagan, J. (1984). *The nature of the child.* New York: Basic Books.

Langmeier, J., & Matejcek, Z. (1975). *Psychological deprivation in childhood* (3rd ed.). New York: John Wiley.

Lowrey, L. G. (1940). Personality distortion and early institutional care. *American Journal of Orthopsychiatry, 10,* 576-585.

Maas, H. S. (1963). The young adult adjustment of twenty wartime residential nursery children. *Child Welfare, 42,* 57-72.

McCall, J. N. (1951). *A comparison of the occupational status of orphanage graduates with national occupational level norms.* Unpublished manuscript, Columbia University, Teachers College, New York.

McNemar, Q. (1940). A critical examination of Iowa Studies of environmental influence upon IQ. *Psychological Bulletin, 37*(2), 63-92.

Mead, M. (1962). A cultural anthropologist's approach to maternal deprivation. In M. D. Ainsworth (Ed.), *Deprivation of maternal care: A reassessment of its effects* (No. 14). Geneva: World Health Organization.

Milk and love. (1952, May 5). *Time, 59*(18), 51.

O'Connor, N. (1956). The evidence for the permanently disturbing effects of mother-child separation. *Acta Psychologica, 12,* 174-191.

Orlansky, H. (1949). Infant care and personality. *Psychological Bulletin, 46,* 1-48.

Pinneau, S. R. (1950). A critique on the articles by Margaret Ribble. *Child Development, 21*(4), 203-228.

Pinneau, S. R. (1955). The infantile disorders of hospitalism and anaclitic deprivation. *Psychological Bulletin, 52*(5), 429-462.

Pringle, M. L. K., & Bossio, V. (1960). Early, prolonged separation and emotional adjustment. *Journal of Child Psychology and Psychiatry, 1,* 37-48.

Provence, S. (1989). Infants in institutions revisited. *Zero to Three, 9*(3), 1-4.

Prugh, D., & Harlow, R. (1962). Masked deprivation in infants and young children. In M. Ainsworth (Ed.), *Deprivation of maternal care: A reassessment of its effects.* Geneva: World Health Organization.

Quinton, D., Rutter, M., & Liddle, C. (1984). Institutional rearing, parenting difficulties, and marital support. *Psychological Medicine, 14,* 107-124.

Rabin, A. I. (1957). Personality maturity of kibbutz (Israeli collective settlements) and non-kibbutz children as reflected in Rorschach findings. *Journal of Projective Techniques, 31,* 148-153.

Rabin, A. I. (1958). Behavior research in collective settlements in Israel. *American Journal of Orthopsychiatry, 28,* 577-586.

Rheingold, H. (1960). The measurement of maternal care. *Child Development, 31,* 565-575.

Rheingold, H. L. (1956). The modification of social responsiveness in institutional babies. *Monograph Social Research on Child Development, 21,* 63.

Ribble, M. (1944). Infantile experience in relation to personality development. In V. Hunt (Ed.), *Personality and the behavior disorders II.* New York: Ronald Press.

Rutter, M., Quinton, D., & Hill, J. (1990). Adult outcomes of institution-reared children: Males and females compared. In L. N. Robbins & M. Rutter (Eds.), *Straight and devious pathways from childhood to adult life.* Cambridge, UK: Cambridge University Press.

Sears, R. R. (1943). *Survey of objective studies of psychoanalytic concepts.* New York: Social Science Research Council.

Skeels, H. M., & Dye, H. B. (1939). A study of the effects of differential stimulation on mentally retarded children. *Proceedings and Addresses. American Association for Mental Defectiveness, 44,* 114.

Skeels, H. M., Updegraff, R., Wellman, B. L., & Williams, H. M. (1938). A study of environmental stimulation: An orphanage preschool project. *Iowa Studies in Child Welfare, 15,* 4.

Spitz, R. A. (1945). Hospitalism: An inquiry into the genesis of psychiatric conditions in early childhood. *Psychoanalytic Studies of the Child, 1,* 53-74; *2,* 113-117.

Spitz, R. A., & Wolf, K. (1946). Anaclitic depression. *Psychoanalytic Studies of the Child, 3/4,* 85-120.

Stone, L. J. (1954). A critique of studies of infant isolation. *Child Development, 25*(1), 9-20.

Tizard, B. (1979). Early experience and later social behavior. In D. Shaffer & J. Dunn (Eds.), *The first year of life.* New York: John Wiley.

Tizard, B., & Hodges, J. (1978). The effect of early institutional rearing on the development of eight-year old children. *Journal of Child Psychology and Psychiatry, 19,* 99-118.

Tizard, B., & Joseph, A. (1970). The cognitive development of young children in residential care. *Journal of Child Psychology and Psychiatry, 11,* 177-186.

Tizard, B., & Rees, J. (1975). The effect of early institutional rearing on the behavior problems and affectional relationships of four-year old children. *Journal of Child Psychology and Psychiatry, 16,* 61-73.

Trotzkey, E. (1930). *Institutional care and placing-out.* Chicago: Marks Nathan Jewish Orphan Home.

Verry, E. (1939). Problems facing children who have had a relatively long period in institutional care. *Bulletin of the Child Welfare League of America, 18,* 2-3, 6-7.

Wellman, B., & Pegham, E. L. (1944). Binet IQ changes of orphanage pre-school children: A re-analysis. *Journal of Genetic Psychology, 65,* 239-263.

Wolkind, S., & Rutter, M. (1973). Children who have been "in care": An epidemiological study. *Journal of Child Psychology and Psychiatry, 14,* 97-105.

Yarrow, L. J. (1961). Maternal deprivation: Toward an empirical and conceptual re-evaluation. *Psychological Bulletin, 58*(6), 459-490.

# CHAPTER 9

# Fostering the Demand for Adoptions

*An Empirical Analysis of the Impact of Orphanages and Foster Care on Adoptions in the United States*

WILLIAM F. SHUGHART II
WILLIAM F. CHAPPELL

The safe and permanent placement of the children committed to its care is one of the chief objectives of the substitute child care system. Ideally, institutional child care facilities (orphanages) and foster homes provide temporary living arrangements for parentless children as a prelude to placing them into stable, traditional family units. The adoptability of children varies considerably, however, with factors such as age, race, and physical and behavioral problems. As a result, children can remain within the substitute child care system for very long periods. Some are never adopted. The longer a child is left in the system, the more likely it is that the system itself will influence his or her adoption prospects.

AUTHORS' NOTE: We thank Hilary Shughart and an anonymous reader for useful suggestions. Helpful advice was also contributed by Gary Anderson, John Conlon, Katherine Daigle, Harold Elder, Paul Pecorino, Keith Womer, and other participants in seminars at the University of Mississippi and the University of Alabama. J. G. Chen and Chuangang Ren provided able research assistance. As is customary, however, we accept full responsibility for any remaining errors.

The substitute child care system in the United States has undergone revolutionary changes during the 20th century. The most obvious change, of course, has been the decline of the traditional American orphanage and its subsequent replacement by a network of foster families. In 1933, for instance, 144,000 children were cared for in orphanages in the United States. The number of children in institutional care declined steadily throughout the following decades. By 1977, only 43,000 children were living in orphanages, and by 1980, the orphanage had for all practical purposes ceased to exist.

Less obvious, but no less important, has been the influence of major changes in the federal welfare system instituted during the 1960s. Specifically, the expansion of a program of government transfer payments to single parents, Aid to Families with Dependent Children (AFDC), has essentially meant that children are no longer removed from the biological mother's care simply because of poverty due to the breadwinner's absence. Abuse, neglect, alcoholism, or other dysfunctional conditions that characterize an unacceptable environment for raising a child are now necessary before the state will intervene. As a result, fewer children enter the substitute child care system and proportionately more of them who do come from backgrounds that make successful adoption less likely.

This chapter explores the determinants of adoption rates in the United States. Of specific interest is the effect of moving from an orphanage-based child care system to a foster family-based system. The linkage between adoptions and the institutional characteristics of the substitute child care system has perhaps seemed irrelevant because many of the children who now enter the system come from backgrounds that promote behavioral problems inimical to successful adoption. Just the opposite is true, however: It is precisely because most parentless children are not adopted quickly that there is a pressing need to understand how the characteristics of the substitute care system impact the adoptability of its wards.

In this chapter, we consider whether successful adoption is better facilitated by an institutional-based child care system or a foster family care-based system. This is accomplished by estimating a pooled cross-section time-series adoption equation in reduced form. Because of data limitations, the analysis focuses on the years 1955, 1957, 1958, and 1959, when both orphanages and foster homes were important components of the substitute child care system in the United States. Observations are collected across states. The model's dependent variable is an adoption rate measured relative to the number of displaced children in a state (unrelated adoptions divided by the number of children in group homes and foster care). Key explanatory variables are the per capita numbers of children in orphanages and in foster care. Other explanatory variables include government welfare payments and state demographic characteristics.

Welfare, birth control, abortion, and a desire on the part of social workers to "deinstitutionalize" parentless children have all played roles in the disappearance of the traditional American orphanage. At the same time, however, these forces may have created a permanent underclass of unadoptable boys and girls who are forced to spend their childhood years being shifted from one foster care home to another.

In the following sections, historical background on the causes and consequences of the decline of the American orphanage is provided, a description of the data is given, our empirical model is specified, and our empirical results are reported.

## ■ Where Have All the Orphans Gone?

There are no longer any orphans born in the United States. Indeed, the only place the word "orphan" appears in the entire *Statistical Abstract of the United States* (U.S. Department of Commerce, 1993) is as an entry in a table headed "Immigrants Admitted, by Class of Admission" in which orphaned children of U.S. citizens are identified as comprising an immigration category exempt from numerical limitations. Slightly more than 9,000 such children were admitted to the United States in 1991 (U.S. Department of Commerce, 1993, p. 10). Apparently, America must import its orphans.[1]

This state of affairs contrasts sharply with circumstances only a few decades ago: There were about 144,000 children in orphanages nationally during the depths of the Great Depression; beginning with the outbreak of World War II, the number fell steadily to 95,000 in 1951, 77,000 in 1963, and 43,000 in 1977. Orphanage care had essentially disappeared by 1980 (Jones, 1993, p. 459).

Three reasons are commonly given to explain the postwar decline of the American orphanage (Jones, 1993). One factor relates to an anti-institutional bias that gradually developed among social workers and public welfare agencies. As early as the first White House conference on children in 1909, the conclusion was reached "that, wherever possible, children should be placed in foster families rather than institutions" (p. 460). The belief that "home life is the highest and finest product of civilization" and that children should not be deprived of it "except for urgent and compelling reasons" reinforced, wittingly or not, the growing movement toward professionalization of social work (*Proceedings of the Conference,* 1909/1971, p. 6).

The origins of the second key factor in the decline of the American orphanage can be traced to the mid-1950s, when the Child Welfare League of America (CWLA), the leading national organization for social workers, issued a series of reports stressing the importance of professionalization and tightening the standards orphanages were required to meet to qualify for CWLA accreditation. These accreditation standards called for the following (Jones, 1993):

> More staff in proportion to children; more professional social workers, that is, with M.S.W. degrees; more social workers with specialty training (usually psychiatric social work); professional social workers as administrators; higher salaries; secretarial help for caseworkers; psychiatric and other consultants; policy manuals; up-to-date personnel policies (provision for sick leave and vacations); and regular case conferences. (p. 468)

These standards raised the average cost of care considerably and, because the rate of public compensation for children placed in their care did not keep pace, they exerted increasingly heavy financial pressure on traditional orphanages. The cost spiral was accelerated by the growing preference for foster care placements, which reduced institutional populations and further raised fixed costs per child.[2] By the late 1960s, "a representative board rate for foster families . . . would have been $120–$150 per month, less than half of the . . . $310 it would have cost to maintain that same child in an institution" (Jones, 1993, pp. 472-473).

AFDC, which began following passage of the Social Security Act of 1935, was the third factor leading to the decline of the American orphanage. The availability of AFDC payments meant that single mothers who might otherwise abandon their children were more likely to continue to care for them at home. That this welfare program had a major impact on the population potentially served by traditional orphanages is evidenced by the fact that from 1950 on, the number of children receiving AFDC payments increased at an average rate of 100,000 per year (Jones, 1993, p. 464).

The Adoption Assistance and Child Welfare Act of 1980 spelled the end of the traditional orphanage, "not because it had anything in particular to say about institutional care, but because it did not" (Jones, 1993, p. 476). To achieve the twin goals of reducing the number of children placed in foster care, which had ballooned from 165,000 to 394,000 between 1961 and 1977, and reducing "the replacement rate to unity, that is, to the point that a child who had to be placed in a foster family either remained with that family for a short while before returning to his or her parents or remained there permanently," the act mandated that children be placed in "the least restrictive (most family-like) setting available" (p. 476).

The 1980 law attempted to deal with a crisis in substitute child care that had been growing since the 1950s and that in many respects plagues the system today. Because the children entering foster care are disproportionately characterized by behavioral problems associated with abuse and neglect,[3] and because the number of foster children needing placement greatly exceeds the number of families willing and able to care for them, most children in foster care are shifted repeatedly from one foster home to another. This "replacement rate" rises progressively with the age of the child, adding yet another source of insecurity to crucial formative years.

Maas and Engler (1959) found that three fourths of the children in foster care never return home. A few years later, Jeter (1963) reported evidence that return home was expected for only about 12% of the 62,000 foster children she studied, whereas adoptive placement accounted for another 13%. The typical foster child in both studies "had been placed at least twice, and as many as 16% had experienced four or more placements. One child in the Jeter study had been placed 22 times" (Jones, 1993, p. 475). When Walter Ambinder (1965) later documented the experiences of 410 boys in foster care homes, he found that "the average number of placements increased regularly from 2.6 at age 8 to 5.7 at age 15" (Jones, 1993, p. 475).[4]

In addition to the fact that by 1980 "most foster families were caring for two or more unrelated foster children" (Jones, 1993, p. 476), the emotional toll levied by such instability is surely quite heavy.[5] Some evidence of this is reflected in available adoption statistics.[6] For example, whereas there were in excess of 12,000 adoptions annually in California during the late 1960s, less than half that number of children were being adopted each year by the mid-1970s. Although adoptions of all types (except intercountry adoptions) trend sharply downward over this period, the decline in the number of children adopted under the auspices of public agencies, which tend to rely more heavily on foster care than on institutional care (Wolins & Piliavin, 1964, pp. 44-46), is particularly noteworthy (Wingard, 1987, p. 306). These changes, which are reasonably reflective of national trends, coincide with a shift in public policy toward abortion (e.g., following passage of the California Therapeutic Abortion Act in 1967, the number of legal abortions in this state increased from 5,031 in 1968 to 116,749 in 1971) and with increases both in the number of births to unmarried women and in the number of single mothers of all ages choosing to keep their children (Wingard, 1987, p. 310).

Adoption has not been a placement priority for social workers for some time. Of the nearly 90% of children in substitute care for which written "permanency plans" existed in 1983, adoption was considered to be the best option for less than 15% of them. The plans for placing children permanently reported by respondents to a 1985 study by the American Public Welfare Association were, in descending order of frequency, "return to parents, relatives, or other caretakers (46.6 percent), long-term foster care (18.4 percent), adoption (14.7 percent), and independent living or emancipation (10.2 percent)" (Stein, 1987, p. 642).[7] Precedence is given to the goal of returning children to their parents' or relatives' homes despite the fact that "the reintegration of children to their biological homes is a difficult process, and reentry to [substitute] care occurs at a fairly high rate—32 percent reentry for children returned to biological families compared to 2 percent for children adopted" (Stein, 1987, p. 648).

Although sociological factors are undoubtedly important, our goal is to isolate the impact of the decline of the American orphanage on adoptions from the background noise generated by changes in welfare policy, the legalization of abortion, the introduction of effective contraceptive techniques, and other such influences. We conjecture that, other things being the same, the substitution of foster family care for institutional care plays a significant role in explaining the decline in adoptions (especially those not associated with the remarriage of a biological parent) by lowering the quality of potentially adoptable children and increasing the cost of adoptions. The reduction in quality is due to the aforementioned forces of self-selection that bias the characteristics of the children entering the substitute child care system away from social norms. This bias is particularly remarkable in adoptions taking place under the auspices of public agencies whose "children are older at the time of placement (median age 48 months vs. less than 3 months), and have more health problems (34% vs. 11% of private agency adoptions)" (Wingard, 1987, p. 307). The increase in cost is due to the dispersion of potentially adoptable children over a relatively large number of foster families, each of which cares for only two or three children,[8] rather than having them housed in a smaller number of larger institutions in which the cost of searching for an adoptable child with desired characteristics is arguably lower.

Previous research on the determinants of adoption has focused on the supply side. Medoff (1993, p. 60) estimates a regression model designed to explain cross-state variations in "the adoption rate (the number of unrelated adoptions of healthy infants as a percentage of live births) for women of childbearing age (defined as fifteen to forty-four years old)" during 1982. He finds that the decision to place a child for adoption is negatively related to the female labor force participation rate, the amount of a state's AFDC payment, and the state unemployment rate. These results are consistent with an economic interpretation of the adoption decision in which working women are less likely to have unwanted births than nonworking women and in which lower opportunity costs of child rearing (higher unemployment rates) and larger welfare payments induce more women to keep their children. Medoff also finds that the decision to place a child for adoption is positively related to the birth mother's marital status, her education, and her religious affiliation. Other things being the same, single women, women with higher levels of educational attainment, and fundamentalist women are significantly more likely to place their children for adoption. Medoff's evidence suggests that the prices and availabilities of abortions do not have statistically significant effects on adoptions.[9] Moreover, the adoption rate is not influenced by the existence of state regulations designed to encourage them.

In the remainder of this chapter, we report evidence suggesting that the decline of the orphanage and the growth of foster care have adversely affected the number of children who get adopted in the United States. That is, in addition to the economic and sociological factors identified in prior research as influencing the decision to place a child for adoption, we find that institutions matter: Adoption rates are lower in those states in which the shift from orphanages to foster care took place earlier. Far from encouraging the permanent placement of parentless or abandoned children in stable family-like environments, the foster care system seems to have accomplished just the reverse.

## ▓ The Data

To explore the relationship between adoption rates and the institutional features of the substitute child care system empirically, observations are needed on three key variables: adoptions, children in orphanages, and children in foster care. Unfortunately, constraints on the availability of data for each of these variables severely limit the time period that can be studied.

Surprisingly, data on adoptions in the United States are virtually nonexistent prior to the early 1950s. Then, as now, there was no uniform data collection system in place for keeping track of the number of adoptions each year. The first generally accessible statistics on adoptions were collated from states voluntarily reporting to the Children's Bureau of the Social Security Administration. Slightly more than half the states supplied data of sufficient accuracy and comprehensiveness to be deemed useful. Thus, adoption data in the United States become available for the first time in the mid-1950s—and then for only about half the states.

Moreover, any analysis of the substitute child care system must take into account the evolving nature of these institutions over time. The children placed in "group care" facilities nowadays almost all tend to be emotionally disturbed, delinquent, or physically challenged. The functions of the traditional orphanage have for all practical purposes been taken over by foster family care.

Hence, we need to go back far enough in time to identify a period in which children who are simply dependent on substitute care (rather than being emotionally, behaviorally, or physically challenged) could be reared either in an institution or in a foster family home. Evidence that such an era existed at least until the early 1960s is provided in Table 9.1.

As reported in Table 9.1, the shift of the U.S. substitute child care system from one in which the majority of children were placed in orphanages to one dominated by foster family care occurred over a time span of approximately 50 years. In 1910, 65% of parentless children were cared for in group homes. This figure dropped modestly over the next 23 years, falling to 58% by 1933. Taken together, the data in Table 9.1 tell a story of a generally steady decline in the percentage of children living in group care homes.

Important for our purposes, however, the orphanage system was still a major institution for caring for parentless children through the 1950s and early 1960s. Thirty-four percent of the children needing substitute care were still being reared in orphanages in 1960 (again, these are not special-needs or delinquent children). Moreover, the data in Table 9.1 are based on all children in the U.S. substitute care system and therefore do not fully capture the important role being played by traditional orphanages in many states as late as the early 1960s. In 1960, for example, 79% of Oklahoma's parentless children were living in group homes; the corresponding figures were 66% in Tennessee and 48% in Illinois (Wolins & Piliavin, 1964, p. 39).

The foregoing discussion suggests that only a relatively narrow time frame exists for which adequate data on adoptions are available and during which orphanages were performing their traditional function of caring for children without special needs. Because of limited adoption data, this period begins in the 1950s; because of the changing nature of group homes, the period

**TABLE 9.1** Children in Group Homes and Foster Family Homes, 1910-1962

| Year | Number in Substitute Care | % in Group Homes[a] | % in Foster Homes |
|------|---------------------------|---------------------|-------------------|
| 1910 | 176,000 | 65 | 35 |
| 1923 | 214,000 | 64 | 36 |
| 1933 | 249,000 | 58 | 42 |
| 1951 | 223,000 | 43 | 56 |
| 1958 | 230,000 | 37 | 63 |
| 1960 | 240,000 | 34 | 66 |
| 1961 | 245,000 | 33 | 67 |
| 1962 | 256,000 | 31 | 69 |

SOURCE: Wolins and Piliavin (1964).
a. Group home data exclude children who were in temporary detention facilities, delinquents in correctional institutions, and children in institutions for the mentally or physically handicapped.

ends somewhere in the mid- to late 1960s. On the basis of these considerations, this study uses observations across a sample of states for the years 1955, 1957, 1958, and 1959.[10]

For this period, observations on all the variables included in the adoption model described in the next section are available for 24 states plus the District of Columbia. A list of these states, along with the corresponding number of unrelated adoptions per capita in 1955, is provided in Table 9.2. With 45 unrelated adoptions for every 100,000 persons in the state, Oregon and Vermont are the most adoption-intensive states on the list. The smallest number of adoptions per capita occurred in Rhode Island, which had 15 unrelated adoptions per 100,000 persons.

## ▨ The Empirical Model

Adoption rates across states vary according to variations in factors that affect the supply of children who are adoptable and the demand for these children. Here, these factors are included in a single-equation linear regression model of the determinants of adoption rates. A simultaneous-equations model specifying separate demand and supply equations is not feasible because there is no empirically practical proxy for the "price" of an adoption. Because of legal and ethical restrictions in the market for adoptions, and because many of the costs of adoption are borne in-kind—arrangements made for the birth mother's medical expenses, resources expended by adoptive parents to estab-

**TABLE 9.2**  Unrelated Adoptions per 100,000 Persons (Available States), 1955

| State | Adoption Rate |
|---|---|
| Arkansas | 17.867 |
| Connecticut | 28.610 |
| Delaware | 25.000 |
| District of Columbia | 32.690 |
| Florida | 38.227 |
| Georgia | 21.076 |
| Indiana | 33.364 |
| Iowa | 30.236 |
| Maine | 43.961 |
| Minnesota | 26.945 |
| Missouri | 20.438 |
| Nevada | 35.802 |
| New Hampshire | 33.454 |
| New Mexico | 42.139 |
| North Dakota | 18.936 |
| Oregon | 45.159 |
| Rhode Island | 15.236 |
| South Dakota | 27.647 |
| Tennessee | 19.606 |
| Texas | 21.600 |
| Utah | 34.375 |
| Vermont | 45.082 |
| Virginia | 28.319 |
| Washington | 44.270 |
| Wisconsin | 23.955 |

lish their financial and emotional qualifications, and so on—there is no observable price for adopted children.

The absence of a market-clearing price means that excess demand or excess supply tend to characterize the market for adoptable children. Anecdotal evidence suggests that although the market for white infants is usually characterized by excess demand, other potentially adoptable children are in excess supply. Because some adoption markets are characterized by excess demand and others by excess supply, we generally avoid referring to the model developed here in terms of either of these concepts.

This study focuses on the influence of group care versus foster family care on adoption rates. As such, we limit our analysis to what are called "unrelated adoptions." A related adoption occurs when a child is adopted by a blood relative other than a biological parent or, more commonly, when a biological parent remarries and the child is adopted by the new spouse. All other cases are considered to be unrelated adoptions.

Our empirical model of adoption rates across states is specified as follows:

$$\text{Adopt}_{it} = f\ (\text{Substitute}_{it},\ \text{Birth}_{it},\ \text{Divorce}_{it},\ \text{Marriage}_{it},\ \text{Agency}_{it},\ \text{Outwed}_{it},$$
$$\text{Income}_{it},\ \text{Unemp}_{it},\ \text{AFDC}_{it},\ \text{White}_{it},\ \text{Educ}_{it},\ \text{Urban}_{it},\ \text{Age}_{it})$$

where $i$ indexes states ($i = 1\text{-}25$) and $t$ denotes the year of observation ($t = 1955, 1957, 1958$, and $1959$). The definition of each of these variables is given and the possible a priori relationships between the dependent variable and the independent variables are discussed now:

*Adopt:* The dependent variable is defined as the number of unrelated adoptions per displaced child (the sum of children in foster care and group homes) for each of the 25 jurisdictions in the sample during each of the 4 years—1955, 1957, 1958, and 1959.

*Substitute:* This variable represents three different measures of the number of children who require care that substitutes for the care normally provided by a biological parent or parents. There are two principal kinds of substitute care available in the time period covered by this study—orphanage care and foster family care. Foster is the number of children in foster care per capita, Orphan is the number of children in orphanages per capita, and Orphan/Foster is the ratio of the number of children in orphanages divided by the number of children in foster homes.

Two different specifications of the adoption equation are estimated. The first specification includes the variables Foster and Orphan. A larger number of children in foster care and orphanages implies a greater supply of adoptable children. Although for supply-side reasons the variables Foster and Orphan are both expected to have positive effects on adoption rates, of key importance is the relative size of these effects. If the estimated coefficient on Foster is larger than the coefficient on Orphan, then it can be argued that foster care promotes the adoptability of displaced children better than a group home-based system. If the coefficient on Orphan is greater than the coefficient on Foster, however, the opposite interpretation is indicated—adoptions are better facilitated by an orphanage-based system than by a foster family-based system.

As an alternative to entering each of the two categories of displaced children separately, we have created a third variable defined as the ratio of these variables. The variable Orphan/Foster is the number of children in orphanages divided by the number of children in the foster care system. If an orphanage-based system of caring for displaced children is more amenable to adoptions, then we expect this variable to be positively related to the dependent variable. A negative sign, however, would indicate that foster care is more adoption friendly than group homes.

*Birth, Divorce, and Marriage:* These variables are defined, respectively, as birth rates, divorce rates, and marriage rates across states. If these life events primarily affect the supply of adoptable children, then Birth and Divorce should be positively related to the dependent variable, whereas Marriage is expected to be negatively related to Adopt.

*Agency:* This variable controls for variations in the mix of institutions through which adoptions are arranged. In particular, Agency is the proportion of adoptions mediated by (public and private) child welfare agencies.[11] If agency adoptions are more restrictive than independent adoptions, or if the children served by agencies are more difficult to place, then it is expected that this variable will be negatively related to adoption rates across states.

*Outwed:* Outwed is the proportion of children born out of wedlock in a state. To the extent that out-of-wedlock births are an important source of supply of adoptable babies, it is expected to have a positive relationship with the dependent variable. The estimated coefficient on Outwed will be negative if illegitimate children are more difficult to place adoptively.[12]

*Income, Unemp, and AFDC:* These variables control for the effects of general economic conditions on the market for adoptions. Income is state income per capita, Unemp is the number of unemployment insurance beneficiaries per capita, and AFDC is the amount of state aid received by families with dependent children per recipient. If these economic variables primarily affect the supply of adoptable children, then Income and AFDC would be positively associated with adoptions across states, whereas Unemp would be negatively associated with adoptions across states. The opposite relationships are expected if these variables are proxies for birth mothers' opportunity costs of rearing their children at home. In this case, we expect adoption rates to be lower in states with lower per-capita incomes, higher AFDC payments per recipient, and more unemployment insurance beneficiaries per capita.

*White, Educ, Urban, and Age:* Adoption rates are linked to any number of general characteristics of the populace, including race and education. White is the proportion of a state's population that is white, Educ is the number of high school graduates per capita, Urban is the fraction of a state's population that lives in an urban area, and Age is the proportion of a state's population that is between the ages of 15 and 44.

From the time the first statistics on adoption were collected in the 1950s, it has been clear that adoptions of white children overwhelmingly dominate nonwhite adoptions. In 1951, for instance, only 6% of total adoptions involved nonwhite children. The variable White is expected to be positively related to state adoption rates for this reason. The effect of education on adoptions is somewhat ambiguous. If education is associated with more "liberal" attitudes toward adoption, then it could be positively associated with adoptions across states. It could be negatively related if more education leads to fewer unwanted births or if more highly educated people are more willing or better able to care for their own children.

Adoptions may be positively related to urbanization for two reasons. First, there may be scale economies in the sense that larger populations are needed to support the institutions (lawyers, child welfare agencies, and so on) that facilitate the adoption process. Second, because the market is thicker, unwed mothers who wish to place their children for adoption may tend to temporarily relocate to large cities for this purpose.

Age, the proportion of a state's population between the ages of 15 and 44, may be positively or negatively related to cross-sectional adoption rates. It will be positively related if this variable reflects the effect of having relatively more women of childbearing age supplying adoptable children; it will also be positive if the variable reflects the effect of having relatively more couples in the age range that tend to demand adoptable children. As the proportion of the population between ages 15 and 44 increases, however, the proportions of the population younger than 15 or older than 44 must necessarily get smaller. If the size of the 15 to 44 age range is inversely related to the size of the less than 15 age range, then Age may be inversely related to Adopt insofar as there will tend to be fewer adoptable children.

Recall that our data set includes observations collected from 24 states and the District of Columbia for the years 1955, 1957, 1958, and 1959 (adoption data are not available for 1956). The means of the dependent and independent variables comprising the data set are reported in Table 9.3.

## ▓ Empirical Results

The empirical results are presented in Table 9.4. Of particular interest are the estimated coefficients on the first three variables—Orphan, Foster, and Orphan/Foster. As predicted, Orphan is positively and significantly related to adoptions per displaced child across states. Somewhat surprisingly, Foster is a negative and significant determinant of adoption rates. Our expectation was that both Orphan and Foster would be positive determinants of adoption rates and that a comparison of their estimated coefficients would indicate which system provided a more favorable setting for adoption. The results are much stronger than our expectation. Adoption rates are positively related to orphans per capita and negatively related to foster children per capita. (The difference in the coefficients is statistically significant on the basis of the relevant Chow test.) These results suggest that traditional orphanages provided an atmos-

**TABLE 9.3** Definitions and Means of the Data[a]

| Variable | Definition | Mean |
|---|---|---|
| Adopt | Adoptions per displaced child | .432 |
| Orphan | Children in orphanages per capita | .267 |
| Foster | Children in foster care per capita | .980 |
| Orphan/foster | Ratio of children in orphanages to those in foster care | .289 |
| Birth | Birth rate | 25.39 |
| Divorce | Divorce rate | 3.494 |
| Marriage | Marriage rate | 17.22 |
| Agency | Fraction of adoptions arranged by public and private adoption agencies | .622 |
| Outwed | Fraction of children born out of wedlock | .423 |
| Income | State income per capita | $1,875.00 |
| Unemp | Unemployment insurance beneficiaries per capita | .032 |
| AFDC | Monthly AFDC payment | $29.23 |
| White | Fraction of the population that is white | .89 |
| Educ | Fraction of the population with a high school education | 8.06 |
| Urban | Fraction of the population living in urban areas | 61.76 |
| Age | Fraction of the population between the ages of 15 and 44 | 40.64 |

SOURCE: *Statistical Abstract of the United States* (U.S. Department of Commerce, Bureau of the Census, various issues).
a. Population is measured in thousands. All per-capita variables should therefore be interpreted as "per thousand population."

phere that instilled characteristics in children that made them more adoptable than did the atmosphere provided by foster family care. Alternatively, orphanages may better facilitate adoptions by lowering the costs of search for prospective adoptive parents.

The remainder of the results in Table 9.4 indicate that only 5 of the remaining 12 explanatory variables are statistically significant in our sample. The percentage of the population that is white is positive and significant in both equations; the proportion of the population that lives in urban areas is positive and significant in one of them. Three explanatory variables have negative and significant coefficients in both regressions—the index of children born out of wedlock, the state unemployment rate, and the generosity of a state's AFDC benefits. The first of these results suggests that illegitimate children are more difficult to place adoptively; the latter two indicate that adoption rates are lower in states in which the opportunity costs of rearing

**TABLE 9.4** Determinants of Adoptions per Displaced Child, 1955, 1957, 1958, and 1959[a]

| Explanatory Variable | Model 1 | | Model 2 | |
|---|---|---|---|---|
| Intercept | −0.533 | (0.520) | −0.934 | (0.938) |
| Orphan | 0.707 | (2.477)* | | |
| Foster | −0.525 | (4.206)** | | |
| Orphan/foster | | | 0.980 | (4.416)** |
| Birth | 0.011 | (0.577) | 0.004 | (0.216) |
| Divorce | 0.033 | (0.709) | 0.050 | (1.102) |
| Marriage | −0.008 | (1.084) | −0.009 | (1.247) |
| Agency | −0.109 | (0.338) | −0.084 | (0.263) |
| Outwed | −1.870 | (3.627)** | −2.138 | (4.505)** |
| Income | 0.0003 | (1.808) | 0.0001 | (0.738) |
| Unemp | −11.531 | (3.081)** | −13.200 | (3.751)** |
| AFDC | −0.020 | (2.474)* | −0.027 | (3.459)** |
| White | 2.534 | (3.753)** | 2.348 | (4.209)** |
| Educ | −0.046 | (0.988) | 0.013 | (0.308) |
| Urban | 0.003 | (0.647) | 0.014 | (3.157)** |
| Age | 0.196 | (0.102) | −0.593 | (0.320) |
| $R^2$ | 0.593 | | 0.603 | |

a. Absolute values of $t$ statistics in parentheses.
*Significant at the 5% level.
**Significant at the 1% level.

children at home are lower. Overall, the regressions explain about 60% of the cross-state variation in adoptions per displaced child.

## ▓ Concluding Remarks

Orphanages had disappeared by 1980 in large part due to social workers' expressed preference for placing children needing substitute care in foster families rather than in large, impersonal institutions. Dickensian scenes of drab regimentation could not possibly compete with pictures of the bucolic freedom and healthy lifestyles supposedly experienced by the streetwise New York City kids Charles Loring Brace sent to work on Midwestern farms in return for room, board, schooling, and the loving attention of caring foster mothers and fathers. Professional preferences aside, however, there has been little or no systematic empirical work hitherto on the relative merits of institution-based versus foster family-based substitute care. Are the children placed in foster care nowadays in fact better off than those formerly placed in old-fashioned orphanages?

At least in terms of their potential adoptability, the answer is "no." On the basis of data from the late 1950s, there is evidence that, other things being the same, children entering the substitute care system in states that relied more heavily on foster family placements than institutional placements were less likely to be adopted by someone other than a blood relative. The lower rate of unrelated adoptions among children placed in foster care can be explained either by the heavy emotional toll levied by the system's relatively high replacement rate, which causes foster children to experience rejection and to develop behavioral problems that reduce their adoption prospects, or by the relatively high costs borne by prospective adoptive parents in searching over more than 100,000 foster families for children with desired characteristics.

In any case, the empirical results presented here call for rethinking the substitute care paradigm universally accepted by the social work profession. If the goal is to place parentless children as quickly as possible into stable, traditional family environments, then orphanages rather than foster families seem to be the institution of choice.

## ▓ Notes

1. With tongue decidedly not in cheek, Cole (1987, p. 69) observes that "there are no recorded cases of American children being sent to other countries for adoption by their citizens."

2. Whether intentional or not, this "preference" for foster care over institutional care was consistent with the self-interests of professional social workers. If casework is subject to economies of scale, more social workers will be employed (and their compensation will accordingly be higher) if orphans are dispersed geographically across many foster care homes than if they are concentrated in a smaller number of larger institutions. This interpretation is supported by evidence that public welfare agencies tend to rely more heavily on foster families than do private ("voluntary") agencies. Approximately three fourths of the 163,000 children receiving casework services in foster homes as of March 1961, for example, were under public agency care (Wolins & Piliavin, 1964, pp. 44-46; see also Chapter 10).

3. As of 1983, "three-fourths of the children entered foster care because of family-related reasons and over three-fourths of these were for abuse or neglect" (Whittaker, 1987, p. 677).

4. These trends seem to have continued. On the basis of 1983 data covering 39.3% of the 251,000 children then in foster care, Stein (1987, p. 641) reports that "a total of 53.1 percent had been in multiple placements, 20.1 percent having been placed two times, 24.2 percent three to five times, and 8.8 percent six or more times." This is due in part to the fact that the age of children in substitute care has been increasing: "The median age in 1977 was 10.8 years compared to 12.6 years in 1983" (Stein, 1987, p. 640).

5. "The child suffers a series of failures, rejections or replacements and he becomes increasingly damaged emotionally from each such experience" (Jones, 1993, p. 465).

6. According to Flango (1990, p. 264), the federal government stopped publishing adoption statistics collected from cooperating state agencies in 1975. Legislation requiring the secretary of health and human services to develop a system for collecting uniform data on adoption and foster care services was passed in 1986, but such data were still not available as of 1993. Flango estimates that a total of 120,069 adoptions took place in 1987. Cole (1987, p. 69) characterizes the "statistical data on adoption" as being "for the most part nonexistent, outdated, or unreliable."

7. Indeed, the Adoption Assistance and Child Welfare Act of 1980 "mandates that any out-of-home placement be undertaken only after 'reasonable efforts' have been made to prevent family breakup" (Whittaker, 1987, p. 673).

8. There were 137,000 such families nationally in 1985 (Jones, 1993, p. 480).

9. Brown and Jewell (1996), however, report evidence from the state of Texas supporting an economic model of fertility choice. In particular, they find that the residents of counties with longer travel distances to the nearest abortion provider have lower abortion and pregnancy rates. For evidence that laws requiring parental consent and 24-hour waiting periods have significantly reduced the number of abortions performed in the state of Mississippi, see Barbour and Shughart (1998).

10. Data on adoptions across states are not available for 1956. For this reason, our data set covers the years 1955, 1957, 1958, and 1959.

11. Data allowing us to distinguish between public and private adoption agencies are unfortunately not available.

12. This might be the case if, as suggested by Cmiel (1995), orphanages refused to accept illegitimate children.

## ▒ References

Ambinder, W. J. (1965, July). The extent of successive placements among boys in foster family homes. *Child Welfare, 44,* 397-398.

Barbour, C. A., & Shughart, W. F., II. (1998). Legal institutions and abortion rates in Mississippi. *Cato Journal.*

Brown, R. W., & Jewell, R. T. (1996, April). The impact of provider availability on abortion demand. *Contemporary Economic Policy, 14,* 95-106.

Cmiel, K. (1995). *A home of another kind: One Chicago orphanage and the tangle of child welfare.* Chicago: University of Chicago Press.

Cole, E. S. (1987). Adoption. In A. Minahan (Ed.), *Encyclopedia of social work* (18th ed.). Silver Spring, MD: National Association of Social Workers.

Flango, V. E. (1990, May/June). Agency and private adoptions, by state. *Child Welfare, 69,* 263-275.

Jeter, H. R. (1963). Children, problems, and services. In *Child welfare* (Publication No. 403). Washington, DC: U.S. Children's Bureau.

Jones, M. B. (1993, September). Decline of the American orphanage, 1941-1980. *Social Service Review, 67,* 459-480.

Maas, H. S., & Engler, R. E., Jr. (1959). *Children in need of parents.* New York: Columbia University Press.

Medoff, M. H. (1993, January). An empirical analysis of adoption. *Economic Inquiry, 31,* 59-70.

*Proceedings of the Conference on the Care of Dependent Children.* (1971). New York: Arno. (Original work published 1909)

Stein, T. J. (1987). Foster care for children. In A. Minahan (Ed.), *Encyclopedia of social work* (18th ed.). Silver Spring, MD: National Association of Social Workers.

U.S. Department of Commerce, Bureau of the Census. (1993). *Statistical abstract of the United States 1993.* Washington, DC: U.S. Government Printing Office.

Whittaker, J. K. (1987). Group care for children. In A. Minahan (Ed.), *Encyclopedia of social work* (18th ed.). Silver Spring, MD: National Association of Social Workers.

Wingard, D. (1987, July/August). Trends and characteristics of California adoptions: 1964-1982. *Child Welfare, 66,* 303-314.

Wolins, M., & Piliavin, I. (1964). *Institution or foster family: A century of debate.* New York: Child Welfare League of America.

# PART III

## problems in bringing back orphanages

# CHAPTER 10

# Social Security, Social Workers, and the Care of Dependent Children

KAROL C. BOUDREAUX
DONALD J. BOUDREAUX

During the past 60 years, the way we care for orphans and abandoned children in the United States has changed dramatically. When Franklin Roosevelt took his first presidential oath, most American children not with their own families were cared for in orphanages; today, such children are routinely placed in foster care homes. Orphanages have fallen from favor. Indeed, as Speaker of the House Newt Gingrich discovered in 1995, the very mention of orphanages today raises the pathetic specter of cold and starving Oliver Twist begging for "more, please."

Reasonable people can disagree on the wisdom of heavier reliance on foster care relative to institutionalized care. This chapter illustrates that America's greater reliance on foster care may reflect not only the general trend toward deinstitutionalization in the 1950s and 1960s but also a change in the way federal funds are used to subsidize the care of orphaned and needy children. That is, by peering through a public-choice lens at the administration of child welfare services, we suggest an alternative approach to the question of why children were moved out of institutions and into foster care.

This chapter begins with a review of the legal norms applicable to orphans in America. We also discuss the impact of the Social Security Act of 1935 on the funding of child welfare services and the amendments to the original act that arguably created incentives to move children out of private institutions and into publicly funded foster care.

In addition, we review the rise of social work as a profession. We argue that changes in the care of orphaned children are explained in part by the emergence of social work as a distinct profession. Two reasons support this conclusion. First, among the more educated and elite social workers at the turn of the century, foster care was embraced as the better way to deal with dependent children. Second, as a result of the Social Security Act, professional study of social work was subsidized by the federal government, thus increasing the numbers of social workers. This growth in the number of social workers (who were primarily government workers from the 1930s on) combined with a professional bias in favor of foster care to increase the use of public foster care in place of private, charitable institutional care.

## ■ Orphans and the Law

Responsibility for the care of orphans in the United States has always been divided among three groups: families and friends of orphans; private, often religious institutions; and the government. Although the importance of the first group invariably outweighs that of the other two groups, we do not discuss familial care for orphans. We instead focus on the care provided by nonfamilial institutions.[1]

### The English Law Background of U.S. Care for Orphans

Early American law governing orphans in the United States closely tracked English practice.[2] Until the reign of Henry VIII, orphaned children not with kin were cared for mostly by the Roman Catholic Church. After Henry seized the church's property, however, church care of orphans largely disappeared. By the reign of Henry's daughter, Elizabeth I, orphaned children not with kin became the responsibility of local governments and the common-law courts. In 1601, Parliament enacted its poor law (43rd Law of Elizabeth), creating a system of public taxation for the support of the poor, destitute, and abandoned. The poor law divided English counties into parishes. Each parish was responsible for collecting the tax for poor relief. The justices of the peace of the parishes appointed overseers responsible for distributing this poor relief.

The kind of relief provided depended on the age and physical well-being of the recipient. The most common form of relief was "outdoor relief." The outdoor relief system either gave monies directly to needy persons or provided subsidized work projects for the needy. This system was called outdoor relief because it provided no shelter for its recipients. Like adults, children received different forms of relief. Older and healthy children were often indentured to a master for the purpose of learning a trade, although these children were occasionally assigned to subsidized work projects sponsored by the parish. Younger or unhealthy children were "farmed out" to low bidders for whatever uses these bidders chose or placed in poorhouses along with destitute adults, drunks, and the mentally ill.

Generally, the colonial American system of caring for the poor and orphans tracked British practices, including the use of outdoor relief. Instead of dividing the colonies into parishes, however, local divisions were cities, townships, or counties. Throughout the 17th century, orphaned children in the American colonies were the responsibility of their families, if they had any, or either of local governments or of local churchwardens. If orphans became the responsibility of the government or the churchwarden, they could be farmed out, apprenticed, or placed in the local almshouse.

Until the mid-19th century, indenture was the most popular means of dealing with orphaned children.[3] Discussing the poor law as it developed in early Massachusetts, Robert Kelso (as quoted in Thurston, 1974) states,

> Cleaning off the account on the treasurer's book by a long-term indenture which for practical purposes amounted to the sale of the child with no guarantee of protection, save public indignation, against enslavement and abuse, was the constant effort of the early town authorities. (p. 14)

Because masters acquired orphan labor at relatively low wage rates, the demand for such labor was high.[4] Apprenticing children, rather than providing some other means of care, relieved the local government of financial responsibility for its charges. This system was cost-effective—at least for masters and taxpayers. Furthermore, although hardly without its faults, the indenture system was arguably a reasonable alternative for children of the period. In addition to learning skills they might not otherwise have acquired, indentured children were at least spared the misery of living in squalid poorhouses filled not only with the poor but also with drunks and the mentally ill.

### *Orphanages and Almshouses*

Early orphanages in what was to become the United States were all private, religiously affiliated institutions. The very first orphanage was founded in 1727 by the Ursuline nuns in New Orleans. In 1739, the Bethesda Orphan House was founded in Savannah, Georgia, by the Methodist Church. Near the end of the 18th century, a handful of other private orphanages were founded in larger cities: Philadelphia's St. Joseph's female orphanage, New York's Society for the Relief of Widows With Small Children, Baltimore's St. Paul's Asylum for Destitute Girls, and Boston's Asylum for Girls.

In addition to these religious orphanages, public almshouses were established in the American colonies during the colonial era. Orphaned children not in private institutions or with their families, and not apprenticed out by local governments, were placed in public almshouses in the 18th century. Because the number of almshouses increased during this time, it is likely that the numbers of orphans and abandoned living in them also increased. It was not until the end of the 18th century that distinct public orphanages were founded. The first public orphanage in the United States opened in 1794 when Charleston, South Carolina, built a facility to care for 115 orphans who were wards of the city. Nevertheless, through the Civil War most orphans were either indentured or housed in public almshouses.

### *Public Institutions and the Rise of Private Charity*

The major development in the care of orphans after the Civil War was the separation of these children from institutionalized adults. This separation took a number of forms: Orphans were put into public orphanages, private free foster care, or private orphanages.

#### *Public Orphanages*

Beginning in the mid-19th century, several states passed statutes directing that orphans be moved out of almshouses and into institutions dedicated exclusively to their care. In some states, such as Ohio, orphans were moved to county children's homes; in other states, such as Massachusetts, orphans were moved to a public "State Primary School"—a centralized institution that cared for all publicly institutionalized orphans in the state (Hall, 1930, p. 130). These statutes created the public orphanage system that lasted largely unchanged until the mid-20th century. (The care of orphaned and pauper children in almshouses did not immediately cease. As late as 1923, approximately 1,900 children in the United States under the age of 15 were living in almshouses [Thurston, 1974, p. 37].)

### Foster Care

The free foster care movement was a reaction not only to the shortcomings of almshouse but also to dissatisfaction with the indenture system. Critics had long suspected that masters abused the indenture system, and by the mid-19th century indentured servitude was loudly decried as cruel to children. The alternative of free foster care meant that foster families would take dependent children free of charge—that is, foster families neither paid for nor were paid to accept foster children. Foster children were expected to work and contribute to the foster family in much the same way that natural children contributed to the family. The idea was to get children into family situations so that they might learn work skills and discipline. The free foster care movement appealed directly to Christian obligations of charity and downplayed the appearance of foster children as servants.

Modern free foster care was the brainchild of Charles Loring Brace, who in 1853 founded the Children's Aid Society in New York City. Brace was moved by the problems of orphaned and destitute immigrant children of New York. He believed that by finding the children homes outside of the city, he could better guarantee that they would grow up in healthy, loving environments. Brace arranged for children, over whom his society maintained legal control, to be taken to New England and to the Midwest, where the children were placed with the families of farmers and merchants.

Brace's Children's Aid Society flourished, placing thousands of children—a total of 22,000 by 1900—into foster families. The society opened several offices along the East Coast. Near the end of the 19th century, the society placed the majority of its children in homes in the West and the South. To keep track of these thousands of children and to ensure their good treatment, the society hired "agents" to travel the country checking on society children. These agents, paid by the society to monitor the welfare of society children, were among the earliest paid social workers in America.[5]

### Private Orphanages

As with public orphanages, the role of private orphanages grew dramatically during the latter half of the 19th century.[6] These private institutions were created for a number of reasons, including to provide a wholesome alternative to almshouse care and to instill particular religious values in children. This latter reason was particularly compelling to Jews and Roman Catholics, who disliked the fact that orphans of their coreligionists were taken in by public facilities and typically raised as Protestants. Additionally, Catholics and Jews objected to placing Catholic and Jewish children in foster care—where these children usually lived with Protestant families. Thus, the desire to bring children up with the religion of their parents led to the very active founding of private orphanages during the several decades following the Civil War.

### Professional Tensions Among Child Care Workers

An interesting ideological split developed in the late 19th century among private charities that cared for orphaned children: Protestant charities pioneered the use of free foster care, whereas Catholic and Jewish charities favored institutional care. By the last decade of the 19th century, this division spawned a major controversy among charitable organizations. Protestant social workers argued strenuously for keeping children in home-like settings. It may be that these social workers recognized that by promoting the use of foster care they stood a better chance of "professionalizing" their field. After all, the requirement that each orphan receive individual supervision by a child welfare worker was more likely to promote the growth of the social work profession than would institutional care that allowed for fewer numbers of custodians to oversee any given number of orphans. In contrast, Catholic and Jewish charities believed that institutions better served the interests of Catholic and Jewish orphans. These charities argued that the foster family system provided inadequate supervision as well as inadequate—and misguided—religious upbringing.

In addition to Catholic and Jewish orphanages, state Children's Home societies became prevalent in the late 19th century. These homes were not state sponsored but rather were statewide private organizations for the temporary shelter of orphaned and dependent children and for the placing of such children in foster families. Unlike the Children's Aid Society, the Children's Home societies often were not the legal guardian of the children they placed. (Each child's local government maintained legal guardianship.)

Another distinction between the Children's Aid Society and the Children's Home societies is that the latter focused less on notions of Christian charity to protect the children they placed than they did on the economic stability of the foster family and follow-up home visits. The Children's Home societies explicitly looked for "well-to-do" families as prospective foster families (Thurston, 1974, p. 150). Importantly, the idea of occasionally visiting the homes of foster families led directly to the development of "casework" by Children's Home society employees. Along with the agents of the Children's Aid Society, the "superintendents" of the home societies were among the earliest social workers.

In summary, by the beginning of the 20th century, the care of orphaned children in the United States was divided between state and local government facilities and private facilities. Funding, however, was mixed, with many states paying a per capita fee to private institutions as well as building and operating public child care institutions. By 1900, state funding of private institutions was highly criticized. Critics of such funding argued that private institutions were inadequately regulated and financially corrupt.[7] State boards of charity were established in most states to oversee the operations of both public and private child welfare institutions. These boards, together with the institutions and agencies they oversaw, determined that children who were placed in private homes needed to be visited regularly so that reliable reports on each child's progress could be made. This insistence, which would have a profound impact on the care of orphaned and abandoned children in the 20th century, was key in the professionalization of social work.

### *Orphans in the 20th Century*

Throughout the 20th century, the number of orphans in the United States steadily fell, whereas the number of children, as a percentage of the overall population, rose. In *The Welfare of Children,* Lindsey (1994, pp. 11-12) reports that there were 750,000 orphans in the United States in 1920. By 1970, this number had fallen to less than 2,000. One overwhelming reason for this happy trend is the decrease in parent mortality rates. Another reason is that, compared to earlier immigrant children, recent immigrant children who lose their parents are more likely to have other family members who can care for them.[8] Thus, the problem of caring for orphaned and abandoned children had almost disappeared by Richard Nixon's presidency.

In the 20th century, however, the public-private split in the care of orphaned children continued. Children cared for by governments were largely placed with foster families (especially after World War II), whereas children cared for by private charities were largely placed in institutions. Additionally, there was a shift in the early part of this century away from local supervision of public institutions and public services toward county and state supervision of these services, with "state departments of welfare assum[ing] increased responsibility for setting standards, licensing, and regulations of public and voluntary child care facilities" (McGowan & Meezan, 1983, p. 61).[9]

The trend begun in the early 20th century toward greater government involvement in the care of orphans was exaggerated by the Social Security Act of 1935. Although in 1929 the *Social Work Yearbook* could truthfully report that "[t]he care of dependent children . . . still rests in large measure in private hands" (Hall, 1930, p. 135), government—especially the federal government—was about to assume a much larger role in the care of dependent children. Because the numbers of orphans fell as the century progressed, the absolute sum spent by the federal government on the care of orphans was not great. The numbers of needy children, however, steadily increased during the century. Although many of these needy children were cared for in their own homes (with the help of Aid for Dependent Children [AFDC] payments and social service programs administered by social workers), a growing number of these children were taken from their homes and placed with foster families supervised by social workers.

We speculate that the increased use of foster care may be partially understood as a rational response by state government agencies to incentives unleashed by the Social Security Act. Three reasons justify this speculation. First, following passage of the Social Security Act, private charitable contributions for relief services (to assist the needy) shrank dramatically relative to public funding. Whereas 25% of relief funds came from the private sector in 1929, by 1939 less than 1% of such funds were private (McGowan & Meezan, 1983, p. 106). Second, states arguably expanded social service agencies to take advantage of Social Security Act provisions that offer federal matching funds, dollar-for-dollar, to defray state agencies' administrative costs. There are no limits on the amounts of these matching funds available to states. Third, to the extent that services provided under a foster care program can be classified as "administrative costs," state agencies have incentives to increase the use of foster care. Foster care programs would be preferred by agencies over public orphanages because staffing requirements at orphanages are lower per child than are staffing requirements for administering a foster care system. Foster care requires close monitoring of foster families, foster children, and of the natural families, whereas institutional care requires only supervision of the child. In short, foster care requires a larger cadre of social workers than does a system of institutional care. Public choice theory suggests that agencies concerned with grabbing federal matching funds would concentrate on providing bureaucrat-intensive services, such as foster care, rather than providing services requiring fewer bureaucrats, such as operating an orphanage.

The following data highlight 20th-century trends in the use of different methods of caring for orphans and for other children not living with family members. (Keep in mind that, since at least World War II, the vast majority of children in institutions and in foster care are not orphans.):

### Children in Institutions, 1933-1970[a]

| Year | Total | Public | Private |
|------|-------|--------|---------|
| 1933 | 144,000 | 23,000 | 121,000 |
| 1950 | 95,000 | 18,000 | 77,000 |
| 1958 | 88,100 | 10,900 | 77,200 |
| 1960 | 83,000 | 11,200 | 71,800 |
| 1965 | 79,400 | 11,100 | 68,300 |
| 1969 | 74,000 | 12,300 | 61,600 |

SOURCE: *Encyclopedia of Social Work* (1987, p. 1655).
a. Includes neglected, dependent, and emotionally disturbed children.

### Children in Foster Care, 1933-1990[a]

| Year | Total | Public | Private |
|------|-------|--------|---------|
| 1933 | 105,000 | 49,000 | 56,000 |
| 1950 | 127,900 | 91,800 | 36,100 |
| 1958 | 143,500 | 106,400 | 36,100 |
| 1960 | 158,900 | 117,800 | 37,100 |
| 1965 | 207,800 | 162,800 | 441,100 |
| 1969 | 249,000 | 205,000 | 45,000 |
| 1970 | 263,000 | 217,000 | 44,100 |
| 1977 | 500,000 | | |
| 1982 | 243,000 | | |
| 1987 | 285,000 | | |
| 1990 | 407,000 | | |

SOURCE: *Encyclopedia of Social Work* (1987, p. 1655).
a. Includes neglected, dependent, and emotionally disturbed children.

### Percentage of Orphaned and Neglected Children in Institutions, 1933-1970

| Year | % |
|------|---|
| 1933 | 58 |
| 1950-1952 | 43 |
| 1958 | 38 |
| 1960 | 34 |
| 1965 | 28 |
| 1970 | 19 |

These data show that although the total number of dependent children in institutions dropped by 57% between 1933 and 1970, the number of such children in foster care increased by more than 150%. Moreover, during the middle part of this century, the reliance on institutional care relative to foster care declined precipitously. Finally, these data show the shift from privately funded to publicly funded caregiving.

Children were deinstitutionalized for the following reasons: (a) The numbers of orphans decreased; (b) funding from the federal government provided incentives to place children in foster homes rather than in institutions (the more children placed, the more money could be demanded from the federal government to oversee these placements); and (c) social work professionals pressed for foster care rather than institutional care. We believe that these latter two reasons provide an important key to understanding the rise of foster care and the decline of orphanages. Each reason is explored in turn.

## ■ The Social Security Act and Its Amendments

The Social Security Act of 1935 created two separate programs affecting child welfare services. The first program, Title IV, was known as Grants to States for Aid to Families With Dependent Children (now known as AFDC). Under Title IV, states received matching federal grants that were used to supplement the income of fatherless homes. Title IV required each state to create a single state agency to administer the program. The program offered block grants, leaving states free to establish eligibility requirements, levels of payments, and administrative procedures. The second program, the Child Welfare Services Program (CWS) (Title V),[10] provided payments to orphaned children. Title V gave responsibility to the Children's Bureau to coordinate the provision of child welfare services to poor rural homeless, dependent, and neglected children. Federal dollars available under Title V created powerful bureaucratizing incentives: "[b]y 1938, all but one state had submitted a plan for the coordinated delivery of child welfare services" (McGowan & Meezan, 1983, p. 69).

### Child Welfare Services Program

Title V, Part 3 of the Social Security Act, which created the CWS program, aimed to help orphaned and dependent children in two ways. First, under the program the federal government paid states to promote the development of child welfare services in rural areas. The target group for these programs was the homeless, dependent, or neglected child—that is, the child traditionally cared for in public or private institutions or through foster care placement. Second, Title V provided these orphaned children with "survivor's benefits," which were designed as a kind of social insurance for "the dependent orphans of deceased wage earners" (Bremner, 1974, p. 535).

The amount of federal funds allocated to this program was small in comparison to other social service programs. Funding was limited to $1.5 million per year in federal grants to states when the program began in 1936, although amendments in 1939 and 1958 increased spending levels. By 1969, funding levels had reached $100 million per year. The federal block grants available under Title V could be used to hire social workers or fund educational leave for social workers; it appears, however, that many states also used the grants appropriated under this program to subsidize foster care payments (McGowan & Meezan, 1983, p. 113).

Important developments under the CWS program included the expansion of the program in 1958 to include all children, not just rural children, and the requirement in 1958 that states match federal funds. In 1962, the program was again broadened to cover expenses for "any social services necessary to promote the well-being of all children, not just for services for homeless, dependent, and neglected children" (McGowan & Meezan, 1983, p. 95). Thus, although the CWS program represented a comparatively small transfer of federal dollars to states, it nonetheless provided incentives to create and expand bureaucracies by funding the hiring and training of social workers (who, we argue later, were professionally disposed to favor foster care over institutional care). Additionally, grants under the program were used to subsidize foster care payments. Both common sense and public choice theory predict that if federal money is made available, agencies will expand to tap into this funding source. Furthermore, the more heavily subsidized a service, the more of that service will be provided. In this case, Title V allowed states to subsidize both the hiring of social workers and the foster care payments; not surprisingly, the number of social workers and children in foster care increased after the act took effect.

### Aid to Families With Dependent Children and Foster Care

Primary financial responsibility for children in institutions or in foster care rested with the states until 1961. At that time, the Social Security Act was amended to extend the AFDC program to children in foster care. The AFDC program was financed through block grants to states, which allowed states to create eligibility guidelines and to govern levels of payment (Bremner, 1974, p. 520). Although originally enacted as a temporary measure, this extension of AFDC to foster children was quickly made a permanent part of the act and was further extended to cover payments to children placed in private, non-profit institutions. These amendments were changed again in 1967 to increase federal funding of foster care payments as well as to require all states to establish what became known as AFDC Foster Care programs by 1969.

Although funds available under the Child Welfare Services Program were limited, this was not the case with AFDC Foster Care program funds. McGowan and Meezan (1983) noted that these funds were

> an open-ended entitlement program. Thus, the states can claim federal reimbursement for the care of as many children as are eligible for the program. Not surprisingly, therefore, expenditures under the program increased rapidly, and support for out-of-home care quickly became the major thrust of federal policy. Particularly troubling was the fact that this legislation provided no checks on the extent to which the federal funds were being used appropriately—whether children in placement did in fact need placement. (p. 96)

Such a program creates clear incentives to place children in foster care families. In addition to the open-endedness of these funds, the fact that under the AFDC program "administrative costs" of social services agencies were shared on a 50/50 basis with the federal government, further encouraged the bureaucratic tendency to grow like kudzu. That is, social services agencies were receiving unlimited funds from federal coffers for AFDC payments, which, as of 1961, included some foster children, and agencies were splitting administrative costs with the federal government. The greater the number of children placed with foster care families, the larger the child welfare agency budget. AFDC's foster care bias is confirmed by the *Encyclopedia of Social Work* (1987), which notes that "[s]tates that were heavily dependent on [AFDC foster care] funds had no incentives to move children out of foster care because funding was lost each time a child was discharged from placement" (p. 642).

Additionally, if agency prerequisites can be classified as administrative costs, then all such subsidized "costs" will surely increase. Also, operating an extensive foster care system requires greater numbers of social workers, who provide elaborate social services to the foster child, his or her natural family, and his or her foster family. As Bremner (1974) reports,

At the urging of professional welfare and social workers, there was recognition in principle of the need for the provision of social services to promote self-help and "strengthen family life." The practical effect of the latter was to make it clear that the costs of services provided by the staff of the state agency could be included among the administrative costs which the federal government shared on a 50-50 basis. (p. 546)

Moreover, although AFDC Foster Care payments were available for children placed in institutional settings, these institutions were primarily private (i.e., not run by public-sector social workers) and so required a much smaller group of government social workers to oversee them and their programs. Given this, such private institutions would likely be disfavored providers of out-of-home care in the eyes of social services agencies eager to capture ever more federal funding.

Probably not coincidentally, the number of children moved out of institutions and into public foster care shifted markedly during the 1960s. During the 1960s alone, the number of children in institutions fell from 83,000 to 62,600, whereas the population of private institutions fell from 71,000 to 55,600. In contrast, the 1960s witnessed a rise in the number of children in foster care from 158,900 to 263,000, with an increase of 100,000 children placed in public foster care programs from 117,000 to 217,000. A child was eligible to participate in the AFDC Foster Care program if a judge determined that remaining in the home posed a threat to the child. Obtaining such judicial determinations was, apparently, not difficult. An unfortunate side effect of this incentive system was that "the availability of federal dollars for foster care resulted in AFDC Foster Care children lingering in 'temporary' care even longer than children for whom the state was paying the whole bill" (McGowan & Meezan, 1983, p. 117).

Taken together, the Social Security Act and its later amendments arguably caused states to shift some of the responsibility for making foster care payments from themselves to the federal government: Under both Title V and the 1961 amendments to the act, states grew more reliant on foster care programs. Furthermore, because the federal government picked up under Title IV fully half of whatever administrative costs states incurred, states had incentives to increase these costs. One way to increase such costs would be to provide services requiring greater numbers of social workers. Therefore, social services agencies placed a higher proportion of dependent children with foster care families rather than with public orphanages. Finally, the act provided incentives to hire and train social workers, who, as government employees, quickly became a powerful special-interest group capable of lobbying for increasing amounts of federal money. The 1961 amendment to the Social Security Act, expanding the AFDC program to foster children, may in part represent the fruits of such lobbying efforts. In the next section, we examine in more detail the effects of the social work profession on orphaned and dependent children.

## ■ The Rise of Social Workers

Although the social work profession began as a predominantly private practice, currently it is overwhelmingly a publicly funded profession. The typical social worker is a state employee. As social workers have moved from private institutions to government offices, they have taken their clients with them so that currently caring for neglected and orphaned children is considered a problem of, first and foremost, government rather than private institutions.

The social work profession began with volunteers. Throughout much of the 19th century, as in earlier centuries, well-intentioned people volunteered their time and resources to help those less fortunate than themselves. Most social workers in the 19th century were of this sort. From approximately mid-century onwards, however, there were an increasing number of professional social workers, employed by public and private institutions.

### The Move Toward Professionalization

The impetus to professionalize social workers gathered steam during the Progressive Era of 1896 to 1912. In this era, social workers, obsessed with social reform, sought to reform both society and their field. Critics dissatisfied with the system of per capita payments by state governments to private child care institutions demanded regulation and licensing of institutions (McGowan & Meezan, 1983, p. 58). At the same time, the National Conference on Charities and Corrections advocated greater public responsibility for dependent children.

Additionally, in the ongoing controversy between advocates of foster care and advocates of institutional care, the foster care contingency scored significant victories. Homer Folds, an influential social work reformer, came out strongly in favor of foster care at an 1896 meeting of the Conference of Charities of New York City. In 1899, at a meeting of the National Conference on Charities and Corrections, "prominent child welfare workers" presented a report that "stated that when a child needed substitute care, consideration should first be given to a foster-family arrangement" (Kadushin & Martin, 1988, p. 350). This position was also adopted in 1909 at the First White House Conference on Children and reinforced at the second such conference in 1919.

Social workers' professional preference for foster care was based on the plausible idea that children receive better and more loving care in familial settings than in institutional settings. However well-intentioned this preference, though, it had the concomitant effect of favoring the more "professional" Protestant approach to child welfare services over the apparently more amateurish Catholic and Jewish approach. The pro-foster care social worker attempted to limit the competition provided by the Catholic and Jewish homes at a time when huge numbers of Catholic and Jewish immigrants were arriving in America. There was no clear evidence, however, that foster care was superior to institutional care. Susan Tiffin (1982) notes, "[F]oster care was accepted by many reformers as self-evident improvement on group care within the institutional framework, despite the paucity of data available to substantiate such a belief" (p. 95).

## The Rise of Casework

The desire to distinguish themselves from competitors led social workers to professionalize by developing formal requirements for professional practice (Ehrenreich, 1985, p. 54).[11] Social workers relied on two primary means to professionalize. They pressed for increased educational requirements of members, and they increasingly emphasized the use and value of psychoanalysis as a tool of their trade.[12] Psychoanalytic tools combined with the casework method to create "psychoanalytic casework"—clearly beyond the capabilities of most volunteers.

In addition to being beyond the scope of most volunteers, psychoanalytic casework had the virtue of concentrating (of necessity) on each individual in need. In other words, professionalization of the industry also shifted its collective focus from broad environmental issues (such as poverty in cities, poor sanitation, or improving education) to narrowly focused individual issues. Social workers argued that more good could be accomplished by providing direct services to individuals than by attempting social reforms. Providing direct services meant providing more social workers.

By the 1920s, individual casework, pioneered by Mary Richmond, dominated social work. New schools were established to meet the need for psychiatrically trained social workers, with the Smith College for Social Work being the foremost among these. As a result of World War I, the Veterans Bureau became, in the 1920s, the single largest employer of psychiatric social workers in the country (Ehrenreich, 1985, p. 70). Throughout the 1920s, the percentage of private funding for charitable relief efforts fell as government spending on these efforts increased.

Another development was the 1912 creation of the U.S. Children's Bureau. This federal agency was ostensibly designed to represent the interests of children (and women) at the national level. It concentrated on research and educational programs dealing with maternal health, dependent children, and other children's issues. In 1921, the Sheppard-Towner Act gave the agency responsibility for administering federal grants-in-aid to states for maternal and child health programs (Tiffin, 1982, p. 60). Such grants-in-aid became a precedent for the extensive provisions of the Social Security Act of 1935.

### The Effects of the New Deal on Social Work

There were 30,500 social workers in the United States in 1930 (up from 19,000 in 1910), and several states were considering licensing statuses for social workers. Casework was the preferred method of social work professionals. Increasingly, social workers were employees of state and local governments rather than of private institutions. Thus, when the Great Depression hit, social workers, many of whom were now public-sector employees, lobbied for the federal government to do more in the name of helping the needy.

The Social Security Act of 1935 provided much of the federal funding social workers sought, including federal funding for social worker training (42 U.S.C. § 626, 1992). Additionally, members of groups that social workers traditionally helped—the poor, the disabled, and the mentally ill—were taken more fully under the public wing in the 1930s. Of course, social workers were in the forefront of those who administered the services these needy groups were given by the states and the federal government. By 1940, the majority of social workers worked for the government.

How did the transition from private provision of social services to government provision of such services affect the social work profession? First and foremost, New Deal legislation dramatically increased the number of social workers. Between 1930 and 1938, the number of social workers doubled to 60,000 (McGowan & Meezan, 1983, p. 108). Not surprisingly, the majority of these new social workers were not considered professionals in the eyes of their senior colleagues. Tensions arose between newly hired workers and more highly trained, more established social workers. These tensions created a rift in the profession, between the "rank-and-file" (i.e., less educated and lower-level) workers and the more senior, better educated, and higher-ranking social workers.

The rank-and-file movement successfully pressed for unionization of government social workers. By the end of the 1930s, more than 80% of all government social workers were members of unions. In addition to lobbying for higher wages and better working conditions, social workers' unions successfully pressed for "more training opportunities for new workers in public agencies" (McGowan & Meezan, 1983, p. 115). Thus, as a result of the Social Security Act of 1935, government social workers became a more powerful special-interest group—desirous of, and often successful in, expanding their professional responsibilities and their budgets.

Throughout the 1940s and 1950s, social workers continued to favor individual care over broad-based reform. This professional preference gave rise to the "diagnostic" school of social work. Diagnostic social workers used a casework method requiring an intensive investigation of each client's environment together with long-term counseling—that is, much social worker time and effort. McGowan and Meezan (1983) noted,

> Most child welfare workers during this period [the 1950s] tended to view the provision of individual casework services as the most prestigious and critical of their professional tasks. . . . Services were geared almost entirely toward placement, and individual casework was the primary interventive modality. (pp. 71, 74)

This focus on the provision of individual service remained a distinguishing feature of social work until the 1960s, when it encountered criticism for being unresponsive to the needs of the poor.

Social workers' concern with "professionalization" and its attendant focus on individual casework may have been a factor driving the increased use of foster care services for dependent children during this period. By placing children in foster care programs, it was easier for social workers to do the kinds of individual casework that increased their professional status. Although the decrease in the absolute number of orphans accounts for much of the drop in the numbers of children in institutions, the rise in the number of children in foster care was almost surely encouraged by social workers' concerns for their own professional status.

### Contemporary Social Work

This cycle of reform-mindedness versus concern with professionalization and casework has plagued social work throughout the 20th century. Social workers in the 1940s and 1950s were concerned with improving their professional image and with providing individual services to clients. In the 1960s, social workers—among the prime beneficiaries of the Great Society legislation because of the tremendous increase in federal funding of social services—once again became interested in broad social reforms.

What are the key characteristics of the social work profession since the 1960s? Certainly, the growth of the industry as a whole is notable. Perhaps the most striking characteristic of post-World War II social work is its reliance on public funding. The provision of social services has become the major task of federal and state governments. Social workers have benefited tremendously from this expansion of services. Even though there has been a substantial movement in recent years toward the privatization of social services, these private institutions are still receiving massive government subsidies.

### Social Workers and Orphans

As noted previously, most U.S. orphans in 1913 were cared for in private institutions, but by 1970 only 19% were in institutions. Expenditures on child welfare casework services, however, rose throughout the 1950s and 1960s, receding somewhat in the early 1970s (after which time data were no longer collected at the national level).

Expenditures on Child Welfare
Services by Public Welfare Agencies[a]

| Year | $ |
|------|------|
| 1953 | 113.2 |
| 1958 | 176.1 |
| 1960 | 211.1 |
| 1962 | 423 |
| 1965 | 532 |
| 1968 | 656 |
| 1972 | 640 |

SOURCE: *Encyclopedia of Social Work* (1987, p. 1654).
a. Total per fiscal year in millions of dollars.

In addition, the number of children receiving casework services increased substantially between 1945 and 1971. For example, in 1945, 236,000 children received such services, whereas in 1972, 530,000 children received such services (*Encyclopedia of Social Work,* 1987, p. 1654). More children received such services and more money was spent to deliver these services.

Thus, since the early 1930s the number of social workers in the United States has increased rapidly, climbing from 30,500 in 1930 to 60,000 in 1938, 125,000 in 1965, and 263,000 in 1972.[13] In addition, the amount of public funding available to support social services and social workers also increased. At the same time, the number of orphans in the United States fell. Some orphaned and many needy children remained, however, and these were increasingly placed with foster care families rather than institutions. Social workers had, from the beginning of this century, expressed a strong preference for foster care over institutional care—a preference that we suggest was at least as much a product of social workers' concerns for their own professional status (and income) as it was of their concern for children's welfare.

## ▓ Conclusion

Changing patterns of federal funding under the Social Security Act of 1935, in combination with the historic professional biases of social workers, arguably are a major factor explaining the movement of orphans from private institutions into foster care homes. Not only would such a move require a higher ratio of social workers to orphans (because each orphan in a foster home requires monitoring by a social worker, whereas a number of orphans in an institution can be monitored by fewer caregivers) but also such a move would capture greater amounts of federal funding, as a result of both Title V grants and the 1961 amendments to the Social Security Act of 1935. Thus, we suggest that the dramatic mid-20th-century decline in the use of orphanages is explained at least in part by the self-interested lobbying of social workers to promote greater reliance on public foster care over institutional care.[14]

## ▓ Notes

1. The following statistic provides a telling example of the tremendous scope of familial care for orphans: In 1920, there were 750,000 orphans in the United States, only 140,000 of whom were in institutions, either private or public (Lindsey, 1994, p. 11).

2. A comprehensive history of orphan care in Europe from ancient times through the Middle Ages is provided by Boswell (1988).

3. Indenturing of orphaned children was still legal in some states as late as 1926 (Thurston, 1974, pp. 107-210).

4. An 1844 account from a worker at the Boston Female Orphan Asylum (Thurston, 1974, p. 57) notes, "The greatest care is always taken in selecting places for those who are old enough to go into families. And this might seem easy to do, as applications for children always greatly exceed the number to be placed out."

5. Even before private charities hired agents to check on the care of foster children, the state of Massachusetts in 1866 employed an agent to oversee the care provided for the orphaned and dependent children of that state who had been indentured (Thurston, 1974, p. 163).

6. In 1851, there were 77 children's institutions in the United States, the vast majority of which were private (Folks, 1902, pp. 52-55). By 1923, there were 1,558 private children's institutions in the United States, with a total population of 140,312 (U.S. Department of Commerce, 1923, Table 22).

7. Criticism was so persuasive that in 1874 New York enacted a state constitutional amendment forbidding the use of money from the state treasury to subsidize private charities. Massachusetts ratified a similar amendment in 1913 (Hall, 1930, p. 131).

8. We thank an anonymous referee for making this point.

9. On the trend toward centralized care of orphaned children, see Chapter 11.

10. Child Welfare Services became Title IV-B in 1967.

11. We do not mean to impeach the motives of all social workers. Many, perhaps most, were (and are) sincere and well-meaning people. Indeed, our hypothesis is consistent with the assumption that all case workers are interested only in the welfare of children and families. All that is needed for our hypothesis to have explanatory power is that enough administrators of social welfare agencies act self-interestedly. Because administrators of agencies enjoy more discretion over the allocation of agency resources, administrators are more likely than are caseworkers to be tempted—and be able—to pursue self-interested goals at the expense of the public welfare.

12. In an interesting comment, Ehrenreich (1985, p. 73) states, "That psychiatry did not yet [in the 1920s] offer much practical value was not serious bar to its use as a basis for professionalization."

13. See the previous table. See also various editions of the *Statistical Abstract of the United States* (U.S. Department of Commerce). The number of social workers in the United States continues to climb. In 1993, there were 586,000 social workers.

14. We also note that during this period (1940-1970) it is very likely that social workers emphasized placing orphaned children in adoptive homes. The number of public agency placements in the United States increased from 14,000 in 1950 to 65,000 in 1971. Of course, agencies receive substantial fees for placing children in adoptive homes. We suggest, however, that this movement may not have been as strong as the movement to use foster care placement because foster care necessitates an ongoing social worker-child relationship and, therefore, continued funding of that relationship.

# ▨ References

Boswell, J. (1988). *The kindness of strangers.* New York: Pantheon.

Bremner, R. H. (1974). *Children and youth in America* (Vol. 3). Cambridge, MA: Harvard University Press.

Ehrenreich, J. H. (1985). *The altruistic imagination: A history of social work and social policy in the United States*. Ithaca, NY: Cornell University Press.

*Encyclopedia of social work*. (17th ed., Vol. 2). (1987). Silver Spring, MD: National Association of Social Workers.

*Encyclopedia of social work*. (18th ed.). (1987). Silver Spring, MD: National Association of Social Workers.

Folks, H. (1902). *The care of destitute, neglected, and delinquent children*. New York: Macmillan.

Hall, F. S. (Ed.). (1930). *Social work yearbook*. New York: Russell Sage.

Kadushin, A., & Martin, J. (1988). *Child welfare services* (4th ed.). New York: Macmillan.

Lindsey, D. (1994). *The welfare of children*. New York: Oxford University Press.

McGowan, B., & Meezan, W. (1983). *Child welfare: Current dilemmas, future directions*. Itasca, IL: F. E. Peacock.

Thurston, H. W. (1974). *The dependent child*. New York: Arno. (Original work published 1930)

Tiffin, S. (1982). *In whose best interest? Child welfare reform in the Progressive Era*. Westport, CT: Greenwood.

U.S. Department of Commerce, U.S. Census Bureau. (1923, February 1). *U.S. Census*. Washington, DC: Author.

# CHAPTER 11

# A Public Choice Analysis of Child Care Dollars

*The Political Bias in Favor of the Status Quo*

DWIGHT R. LEE

O rphanages provided much more than material assistance to young people in need. They also provided companionship, love, instruction, responsibility, and a sense of permanence and place for children who otherwise would have lacked these important ingredients in growing up. Orphanages are not institutions that can be effectively run from afar, subject to standardized rules and procedures formulated by remote authorities. They are local institutions best run by people who possess the local information of time and place. They may be primarily private or primarily public, but they are almost by necessity local.

The local nature of orphanages is an important element in understanding why they have declined in importance and why this decline has corresponded closely with the increased centralization of government efforts to fight poverty. Political forces behind the centralization of government poverty programs, and behind government centralization in general, have resulted in spending more money in the name of helping the poor, particularly poor children, but have also resulted in less being done to actually help. The poor have become treated less as people in need of our responsible compassion and more as pawns in a competition for government largess. This is not a political environment in which orphanages can expect to thrive. For the very reasons that orphanages are better (not perfect) than centralized transfer programs for delivering responsible compassion to children most in need, they no longer play the important role in social welfare they once did.

## ■ The Politics of Centralization

Why was there a political takeover and centralization of antipoverty efforts, which began in earnest during the 1960s? Surely one reason was that many sincere, well-intended, and highly credentialed people believed that poverty was not being adequately confronted by private organizations, local governments, or the combined efforts of the two. Certainly, such a belief could be supported with empirical studies and plausible arguments. Poverty, after all, is a resilient condition in all societies. Indeed, this resiliency has traditionally moderated public expectations about any arrangement to eradicate poverty. The persistence of poverty, however, became harder to accept as the contrast between this poverty and the postwar prosperity enjoyed by most became a tempting topic for emotionally gripping television reports. Also, in the 1960s and 1970s many people believed that the successes in the physical sciences could be duplicated by the social sciences if only social scientists were given sufficient resources and empowered to guide enough federal government programs with their expertise. Who over the age of 25 has not heard, "If we can send a man to the moon, then we should be able to revitalize our cities, fine-tune the economy, rehabilitate criminals, and, of course, eliminate poverty"?

More than good intentions and optimism, however, were behind the shift to more federal responsibility for helping the poor. Failing to recognize the political influence of private interests on all government policy, regardless of how much that policy is justified in the name of concern and compassion, would be hopelessly naive. The poor, who are the putative recipients of assistance from poverty programs, have a clear private interest in the generosity of these programs. The interest of the poor, however, is not the only, or even the most important, interest influencing government policy affecting the poor. Government employees of agencies administering poverty programs benefit from expanding budgets for those agencies. Suppliers of goods and services that government programs provide in-kind to the poor (such as medical care, housing, food, and education) obviously gain when their products are more generously provided. Also, apart from their role as suppliers of education, many academics benefit from expansions in government poverty programs as researchers and consultants.

There is no need to argue that these interest groups were more important than genuine public concern in initiating significant federal funding of poverty programs. The important point is that once funding is initiated, interest groups discover private advantage in political efforts to influence its size and distribution. On one level, these groups are competing with one another. For example, agricultural interests, when lobbying for an expanded food stamp program, are in competition with the medical interests lobbying for an expanded Medicaid program. On another level, however, all these groups share a common objective: more government funding for poverty programs in general. In this sense, the organized interests that have coalesced around poverty programs are more in competition with taxpayers than with each other.

This is not to argue that taxpayers are unwilling to pay for a reduction in poverty. Clearly they are willing to do so. Most citizens feel remorse, or at least discomfort, knowing that some of their fellow citizens, particularly children, are suffering from deprivations that could be rather inexpensively overcome if the burden were shared by the more fortunate. The interests of taxpayers paying for poverty programs and the interests of groups benefiting from them as suppliers diverge in important ways, however. Taxpayers are more concerned with controlling the costs of the programs than are suppliers. The lower the cost of achieving a given reduction in poverty, the better off are taxpayers. This is not the case with suppliers. Costs are really benefits to the suppliers of government poverty programs, with higher costs equivalent to more demand for their products and services. Relatedly, taxpayers are more concerned with the effectiveness of poverty programs than are suppliers. The only benefit taxpayers realize from these programs comes from their effectiveness at reducing poverty. Not so for the suppliers. As concerned citizens, suppliers will prefer effectiveness over ineffectiveness, but as suppliers to poverty programs they will benefit from the programs even if they are less effective than they could be. Indeed, poverty programs (and other government programs) are often funded more generously if they are less effective. Therefore, suppliers will be more concerned with expanding the budgets of poverty programs and less concerned than are taxpayers with the effectiveness of these programs.

The desire of organized interest groups for more government funding of poverty programs helps explain the pressure from these groups for more federal control and funding of these programs. They gain several advantages from centralizing political decisions in the competition against taxpayers to expand funding for government programs.

First, taxpayers always have a serious disadvantage against organized interest groups in political competition because the cost of government programs is spread over many, whereas much of the benefit is concentrated on a few. Therefore, each taxpayer gains little from opposing the expansion of a government program, whereas each member of the benefiting interest group gains a great deal. Not surprisingly, when people mobilize for political action, they invariably do so to support a program that benefits them rather than oppose a program that benefits others. This bias in favor of expanding programs increases when funding for a program is transferred from the state or local level to the federal level because this transfer spreads the cost of the program over many more taxpayers. The reduction of the per taxpayer cost of expanding the program increases the difficulty of motivating political resistance to the political influence of organized interest groups.

Second, transferring control of a program to the federal level reduces the political transaction costs faced by interest groups. Mastering control of a few centrally located special-interest levers is much easier than dealing with a multitude of such levers spread over different government levels and jurisdictions. Also, control over how poverty programs are designed and implemented is very important to the organized interests that benefit from them. Although these groups always lobby on behalf of the poor, they benefit from altering poverty programs in ways that do more to help themselves than to help the poor.[1]

Third, the more centralized the funding and control of poverty programs, the less the taxpayer benefits from competition in the cost and supply of those programs. Consider the effect of the centralization of taxes and political control. Since 1929, the percentage of all tax revenues in the United States that the federal government receives has increased sharply.[2] When most of the tax revenue was raised within the states, the ability to acquire that revenue was limited by competition between the states. If one state tried to charge too much for its services, taxpayers could "shop" elsewhere by locating in another state. By assuming central control of most tax revenue and then returning much of it to the states, the federal government is, in effect, enforcing a tax cartel.[3] States now acquire a much lower proportion of their revenue from a taxing authority that taxpayers cannot escape by moving, unless they are willing to move out of the country. Not surprisingly, as centralization in tax collection increased, so did the percentage of national income paid in taxes.

Fourth, more federal control over tax revenues motivates state and local officials to demand more federal spending and reduces their concern regarding the efficiency of that spending. Local taxpayers realize that their federal taxes will not be reduced if their political representatives fail to bring home large amounts of federal money; they will continue to pay, but their money will be spent elsewhere. Thus, even the most fiscally conservative congressional districts expect their political representatives to secure as much federal funding of local projects and programs as possible. The understandable attitude of local taxpayers is that it is better to waste federal tax dollars at home than have them wasted somewhere else, and politicians who do not cater to this attitude are soon replaced by those who do. Obviously, local officials are not in a strong position to insist on federal funding for only those programs that most efficiently serve local needs. If federal experts decide on an approach to a problem, and insist that that approach be implemented by imposing restrictions and mandates on the use of federal money, local officials are not likely to object. They are under strong pressure to accept the federal funding, along with the restrictions and mandates, even though local conditions and circumstances call for alternative approaches.

The previously discussed four effects of increased centralization of political decisions help explain the persistent pressure in favor of more centralization. Centralizing political decision making shifts the advantage to organized interest groups desiring more government spending in their competition with taxpayers. More centralization also shifts more control to organized political interests and government experts regarding how, and how much, taxpayer dollars are spent. The common feature in all four effects is a reduction in the control of those who are paying for a government service relative to the control of those who are supplying the service. Taxpayers tend to defer to government experts, and pay little attention to the effectiveness of the programs they run, when control is shifted to the federal level, especially in the case of charitable programs such as those to help the poor.

## ■ The Disengaged Consumer

Even when people contribute voluntarily to local charitable efforts, they often do not pay close attention to the effectiveness of those efforts. When people pay for a service that they expect to benefit from directly, they have a clear motivation to determine if the benefit justifies the cost and can usually make this determination easily. In this case, the consumers of the service are actively engaged. Charitable services are different. Those who pay for charitable services (consumer donors) are not those who receive the primary benefit (the poor, the infirm, orphans, etc.). Why then do people donate to charities? The reasons are surely many and complex. Simply stated, people contribute to charities because of the private benefits from doing so, both the positive benefits that come from feelings of virtue and the not-so-positive benefits that come from social pressure. Donors also receive the benefits of living in a society with less poverty, better care for the young, and so on if their donations are used wisely, but these are public goods (benefiting both those who donate and those who do not) and in most cases do little to motivate charitable contributions. Therefore, the primary benefits from contributing to a charitable cause are realized from the act of making the contribution, and once it is made the donor has little motivation to determine how the money is actually spent.[4] Indeed, one may not want to know how effective his or her donation is at achieving its stated purpose. Information on what is actually done with one's donation may jeopardize the sense of virtue one received from making it.[5] Therefore, at best, the consumer of charitable activities tends to be disengaged.

This consumer disengagement is far greater when charitable services are paid for through general taxation and the decisions are made by remote authorities. Why should people be engaged in decisions when they cannot use any knowledge they acquire to significantly affect them, which is the case with political decisions, particularly those made at the federal level. In the case of private charities, a donor knows how much he or she is donating and can always quit donating, or donate to a competing charity, if the individual discovers that his or her donations are not being used effectively. In the case of public charity, only with great effort could a taxpayer find out how much of his or her tax bill is going to a particular charitable program. Furthermore, if the taxpayer discovers that the programs he or she is paying for are ineffective, he or she could quit paying for them only by moving, and it would be an extremely costly move if the programs are being funded by the federal government.

This shift in control from consumers to suppliers and experts as government has become more centralized explains why government spending has become almost synonymous with waste and inefficiency. The joke "I'm from the government and I'm here to help" is funny for a reason. No matter how expert, government authorities will have too little motivation to pursue those policies that best help others and too much latitude to pursue those that best help themselves, unless they have to cater to the demands of those paying the bill. Nowhere is this more evident than in the case of government efforts to help the poor.

## ■ The Difficulty of Helping the Poor

Helping the poor is difficult, and helping poor children is especially difficult. The fundamental problem is unavoidable, and mitigating it is the best that can be expected. Helping people in unfortunate situations necessarily lowers the cost of getting into, and lowers the benefit of getting out of, those situations.[6] This is not to deny that people often find themselves in unfortunate situations through no fault of their own; this is especially true of children who are orphaned or born into dysfunctional families. Such children cannot be expected to overcome their situations without help. The type of help, however, is surely more critical for children than for adults. The basic attitudes of adults are essentially formed and fixed. Helping adults is not likely to undermine a sense of personal responsibility in those who have it or to prevent the late development of such a sense in those who do not. Children are far more affected by the type of help they receive. The right kind of help can instill attitudes that allow children to develop into productive adults, and the wrong kind of help can breed a sense of dependency that lasts a lifetime.

The point is that the way we help children is of special importance, not that the type of help given adults is of no consequence. Indeed, there was a long tradition of helping the poor in America based on the recognition that such help can be either constructive or destructive. This tradition emphasizes the importance of responsibility and is almost as concerned with a lack of responsibility by the providers as that by the recipients.

According to Marvin Olasky (1992), there was an understanding in the 19th century that "those who gave material aid without requiring even the smallest return were considered as much a threat to true compassion as those who turned their backs on neighbors and brothers" (p. 21). Nineteenth-century Americans were harshly realistic about helping the poor, recognizing that for compassion to be effective it had to be responsible—what might today be called "tough love." Using quotes from the 1835 issue of *American Quarterly Review,* Olasky (1992, p. 44) conveys the prevailing wisdom that "government subsidies lead individuals to become 'degraded, dissolute, wasteful, profligate, and idle, by promising them a support if they do so.' Children

would learn that income came without work, and the result would be 'generation after generation of hereditary paupers.' "

Attempts were made to distinguish between the deserving poor and the
undeserving poor, with help being denied the latter. This distinction was not
motivated by a lack of compassion but by a responsible recognition that
refusing help to the undeserving poor would mean there would be fewer of
them. On the basis of her experience as a leader of charitable efforts in
19th-century New York, Josephine Lowell (as quoted in Olasky, 1992) stated,

> The problem before those who would be charitable, is not how to deal with
> a given number of poor; it is how to help those who are poor, without adding
> to their numbers and constantly increasing the evils they seek to cure. (p. 110)

Relatedly, Indiana officials observed, "Nothing creates pauperism so rapidly
as the giving of relief to [able-bodied] persons without requiring them to earn
what they receive by some kind of honest labor" (p. 109). Work requirements
not only helped aid recipients maintain a sense of responsibility but also
helped separate the deserving from the undeserving. In the 1890s, an able-
bodied man who wanted relief in most U.S. cities was expected to chop wood
or whitewash buildings in return. Women were commonly required to work
in a "sewing room" or assist in a nearby child care room. The sense of dignity
the able-bodied poor received from performing useful work was often enhanced from knowing that their efforts were helping others, with the wood
and garments they made commonly going to aid the helpless poor (p. 105).

Another goal of the responsible compassion of 19th- and early 20th-
century charitable efforts was contributions that went beyond simply giving
money. The most effective help occurred when recipients felt that others cared
and felt some appreciation and obligation for those who provided them
assistance. This view was reflected by the minister William Ruffner, who
wrote in 1853 (as quoted in Olasky, 1992),

> There must, of course, be officers, teachers, missionaries employed to live in
> the very midst of the wretchedness, and to supervise and direct all the efforts
> of the people. [But] Mark you! These officers are not to stand between the
> giver and receiver, but to bring *giver and receiver together.* (p. 31)

Government assistance to the poor, though small by today's standards,
was provided in the 19th century, but clear concern was expressed about the
effectiveness of this assistance. In his massive 1894 report, *American Chari-*

*ties: A Study in Philanthropy and Economics,* Amos G. Warner (as quoted in Olasky, 1992) commented on the deficiencies of government efforts to help the poor. Among his concerns about government charity were that it is "necessarily more impersonal and mechanical than private charity or individual action" and "there is a tendency to claim public relief as a right, and for the indolent and incapable to throw themselves flat upon it" (p. 111).

## ■ Orphanages and Responsible Compassion

The primary advantage realized from the tradition of responsible compassion was the recognition of the inevitable pitfalls when attempting to help the needy. No one would argue that any charitable effort, private or otherwise, can completely avoid these pitfalls. Knowing about them, however, made it possible to avoid some and mitigate the effects of others. Orphanages were prevalent during the period of responsible compassion, which lasted well into the 20th century, and they satisfied many of the requirements for responsible and effective assistance to the disadvantaged. Orphanages were obviously not ideal environments for raising children. They were, at best, second-best arrangements for taking care of children for whom the ideal of living with competent and loving parents was not an option. No one would deny that some orphanages were woefully deficient even by the standards of second best. In general, however, they were effective arrangements for providing care in ways that not only took care of temporary material needs but also taught and encouraged responsible behavior.

Children raised in orphanages were provided with the basic requirements of food and shelter and given access to education. More than these basics were provided, however, because they were not provided impersonally and with nothing expected in return. Orphans quickly learned that the necessities and conveniences of life had to be earned and not simply expected. The children were required to work, and through that work they developed attitudes conducive to a life of responsibility rather than indolence. In recounting his experiences growing up in an orphanage, McKenzie (1996, p. 167) tells of voluntarily going to bed by 8 p.m. because he knew that Mr. Panns would be knocking on the door at 3:30 a.m. to make sure that he, and the others on the milking team, completed their tasks of filling the milk canisters, "transporting [them] to the milk room, cleaning the gutters behind the cows in the barns, and scrubbing the place down." Obtaining spending money typically required additional jobs on weekends or after schoolwork and the required chores were completed. McKenzie recalls working on Saturday afternoon for a local farmer, delivering papers, and cutting hair to earn a little money (pp. 172-173). Much of this money he saved for college expenses. Although McKenzie's orphanage helped with some college expenses, it was expected that the student who was college bound would pay for much of those expenses himself or herself (p. 187).

The requirement of work reduced the risks that children raised in orphanages would think of themselves as helplessly dependent on the charity of others. Reducing this risk further was the expectation that the children would help others. Very much in the tradition of responsible compassion, with recipients of assistance expected to cut wood or sew garments for others, orphans were expected to help others. Much of this was simply the result of the work required to keep the orphanage clean and the children fed. Part of it was the expectation that the older children at the orphanage would extend help to the younger children, not only by taking on more responsibility in general but also by such acts as helping the younger ones with lessons and schoolwork. Children in orphanages, however, were typically encouraged to provide what modest help they could for others in need. McKenzie (1996) recalls this aspect of his life in "The Home" with some amazement. He tells the story of his first Christmas there, when, after the Christmas tree had been decorated, "we each were encouraged to drop a contribution in a stocking as we passed by the tree. Here was a group of orphans encouraged to give to the disadvantaged!" (p. 80).

Maybe it should not be surprising that children who grow up in an orphanage often do not feel as though they are particularly different or disadvantaged. They are when compared from a distance, but from the perspective of the children in orphanages, the differences often do not seem important. According to McKenzie (1996),

> Much of life at The Home was decidedly different from the way other children grew up in the 1950s, but much of it was ordinary, taken as a matter of course and routine, as other children take the daily events of their lives. . . . We knew we lacked many things, but what we didn't have in the way of opportunities and material things were no big deal, at least at the time. (p. 165)

Also, compared with the disruptive and dysfunctional situations that most children raised in orphanages had previously experienced, and which they considered their most likely alternative, orphanages provided a sense of place, permanence, and security. Orphanages surely did not provide the love and warmth of normal family life (McKenzie mentions several times in *The Home* that he did not get enough hugs), but they consisted of people helping children, often with genuine concern and compassion. They attempted, generally successfully, to avoid the "impersonal and mechanical" charity that was anathema in the tradition of responsible compassion discussed by Olasky (1992). McKenzie did not get the hugs he craved and that he would have received in an ideal world. He does, however, remember fondly

> Mrs. Kay, who was my housemother for . . . three years . . . and who made more cookies for us at her own expense than she should have, sent me a birthday card every year after I left The Home until she died. . . . My aunts had stopped sending cards when I was in my early teens. (p. 186)

The prevailing view of the decline of orphanages is surely that they declined because society would no longer tolerate the Dickensian squalor children experienced. This view cannot be supported by the evidence of what at least the vast majority of orphanages were really like. Certainly, growing up in an orphanage was not what most people would describe as ideal, and many would describe it as harsh. The path from a dependent child to a responsible adult, however, is seldom an easy one, no matter what the setting. Much of what appeared harsh in the lives of those in orphanages (e.g., the work requirements) was not only necessary if poor children were to be provided for materially but also an essential part of the responsible compassion that gives poor children the best chance of becoming productive adults.

## ▓ Conclusion

Why, if orphanages were providing a vital function, and providing it well, did they decline? My thesis is that they succumbed to the centralization of government functions in general and charitable functions in particular. The rationale put forth for much of this centralization was that efforts to solve problems privately, and at the state and local levels, were not adequate, and therefore the federal government had to assume responsibility. Leaving aside for the moment the sincerity or validity of this rationale, it was acted on and, as it was, became something of a self-fulfilling prophesy. Consider the following observation of Fukuyama (1995):

The original argument for the expansion of state responsibilities to include social security, welfare, unemployment insurance, training, and the like was that the organic communities of preindustrial society that had previously provided those services were no longer capable of doing so as a result of industrialization, urbanization, decline of extended families, and related phenomena. But it proved to be the case that the growth of the welfare state accelerated the decline of those very communal institutions that it was designed to supplement. Welfare dependency in the United States is only the most prominent example. (p. 313)

Surely, orphanages, communal institutions that were nourished primarily by local efforts, were victims of the centralization of welfare.

The centralization that has done so much to hamper, and diminish, local arrangements for addressing problems has not been motivated solely by good, if often misguided, intentions. The desire of organized interest groups for more taxpayer dollars has been at least as important as concern over the efficient and compassionate use of these dollars in explaining the persistent pressure to shift government decisions and programs to the federal level. After the shift and after politically influential groups alter their actions to best take advantage of the centralized power, the pressure to maintain the centralization intensifies.

Certainly, this describes the politics of orphanages. Child care and public welfare professionals are close to uniform in opposing any suggestion that improvements can be made in child care with policies encouraging more reliance on orphanages as an alternative of maintaining children in dysfunctional families.[7] The opposition to orphanages is typified by Belinda Hare, regional recruiter for children protective services in Austin, Texas, when she said (as quoted in "Newt May Need Home," 1994, p. 10), "All research out there shows that childhood institutionalized care has adverse effects on a child's psychological and emotional well-being."[8] No doubt, child care and public welfare professionals sincerely believe that their views on orphanages are in the best interests of children. It would be naive, however, not to recognize how easy it is for all of us to sincerely believe that what is good for us is in the public interest. The larger the number of children placed in orphanages, the more difficult it would be to maintain the necessary political support for continuing, and expanding, public funding for existing government programs that provide assistance to families. Also, as suggested earlier, these public assistance programs, even when they were far worse for children than an orphanage would have been, helped undermine the orphanage alternative. With checks going to families to maintain children at home, parents (often single parents without the ability or interest to care adequately for a child) are given an incentive to keep at home children who would be better served in an orphanage.

It cannot be overemphasized that my argument is not that orphanages can ever be better than a stable and loving family. Such families, however, are not a realistic option for many children. Not all families are stable and loving, and they can, and often do, deprive children of the stability, discipline, and material well-being they need to develop into responsible adults. Orphanages have been able and can continue to offer the best opportunity for many children to realize some of the advantages that loving intact families would, in an ideal world, provide all children.

## ▓ Notes

1. One way to accomplish this is to impose credentialing requirements on those who provide care for the poor, with these requirements often having more to do with increasing costs and restricting the competition faced by the "experts" than with helping the poor.

2. In 1929, total government receipts were $11 billion and total federal government receipts were $3.8 billion—the federal government received 34.5% of all government receipts. In 1991, total government receipts were $1,746.8 billion and total federal government receipts were $1,122.2 billion—the federal government received 64.2% of all government receipts. Data were taken from U.S. Department of Commerce, Bureau of Economic Analysis (1993, Tables 3.1 [p. 55] and 3.2 [p.56]) and from U.S. Department of Commerce, Office of Economics (1992, Tables 3.1 and 3.2 [p. 66]).

3. For a more complete discussion, see McKenzie and Staaf (1978).

4. For a consideration of some of the implications of the benefits from the act of giving for private charity, see Lee and McKenzie (1990).

5. According to economists Bennett and DiLorenzo (1994, p. 96), "Only a minuscule proportion of donors takes the effort to check out charities to which they contribute."

6. Charles Murray brilliantly illustrates this problem in his 1984 book *Losing Ground* when he discusses the considerable difficulty that would be encountered in designing a government program (even an extremely well-financed program) to help people quit smoking.

7. We know of no study aimed at determining the percentage of child care and public welfare professionals who dismiss orphanages as an acceptable alternative to such programs as Aid to Families with Dependent Children, but this is probably because the results of such a study would surprise no one.

8. For evidence that Ms. Hare overstated her case, see McKenzie (1995).

## ▓ References

Bennett, J. T., & DiLorenzo, T. J. (1994). *Unhealthy charities: Hazardous to your health and wealth.* New York: Basic Books.

Fukuyama, F. (1995). *Trust: The social virtues and the creation of prosperity.* New York: Free
    Press.
Lee, D. R., & McKenzie, R. B. (1990, January). Second thoughts on the public-Good justification
    for government poverty programs. *Journal of Legal Studies, 19*(1), 189-202.
McKenzie, R. B. (1995). *Orphanages: Did they throttle the children in their care?* Minneapolis,
    MN: Center of the American Experiment.
McKenzie, R. B. (1996). *The Home: A memoir of growing up in an orphanage.* New York: Basic
    Books.
McKenzie, R. B., & Staaf, R. (1978). Revenue sharing and monopoly government. *Public Choice,
    33,* 93-97.
Murray, C. (1984). *Losing ground: American social policy, 1950-1980.* New York: Basic Books.
Newt may need home [Editorial]. (1994, December 14). *Waco Tribune-Herald,* p. 10.
Olasky, M. (1992). *The tragedy of American compassion.* Washington, DC: Regnery.
U.S. Department of Commerce, Bureau of Economic Analysis. (1993, February). *National income
    and product accounts of the United States: Volume 1, 1929-1958.* Washington, DC: U.S.
    Government Printing Office.
U.S. Department of Commerce, Office of Economics. (1992, July). *Survey of current business.*
    Washington, DC: U.S. Government Printing Office.

# CHAPTER 12

# Who Will Mow the Lawn at Boys Town?

## Child Labor Laws in an Institutional Setting

MARGARET MACFARLANE WRIGHT

W hen asked to explain why they are supportive of childhoods spent in both public and private institutions, orphans respond over-whelmingly that the discipline and work ethic by which they were reared proved to be a valuable tool in shaping both character and career (see Chapter 7). The responsibility of domestic chores and horticultural duties equipped these young people early on with emotional skills to carry the burden eventually placed on them as adults as productive members of society. Although abuses may have existed, orphans report that, on the whole, the system worked.

Growing frustration with a foster care system, which to many apparently "fosters" only the routine waste of human potential, has led to a reconsidera-tion of the child care institution,[1] or orphanage, as a viable alternative (Morganthau, 1994). Given the emphasis prior inhabitants placed on "hard work" as an integral component of their institutional care success, any reconsideration of the orphanage must contain, as a foundational inquiry, the viability of incorporating those work practices of the orphanages of "yester-year" or their present-day equivalents into a revamped institutional setting. The title of this chapter, "Who Will Mow the Lawn at Boys Town?" is appropriate simply because directors of homes must be concerned with whether or not the laws and regulations in their particular states will allow their children residents to mow the grass (and more demanding jobs relating to campus farms and maintenance shops) and, if so, with the size and power of the lawn mowers (and other pieces of equipment). These issues are critical to the question of whether or not orphanages will be resurrected because they will affect the cost of orphanage care. The more work children are allowed, and required, to do, the lower the cost of orphanage care and the greater the number of children who can be cared for in orphanages. Also, some work experience can be beneficial to the children, as the alumni report their work experience was beneficial to them.

This chapter examines what work activities were part and parcel of the "traditional orphanage" and whether these same activities could be undertaken in a "reconsidered" orphanage system given present-day child labor laws. This chapter also provides recommendations to enable these work activities to be incorporated into a revamped orphanage child care system. The emphasis herein is on whether, legally speaking, we "can go home again" and not whether we should do so.

I have found that homes do have (depending on the state) wide latitude in asking the children to work. Some work activities undertaken by children in orphanages decades ago, however, cannot be done by children today without a change in the law. Also, even the most favorable reading of the covered laws relating to child labor suggests that children in resurrected orphanages are not allowed to work as much and for as long and as hard as can children in families. Also, the orphanages' liability for damages in the event children are hurt while working may preclude many institutions from working their children as much as the law allows. Obviously, reforms in liability laws should be considered.

## ▓ The Traditional Orphanage

The "traditional orphanage" as referred to in this chapter consists of a structured living environment. Children are housed in buildings that provide abode to a number of inhabitants in somewhat barracks-like organization, and several adults supervise these children. Children are segregated in the housing units typically by age and gender. The orphanage provides schooling to the younger children in its care. Attendance at public schools by older children entering junior high and high school is normally mandatory to integrate the children into a "typical" school atmosphere (see Note 1).

Children are provided vocational training at the orphanage site. Older children, however, are encouraged to seek outside employment where possible. The orphanage may be located in a city setting, but more likely than not the traditional orphanage is located in a rural setting, with substantial property and grounds that must be maintained. These grounds in turn provide crops and farm products that aid the institution to be partially, if not fully, self-supporting.

The traditional orphanage is usually private, often sponsored and financially supported in large part by charitable or religious groups. Accordingly, religious instruction is normally part of the children's rearing.

## ▨ Types of Activity

The previous description of the traditional orphanage was modeled after Barium Springs Presbyterian Home for Children, Barium Springs, North Carolina. Barium Springs was founded in the late 1800s. This institution operated according to the previous description until approximately the mid-1960s. At that time, the focus of Barium Springs changed, taking on the characteristics of current child care institutions.[2] Prior to this shift, the work activities of Barium Springs were typical of the traditional orphanage of that period. The following is a list of some of the more common work activities undertaken by the orphans at Barium Springs in the 1950s:[3]

1. Operation of tractors, haymakers, trucks, and other motorized farm equipment
2. Operation of a school printing press
3. Cobbler duties (use of repair equipment, including hammer and nails)
4. Operation of motorized sewing machines
5. Care and maintenance of vegetable gardens
6. Harvesting crops in the fruit orchards (excess sold for profit)
7. Ditch digging in conjunction with outside pipe and sprinkler installation and repair
8. Mowing lawns surrounding Barium Spring's acreage on motorized small "John Deere-type" residential tractors
9. Care and feeding of dairy cattle and other farm animals (dairy products were sold for profit)

10. Light and heavy carpentry and painting
11. Yard maintenance with nonmotorized tools including tree trimming
12. Housekeeping, including making beds, folding clothes, dishes, and so on

The performance of these chores by children at Barium Springs differed according to the age of the child. Normally, the "older" children took part in the more hazardous type of activities—those associated with both light and heavy motorized machinery, such as operation of tractors, haymakers, and manure spreaders. It was not unusual, however, for children under the age of 16 to participate in the operation of small motorized mowing equipment, operation of a printing press, and strenuous manual labor in the form of assisting in picking crops and fruits grown on the orphanage grounds. Both younger and older children participated in caring for the farm animals and in undertaking household chores.

As mentioned previously, during approximately the mid-1960s, these work activities at Barium Springs were discontinued due to not only a philosophical change of focus but also economic and legal concerns. Assuming, as this discussion does, that these types of chores or their present-day equivalents are desired to be reinstituted in the modern-day, reformatted orphanage, however, to what degree would present-day child labor laws prohibit this inclusion?

## Federal Child Labor Law

The federal body of law that governs child labor practices in the United States is the Federal Fair Labor Standards Act of 1938 (FLSA) (Ireland, 1937).[4] The federal law was designed as a "safety net" with regard to child labor; the purpose of the FLSA was to set a "minimum" standard that employers must obey for the employment of children. Although states can enact more stringent guidelines, they cannot enact lesser standards of child labor conditions.[5]

## Application of the FLSA to Orphanages

The FLSA (1997, 29 U.S.C.S. § 201, *et seq.*) contains a number of provisions that, when taken together, cast a broad prohibition of employment of child labor in interstate commerce. In particular, FLSA prohibits any producer, manufacturer, or dealer from shipping or delivery for shipment in commerce any goods produced in an establishment situated in the United States in or about which within thirty days prior to the removal of such goods therefrom any *oppressive child labor* [italics added] has been employed. (29 U.S.C.S. § 212)

Oppressive child labor is defined (29 U.S.C.S. § 203 (l)) essentially as a condition in which any employee under the age of 16 years is employed by an employer in any occupation or any employee between the ages of 16 and 18 years is employed in an occupation found by the secretary of labor to be particularly hazardous to their health or well-being.

The avowed purpose of the FLSA's broad prohibition was not merely to regulate oppressive child labor but also to abolish it (*Mitchell v. Munier,* 1958). The abolishment was to serve essentially a threefold purpose: (a) to protect life and limb of children, (b) to promote school attendance, and (c) to prevent inexpensive child labor from depressing wages of adult counterparts (*Shultz v. Brannon,* 1970).[6]

## ▓ Child Labor as "Commerce" to Warrant FLSA Application

Although the reach of the federal child labor statutes is substantial, they are not without limits. This statutory scheme comes into play only when and if the employment of the child is rendered in "interstate commerce," the constitutional authority or "hook" for federal intervention in this area. At the time of passage of the FLSA, opposition to abusive child labor had become a particularly attractive political cause to foster. Consequently, when Congress defined "commerce" in the FLSA, the intent was to give the broadest possible meaning so as to include all transactions, conditions, and relationships known and acknowledged as constituting commerce in the constitutional sense (*Bell v. Porter,* 1946; *United States v. Darby,* 1941).[7] The result was a definition that includes all "trade, commerce, transportation, transmission, or communication among the several States or between any State and any place outside thereof" (FLSA, 1997, 29 U.S.C.S. 203(b)). Given this broad definition of commerce, would the previously listed work activities undertaken at Barium Springs be precluded from incorporation into the reformed orphanage of today by FLSA interference?[8] Courts generally look to whether the "interstate activities" are "substantial in character."[9] More than likely, these activities would be found to be of a truly local nature, either because they were undertaken solely on the grounds of the orphanage facility and sold for local consumption or because they were of an isolated and infrequent nature. It is doubtful, therefore, that the FLSA would apply.

Because of the repugnant nature of child labor, however, courts may be willing to find commerce not otherwise fitting within a traditional definition. To this end, judicial scrutiny of the previously listed activities might find commerce present in Item 6, crops grown and harvested by the children. Commerce might also be found in the production and sale of surplus dairy products (Item 9) if these products ended up in the stream of commerce for profit. Although judicial interference may be unlikely, the uncertainty of court intervention and the dire consequences of violating the FLSA may in fact effectively preclude the "reformed" orphanages from allowing children to participate in these activities.

### ▓ Institutional Children as "Employees"

Even assuming a court's finding that the products of a child's labor, either crops or dairy products and the like, are put into interstate commerce, the FLSA may still not apply unless it can be found that orphanages are in fact "employers" of employees under the age of 16 years.

The FLSA defines employee as "any individual employed by an employer" (FLSA, 1997, 29 U.S.C.S. § 203 (e) (1)). The categorization of employee is generally determined by the underlying economic realities of the situation. This is illustrated in *Bernal v. Baptist Fresh Air Home Soc.* (1949). In this case, a child older than 14 but younger than 16 years of age attended a free fresh-air camp run by a charitable society and performed chores without compensation; such chores were reciprocated by other campers in the same age group. After the youth was injured in the kitchen while doing chores, a lawsuit was brought claiming a violation of the FLSA.

The court refused to impose liability on the camp, holding that the youth was not an employee within the meaning of the term employee in the federal labor law. The *Bernal* court[10] found that

> [t]he words employer and employee are used in the act in the common-law understanding of those words. They denote a contractual relation, not a mere casual voluntary rendition of a slight service or favor reward by a gratuity. . . . A relationship of employer and employee must be shown to exist before either the Labor Law or Education Code will be applicable. In this case there was no contract of hire or master and servant relationship between plaintiff

and defendant; conducting the camp was not a business or an enterprise of a commercial character self-supporting and available to the general public; no alternative of payment was permitted; and the attendance here unlike attendance in penal or quasi-penal institutions, was purely voluntary. (*Coverage Under the Fair Labor Standards Act,* 1996)[11]

Although *Bernal* found the employment relationship lacking, other courts have not hesitated to find an employment relationship to serve the avowed purpose of the FLSA—to eliminate child labor. One court imposed FLSA restrictions on the labor of children where there was neither actual knowledge of the child's labor on behalf of the employer nor an agreement, express or implied, to compensate the child. In *Mitchell v. Howard* (1959), a minor was deemed employed within the meaning of the child labor provisions of the FLSA (1997, 29 U.S.C.S. § 203(g)), when the employer raised no objection to one of his truck-driver employees letting a brother under the age of 18 ride on the truck and give some assistance. Although the details of the pay arrangement between the brothers were unknown to the employer, it was nonetheless found that the employer did know that the minor was riding with, and assisting, his brother.[12] Hence, an employment relationship was found for purposes of the FLSA.

## ▓ Institutional Labor

Courts have routinely applied the provisions of the FLSA, both with regard to permissible child labor and minimum wage and hour standards, to "civilly committed" persons, be they at mental institutions (*Souder v. Brennan,* 1973; *Wyatt v. Aderholt,* 1974; *Wyatt v. Stickney,* 1972) or children adjudged wards of the juvenile court.

In *King v. Carey* (1975), the New York Federal District Court found that a child civilly committed to a state camp operated by the state's division of youth had the benefit of the child labor laws.[13] Arguments that labor of the inhabitants of such institutions (and by analogy, orphanages) was therapeutic and beneficial such as to exempt it from the federal statutory scheme was soundly rejected by the King court:

The fallacy of the argument that the work of patient-worker is therapeutic can be seen in extension to its logical extreme, for the work of most people, inside and out of institutions, is therapeutic in the sense that it provides a sense of accomplishment, something to occupy the time, and a means to earn one's

way. Yet that can hardly mean that employers should pay workers less for
what they produce for them. (p. 813, 367 F. Supp. 808)[14]

Given these parameters, it is feasible that work performed at the insistence of
the orphanage, supervised by the orphanage staff, and for which the orphanage
derives some economic benefit may result in the orphan being classified as
an employee for FLSA purposes. Of the 12 work activities listed previously,
activities that might fit within this "economic reality" are those with some
direct or indirect benefit to the orphanage employer. Harvesting of fruit
orchards, gathering of dairy products, and perhaps collection of vegetables
from orphanage gardens for resale may be a precursor to FLSA inclusion. To
the extent that any of the work activities mentioned are found within the
umbrella of the FLSA, all of the other activities are subject to FLSA regulation
as well.[15]

## ▩ The FLSA in Application

Application of the FLSA to work activities of children does not result in an
absolute ban on child labor per se. On the contrary, the FLSA specifically
authorizes a number of work activities that children can undertake. Furthermore, the FLSA provides a number of exclusions, exceptions, and exemptions
that permit children to undertake what might otherwise be considered more
strenuous or hazardous "adult" labor.

### Specifically Permitted Activities

The statutory provisions of the FLSA are supplemented and further
defined by the Code of Federal Regulations (CFR). To the extent the FLSA
either refers to or is silent as to specifics and definitions, the CFR may
supplement its provisions. For instance, the FLSA (1997), in 29 U.S.C.S. §
212, states that employment by youths between the ages of 16 and 18 in
occupations that are found by the "secretary of labor to be particularly
hazardous" are prohibited. To determine what exactly the secretary of labor
has deemed particular hazardous, one must resort to the CFR.

In this regard, the secretary of labor has determined not only what
occupations are hazardous (discussed later) but also what occupations are not.
Both categories of prohibited and nonprohibited activities are specified by the
secretary of labor in various provisions of the CFR. Consequently, even

assuming that all the listed work activities of Barium Springs are within the reach of the FLSA, not all are automatically prohibited as a result.

### Traditional Teenage Employment

The regulations contained in the CFR permit minors between the ages of 14 and 16 (29 CFR § 570.34) to undertake the more traditional type of nonmanufacturing jobs. Permitted activities include office and clerical work, including the operation of office machines; errand, bagging, and delivery work, including carrying out customers' orders and delivery work by foot, bicycle, and public transportation; and light to heavy housekeeping chores, including use of vacuum cleaners and floor waxers.

Also, traditional types of yard maintenance activities normally associated with gainful youth employment are permitted. The use of power-driven mowers or cutters, however, is prohibited. Kitchen work, which permits children to work in food service establishments, is also permitted, as is preparation and serving of food and beverages. Regulations permit the children of this age group to operate machines including dishwashers, toasters, dumbwaiters, popcorn poppers, milk shake blenders, and coffee grinders.

Automotive service and repair work is also authorized by the CFR. This permits children in this age group to work in connection with cars and trucks if confined to the dispensing of gasoline and oil, courtesy service, and car cleaning, washing, and polishing (but this does not include the use of pits, racks, or lifting apparatus or the inflation of any tire mounted on a rim equipped with a removable retaining ring). Finally, children are permitted to participate in limited retail agricultural work including cleaning vegetables and fruits, and wrapping, sealing, labeling, weighing, pricing, and stocking goods when performed in "safe areas."[16]

As can be seen, those nonmanufacturing, less hazardous activities traditionally associated with "teenage employment" are authorized by the FLSA. With these permitted activities in mind, several items on the list of "chores" at Barium Springs would be permitted under the FLSA and concomitant CFR regulations. Care and maintenance of vegetable gardens (Item 5), yard maintenance with nonmotorized tools (Item 11), and housekeeping (Item 12) would all be permitted under the current FLSA restrictions and guidelines.

### Prohibited Activities Under the FLSA

The emphasis of the FLSA is clearly to shield the child from harm due to instruments and machinery that the child is simply too young to master and that can result in great bodily harm. The provisions of the FLSA reflect this congressional concern. Occupations that are forbidden to minors between 14 and 16 years of age include those tasks traditionally associated with manufacturing, mining, or processing that normally require the operation of power-driven machinery other than office-type machinery (29 CFR § 570.33).[17]

Many of the work activities engaged in by the children of Barium Springs fall within these otherwise prohibited activities. Operation of haymakers, tractors, and other heavy farm-type equipment would not be allowed by children 14 to 16 years of age under the CFR regulations unless an exemption, exception, or exclusion was available.

## ▓ Exclusions From the FLSA

### *The Parental Exception*

Excepted from the definition of "oppressive child labor" is the employment of any employee under the age of 16 who is employed by "a parent or person standing in place of a parent" in an occupation other than in manufacturing, mining, or an occupation deemed by the secretary of labor to be particularly hazardous for children between ages 16 and 18 (FLSA, 1997, 29 U.S.C.S. § 203 (l)). This exclusion focuses on allowing children to work for and with the supervision of a parent or similarly situated adult. Many of the more hazardous activities involving operation of motorized vehicles would fall under this exclusion. This exclusion does not consider where and the type of work that is performed (other than manufacturing) but only whether the child is employed by the parent.

### *Family Farm Exclusion*

In addition to a "parental" exclusion, the FLSA contains a "family farm" exclusion (FLSA, 1997, 29 U.S.C.A. § 203 (c)), permitting children less than 12 years of age to be employed in agriculture (outside of school hours) if such employee is employed by a parent or a person standing in the place of a parent on a farm owned or operated by such parent or person. Such exclusion is extended if the child is employed with the consent of his or her parent or person standing in the place of his or her parent on a farm that does not routinely employ more than 500 workers.

Neither the FLSA nor the CFR regulations define the term *farm.* Conceivably, a farm could be defined with regard to acreage or the principal use of that acreage. Given that this definition does not exist, however, it is also conceivable that farm could be acreage, any part of which is committed to the production of crops or products for input into the stream of interstate commerce. Again, because there are no specific legal guidelines in this regard, orphanages such as Barium Springs might qualify for this exclusion due to the farm-like nature of the chores and the potential qualification of parent status for purposes of the FLSA.

### Assisting a Parent Exclusion

In addition to the parental exclusion (employing your child) and family farm exclusion (employing your child to work on a farm), another exclusion from the definition of oppressive child labor exists. A child 12 or 13 years old may be employed with the consent of the parent or person standing in the place of the parent, regardless of the ownership or type of farm, if he or she works along side his or her parents or a person standing in such stead. Literally, children in this age category may accompany their parents or persons standing in the place of parents in agricultural pursuits, regardless of the nature of hazardous activity undertaken.

Because parental supervision and not ownership of the farm at which the labor is being rendered appears to be the prerequisite for this exclusion, if the child's work is performed in conjunction with and under the supervision of a caregiver, ostensibly standing in the place of a parent, children in this age group could undertake the more arduous and strenuous farm-type chores undertaken by their Barium Springs counterparts. Note that in this particular category, there are no restrictions with regard to participation of the child in agricultural activities otherwise deemed hazardous.[18] If the child is under age 16, he or she may be employed in an agricultural occupation declared hazardous for children under 16 if such child is employed by his or her parent or by a person standing in the place of his or her parent on a farm[19] owned or operated by such parent or person.

## ■ The Institution as Parent Under the FLSA

Neither the FLSA nor the CFR define "standing in place of a parent." Orphanages, although serving the functional equivalent of a parent regarding the day-to-day activities of child rearing, are not normally charged with the role of legal guardian. In determining the type of care for a child or institution in which a child will be placed, state procedures normally require that the child become a ward of the juvenile court, which retains jurisdiction over the child in the strict legal sense.[20] Once a ward of the court, a social worker is appointed for the child who has limited consensual rights as to such child. Notwithstanding the reservation of legal jurisdiction over the child by the courts and social workers, however, parental rights, including the right to consent, are generally not terminated save formal adoption of the child.[21] Consequently, while the child is in the custody of the institution, the "legal" status of parent is retained by the parent if available or by the court if the parent is not available. It is doubtful that the institution would stand in the stead of a parent, effectively precluding the institution from engaging the child in a number of the activities that might otherwise be available upon parental oversight[22] or consent,[23] unless formal steps were taken by the institution to become the child's guardian.

### Nonparental Exemptions

Although much more limited than the parental exclusions, nonparental employers can also employ children in agriculture in certain circumstances by virtue of educational and work-related exemptions.

A detailed statutory scheme is set forth in 29 CFR § 570.72 that exempts children below the age of 16 from child labor law constraints in the agricultural setting, provided all conditions are met. These conditions include enrollment by the minor in an approved vocational education training program.

Furthermore, pursuant to the Federal Extension Service, minors 14 years old or older may undertake otherwise hazardous activities, such as the operation of tractors and other farm machinery, upon completion of the requirements of education and training set forth in the regulation, including both written and practical training on the use of the vehicles and machinery.[24]

## ▓ State Child Labor Laws

Each of the 50 states has enacted laws prohibiting the employment of children in hazardous occupations within its borders. These state statutes are remedial[25] in nature and are directed at the employer, both in obligations and liability,[26] and not at the child or his or her parent or guardian. As mentioned previously, state child labor standards cannot fall below federal child labor legislation, but there is no restriction on the upward standards set by each state (FLSA, 1997, 29 U.S.C.S. § 218 (a)). State laws generally follow the same legislative scheme as the federal law, although several states have far stricter standards.

Like the FLSA, many state child labor laws prohibit child labor below the age of 16 or between the ages of 16 and 18 in activities categorized by the secretary of labor as hazardous. Like the FLSA, state laws routinely provide exemptions and exclusions from child labor prohibitions. The exemptions, however, are based primarily on work and educational permits rather than broad parental exclusions. An examination of all states is prohibitive.[27] California laws, indicative of a majority of the state labor laws, will be briefly discussed.

### California Labor Law

The general rule regarding the work activities of minors in California is found in California Labor Code § 1290 (1997). This section states that no minor under the age of 16 years shall be employed, permitted, or "suffered to work" in connection with any manufacturing establishment or other place of labor or employment at any time except pursuant to specific statutory exemptions.[28]

California Labor Code § 1292 (1997) specifically sets forth activities in which persons under age 16 are prohibited from being employed, primarily including any occupation requiring the operation of motorized equipment and machinery.[29] With regard to the listed activities undertaken by the children of Barium Springs, under California state law, Items 1 (operation of tractors, haymakers, and motorized farm equipment), Item 2 (operation of a school printing press), Item 4 (operation of motorized sewing machines), Item 8 (lawn mowing with small motorized lawn mowers), Item 9 (care and feeding of farm animals), and Item 10 (light and heavy carpentry and painting) would more than likely be prohibited.[30]

### Permitted Activities Under California Law

Like the FLSA, California statutes specifically provide for areas of employment in which minors, within certain age limits, can engage. These activities are set forth in California Labor Code § 1294.3 (1997) (minors 14 and 15 years of age may be employed in the listed occupations not otherwise prohibited). The list confines child labor to the traditional type of nonmanufacturing work, including office, clerical, bagging, and delivery work (by foot, bicycle, and public transportation). Like the federal law, cleanup work, including the use of vacuum cleaners and floor waxers, is permitted, as are traditional types of nonmotorized lawn maintenance. Kitchen work and light housekeeping are also permitted. Again, like the federal law, limited or "light" types of retail agricultural activities, such as cleaning vegetables and fruits and stocking goods, are also permitted.

### Parental Exclusions

Although California law is stringent with regard to manufacturing and child labor, California law, like federal law, does not take such a stance with regard to child labor performed with the supervision or oversight of a parent. Excluded from the definition of prohibited child employment activity is employment of minors in any agricultural, horticultural, viticulture, or domestic labor during the time the public schools are not in session or during other than school hours, when the work performed is for or under the control of his or her parent or guardian (California Labor Code, 1997, § 1394). This exemption does not require that the work be done in or on a family farm-type setting. Rather, it envisions the child working in a family-owned or -operated business, no matter where it is located.

### Agricultural Exemption

Like federal law, California has an agricultural exemption that is broad and was initially designed to facilitate the "family farm" environment. As long as a child is under the care of his or her parent or guardian, the child can engage in agricultural hazardous activity. Those activities listed previously undertaken at Barium Springs, including the use of motorized equipment, carpentry tools, and the like, would be permissible if the orphanage or institutional setting acted in the capacity of a guardian.[31]

### Exemptions

Children under the age of 16 are permitted to engage in otherwise prohibited activities pursuant to certain specialized programs. Of particular interest is the exclusion found in California Labor Code § 1295 (1) (1997), which exempts courses of training in vocation or manual training schools or in state institutions. Although penal institutions may in fact have been the intended recipient of this exemption, the statute does not differentiate between civilly and criminally committed institutional occupants. These work and training exemptions theoretically permit children in institutional care in this state to undertake most if not all the activities set forth on the previous referenced list.[32]

## ▓ Guardian Under State and Federal Law

Like the FLSA term "standing in the place of a parent," the term "guardian" is not defined in the body of law that regulates child labor. Family law including guardianship of children, however, has always been a highly local form of law in the American federalism scheme. Consequently, the term guardian is defined under local law. Most likely, the FLSA term standing in the place of parent would be construed pursuant to local law as well.[33]

California Probate Code § 2350 (1997) defines guardian as the "guardian of the person" (rather than conservator of "property"). The appointment of a guardian requires a court order after hearing.[34] The California Probate Code provides for the appointment of both nonprofit charitable corporations and individuals or entities who qualify as a "private professional guardian" to be appointed as guardians.[35] If the child does in fact have a surviving parent or parents, guardianship may still be an option by the institution, provided the parents consent or the courts deem it to be in the best interests of the child (California Welfare and Institutions Code, 1997, § 3041). Appointment as a guardian carries with it the full force of parental authority and, as a result, the option for the child to undertake otherwise excluded work. The child, under the supervision of institutional caregiver or guardian, could have opportunity to undertake chores and duties requiring more responsibility.

### *Liability Considerations*

It is clear that a child care institution has a number of avenues that can be pursued to afford children in its care the opportunity to engage in work that prior occupants have deemed beneficial. Generally, children can work in certain service-type occupations traditionally associated with youth without qualification. Furthermore, if training and education permits are obtained, even more demanding types of activities requiring further skill can also be performed. Finally, if the institution desires to become the legal guardian of the child, all the parental exclusions and exemptions are available as well. In reality, any child at Boys Town can mow the lawn—some using a non-power-driven mower and others, with additional certification and skill, using power-driven mowers—and this is perfectly legal under child labor laws—state and federal.

Compliance with federal and state child labor laws by institutions does not seem to be the problem with reinstituting the chores of Barium Springs into a revamped orphanage of today. The problem, in reality, is twofold: the type of child being placed in the institution of today and the cost to the institution of potentially placing the child and others in harm's way.

### The Institutional Child

The type of child placed in the institutional setting of today is vastly different from the inhabitant of institutions such as Barium Springs or Boys Town. Children placed in the traditional orphanage came to that organization as a result of parental abandonment rather than physical abuse. Abandonment, more often than not, was the result of the inability of the parent or family members to financially care for the child. Although "emotional" abandonment was certainly a by-product of eventual physical abandonment, placement in the orphanage was rarely a result of intervention by authorities for the protection, safety, and physical well-being of the child. Today, most children come into the caregiving "system" as a result of such intervention by authorities. Furthermore, because of the organization of the current system, children who are placed with institutional caregivers are the most emotionally damaged.

For the emotionally healthiest children, attempts are first made to place them in a foster home. If a child has emotional disorders requiring psychiatric aid, the child will be sent to a group home setting in which such help is available. If the child requires additional mental health professionals, it is only then that the child is placed with an orphanage-type institution. Currently, an institution is considered as a last resort. The general hope is that the child will receive the help he or she needs and be placed back into the group home or foster home or be returned to a parent or guardian. With this structure in mind, the notion that the institutional orphanage setting can support minors engaging in work around sometimes dangerous instrumentalities is seen by such caregivers as untenable. The predominant theme discerned from conversations and interviews with institutional child caregivers is that the potential for harm, both to the child and to those who come into contact with him or her, is simply too great. Allowing these children to handle motorized equipment and instruments of agriculture, such as rakes, hammers, hoes, and so on, presents too many hazards. Routine chores normally associated with adolescence, such as household duties, are by far a safer alternative.

## *Liability*

Violation of a state labor statute or a provision of the FLSA by an institution can have severe consequences. The federal and state statutory schemes will exact penalties from the violator. Furthermore, if a child is employed in violation of either a state or federal child labor law, should harm come to the child or a third person the imposition of liability on the institution will be swift and grave.

An institution can be liable for negligence per se or negligence as a matter of course if it is found that the child was illegally employed in violation of a state or federal child labor statute. For instance, in *Tesche v. Best Concrete Products, Inc.* (1958), the father of a boy who had been killed while engaged in work found to be prohibited under California law requested that if the jury found that his son was employed in violation of California Labor Code § 1290, liability would be imposed on the employer per se. Liability would be imposed notwithstanding that there may in fact have been no negligence in the manner in which the deceased boy was supervised by the employer or in the manner in which the boy undertook his activities. In other words, violation of the labor code section itself, regardless of the finding of any further error or fault, was legally sufficient to impose liability on the employer.

In *Tesche* (1958), the court found that such a request was proper, notwithstanding that the son was killed in a cement-mixing machine during the time in which his father was in charge of cleaning up machinery and loose cement at the employer's concrete company's plant. Liability was imposed in *Tesche* notwithstanding the father's consent to his son's "illegal" employment in violation of the California labor statute (dangerous machinery). Consequently, obtaining the parent's consent to an act that is otherwise in violation of a statute is no shield.[36]

Parental consent was found not to be a bar to liability by a South Dakota court as well. In *Strain v. Christians* (1992), a 14-year-old, with the knowledge and consent of his parents and in compliance with federal child labor laws by the employer, was operating a tractor when it overturned and the boy was killed. The parents sued for wrongful death, citing noncompliance with state child labor laws of South Dakota. The defendant employer, in turn, defended on the basis of compliance with federal law and the parent's consent to the boy engaging in operation of the tractor. Noting that the federal law is a floor and not a ceiling, the South Dakota court sided with the parents and rejected all asserted defenses.

In *Strain* (1992), the court acknowledged that the legislature's intent was to discourage employers from hiring children to work in dangerous occupations and not to discourage parents from permitting it. Consequently, even in those situations in which parental consent is obtained, there is no guarantee that liability will be averted on that ground alone (see *Contributory Negligence as a Defense,* 1995; *Liability of Youth Camp,* 1995; *Master's Liability to Servant,* 1995).

If further consideration could be made to placing children in the Boy's Town type of environment as a first resort rather than a last, the type of child that occupies the institution may be better equipped to undertake the more rigorous chores. The entire focus of the foster care system, however, would have to be changed. Occupants of Barium Springs report that the home attempted to foster in the children under its care a sense of independence, to make their way in the world, separate and apart from the family that was unable to care for them. Currently, the foster care system, with its focus on returning the child to the very family unit that was unable to care for him or her, seems to foster dependence. It may not be possible to have it both ways.

With regard to liability, consideration should be given to some method of tempering the liability of the institution that assumes an otherwise parental risk. Because of the potential for liability, most institutions will undoubtedly shy away from engaging a child in the activities undertaken at Barium Springs, especially those dealing with motorized instruments in which the chance of harm is the greatest.[37] Limitations of liability—setting specific dollar amounts that either a child or a third party may obtain from the institution—may be a solution, albeit a harsh one.

This remedy would have to be weighed against the cost that society as a whole would be willing to pay for harm that might be caused by individuals in their learning attempts. The cost of encountering harm in attempts to learn and become self-sufficient may be substantially less than the cost of care for these children who, when they reach adulthood, have not acquired such skills.

## ▓ Notes

1. The term *child care institutions* or orphanages is synonymous with what is known as a "campus" environment. The facility provides children room, board, education, play activities, church, and so on. The reference is to the more self-contained large facility, similar in character to the "Boys Town" model in Nebraska (McKenzie, 1996).

2. The traditional orphanage essentially evolved from an institution that provided room, board, and instruction to children to an institution that provided therapeutic and psychiatric services to emotionally troubled youths.

3. Life at Barium Springs circa 1955 was depicted in the film, *When the Bough Breaks* (n.d.), made during that era. It shows the types of activities undertaken by the children at Barium Springs during that period.

4. The first major attempt to enact child labor legislation was in the Owens-Keating Law of 1916, which prohibited the shipment of goods produced under conditions employing children aged 14 to 16 for more than 8 hours a day. The law was declared unconstitutional 9 months after its adoption by *Hammer v. Dagenhart* (1918). The Federal Child Labor Tax Law of 1919, which prohibited child labor through the taxing power, was also declared unconstitutional in *Baily v. Drexel Furniture Co.* (1922). In 1924, Congress approved the Child Labor Amendment crafting legislation within the confines set out by the Court in the previous decisions. Although popular with a depression-weary populous, the amendment failed to be ratified by eight states. The National Industrial Recovery Act of 1933, drawn as a prohibition on the labor of children under 16 years old, approached child labor from fair competition grounds but was also declared unconstitutional by the Supreme Court. Finally, in 1938, the federal law was passed that is now in place.

5. 29 U.S.C.S. § 218 (c) provides in part: "(a). . . no provision of this Act relating to the employment of child labor shall justify noncompliance with any Federal or State law or municipal ordinance establishing a higher standard than the standard established under this Act."

6.The impact of this third factor cannot be understated. Strong economic concerns, such as the Grange Movement in the late 1800s and early 1900s, effectively prohibited any meaningful enactment of child labor law. It was only with the advent of the political and economic clout of labor unions that the child labor laws were enacted on both a federal and a state level.

7. In determining whether a child labor practice is an activity in commerce, the courts are guided by practical considerations and not by technical conceptions; the test applied is whether the work is so directly and vitally related to the functioning of the instrumentality or facility of interstate commerce as to be, in practical effect, part of it rather than an isolated, local activity.

8. The FLSA was enacted in 1938. To the extent that the activities at Barium Springs would have been found encompassed by the FLSA, the activities would have been prohibited unless arguably within an FLSA exclusionary or exemptive provision. Whether in fact the FLSA standards were enforced during the period in question at Barium Springs or in this general region is another issue and beyond the scope of this discussion.

9. In *Mile High Poultry Farms, Inc. v. Frazier* (1945), the court reasoned that such statutory phrases as "engaged in commerce" or "in the production of goods for commerce" should be qualified by the word substantially or some similar qualifying words (see also *Keen v. Mid-Continent Petroleum Corp,* 1945).

10. Relying in part on *Ferro v. Shinsheimer Estate, Inc.* (1931).

11. Other courts finding an employment relationship lacking include *Wirtz v. Mitchell* (1962), in which it was held that a "colored minor" was never in the employment of a wholesale produce distributor. Regarding the secretary of labor's charge that this minor was employed, the court noted that the distributor had found the minor to be in want of the necessities of life when the minor was but 7 years old. From time to time thereafter, the distributor provided the minor with food and clothing. The distributor took a liking to this child, and this child and the distributor's son played together, often around the stall operated by the distributor at the state farmers market. In addition to giving clothing and food, the distributor, prompted by motives of charity, gave money to the child. On rare occasions, the minor rode, for pleasure, with one of the truck drivers of the distributor but never as an employee of the distributor. The court held that the record was clear that there was no substance to the secretary of labor's charge of employment. In *Shultz v. Hinojosa* (1969), it was

held that the evidence was insufficient to show that minors were "in any sense of the word" employees of a meat processor, where the minors, on occasion, assisted their adult relatives (two girls helping their father and mother, and one boy helping his uncle) in cleaning the killing floor of a meat-processing plant, for which work the adults had been hired on a contract basis.

12. In *Wirtz v. Hart* (1965), it was found that a defendant cotton farmer, with knowledge that at least several minor boys were working as cotton pickers on his farm, "suffered" (to use the statutory language of 29 U.S.C.S. § 203(g)) the employment of child labor, contrary to the provisions of the Fair Labor Standards Act, by allowing the continuation of such labor. The defendant farmer's contention that the children were recruited for such labor by another person, acting in the capacity of an independent contractor, was rejected as "unsound and repugnant in law" because this other person was not engaged in the business of harvesting cotton crops and because the children's work was for the benefit of the defendant farmer. In *Gulf King Shrimp Co. v. Wirtz* (1969), the defendant employer did not contest the fact that minors under the age of 16 did, in fact, work in the company's shrimp-heading shed but argued that an employer must have actual knowledge that another is working for him for that other to be an employee under the act. The court found that the difficulty with this argument was that it placed the employment relationship, and through it the very coverage of the act itself, at the mercy of an employer's subjective understanding. The court stated that employment under the act was as much a matter of circumstance as it was of consensual agreement. The court believed that it need only inquire whether the circumstances were such that the employer either had knowledge that minors were illegally in his employ or else had the opportunity through reasonable diligence to acquire such knowledge. As long as the defendant employer indulged in "conscious myopia and studied indifference," this illegal labor supply, believed the court, would have continued (see also *Wirtz v. Keystone Readers Service, Inc.,* 1968).

13. Such is not the case with regard to penal institutions. Adult prisoners, unlike children of a juvenile court, are presumed to have the mental capacity in undertaking their crime of choice. Hence, with regard to criminally committed inmates, FLSA rules do not normally apply (see *Coverage Under the Fair Labor Standards Act,* U.S.C.S. § 201 of Prisoners Working for Private Individual or Entities Other Than Prisons, Timothy M. Hall, 110 A.L.R. Fed. 839, 1996).

14. See *Nonprofit Charitable Institutions as Coming Within the Operation of Labor Statutes,* 26 A.L.R.2d 1020; *Immunity of Nongovernmental Charity From Liability for Damages in Tort,* 25 A.L.R.2d 29; and 25 A.L.R. 4th 517).

15. Assuming that only Items 6 and 9 of the of 12 activities undertaken involved interstate commerce, the employer will nevertheless be subject to the FLSA as to all activities undertaken (*Abram v. San Joaquin Cotton Oil Co., 1943; Guess v. Montague,* 1943).

16. Areas that are deemed unsafe include work performed in or about a boiler or engine room; work in connection with maintenance or repair of the establishment, machines, or equipment; outside window washing that involves working from window sills; all work requiring the use of ladders, scaffolds, or their substitutes; cooking (except at soda fountains, lunch counters, snack bars, or cafeteria-serving counters) and baking; occupations involving operating, setting up, adjusting, cleaning, oiling, or repairing power-driven food slicers and grinders, food choppers, cutters, and bakery-type mixers; work in freezers and meat coolers and all work in the preparation of meats (with some exceptions); loading and unloading goods to and from trucks, railroads cars, or conveyors; and all occupations in warehouse except office and clerical work.

17. For further prohibited hazardous activities regarding children between the ages of 16 and 18, see 29 CFR § 570.51-63.

18. Activities in agriculture that have been declared hazardous include the following: operating a tractor of over 20 PTO horsepower or connecting or disconnecting an implement or any of its parts to or from such a tractor; operating or assisting to operate (including starting, stopping,

adjusting, feeding, or any other activity involving physical contact associated with the operation) a corn picker, cotton picker, grain combine, hay mower, forage harvester, hay baler, potato differ or mobile pea viner, feed grinder, crop dryer, forage blower, auger conveyor, or the unloading mechanism of a nongravity-type self-unloading wagon or trailer power posthole digger, power post driver, or non-walking-type rotary tiller; operating or assisting to operate (including starting, stopping, adjusting, feeding, or any other activity involving physical contact associated with the operation) trencher or earthmoving equipment, fork lift, potato combine, or power-driven circular band or chain saw; working on a farm in a yard, pen, or stall occupied by a "bull, board or stud horse maintained for breeding purposes, a sow with suckling pigs, or cow with newborn calf (with umbilical cord present)"); felling, bucking, skidding, loading, or unloading timber with butt diameter of more than 6 in.; working from a ladder or scaffold (painting, repairing, or building structures, pruning trees, picking fruit, etc.) at a height of over 20 feet; driving a bus, truck, or automobile when transporting passengers or riding on a tractor as a passenger or helper; working inside a manure pit or a horizontal silo while operating a tractor for packing purposes; manufacturing and storing of explosives; motor vehicle driver and outside helper; coal mining, logging, and sawmill activities; power-driven woodworking; exposure to radioactive substances; power-driven hoisting apparatus; power-driven metal forming; mining other than coal mining; slaughtering and meatpacking; operation of bakery machines; operation of paper-products machines; manufacturing of brick and tile; operation of power-driven saws and shears; wrecking and demolition; roofing; and excavation and certain activities in agriculture (29 CFR § 570.71).

19. The FLSA does not define farm; rather, agriculture is defined in 29 U.S.C.S. § 203 (f) as follows: "Agriculture" includes farming in all its branches and among other things includes the cultivation and tillage of the soil, dairying, the production, cultivation, growing, and harvesting of any agricultural or horticultural commodities (including commodities defined as agricultural commodities in section 15(g) of the Agricultural Marketing Act, as amended [12 U.S.C.S. § 1141j(g)], the raising of livestock, bees, fur-bearing animals or poultry, and any practices (including any forestry or lumbering operations) performed by a farmer or on a farm as incident to or in conjunction with such farming operations, including preparation for market, delivery to storage or to market or to carriers for transportation to market.

20. See California Welfare and Institutions Code § 300, *et seq.,* which sets forth the statutory scheme for adjudging minors as wards of the court together with the further disposition of these children as to foster homes, group homes, and institutional settings.

21. Indeed, the parents remain financially responsible for the child while in the "custody" of the juvenile court (California Welfare and Institutions Code § 202).

22. To further complicate the issue, there is no definition in the FLSA as to what constitutes "standing in the place of a parent."

23. Consequently, if a director of an institution desires to have a child undertake an activity that is exempt with parental consent (or with the consent of a person standing in the place of a parent), the better reasoned approach would be to attempt first to contact the child's parent either directly or through the social worker appointed to the child's case by the court. Should the institution be unable to locate the parent for consent, the next logical step would be to contact the child's social worker to obtain permission from the court for the child to undertake the activity.

24. 29 CFR § 570.50 also provides that children between the ages of 16 and 18 can be employed as apprentices supervised by journeymen or as student learners.

25. For example, in *Cernadas v. Supermarkets Gen* (1983), in determining that the New Jersey statute must be liberally construed, the court found that the child labor law was primarily a piece of remedial social legislation rather than a penal statute.

26. See *Child Labor Laws* (1975). The appendix providing a summary of each state's child labor laws is appended hereto. Although hazardous activity may be defined by each state somewhat

differently, all 50 states' child labor laws, whether enumerating hazardous occupations or not, provide "catch-all" provisions prohibiting employment that is dangerous to the life, limb, health, or morals of the child.

27. See Note 25 for reference to a summary of state child labor law.

28. California Labor Code § 1290: "No minor under the age of 16 years shall be employed, permitted, or suffered to work in or in connection with any manufacturing establishment or other place of labor or employment at any time except as may be provided in this article or by the provisions of Part 27 (commencing with Section 48000) of the Education Code."

29. Further prohibitions are found in California Labor Code § 1293. Pursuant to this particular provision, no minor under the age of 16 years may be employed or permitted to work in any capacity in operating or assisting in operating any of the following machines: (a) Circular or band saws, wood shapers, wood jointers; planers, sandpaper or wood-polishing machinery, and wood-turning or boring machinery; (b) picker machines or machines used in picking wool, cotton, hair, or other material; carding machines; leather-burnishing machines; and laundry machinery; (c) printing presses of all kinds; boring or drill presses; stamping machines used in sheet metal and tinware, paper and leather manufacturing, or in washer and nut factories; metal or paper-cutting machines; and paper-lace machines; (d) corner-staying machines in paper-box factories; and corrugating rolls, such as are used in corrugated paper, roofing, or washboard factories; (e) dough brakes or cracker machinery of any description; and (f) wire or iron-straightening or -drawing machinery; rolling-mill machinery; power punches or shears; washing, grinding, or mixing machinery; calendar rolls in paper and rubber manufacturing; and steam boilers in proximity to any hazardous or unguarded belts, machinery, or gearing.

30. California Labor Code § 1294.1 refers specifically to prohibitions contained in the federal code: "(a) No minor under the age of 16 years shall be employed or permitted to work in either of the following: (1) Any occupation declared particularly hazardous for the employment of minors below the age of 16 years in Section 570.71 of Subpart E-1 of Part 570 of Title 29 of the Code of Federal Regulations, as that regulation may be revised from time to time; (2) Any occupation excluded from the application of Subpart C of Part 570 of Title 29 of the Code of Federal Regulations, as set forth in Section 570.33 and paragraph (b) of Section 570.34 thereof, as those regulations may be revised from time to time. (b) No minor shall be employed or permitted to work in any occupation declared particularly hazardous for the employment of minors between 16 and 18 years of age, or declared detrimental to their health or well-being, in Subpart E of Part 570 of Title 29 of the Code of Federal Regulations, as those regulations may be revised from time to time. (c) Nothing in this section shall prohibit a minor engaged in the processing and delivery of newspapers from entering areas of a newspaper plant, other than areas where printing presses are located, for purposes related to the processing or delivery of newspapers."

31. California law, unlike the FLSA, does not make provision for a child to work in hazardous activities with parental consent.

32. "Exempt from the prohibitions of Cal. Lab. Code § 1292, 1293, 1294, and 1294.5 are:

1. Courses of training in vocational or manual training schools or in state institutions.

2. Apprenticeship training provided in an apprenticeship training program established pursuant to Chapter 4 (commencing with Section 3070) of Division 3.

3. Work experience education programs conducted pursuant to either or both Section 29007.5 and Article 5.5 (commencing with Section 5985) of Chapter 6 of Division 6 of the Education Code, provided that the work experience coordinator determines that the students have been sufficiently trained in the employment or work otherwise prohibited by these sections, if parental approval is obtained, and the principal or the counselor of the student has determined that the progress of the student toward graduation will not be impaired.

Exempt from the prohibitions of Cal. Lab. Code § 1294.1 (Hazardous Activity) as provided by Section 570.72 of Title 29 of the Code of Federal Regulations:

1. Student-learners in a bona fide vocational agriculture program working in the occupations specified in paragraph (1) of subdivision (a) of Section 1294.1 under a written agreement that provides that the student-learner's work is incidental to training, intermittent, for short periods of time, and under close supervision of a qualified person, and includes all of the following:

   A. Safety instructions given by the school and correlated with the student-learner's on-the-job training.
   
   B. A schedule of organized and progressive work processes for the student-learner.
   
   C. The name of the student-learner.
   
   D. The signature of the employer and a school authority, each of whom must keep copies of the agreement.

2. Minors 14 or 15 years of age who hold certificates of completion of either a tractor operation or a machine operation program and who are working in the occupations for which they have been trained. These certificates are valid only for the occupations specified in paragraph (1) of subdivision (a) of Section 1294.1. Farmers employing minors who have completed this program shall keep a copy of the certificates of completion on file with the minor's records.

3. Minors 14 and 15 years old who hold certificates of completion of either a tractor operation or a machine operation program of the United States Office of Education Vocational Agriculture Training Program and are working in the occupations for which they have been trained. These certificates are valid only for the occupations specified in paragraph (1) of subdivision (a) of Section 1294.1. Farmers employing minors who have completed this program shall keep a copy of the certificate of completion on file with the minor's records."

33. Suggestion is made that the FLSA specifically requires this definitional phrase to be decided under the law of the applicable state.

34. See California Probate Code § 2100 *et seq.* for the law governing guardianships and conservatorships.

35. California Probate Code § 2104 (3) provides for a nonprofitable charitable corporation to be appointed as guardian or conservator of a person in this state in certain defined circumstances. California Probate Code § 2341 provides for the appointment of a private professional guardian in defined circumstances.

36. Under the prior statute, a contract employing a minor of the age of 15 years in forbidden places that was entire and required the employee to work 6 days a week for the whole day and while school was in session was prohibited, and the fact that the employee might have been legally employed after school hours on the day on which he was killed while at work did not cure the illegality (*Maryland Cas. Co. v. Industrial Acc. Com.,* 1919). In *Shannon v. Fleishhacker* (1931), no liability was imposed.

37. Children who are in institutional care will find it difficult to obtain a driver's license to operate a motor vehicle because the institution is more likely than not to decline the voucher of liability required of the parent or guardian.

# References

Abram v. San Joaquin Cotton Oil Co., 49 F. Supp. 393 (1943).

Baily v. Drexel Furniture Co., 259 U.S. 20 (1922).

Bell v. Porter, 159 F.2d 117 (1946).

Bernal v. Baptist Fresh Air Home Soc., 275 App. Div. 88, 87 N.Y.S.2d 458, *aff'd* without opinion, 300 N.Y. 486, 88 N.E.2d 720 (1949).

California Labor Code, § 1290, 1292, 1293, 1294, 1295, 1394 (1997).

California Probate Code, § 2100, 2104, 2341, 2350 (1997).

California Welfare and Institutions Code, § 202, 300, 3041 (1997).

Cernadas v. Supermarkets Gen, 471 A.2d 73, 75 (N.J. Super. 1983).

*Child Labor Laws—Time to Grow Up,* 59 Minn. L. Rev. 575 (1975).

Code of Federal Regulations, 29 CFR § 570.

*Contributory Negligence as a Defense to a Cause of Action Based Upon Violation of Statute 10,* A.L.R.2d 853 (1995).

Federal Fair Labor Standards Act of 1938, ch. 676, 52 Stat. 1060, 29 U.S.C.S. § 201, 203, 212, 218, 219 (1997).

Ferro v. Shinsheimer Estate, Inc., 256 N.Y. 398, 401-402 (1931); 176 N.E. 817.

Guess v. Montague, 140 F.2d 500 (1943).

Gulf King Shrimp Co. v. Wirtz, 407 F.2d 508, 21 A.L.R. Fed. 376 (Tex. Ct. App. 5 1969).

Hammer v. Dagenhart, 247 U.S. 251 (1918).

Ireland, T. (1937). *Child labor, as a relic of the Dark Ages.* New York: G. P. Putnam.

Keen v. Mid-Continent Petroleum Corp, 63 F. Supp. 120 (1945).

King v. Carey, 405 F. Supp. 41, 78 CCH Lab. Case 33354 (W.D. N.Y. 1975).

*Liability of Youth Camp, Its Agents or Employees, or of Scouting Leader or Organization for Injury to Child Participating in Program,* 88 A.L.R.3d 1236 (1995).

Maryland Cas. Co. v Industrial Acc. Com., 179 C. 716, 178 P. 858 (1919).

*Master's Liability to Servant Injured by Farm Machinery,* 67 A.L.R.2d 1120 (1995).

McKenzie, R. (1996). *The Home: A memoir of growing up in an orphanage.* New York: Basic Books.

Mile High Poultry Farms, Inc. v. Frazier, 113 Colo. 338, 157 P.2d 125 (1945).

Mitchell v. Howard, 37 CCH Lab. Case 65554 (D.C. Ga. 1959).

Mitchell v. Munier, 38 CCH Lab. Case 65781 (D.C. Cal. 1958).

Morganthau, T. (1994, December 12). The orphanage, is it time to bring them back? *Newsweek,* 28-33.

Shannon v. Fleishhacker, 116 C.A. 258, 2 P.2d 835, 3 P.2d 1020 (1931).

Shultz v. Brannon, 62 CCH Lab. Case 32325 (D.C. Okla. 1970).

Shultz v. Hinojosa, 63 CCH Lab. Case 32369 (D.C. Tex., 1969), *affd* in part and *revd* in part on other grounds (Tex. Ct. App. 5) 432 F.2d 259.

Souder v. Brennan, 367 F. Supp. 808 (D.D.C. 1973).

Strain v. Christians, 483 N.E.2d 783 (1992).

Tesche v. Best Concrete Products, Inc., 160 Cal. App. 2d 256, 325 P.2d 150 (1958).

United States v. Darby, 312 U.S. 100, 61 S. Ct. 451, 85 L.Ed. 609 (1941).

*When the Bough Breaks.* (n.d.). Barium Springs, NC: Barium Springs Home for Children with American Film Services.

Wirtz v. Hart, 52 CCH Lab. Case 31733 (D.C. Tex. 1965).

Wirtz v. Keystone Readers Service, Inc., 282 F. Supp. 871, *affd* (Fla. Ct. App. 5) 418 F.2d 249, 7 A.L.R. Fed. 604 (D.C. Fla. 1968).

Wirtz v. Mitchell, 46 CCH Lab. Case 31387 (D.C. Ga. 1962).

Wyatt v. Aderholt, 503 F.2d 1305 (5th Cir. 1974).

Wyatt v. Stickney, 344 F. Supp. 373, 381 (N.D. Ala. 1972).

# CHAPTER 13

# The Regulation of Orphanages

## A Survey and Critique

MICHAEL DeBOW

Orphanages are subject to extensive regulation—particularly by state governments in the exercise of their licensing authority. As a result, care for children in need is "delivered through a thicket of rules and regulations that are often unnecessary, usually obstructive, and always expensive" (Jones, 1994, p. 18).[1]

This chapter explores the nature of these regulations and offers a starting point for considering how costly these regulations are, how effective they are, and the extent to which government regulations could be expected to impede any revival of orphanage-based child care.

To put these questions in perspective, recall that critics of the revival of orphanages often point to the relatively high costs of orphanage care compared to foster home care. One estimate widely noted is that for Boys Town, which apparently spends approximately $47,000 per year per resident (including educational and treatment operations) (Jendryka, 1994, p. 44). Another estimate, from the pro-foster care Child Welfare League of America, indicates the per child cost of room and board is $36,500 (Collins, 1994, p. 55). How much of the current cost structure of orphanages is dictated by regulatory burdens? How much of this burden could be safely lifted?

## ▪ History of Orphanages and the Structure of Regulation

As explained by Boudreaux and Boudreaux in Chapter 10, the nation's attitude toward orphanages changed dramatically during the period from 1930 to 1960 from one of support and acceptance to one of hostility to such "institutionalized" child care compared with the alternative of foster care. As a result, the number of children in orphanages shrank over this period, and the number of children in the foster care system rose dramatically.[2]

Foster families were said to be the more appropriate placement for the vast majority of children in need of care, with institutional care appropriate only for children with "special needs." For those who shared this outlook— including the social work profession, as described by Boudreaux and Boudreaux in Chapter 10—orphanages "should be turned into smaller, more intensely therapeutic environments for emotionally disturbed children, [whereas] the overwhelming majority of dependent children" belonged in foster homes (Cmiel, 1995, p. 125).

These two ideas—the orphanage as therapeutic and the preference for "home"-like as opposed to institutional environments—can be seen in the regulation of orphanages. Indeed, the most significant regulations can be traced to one or the other of these ideas. (These two ideas are, accordingly, responsible for some portion of the large per child costs of orphanage care noted previously.)

## ▪ The Substance of the Regulations

The regulation of orphanages is primarily the responsibility of state governments.[3] Typically, a state's statutory code will contain a set of statutes dealing with child welfare matters, including the regulation of child care facilities. The statutes generally set out the requirement that such facilities be licensed by the state.

Although the licensure statutes themselves may impose regulatory requirements, very often the statutes delegate the responsibility for fleshing out the regulatory scheme to the state's department of human resources or the like. Pursuant to this delegated authority, the welfare bureaucracy announces the detailed regulations that will govern the creation and operation of orphanages and other child care institutions.

My research focused primarily on the statutes and regulations in six states: Alabama, Florida, Georgia, Massachusetts, South Carolina, and Tennessee. The following descriptions of the main areas of regulation show a good deal of variation among the states. The good news seems to be that there is no "one way" of regulating orphanages. Accordingly, states that now have more expensive regulatory schemes can find models from lower-cost states that presumably do not condemn the children in those jurisdictions to a Dickensian existence. At a minimum, the more demanding states should adopt the standards of the less demanding states. Beyond that, it seems clear that all states should give serious thought to reassessing their general regulatory approach to orphanages.

### Facility Requirements

Traditionally, most orphanages employed barracks-style sleeping arrangements, such as the 1950s living quarters described by Richard McKenzie (1996):

> Sleeping? No private or semiprivate rooms at Larr's, to say the least. We had "sleeping porches"—rooms that extended from three sides of the second floor of the cottage, made of wood and windows, each lined with eight or more beds, each be so tightly made that a quarter would bounce off. There was nothing else—no pillows, no bedspreads—only an old-fashioned quilt folded neatly at the foot of each bed. (p. 35)

Today, regulations often specify a number of attributes that an orphanage's buildings must possess, particularly with respect to the sleeping area and bathroom facilities. These requirements tend to reflect the idea that the orphanage should be, as much as possible, like a "home" environment. This connection is made explicitly in Massachusetts's regulations (Massachusetts Regulations Code, 1998):

> The licensee shall design the living units to simulate the functional arrangements of a home and to encourage a personalized atmosphere for small groups of residents, unless it has been demonstrated that another arrangement is more effective in maximizing the human qualities of the specific population served. (p. 7a)[4]

Similarly, Tennessee's regulations (Tennessee Comp. Rules and Regulations, 1998) state "There must be a family type setting and living arrangements which enhance family living." Requirements designed to attempt a replication of a home-like atmosphere, however, almost certainly have the effect of raising the per child cost of operating orphanages compared with the barracks-type arrangement.

For example, both Florida and Tennessee provide that there can be no more than four children per sleeping room (Florida Administrative Code, 1998). Alabama's regulation states that "Two children per bedroom is recommended, but there shall be no more than three children per bedroom." In addition, no more than 12 children can be housed in any "living unit," and there can be no more than two living units in a single building (Alabama Administrative Code, 1998).

Furthermore, the regulations generally specify a minimum living space in the sleeping area per resident. Florida and South Carolina (South Carolina Code Regulations, 1998) require 50 square feet per resident, whereas Massachusetts requires 50 square feet per person in bedrooms housing two or more children and 70 square feet for single bedrooms. Alabama requires 70 square feet per resident, and Georgia requires 63 square feet in bedrooms housing two or more children and 75 square feet in single bedrooms (Georgia Comp. Rules and Regulations, 1998). (Generally, square footage requirements rule out the counting of closet space toward the total.)

These regulatory schemes also specify minimum bathroom facilities. For example, in Georgia there must be one sink and toilet for every 8 residents and one shower or bathtub for every 10 residents. Alabama's and Massachusetts's requirements are more demanding: one sink and toilet for every 6 residents and one shower or bathtub for every 6 residents.

Some states include aesthetic requirements. Massachusetts directs that "furniture and furnishings" used by the residents be "safe, appropriate, comfortable, and home-like" and "substantially the same as those provided to staff." Furthermore, the orphanage must "provide a means for residents to mount pictures on bedroom walls, for example, by means of peg-board or cork strips, and to have other decorations." Similarly, Florida provides that "[c]hildren shall have the opportunity to personalize their bedrooms with furnishings and possessions."

The combination of these regulations has the effect of ruling out a barracks-type sleeping arrangement for the residents of orphanages. It seems reasonable to assume that the construction costs for the types of residential facilities required by present-day regulations exceed those of the older, barracks-style residences.

## Staffing Requirements, Volunteers, and Residents' Work Assignments

State regulations in each of these areas put pressure on operating costs.

### Staffing Levels

States generally specify minimum staff-to-resident ratios. In Florida, a distinction is made between institutions caring for children under the age of 6 and those caring for children 6 years old or older. In the latter, there must be "[o]ne direct care staff member or trained volunteer to 6 children, when [the] children . . . are awake, and 1 to 12 when children are sleeping." In the former, there must be a "staffing ratio of 1 to 4 when children are present and awake and 1 to 6 when children are sleeping."

Georgia's scheme is simpler: "There shall be one child care worker for every ten children, or fraction thereof, in a living unit." In Tennessee, the ratio is one to eight. Oddly, Massachusetts provides only that the institution "shall assure a staff-child ratio appropriate to the age, capabilities, needs, and service plans of the residents in the facility." The Alabama and South Carolina regulations appear not to address this point.

Beyond requiring certain minimum numbers of employees, most states go to great lengths to specify particular positions that must be filled and the qualifications of those who fill them. For example, all the states I studied require the lowest-ranking category of employees (usually referred to as "child care staff") to hold a high school diploma or its equivalent.

Moving up the pecking order, Georgia defines a class of employees "human services professionals" and requires "one human services professional . . . for every thirty children in care or fraction thereof." Florida requires "one social services worker for every 25 children in care."

Georgia human services professionals must either hold a master's degree in social work, psychology, childhood education, education counseling and psychology, or a related field or hold a bachelor's degree in one of these fields and have either 2 years of experience in the field or be supervised by another human services professional with a master's degree or above in one of the fields already noted. In Florida, social services workers who "perform direct counseling to children and their families" must hold master's degrees in social work, counseling, or a related area and have at least 2 years of experience. Social workers in supervisory positions must have either a master's degree or a bachelor's degree plus 4 years experience working with children.

Alabama's requirements with respect to social workers are set out in terms of licensing requirements. Tennessee requires "caseworkers" to hold at least a bachelor's degree in social work or a related field.

In Georgia, the director of a child care institution must hold a bachelor's degree in social sciences, social work, childhood education, or business or public administration, or a related field and have 4 years of experience in child care. In Florida, the requirements are a bachelor's degree and 3 years of experience in management or supervision; in Tennessee, a bachelor's degree and 10 years of "administrative experience" are required. Many states also require operators of child care institutions to provide a minimum amount of in-service training to their employees.

These requirements are very likely to drive up the personnel costs of orphanages. The minimum staffing ratios appear to require larger numbers of employees than those of the traditional (pre-World War II) orphanages, and the educational requirements require orphanages to employ people with particular backgrounds at what are likely to be higher salaries than would be demanded by people with lesser credentials.

Beyond these requirements, some states' regulations also show a skeptical attitude about two alternatives to paid employees—volunteer and resident labor.

### Volunteers

The use of volunteers is subject to numerous restrictions. In Florida, volunteers who work more than 40 hours per month must have the same qualifications and training as paid employees doing the same work, must be supervised and evaluated in the same fashion as paid employees doing the same work, and are subject to background checks in the same fashion as paid employees. Furthermore, any college student accepted for uncompensated "fieldwork" at an orphanage as part of a degree program cannot be expected by the orphanage "to assume the total responsibilities of any paid staff member."

Alabama's provisions for volunteers state at the outset that "Volunteers shall not be permitted to assume total responsibilities or duties of any paid staff member." The meaning of this requirement is not clear, and it is probably given meaning only through the real-world inspection and enforcement actions of the relevant state agency. At the extreme, however, it could be argued to mean that no volunteer or volunteers can be substituted for a paid staff member. This inflexibility obviously puts pressure on costs by requiring the employment of more people than is necessary.

Beyond this statement, Alabama's restrictions on the use of volunteers are less onerous than Florida's in that there are no requirements as to qualifications, prior training, and so on. The orphanage need only provide for orientation and training of the volunteers, supervise their work, and keep records of the hours and activities of the volunteers.

South Carolina takes a similarly relaxed view of the matter, requiring only a background screening of volunteer applicants and recommending ongoing training of volunteers. South Carolina has no requirement analogous to Alabama's warning about permitting volunteers to assume the "total responsibilities" of paid staff.

Massachusetts also requires background screening and ongoing supervision of volunteers but does not otherwise seek to prevent their use. Georgia's regulations mention volunteers but do not appear to make any demands on their use other than that they be "supervised to ensure that assigned duties are performed adequately and to protect the health, safety, and well-being of the children in care." Tennessee's regulations are in the same vein.

States that wish to promote the development of orphanages should limit their regulation of volunteers. Assuming that there is no evidence of serious negative consequences in Georgia, Massachusetts, South Carolina, and Tennessee from their more hospitable stance toward volunteers, states with more restrictive schemes should follow their example. At the very least, states should drop any prohibitions on allowing volunteers to replace paid employees.

### Residents' Work Assignments

Work assignments for residents provide another substitute for paid employees in the orphanage. In the traditional orphanage, much use was made of child labor, as in Richard McKenzie's (1996) North Carolina orphanage in the 1950s:

> Outside the classroom, work needed to be done. Cows needed to be milked. Crops needed to be grown and harvested. Meals needed to be cooked. Things needed to be fixed. The Home tried to feed itself—well, not totally, but as much as child labor, with the help of a few grownup hands, or "bosses," would allow. Even if work had not been required to put food on the table, Mr. Shanes would have required it. He thought that idle hands were the Devil's workshop. Work, in itself, he thought, was good. (p. 70)

McKenzie's description of his orphanage's schedule indicates that work was performed during weekday afternoons and Saturday mornings.

Today, however, there are numerous regulatory obstacles to the substitution of resident labor for employee labor. The matter of the child labor laws—including the wage and hour provisions—is discussed elsewhere in this book (see Chapter 12). In addition, the states' regulations dealing with on-grounds work assignments also limit this substitution.

Alabama's regulations begin with an admonition similar to that against the overuse of volunteers: "Children shall not be considered as substitutes for employed adult staff, nor shall they be employed as a means of avoiding the hiring of adult staff." This language, like the admonition to volunteers, is unclear, particularly because it is followed by provisions that clearly anticipate that work assignments will be made. The regulations require that work assignments "be made in accordance with the age and ability of the child" and that they not "conflict with schooling, playtime, extracurricular activities, or normal community visits or visits with their families and friends." Furthermore, children must be given "some choice in their chores, and a change of routine duties shall be offered periodically to reduce monotony and to provide a variety of experiences." Without an understanding of how these regulations are actually enforced, it is hard to know how much of a barrier they are in practice to the use of student labor. It is clear, however, that a demanding regulatory agency could use these requirements to reduce the use of student labor substantially.

Georgia's regulations are similarly vague but threatening. The relevant language provides, in its entirety, that "children shall not be held solely responsible for the accomplishments of any work activity of the institution such as food preparation, laundering, housekeeping, or facility maintenance. Children shall not be considered substitutes for employed staff."

Florida also cautions that "[c]hildren's participation in work activities, within the facility, shall not be used as a substitute for the duties or assignments of staff members." South Carolina provides that "[c]hildren shall not substitute for staff nor regularly perform tasks assigned to staff" while allowing the assignment of tasks to children "appropriate to the age and abilities of the child." Massachusetts's and Tennessee's regulations, however, do not appear to address child work assignments at all.

Taken together, the requirements regarding employee numbers and qualifications, volunteers, and child labor very likely have saddled orphanages with higher labor costs than necessary. More flexibility as to numbers and qualifications of paid staff, and greater freedom to use volunteers and residents to do work that would otherwise be performed by paid employees, would obviously help orphanages contain their labor costs. The current system of regulations seems to exhibit more concern for the salaries and job security of social workers and other employees than for the financial viability of these institutions.

## Casework Regulations: The Requirement
## of "Therapy" in Orphanages

### Some History

States generally place what appear to the nonspecialist to be extensive requirements on orphanages as to the "casework services" provided their residents. Without a knowledge of the content and methods of the social work industry, it is difficult for an outsider to evaluate the nature of these requirements. The fact of their existence cannot be denied, however.

In a very important sense, the historical trend in favor of the therapeutic approach has progressed at the expense of the traditional orphanage. The rise of the former caused the decline of the latter. This was in large part the result of the efforts of social workers and others to "professionalize" the care of children, taking it out of the hands of charities and their supporters (Jones, 1994).[5]

Currently, there exists, alongside the state statutes and regulations, another regulatory system—through "private" accrediting agencies—that has as its primary goal the promotion of the therapeutic approach. The most significant private accrediting body is the Council on Accreditation of Services for Families and Children, Incorporated (COA). The COA accredits approximately 1,000 behavioral health care programs and 3,000 social service programs delivered by approximately 700 providers in the United States and Canada, including residential centers for children and youth.[6]

Membership in COA is voluntary but is important in at least two respects. Some private insurance companies condition reimbursement of mental health costs (particularly drug and alcohol rehabilitation) on COA membership, and some state governments pay a higher rate under contracts for the provision of care—particularly mental health services—to COA-accredited providers. The basic rationale for this favored treatment of COA members is that they provide more therapy than do nonaccredited providers and thus earn a higher reimbursement rate.

As a result, any orphanage that is in the business of providing mental health treatments, such as drug and alcohol rehabilitation, may wish to seek COA accreditation. Because the COA's requirements go beyond the licensure requirements of most states, particularly with respect to the therapeutic offerings of its members, COA membership involves even higher costs than compliance with the state requirements.

In the material that follows, I focus on the state requirements because my concern is with the traditional orphanage and its focus on helping disadvantaged children, as distinguished from severely disturbed children in need of specialized therapy.

### Typical Requirements

To get a sense of the state requirements regarding therapy, consider the rather detailed set contained in the Massachusetts regulations. Within 6 weeks of the admission of a new resident, the regulations direct that the orphanage "shall assess the needs of the resident and prepare an individual goal-oriented service plan for services and treatment for the resident." A team composed of various professional and staff employees assesses

> the needs of the resident in the areas of education; health, including medical, dental, and ancillary services; social services, including family work; psychological and psychiatric services, including individual and group counseling; and behavior management, recreation, life skills, and vocational training.

As a result of its assessment of the needs of the resident, the team develops a "written service plan" that includes a "statement of goals for the resident and family," a listing of "all services to be provided" the resident, and a listing of all the individuals providing these services. Thereafter, at least every 6 months the team must conduct a progress evaluation and revise the service plan as necessary.

It is hard to know how time-consuming and costly such an approach may be. That said, it is also hard not to wonder if a certain amount of this process is just bureaucratic paper shuffling that produces very little with regard to benefits. In other words, it would seem that the resident care process is an appropriate candidate for some amount of deregulation—which would also yield the added benefit of a reduction in the number of social workers necessary to the operation of the orphanage.

This raises a much broader, and potentially a much more financially significant, question: Couldn't orphanages that were allowed to concentrate on serving disadvantaged children, rather than children with severe emotional and psychological problems, eliminate most or all of this "therapeutic" orientation? This seems a very promising possibility—a "back to the future" move in which the traditional view of the orphanage is once again embraced and the social worker and therapeutic view limited to those institutions that are committed to the care of severely disturbed (compared to disadvantaged) children. In summary, it seems quite feasible to avoid much of the cost generated by today's emphasis on social worker intervention in "new" orphanages that define a less therapeutic mission for themselves.

## ■ An Alternative: Licensing Providers of Services Rather Than the Services Provided

States currently impose regulations on the operation of orphanages that, to a greater or lesser degree, raise their costs of operation. The most salient regulations with respect to this upward pressure on costs appear to be those dealing with facility requirements, minimum numbers and qualifications of paid staff, the use of volunteers, the assignment of work to residents, and the extent of casework given to each resident. All these requirements can be explained as a result of the two themes identified at the beginning of this chapter—the preference for home-like environments (as opposed to institutional environments) and an emphasis on a therapeutic environment for those children who are placed in institutional settings rather than in foster homes.

The push for home and therapy thus increases orphanages' operating costs. It cannot be said, at this point, that the regulations described previously produce no benefits to the children currently in orphanages. This is not the end of the matter, however. Rather, the question is whether the regulations can be relaxed—and operating costs thus lowered—to a degree without generating offsetting harm to the children.

I submit that the regulations described previously, considered in light of the historical evidence presented elsewhere in this book regarding the performance of traditional orphanages prior to the ascension of the home and therapy models, can be greatly modified or even eliminated without significant harm to the children in question. The resulting decrease in per resident costs of operation would allow both government subsidies and private charity to accomplish more—to provide a home for more children than the current, more expensive, system can afford to provide.

Clearly, there would be, in this scenario, characteristics of life in orphanages that would be less than ideal from the point of view of the children, administrators, or social workers. This, however, obviously does not resolve the issue. For example, regarding therapeutic care, if a state were to allow orphanages that serve disadvantaged—as opposed to severely emotionally distressed—children to "opt out" of the casework approach to the care of their residents, then those orphanages' costs would decrease but they might not offer psychological and other services that would, in a perfect world, still be advisable even for their less troubled residents.

The real choice, however, is not between a hypothetical perfect system and a real-world system that is flawed. Although improvements to an institution such as an orphanage are always possible, the decision to require the improvements via regulation should only be taken if it is determined that the costs of imposing the regulation—including the negative effect that cost increases have on the size of the population that can be served—are more than outweighed by the benefits of the regulation.

When the performance of traditional orphanages, which did not operate under such regulatory constraints, is considered, it is far from clear whether there have been any significant benefits from the imposition of the regulations discussed previously. Surely there have been significant cost increases as a result.

How can we begin to move from a regulated to a substantially deregulated regime in this field? I offer a modest proposal that would move us toward this goal.

Rather than regulating particular details of the services provided by orphanages—the number of beds and toilets, the number of child care workers, the amount of work required, and the amount of social work intervention—the state should instead license particular operators of orphanages, and then allow each operator very substantial latitude in designing its facility, staff, and a "treatment" regimen. The idea is a simple one: The provider—for example, a church group or other charitable organization—has the interest of its residents at heart. The state should rely to a very large extent on the motivation of the care providers and intervene only when there is a significant problem demonstrated with respect to the operation of any given orphanage.

If a state adopted this approach to orphanages, then the entrepreneurial efforts of orphanage managers—including the nonprofit providers—would lead to the identification and elimination of unnecessarily costly regulations and the substitution of a more sensible and less costly approach to the question at issue. It seems reasonable to predict that changes could be made very quickly to take advantage of greater flexibility in the design of facilities (taking advantage of economies of scale), in the hiring of paid staff (reducing number and cost), in the use of volunteers and resident labor (increasing both), and in the treatment of the residents (reducing the therapeutic component and thus lowering costs).

There is some precedent for such a change. Two states—Mississippi and Florida—have created an alternative to licensure. In these states, an orphanage can "register" with the state government by satisfying much less intrusive requirements than those for licensure. In addition to fewer regulations, registered orphanages are able to make greater use of volunteers than their licensed counterparts. The main drawback to registration is that this does not entitle the orphanage to receive state moneys—that is, the registered orphanage must generate its operating budget on its own, without state support.

Although I do not agree with the differential treatment regarding state funding, the registration idea has much to recommend it. It may offer a way out of the therapy-driven model of children's homes that has dominated the field for a half century.

How much would such changes lower the costs of orphanage care? I can offer only one data point here. The Palmer Home of Columbus, Mississippi, a Presbyterian orphanage, is registered, rather than licensed, under Mississippi law. According to the home's director, Ed Waldron, total per child cost of operations is approximately $24,000 per year. This is one third less than the Child Welfare League figure of $36,500 and roughly one half the Boys Town figure of $47,000 cited at the beginning of this chapter.

There is reason to believe that significant cost savings are possible as a by-product of deregulating orphanages. Even with substantial improvements in operating costs, orphanage care is likely to remain relatively more expensive than foster care. Given the severe shortcomings that the foster care system exhibits and the dramatic increases in the number of children in need,[7] some experimentation is clearly in order. Deregulation could help revive traditionalist orphanages that would provide a preferable alternative to the failing foster care system—contrary to almost a century of social work protestation to the contrary—and private charities could once again become interested in subsidizing this care in a deregulated, traditionalist environment.

Why not experiment with this approach to licensing the operator rather than the operation? A state could allow one or more orphanages to open their doors to disadvantaged, rather than severely disturbed, children under this relaxed regulatory plan. The orphanages' operations could be audited from time to time, and serious deviations from the state's expectations regarding the care of the children could be remedied on a case-by-case basis. (True abuse, of course, would not be tolerated under the new regime any more than it would under the current regime.)

I strongly suspect, however, that poor care would be no more of a problem in the future than it was in the past, and that the performance of the new traditionalist orphanages in terms of the marks given them by their graduates would rival those given the old traditionalist orphanages by their graduates.

## ▓ Notes

1. Currently, Jones is chair of the Department of Behavioral Science at the Pennsylvania State University College of Medicine in Hershey.

2. As Boudreaux and Boudreaux explain in Chapter 10, this shift was no doubt reinforced by changes in the Social Security Administration's funding of the states' child welfare services.

3. In addition, there are also private accrediting agencies that accredit child care providers according to standards similar to, but more demanding than, most state regulatory requirements. The private accrediting agencies are discussed later in connection with the therapeutic emphasis of state regulation.

4. Rather than overwhelm the reader with citations to specific subsections of the states' regulations for each statement made in the text, I provide a citation to the first regulation discussed for each state. This single citation provides a guidepost for the reader interested in further researching a given state's regulations of child care providers.

5. Jones (1994) provides a pithy description of the early social workers' attitude toward traditional orphanages: "Traditional charity work was sloppy, sentimental, counterproductive— and the 'Ladies bountiful' who did it were amateurs, untrained, and emotional. Social work professionals would be another breed altogether. They would be 'doctors to society' and 'social engineers' " (pp. 12-13).

6. A review of the COA membership list yields many entries for such agencies as Catholic Family Services of Birmingham, Alabama, and Family and Child Services of Washington, D.C. Indeed, the vast majority of COA members appear to be such family service agencies. There are numerous residential child care members, such as Florida Sheriffs' Youth Ranch, Idaho Youth Ranch, and Bethel Bible Village of Hixson, Tennessee. I counted, however, only 83 "homes" and "schools" on the COA's list of U.S. members. Clearly, most homes are not members of COA.

7. See Jones (1994, pp. 17-18), who describes the decline in the number of foster homes since 1980 and the increase in juvenile runaways and drug use.

## ▓ References

Alabama Administrative Code, ch. 660-5-37-.06 (1998).

Cmiel, K. (1995). *A home of another kind: One Chicago orphanage and the tangle of child welfare.* Chicago: University of Chicago Press.

Collins, S. (1994, December 19). There are no free lunches. *U.S. News and World Report,* 55-56.

Florida Administrative Code Ann., 10M-9.052 (1998).

Georgia Comp. Rules and Regulations, 290-2-5-.18 (2) (1998).

Jendryka, B. (1994, Summer). Flanagan's island. *Pol'y Review.*

Jones, M. B. (1994, Summer). The past and future of child welfare: Voluntary benevolence. *Caring.*

Massachusetts Regulations Code, title 102, § 3.06 (1998).

McKenzie, R. (1996). *The Home: A memoir of growing up in an orphanage.* New York: Basic Books.

South Carolina Code Regulations, 114-590 (1998).

Tennessee Comp. Rules and Regulations, ch. 1240-4-5-.09 (1998).

# CHAPTER 14

# Funding Our Children's Future

## *The Interplay of Funding and Regulatory Philosophies on Private Children's Homes*

JOSEPH L. MAXWELL III

E aster 1907 had just passed, and a Mississippi summer was at hand. The lawn surrounding two large, brick buildings at Palmer Orphanage in Columbus, Mississippi, was a carpet of green, "so inviting to the little ones," wrote Florence Frierson, the orphanage's head matron and wife of Palmer superintendent William V. Frierson. Mrs. Frierson was a devout Presbyterian who loved a summer rainstorm, watching new growth break out of the winter soil, or hearing children recite their catechism from beginning to end for the very first time. On this April day, she rode to the local train station with a cheerful heart. In seconds, however, it was broken. Mrs. Frierson heard a baby cry and ran to the steps of the arriving train; there, the frail form of a dying woman trembled with each descending step, as two "older tots" stayed close by her. A man accompanied her, carrying her crying infant. "My heart leaped into my throat, and for a moment I seemed ready to yield to a flood of tears," Mrs. Frierson later wrote to some friends.

The Christian mother was bringing her children to Palmer Home before she died of cancer. Mrs. Frierson later reported in her letter, "These three little girls, although badly spoiled—having had a sick mother so long—are promising children." In the following minutes, the sickly mother told her offspring good-bye.

Mrs. Frierson could only watch and pray. Then, the woman turned to Mrs. Frierson and, with tears streaming down her face, made this last request: "Teach my children to meet me in heaven." That said, she returned to her home to die. Mrs. Frierson, however, took the three children to Palmer Home and fulfilled their mother's last request (Maxwell, 1995, pp. 28-29).

Such stories fill accounts from thousands of privately run American orphanages that a century ago led the way in caring for destitute children. The first private orphanage originated in 1729 in the United States to care for orphans from an Indian massacre in Natchez, Mississippi; orphanage numbers grew commensurate with cataclysmic times of war and epidemics of tuberculosis, cholera, and yellow fever. Such homes, or children's villages, may again be the answer to potential new national cataclysms. In *The Atlantic Monthly,* journalist Mary-Lou Weisman (1994) writes,

> Contemporary epidemics such as AIDS, the resurgence of tuberculosis, and the rampant use of crack cocaine have the potential to create another orphan crisis in the twenty-first century. By the Year 2000, it is estimated 100,000 children, most of them from female-headed households, will lose their mother to AIDS. Senator Daniel Patrick Moynihan, among others, foresees the return of the orphanage as inevitable. (p. 44)

Today, however, few administrators of children's homes would be able to operate as Mrs. Frierson did at Palmer Home; a paucity could make such promises of spiritual instruction to comfort a dying woman. On the contrary, an elaborate modern system of government controls and alliances now predominate much of what is left of the children's home landscape; money is exchanged for regulatory control. There may be times when such public-private alliances benefit more children due to greater funding access; often, however, such deals have proven Faustian.

It would have been hard for Palmer Home's Mrs. Frierson to foresee what was to become of her turn-of-the-century orphanage movement. Indeed, by the time her son, John, took the reins of the Columbus, Mississippi, Presbyterian home in 1911, things were rapidly changing. Frierson, a noted lawyer and state legislator, was caught in the middle of social and philosophical upheaval; he attended one of the early Child Welfare Conventions in Washington, D.C., initiated by Theodore Roosevelt and continued during Frierson's time by Herbert Hoover, and wrote later that he was the only orphanage representative in attendance. Throughout America, new "professional" social workers, most with government ties, were arguing that traditional, church-run efforts were sloppily sentimental (Jones, 1993). A new wave of professional social workers took the reins in cooperation with a growing government entrance into the child care business.

Today, professionals from both ends of the spectrum—the nonprofit end and government-funding end—note that the sources of government funding available for private children's homes can be mind boggling and computer glutting. Of less concern to the government officials, and of more concern to those operating nonprofit and private children's homes, is the tangle of regulations that federal or state funding or both creates for private recipients; indeed, a top professional at one of the nation's largest charitable advisory agencies told me that there is no way to itemize neatly the "do's and don'ts" that taking federal or state funding necessitate for a home (several other leaders in the nonprofit field back this claim) because regulations vary depending on the agency or governmental entity giving the grant or funding. This is the very thing that makes taking such money so unwieldy and impractical for many private children's homes: These often-small children's homes are left to do what no expert on either the national nonprofit or government regulatory side has yet to do—decipher and systematize the multifarious regulatory codes that come with receiving any public money. It is questionable whether the century-long shift from private to public funding of children's homes has been on the whole positive; as the century winds down, new efforts at public-private partnerships demand that we begin unraveling our past concerning the influence of public funding on private child care philosophies.

## ▓ A Cataclysmic Shift

An example of the kind of shifts that can occur in the funding and philosophy of a children's home is Father Flanagan's well-known Boys Town in Omaha, Nebraska. Boys Town still exists but not without currying the favor of government as well as private funding sources. As a result, Boys Town is much different than the originally acclaimed version. Weisman (1994) notes, "When it was an orphanage, Father Flanagan's Boys Town put its faith in God and the work ethic. . . . Now that it's a residential treatment center, it also believes devoutly in science and technology" (p. 53).[1] Boys Town changed with the times, but has it changed for the better or for the worse? This question remains unanswered.

Today, private children's homes have a choice: (a) reject public funding and face ongoing angst over where funds will come from (fund-raising is not easy!) or (b) take government funds and face anxiety over when government social workers will next visit and for what purpose. Indeed, there is no assurance that government officials will not attempt to enforce even nonapplicable regulations on a home that refuses all public funding.

Curiously, although legal history indicates that scrutiny of charitable enterprises involving children is much heavier than that of charitable groups working with adults, the practice of taking state or federal funds actually is more common among private child care agencies than among adult-oriented charitable groups, such as private relief agencies, colleges, or universities, according to a study of 286 child care agencies conducted by Stephen Monsma (1994, p. 5).[2]

A great many small child care agencies receive government funding. Monsma (1994) notes, "A majority of the agencies with only 15 to 49 employees receive over 60 percent of their budgets from government sources" (p. 5). Monsma's study found that agencies created during the big-government era from 1965 to 1980 receive more public funding than agencies founded earlier or later. Many child care agencies studied by Monsma that once had a religious orientation, but then began taking public funds, now have abandoned their religious orientation. Meanwhile, those existing children's homes and agencies that have maintained their religious orientation report being much less likely to take money from government sources (Monsma, 1994, p. 6).

Of the 286 child care agencies polled in Monsma's (1994) study, a startling paucity—only 13—reported taking no government money at all (p. 5). This probably reveals the pressure agency heads feel to "make ends meet." When a child care home is constantly on the ropes financially, it becomes harder and harder to decline the "means of escape" that public funding seems to present, especially when decisions are cast in the light of providing necessities for living, breathing children in the immediate present.

Those children's homes and agencies that do remain doggedly opposed to such government reliance must have strong reasons for their determination. Thirty of the 286 agencies polled by Monsma (1994) took no government funds at all; of those 30 agencies, 70% (21) cited their religious commitments as a chief reason for refusing public funding (p. 7).

Why would a children's home so adamantly refuse government funds? There are at least four reasons.

## ▓ Four Reasons for Eschewing Public Funds

### *Government Funding Can*
### *Restrict Religious Emphasis*

Throughout the United States, stories abound of private child care agencies yielding to the warning of government officials to steer clear of religious instruction. In Monsma's (1994) study of child care agencies, 24 reported that government officials had pressured them to relax their requirement of Sunday church attendance. The heads of these private child care agencies sought to address such pressure in various manners. One agency head wrote that his children's home nuanced regulations: "In the past, religious services were mandatory, but we can no longer do that. However, we give incentives for attendance and encourage them to attend their own church" (p. 21). Meanwhile, an official of another agency contacted by Monsma said that in their case the system could not be massaged by incentive or other alternative plans: "We used to encourage church attendance by giving children extra free time if they went to church. We had to discontinue the practice. We may encourage church attendance but may not reward for church attendance" (p. 21). A third private agency head said, "[We experience] some informal leaning [on us] that youth should not be required to attend church—they say federal law mandates this, but no one has pushed us or other agencies yet" (p. 21).

### *Government Funding May Unduly*
### *Promote Unproven Models of Child Care*

As stated earlier, history indicates that among those homes that have begun taking government money, the trend is toward the homes' compromising their initial child care philosophy rather than government bending on its regulations. It has been a slow process of change in many cases; like a glacier, movement is measured over longer period of times, but with many homes, shifts can suddenly appear in startling degrees. Marshall Jones (1994) writes,

In the 1920s, social workers were not ready to deinstitutionalize child welfare in America; but they were able to persuade or induce many child caring agencies either to cooperate with local casework agencies or to hire caseworkers of their own, among other ways, by means of community chests (forerunners of the United Way). These depersonalized organizations were a powerful instrument in the hands of the social workers who staffed and controlled them. Agencies that refused to professionalize were not likely to qualify for support from the community chest. When the professional presence in an agency had increased sufficiently and especially if the director was a social worker, the next step was to insist that the board of trustees defer to the staff in what were, after all, best understood as technical decisions. (p. 13)

Where does that leave us today? Children's home officials must be more studious than ever in considering their government funding. Often, to receive public funds a private home must disassociate from its original philosophical base; there are numerous incidents of homes, either cataclysmically or glacially, moving along with the social science trend of the day in child care. The Villages, a group of children's homes in Kansas, is an example of an all-private group that chose to take public funding; today, 78% of its operating expenses come from the state. As a result, it is constantly adapting its program to move from traditional orphanage philosophy that favors consistency of environment to accommodating the government-led mantra of "family preservation." The Villages is now creating a family-preservation program to accentuate its group foster care program. Weisman (1994) notes,

One of the eight Kansas residences will be rededicated as a ninety-day 'home away from home' for abused children. Meanwhile, therapists trained by The Villages will work with the abusing parents and the abused children in an effort to reunite the family. (p. 62)

The bottom-line reason for the shift, as Village official Mark Brewer (as quoted in Weisman, 1994), is that "we want to provide the services that the state wants to purchase. . . . We'd be foolish not to" (p. 62).

It appears that a subtle, or maybe not-so-subtle, shift has occurred at the Villages: Getting funding has prevailed over setting policy; the practical has overruled the philosophical. Eventually, such homes often find a hole in their soul: They are still operating, but just what they are operating is less clear.

## *Government Funding Can Create Dependency and Loss of Self-Rule*

As mentioned earlier, most orphanages originally were denominational and often ethnic as well. History has shown, however, that government subsidy of children's homes has the same effect as government subsidy of unwed mothers. Unless historic orphanages and children's homes developed strong ties to committed private funders, they were all too likely to exhibit one of two forms of government dependency, both arguably unhealthy: (a) Private homes became heavily reliant on the government's coffers or (b) private homes deemed their own private efforts altogether unnecessary given the growth of government programs. Private children's homes, especially those centered on inculcating religious principles, open a dangerous door when they visit Uncle Sam's bank. As Julie Segal, legislative council for Americans United for the Separation of Church and State, states (personal communication, November 1996), "With the shekels come the shackles. And that's the problem. Religious organizations are private for a reason."

In 1996, federal welfare reform legislation was hailed as a step in the right direction to moving back toward private organizations providing more personal, truly compassionate care. One of the hallmarks of reform legislation passed by the U.S. Congress was provisions allowing more cooperative efforts via government funding of already effective privately run groups. A "charitable choice clause" lets a state contract with religious organizations to conduct its social services—a sort of out-sourcing by the government.

This certainly sounds like a step in the right direction; if someone is going to get the dollars, why not let that someone be a proven care agency that nurtures the heart as well as the body? Even better, the law lets private agencies continue with "control over the definition, development, practice, and expression of its religious beliefs."

Even this measure, however, raised questions about possible government strings attached. As Stephen E. Berger, executive director of the International Union of Gospel Missions, states (1996),

> The devil (if you will) is in the details. A "limitations" clause states that "no funds provided directly to institutions or organizations to provide services . . . shall be expended for sectarian worship, instruction, or proselytization." . . . Now, what exactly does that mean? For example, in Schenectady, New York, the state's Department of Social Services cited the City Mission because

it prohibited pornography in its facilities. "We determined that on health and safety issues, we would submit to government regulations," says Eivion Williams, executive director. "But this was an issue of morality." Only after three months of negotiations did the state relent. . . . But, of course, even when a faith-based charity wins a lawsuit, it still has lost precious time and money defending itself—resources better devoted to helping [those in their care]. (p. A13)

## Public Funding Can Create Job Stress, Creating an Unhealthy Work Climate

No one enjoys the feeling that one must always be looking over one's shoulder, wondering if what one is doing is being monitored or, moreover, sieved for acceptability according to a standard other than one's own. Perhaps no organization knows this feeling more intimately than the Massachusetts Society for the Prevention of Cruelty to Children, which is the oldest such society in America, having been in operation since 1878. Kowal and Robinson (1991) noted,

> When the Society began its efforts to respond to the needs of children, all of the Society's resources were directed toward service delivery. Today, the legal, insurance, and auditing requirements and functions are so complex, that if attorneys and insurance brokers knew about [the society's earlier] work in the nineteenth century, the Society probably would never have survived to become venerable and respected. . . . As a modern child welfare and mental health agency . . . the Society requires legal subspecialists due to the continuing complexity of the various components of a modern organization. . . . For example, a labor attorney is kept busy by the increasingly complex life circumstances and characteristics of staff who are more outspoken about their needs from employers. The Society also has an attorney who assisted in complying with the confusing, if not contradictory, regulations necessary to open eight mental health clinics. Another attorney reviews contracts for fund-raisers and special events. Still another attorney revises the pension plan, while another helped review and define conflict of interest for board members. These attorneys handle our business and protect the agency from harm. They prevent trouble for board, administration, and staff.
>
> That does not exhaust the need for legal services in a private child protective and treatment agency. Recently the Society has hired over five attorneys whose primary responsibility involves representing [the society] in court petitions for care and protection of vulnerable children and other child welfare case-related matters. The evolution of salaried child welfare attorneys from fee for service arrangements was justified by the escalating expense of

the former arrangement without a commensurate perception of control: Fee for service attorneys were just not working well enough. These staff attorneys also keep us aware of legal changes in case practice (confidentiality, duty to warn, privacy issues).

Having described all that, there are some special risks to doing business with the state. Over the past 6 years, the Society has been sued by one client [regarding services rendered for the state by the society]. . . . The case record documentation is professional, includes only behavioral observations, and, as an example of the best of protective services investigations, could be used as a training guide. Nevertheless, the Society has spent $5,000 in legal fees to move all the paper around a courthouse for a case that has no merit, but is a nuisance and may drag on for years.

Arguments can be made for making sure that the private provider [working with the state] . . . has all the protection required. . . . Yet the government agency is too often eager to contract with providers that lack internal credentials and internal standards, and insurance. (pp. 35-36)

No private agency should operate as though the state will provide protection from liability. The protection of clients, staff, and board is the responsibility of the private agency. The state can delegate authority, but the responsibility is and should be with the provider; otherwise, the private agency is not acting as an independent entity. A private entity must be accountable as a free-standing unit regardless of the states' authoritative role vis-à-vis other responsibilities.

The previously described experience is not uncommon for those working in the private child care industry. In fact, 16% of child care agencies that responded to Monsma (1994) said they had been pressured or threatened with legal action and so on for exercising some form of religious activity on site; such action ranged from observing a religious holiday to not exercising "religious diversity" in hiring practices (p. 24).

In today's litigious climate, whether a private children's home takes public funds or not, it will find itself constantly on the lookout for areas of vulnerability. For those private agencies that choose to receive federal funding, excessive opportunities for litigation are created because outside scrutiny (justified or not) increases. Kowal and Robinson (1991) provide the following partial but daunting list of allegations private homes can face:

Failure to report maltreatment; failure to accept the report of maltreatment; failure to timely investigate the report; failure to adequately investigate the report; conducting an unnecessary or overintrusive investigation; wrongful removal of a child from his home; removal of a child from the home without

due process (1983 action); slanderous investigation; malicious filing of abuse
petition; failure to transport client safely; . . . breach of confidentiality; . . .
sexual impropriety; failure to supervise client properly; incorrect treatment;
failure to refer client for treatment; treatment without consent; failure to
provide treatment, case plans, etc.; . . failure to make proper diagnosis;
failure to hire qualified staff; abandonment of client; failure to prevent client's
suicide; causing client's suicide; failure to warn of client's dangerousness.
(pp. 41-43)

## ▓ Negotiating the Public Funding Maze

At the time of founding of America, the relationship of the public and private
(namely, religious) sector was entirely different than it is today. The nation
had an early reliance on mostly private sources of child care until, earlier this
century, there was a nearly all-out launch toward government control of child
care. Today a hybrid form of public-private cooperation is emerging. Nonetheless, the legalities of government involvement in a private, religious
children's home, hinge on interpretation of the First Amendment's Free
Exercise and Establishment clauses. Regarding application of the First
Amendment to operation of children's homes, the Free Exercise clause generally mandates that government protect a child from being forced to engage
in religious practices against his or her will, and that government protect a
child's right to practice the religion of his or her choosing. The Establishment
clause prohibits government from exercising undue or overbearing influence
or interference regarding religious beliefs or practices appropriately deemed
fundamental by a children's home while restraining government from advancing via funding any home's religious beliefs.

   With the First Amendment Free Exercise and Establishment clauses as a
guideline, children's home and government officials today are given the task
of interpretation and application in the modern world of child care. How has
the American religious and nonprofit community responded? Legal expert
Carl Esbeck (1984) offers the following evident modes of response:

   Secularization of children's home: "Some were eager to secularize, thus trading
   their faith distinctives for government dollars. This was little loss for some,
   because the ecclesial leadership no longer held to the proselytizing purposes on
   which the ministry was founded." (p. 352)
   Separationist resistance: Still others resisted and refused to participate at all in the
   government programs. Such resistance was either to maintain the integrity of

the religious program or because the leaders themselves agreed with the strict separationist view as the only sure means of keeping religion from being compromised by too close an involvement with government. Unless the devotees of a religion, these leaders argued, are willing to finance the entire budget of its charities by sacrificial giving, it is better that the ministry close its doors than go on the dole. (p. 352)

Accommodation to government: "Others sought to qualify for the state aid, but asked for accommodation and tolerance of the agency's sectarian distinctives where the religious practices could be segregated from the delivery of 'secular' services." (p. 352)

Of these three approaches, the first two—secularization and separation—yield somewhat obvious consequences. In the case of secularization, a children's home virtually ceases to exercise any sense of personal autonomy regarding religious inculcation and values-based discipline and behavior modification; in exchange, the home has the comfort of ready funding. Those choosing separation cling tenaciously to their autonomy regarding teaching matters of faith and values and conduct, with the trade-off usually being an ongoing frustration of having to muster all their financial support from the private sector.

For purposes of this chapter, the third approach—accommodation—requires the greatest amount of nuance and expertise from children's home officials. Those choosing this route—taking public funds while still seeking to maintain some sense of religious and disciplinary autonomy—must negotiate a maze of federal and local regulations.

The legal key, or set of guidelines, most used today by judges, legislators, and children's home officials to decipher the map of accommodation was provided in the Supreme Court ruling, *Lemon v. Kurtzman*. Specifics of the *Lemon* ruling are not important at this point; what is important is the three-pronged set of guidelines that the Supreme Court justices offered in their ruling for deciphering the legalities and illegalities of contact between church and state. This set of guidelines has come to be called the Lemon Test, and the guidelines are as follows: Any funding of a private religious enterprise by a government entity (a) must have a secular legislative purpose, (b) must neither advance or inhibit any religious belief, and (c) must not foster excessive governmental entanglement with religion.

Armed with this three-pronged set of guidelines, church and state officials exercising efforts to accommodate religion to government standards and government to religious standards must apply the Lemon Test to a host of federal, state, and local regulatory laws.[3]

### The Federal Level

According to Esbeck (1992), "the federal law can be usefully divided into the following regulatory categories: (a) labor law and employee benefits legislation; (b) taxes, tax regulation, and tax benefits; (c) civil rights acts prohibiting discrimination in employment and public accommodations; and (d) spending power legislation" (p. 361).

### The State and Local Level

Children's home officials must master a conglomerate of state and local regulations, which can vary from state to state but usually consist generally of three basic categories, according to Esbeck (1992): "comprehensive licensing schemes; child abuse reporting laws and their interaction with the clergy-counselee privilege; and religious preferences in adoption and foster placement agencies" (p. 381).

Social services ministries, however, are regulated in numerous other ways: professional and occupational licenses; workers' compensation statutes; labor relations; state Occupational Safety and Health Administration and other safety laws; incorporation and registration of foreign business statutes; taxes (use, sales, property, income, and business licenses); state human rights acts and city ordinances concerning discrimination in employment and public accommodations; financial solicitation ordinances; lobbying and political activity regulation; zoning; landmarking, and other land-use controls; health, sanitation, food handling, and environmental regulation; and building and fire codes (Esbeck, 1992).

Implications and variations of application abound from this bevy of laws. Suffice it to say that when public money makes its way into private charities, the courts will be watching with magnifying glass in hand. In the following sections, I provide examples of the most common areas of controversy between children's homes attempting to hold onto elements of religious or disciplinary distinction or both in the face of government regulation: (a) licensing conflicts, (b) employment conflicts, (c) funding conflicts, and (d) philosophical conflicts.

### Licensing Conflicts

Currently, most states require children's homes to earn a state license by meeting certain state-determined criteria for operation. Some states allow homes to operate without licenses, but in these cases, these homes report attempts by state officials to monitor and sometimes coerce their operations as well as pressure to voluntarily apply for a state license. Such children's homes must decide whether to seek licensing by their resident state or eschew it. In fact, cases of high court rulings concerning licensing of children's homes outnumber those regarding state licensing of boarding homes, rescue missions, nursing homes, mental retardation wards, and religiously affiliated hospitals (Esbeck, 1992).

The following are examples of litigation in which a children's home was given relief (all cited in Esbeck, 1992):

> The Louisiana case—*State v. New Bethany Baptist Church* (1988): State officials sought to conduct mental and physical exams on children and employees of a children's home operated by New Bethany and, if necessary, remove children from the home's care. The federal courts ruled that state officials had the right to "access" the children's home but no right without home permission to conduct tests or remove children. (pp. 385-386)
>
> *Tabernacle Baptist Church v. Conrad*: The courts ruled that because the religious nature of an unlicensed home operated by Tabernacle was vital to its operation, insistence by the state of compliance with basic regulations such as fire and health codes was permissible. The court declared, however, the state had inappropriately applied certain "broadly phrased" elements of the Child Welfare Agencies Act, including requiring licensing, setting minimum standards for a home's well-roundedness and community involvement, filing reports defining the home's purpose and relevancy, and requiring government inspections. (p. 387)
>
> *The State ex rel. O'Sullivan v. Heart Ministries*: The court sided with state efforts to regulate the makeup of the governing board of Heart Ministries' children's home, the state-approved training of staff, and assurances of "sound and adequate" financing. (p. 388)

The following are examples of litigation in which courts upheld state actions against a home:

> *Darrell Dorminey Children's Home v. Georgia Department of Human Services*: A pastor operating a home opposed state-mandated licensing, but the courts upheld the states' mandatory licensing law. (Esbeck, 1992)
>
> *State ex rel. Roberts v. McDonald*: The courts upheld an operational injunction against a church-affiliated boy's ranch saying that the state was rightly requiring assent to basic standards, among others, including provision of details for a "constructive program," evidence that employees are of "good moral charac-

ter," and proof that the home's facilities provided "full . . . religious opportunities." (Esbeck, 1992, p. 389)

## Employment Conflicts

Whether a private children's home takes government money or not, it is subject to compliance with numerous labor laws. For instance, in the New York State case, *Wilder v. Sugarman* (Noonan, 1987),

> The state Civil Liberties Union and the Legal Aid Society of Brooklyn sued about thirty orphanages in the New York City area—some municipal, others private (including a Jewish home, a Lutheran home, and a Catholic home)—claiming that the state's placement standards discriminated against blacks and Protestants. The plaintiffs challenged the public funding of the specified sectarian orphanages—which totaled about $194 million—as a violation of the First Amendment's Establishment clause, arguing that the practice amounted to government subsidy of certain religions over others. (pp. 283-284)

The court ruling cited New York State's early history of legally mandating state funding of religious orphanages. Moreover, it noted that although the Free Exercise clause set an ideal of matching a child's own religious preferences in his or her placement, realistically this is not always possible in New York City simply due to availability of preferable homes placements. Having considered both Free Exercise and Establishment concerns, "The court said it would opt for the 'benevolent neutrality' " argument, a precedent set in an earlier federal ruling. Basically, this meant that the court opted for an effort to accommodate both Free Exercise and Establishment concerns; it ruled that because no reasonable alternatives existed for placement of the plaintiffs, their placement in "pervasively religious" homes was warranted (Noonan, 1987, pp. 283-284).

## Funding Conflicts

In *National Labor Relations Bd. v. Hanna Boys Center* (1991), the National Labor Relations Board sought to represent several "lay non-teaching employees," including cooks, maintenance, and child care workers, at the boy's center, which was owned and operated by the Roman Catholic Church. The church opposed the National Labor Relations Board's intent, claiming that the school was "closely supervised by the church, its religious mission pervades its operations, and that every employee plays a role in furthering that mission" (*National Labor Relations Bd. v. Hanna Boy's Center*, 1991, pp. 312-313). The *Religious Freedom Reporter* noted,

> The court concluded that: (a) The National Labor Relations Act (NLRA) applies to the school's nonteaching employees; and (b) there was no constitutional question raised by the board's exercise of jurisdiction over the relationship between the school and its secular employees who are significantly involved in teaching. To pass constitutional muster under the Establishment clause, the board's application of the NLRA to the school's nonteaching employees must: (a) have a secular purpose; (b) have a primary effect that neither advances not [sic] inhibits religion; and (c) not foster excessive state entanglement with religion. The court determined that the board's exercise of jurisdiction over the school did not deviate from secular purpose or primary effect. The court further explained that the government involvement through the board will consist only with respect to the specific charges filed on behalf of the employees and will not involve the systematic monitoring or supervision of the church's activities or free exercise of the religious beliefs of anyone at the school. (pp. 312-313)

## Philosophical Conflicts

Whenever a private children's home takes government money, it should expect that strings will be attached: The home will be expected to cooperate in caring for government-assisted children; moreover, the home will be subject to public scrutiny concerning its internal operational standards.

One example of such conflict is the 1988 State of New York case, *Arneth v. Gross*. Regarding this case, the state had placed two foster children in a Roman Catholic home that took public funding. The two girls sued the home because Catholic workers there confiscated their contraceptive devices and pills due to religious restrictions. In this case, the courts faced a clear clash between applying the First Amendment's Free Exercise and Establishment clauses. On the one hand, the courts were charged under the Free Exercise clause with protecting the children from being coerced into a religious practice. On the other hand, the Establishment clause dictated that the state not unreasonably restrict the home's fundamental religious practices. The court found in favor of the home, substantially because the child-plaintiffs had been placed in the home by the state; having so freely decided on the girls' placement there, the state should not be able to force the home to change fundamental religious standards (Esbeck, 1992).

The previously discussed categories are the primary ones in which government funding of private children's homes can create sparks. There are,

of course, others, including charitable solicitation.[4] As these cases show, no
children's home enterprise is totally immune from government scrutiny. It is
true, however, that choices made by a children's home will have immense
consequences regarding how it will seek funding.

## ■ Taking the "Narrow Way"

*Model Disciplined Goodness*
*Versus Error-Proned Ease*

Evelyn McPhail grew up learning how to care for herself, learning how
to stretch $1 into $2, learning how to cook from a garden and pluck feathers
off a chicken, learning how to sew, and wearing hand-me-down clothes. Are
these things bad? In some circles today, philosophers, practitioners, and
politicians would argue so—claiming that a child should not be burdened by
such cares, that such "hardships" violate child labor laws, that they warp
self-esteem, and so on.

On the contrary, Evelyn McPhail credits such an environment as the main
factor in molding her into the person she is today—a top national leader in
the Republican Party, who served as cochairman of the Republican National
Committee from 1993 to 1996. McPhail grew up at Palmer Home for Children
in the 1940s and 1950s; to this day, she says a day rarely goes by when she
does not think about those at Palmer Home who cared for her and modeled a
life of high moral character and personal responsibility. John Frierson, mentioned earlier, was the superintendent during her years at Palmer; he remains
McPhail's hero:

> If we ever get to the point that we take government assistance, that's the end
> of the value of Palmer because the government that gets involved in these
> social things, such as orphanages and organizations . . . it is a sure sign of
> failure. It's not going to last because there is no continuity to government. As
> good as it is, and I love America and I love government, but I like a
> government that does not interfere with our private lives. Government [today]
> is at the point of administering programs by bureaucrats paid to do so. That
> means that they may or may not know how to administer it; they may or may
> not dedicate their life to it; they may or may not have compassion and care.
> It's simply a job. (E. McPhail, personal communication, June 1995)

## *Gauge Success by Children's Maturational, Not Numerical, Growth*

Donnalee Velvick runs Hope House—literally. The home for abused children has her heart and her time. Others must wait in line. "Those who've taken an interest in her story—congressmen, TV executives, movie agents, and literary agents . . . often must wait while Velvick attends to a child's needs" ("Hometown Heroes," 1996, p. 14).

Velvick's facility is overflowing with 42 children, most of whom will live there until they become adults. *Citizen* magazine ("Hometown Heroes," 1996) noted,

> Velvick believes these children benefit more from a permanent home than from the instability of foster care. "I'd rather have orphanages and children's home available than have children unwanted," said Velvick, 54, who grew up in an orphanage and vowed as a young girl to someday help other orphans. (p. 14)

Hope House runs its own day school, with life skills training for older children. It also has morning and evening Bible devotions and mandatory church on Sundays.

> Pro-family politicians and Christian activists see in Hope House a working model for welfare reform. State-paid children's homes in Idaho spend $21,600 per child per year, compared to $5,112 per child at Hope House. The gap would be even wider in other states; California spends $40,000 a child.
>
> Hope House is a situation where compassionate care and budget balancing can work together," said Marvin Olasky, senior scholar at the Center for Effective Compassion, a welfare-reform think tank in Washington, D.C. "I hear in Washington all the time that if you're serious about helping kids, you need more money. The fact is, if you're serious about kids, you spend more time. (p. 14)

Velvick is not running a large organization and she does not have a large budget. One thing is for sure: Velvick's Hope House is effective.

The glut of government-funded child care facilities in America has created numerous unfortunate side effects; one of those not often considered is the cookie-cutter effect such funding promotes. To get funds, a home must comply with so many government regulations that when all is said and done, all the homes end up practicing the same type of child care philosophy with little room for innovation and positive experimentation.

On the contrary, homes such as Velvick's are finding effective ways to raise children without public money and at a fraction of the cost. In other words, those children's homes with courageous vision can dare to be different, to try new—or often old—ways of child care, and to even be small and effective versus big and bloated. Marchetti (1996) states,

> The best way to fight poverty is by supporting the efforts of small, private charities that are practicing "effective" compassion—that is, encouraging people to change their behavior rather than just giving handouts. And the charities that are doing the best work . . . are typically those that take no government money and that stress spiritual rehabilitation as part of their program. (p. 9)

To the degree that a home takes government funds, it will often forfeit opportunities for creative care. Moreover, in today's climate, to the extent that a children's home relies on government agencies to supply its children versus referrals from private groups, including churches, individuals, and charities, it may find itself encountering a sense of growing insignificance.[5]

Homes should doggedly defend what makes them special and effective—be that a religious orientation, disciplinary code, employee standards, and so on. To the extent that a home trades elements of its core philosophy for money (and the false god of numerical growth), administrators may well regret it. Administrators of private children's homes would do well to heed Berger's (1991) words:

> Any institution remains "relevant" as long as it has something to offer. Religious institutions are no exception. The religious institution that becomes indistinguishable from other institutions, such as political lobbies or therapeutic agencies or radical caucuses . . . in very short order has great difficulty answering the question of why it should exist as a separate institution at all. At this point it has become "irrelevant" in the strictest sense of the word—the sense of redundancy and obsolescence.

A growing number of leaders in compassion ministries throughout the United States are reawakening to a vision of child care that ensures care for the long-term emotional, physical, and spiritual needs of children; many view privately funded children's homes as a viable answer to this need. Indeed, in this sense, this growing delegation is returning to the nation's roots.

The first public orphanage in the United States was not founded until 1790, in Charleston, South Carolina. At that time, the state benefited greatly from the free exercise of religion, as Charleston's Bethesda orphanage proved. The Bethesda Orphan House was not founded by the city of Charleston, the South Carolina Department of Human Services, or any arm of the federal government. On the contrary, it was established by the noted English evangelist George Whitefield, a contemporary and former college roommate of John Wesley. Both Whitefield's Bethesda home and the Ebenezer Home were modeled after the great orphanage at Halle, Germany, founded by August Franke.

Commenting on his orphanage's location approximately 10 miles from Savannah, Georgia, Whitefield once said,

> I choose to have it so far of the town because the children will be more free from bad examples and can more conveniently go up on the land to work. For it is my design to have each of the children taught to labor, so as to be qualified to get their own living. Lord, do Thou teach and excite them to labor also for that meat which endureth to everlasting life. (Waldron, 1991, p. 9)

Sadly, Whitefield would have found it extremely difficult to fulfill his dream in today's regulatory climate. Surely his eternal vision would have provided him with the muster to meet the task, the same sort of vision that found him at the evangelistic forefront of the historic "Second Great Awakening" in America. Perhaps there are new Whitefields today who will muster the resolve to usher in yet another great awakening—that of the need for quality children's homes committed to religious and philosophical principle as well as the principal of capital income.

## ▓ Notes

1. Weisman (1994) notes, "Orphanages . . . virtually disappeared by the late 1970s as a result of a decrease in the number of orphans and a growing conviction that children belong in families. That every child needs parents and a home has become an article of faith and a guiding principle for social-policymakers and a matter of federal law as well. The philosophy of 'permanency planning,' as set forth in the Adoption Assistance and Child Welfare Act of 1980, considers the goal of the foster care system to be keeping children in families. The law allows for but discourages 'out-of-home placement'—institutionalization in group homes or residential treatment centers—and calls for the return of the children to a family, biological or otherwise, whenever possible and as quickly as possible" (p. 46).

2. This article constitutes preliminary findings from Monsma (1996).

3. Esbeck (1992) provides the following useful list by category of the primary federal regulatory laws that operators of a children home should be aware of:

1. "Principal examples of the interaction between social ministries and federal labor law and employee benefits legislation are: (i) the Federal Unemployment

Tax Act; (ii) the Fair Labor Standards Act and Child Labor Law Act; (iii) the National Labor Relations Act; (iv) the Immigration Reform and Control Act; (v) the Social Security Act and ERISA, and (vi) the Occupational Safety and Health Act" (pp. 361-362).

2. "Principal examples of the interaction of social ministries and federal taxes, tax regulation and tax benefits are: (i) regulations governing the lobbying and political activities of Internal Revenue Code Section 501 (c)(3) organizations; (ii) the case law resisting the IRS requirement to annually file Form 990; (iii) the Church Audit Procedures Act; (iv) the utilization of IRC Sections 170 and 501(c)(3) to disfavor religious organizations acting contrary to 'public policy' " (pp. 362-364).

3. "Principal examples of the interaction of social ministries and federal legislation prohibiting discrimination in employment and public accommodations are: (i) Titles II and VII of the Civil Rights Act of 1964; (ii) the Equal Pay Act of 1963; (iii) the Age Discrimination in Employment Act of 1975; and (iv) the Americans with Disabilities Act of 1990" (pp. 364-365).

4. Principal examples of the interaction of social ministries and federal spending power included: (i) The Adolescent Family Life Act; (ii) Title VII of the Civil Rights Act of 1964; (iii) The Child and Adult Care Food Program of 1991; (iv) The Child Care and Development Block Grant of 1990; (v) The Civil Rights Act of 1964; (vi) The Age Discrimination Act of 1975; (vii) The Rehabilitation Act of 1973. The last three acts were amended by Congress in 1987 by what is commonly known as the Grove City College Bill, or "Restoration Act," which extended antidiscrimination statutes to apply with greater expansiveness within private organizations accepting federal funds (pp. 365-381).

4. For a comprehensive overview of issues regarding charitable funding, see Johansen and Rosen (1979, pp. 116-135).

5. Weisman (1994) recounts the following comments of a staffer at the Villages regarding what is at stake: " 'The lines have been drawn. When the words preventive service got applied to everything up to the doorstep of residential care, some of us had apoplectic fits. We all would have told you that what we did here was preventive. We prevent lifetimes in mental hospitals, lifetimes in prisons. All of a sudden some bureaucrat in Washington defines preventive service as preventing placement outside the home, and we become the thing to be prevented.' For the first time in anyone's memory The Children's Village, one of the largest and considered one of the best residential treatment centers in the country, has no waiting list. Dale says that children who might once have been sent there are being diverted to less restrictive, less expensive, and less appropriate options, such as foster home care, on the presumption that a family setting is always better" (p. 62).

## ■ References

Berger, P. L. (1991). The serendipity of liberties. In R. J. Neuhaus (Ed.), *The structure of freedom: Correlations, causes, and cautions* (pp. 1-16). Grand Rapids, MI: Eerdmans.

Berger, S. E. (1996, September 3). New hope for gospel missions? Devil's in the details. *USA Today*, p. A13

Esbeck, C. H. (1984, April 5-8). *The neutral, secular state: Imperative or impossibility?* Paper presented at the Christian Legal Society, Faith and Freedom Conference.

Esbeck, C. H. (1992). Government regulation of religiously based social services: The First Amendment considerations. *Hastings Constitutional Law Quarterly, 19*(2), 343-412.

Hometown heroes. (1996, May 27). *Citizen, 10*(5).

Johansen, R. B., & Rosen, S. J. (1979, November). State and local regulation of religious solicitation of funds: A constitutional perspective, The uneasy boundary: Church and state. *Annals of The America Academy of Political and Social Science, 46,* 116-135.

Jones, M. (1994). The past and future of child welfare: Voluntary benevolence; America's history of caring for children in need—Part IV. *Caring, Summer,* 10-19.

Kowal, L. W., & Robinson, D. S. (1991). Child welfare liability from the private agency perspective. In M. Sprague & R. M. Horowitz (Eds.), *Liability in child welfare and protection work: Risk management strategies.* American Bar Association Center on Children and the Law.

Marchetti, D. (1996, March 7). A private war against public welfare: Group highlights charities that offer "effective compassion" as an alternative to government aid; Effort draws mixed reaction. *Chronicle of Philanthropy,* p. 9.

Maxwell, J. (1995). *Palmer home for children: A century of hope, a passion to care.* Columbus, OH: Palmer House.

Monsma, S. V. (1994). *Religious nonprofits and public money: Patterns.* Malibu, CA: Pepperdine University Press.

Monsma, S. V. (1996). *When sacred and secular mix: Religious nonprofit organizations and public money.* Lenham, MD: Rowman & Littlefield.

National Labor Relations Bd. v. Hanna Boy's Center (1991, August). *Religious Freedom Reporter, 11,* 312-313.

Noonan, J. T., Jr. (1987). *The believer and the powers that are: Cases, history, and other data bearing on the relation of religion and government.* New York: Macmillan.

Waldron, E. (1991). *The history of child care in America from colonial days through the nineteenth century.* Presented to the Noxubee County (Mississippi) Historical Society.

Weisman, M.-L. (1994, July). When parents are not in the best interests of the child. *Atlantic Monthly, 274*(1), 43-63.

# CHAPTER 15

# The Cost of Care in Institutions and Families

DEL BRADSHAW
DONALD WYANT
RICHARD B. McKENZIE

**W**hat is the cost of care for children in an institutional setting? Is there a differential in the cost of care for the disadvantaged child compared to the cost of care for the severely troubled child, as might be expected? If there is, what is the cost differential?

This chapter seeks to address these questions. We provide actual and some estimates of the cost of institutional child care over time and then evaluate the difference in the cost of care for severely troubled and disadvantaged children.

Child care professionals often maintain that the annual cost of institutional child care is in excess of the full cost of a year at Harvard University. They fail to note, however, that the cost figures cited often relate to the cost of care for severely troubled youth and that the cost of care for disadvantaged children was not always as high in real dollar terms as it is today (Ford & Kroll, 1995). We analyze the accounting records of two homes for children—one of which provides permanent residential care for disadvantaged children (or children who suffer the effects of poverty and neglect or the loss of one or both parents but who are otherwise fairly "normal") and one of which provides temporary residential treatment for severely troubled children (or children who are scarred physically and emotionally by family abuse and neglect, who are criminally delinquent, who are in need of medical and psychological treatment, or all three)—that appear to be reasonably representative of similar institutions throughout the United States.[1] We find support for the following conclusions:

1. It is indeed true that the annual cost of care for disadvantaged children in the mid-1990s exceeded the cost of tuition, fees, and room and board for a year at Harvard, or more than $30,000 a year. The cost of care in conventional two-parent families, however, is equally costly. The cost of institutional care within the children's institutions studied does not appear to be radically out of line with the full cost of care per child within two adult/two children families—when the opportunity value of parental time is included in the cost of family care.

2. The cost of care for severely troubled children was much higher—in our comparison, it was twice the cost of institutional care for disadvantaged children. Of course, the cost of care for severely troubled children is substantially higher for an easily understood reason: The cost structure includes an array of professional services in addition to the basic living costs incurred in the care of disadvantaged children.

3. The cost of care in real (or inflation-adjusted) terms for both severely troubled and disadvantaged children has risen dramatically during the past half century. In 1995, the real annual cost of care of disadvantaged children, after adjusting for inflation, was one third higher than it was two decades ago. The real annual cost per child in 1995 was more than four times that in 1950. The real annual cost of care for severely troubled youth in one of the two institutions was nearly nine times the cost of care for disadvantaged children in 1950.

4. The increase in the cost of care has obviously been associated with the decline in the number of children in institutional care, but it is, no doubt, also associated with a decline in the work the children can do and with the growth in regulatory and accreditation requirements for the care of institutionalized children.

To provide complete confidentiality for the two homes in this study, the names of the homes are not given. Instead, we refer to the home for severely troubled children as "Facility ST" and the home for disadvantaged children as "Facility D."

## ■ Historical Cost at Two Homes for Children

We began by studying the available accounting records of Facility ST from 1935 through 1995. This facility began operating in the late 1800s and was affiliated with a major Protestant denomination. After studying the records of Facility ST, we expanded our study by evaluating the accounting records of Facility D, which also opened its doors in the late 1800s. The accounting records for Facility D, however, were available only from 1950 through 1995.

On the basis of our studies, we note that during the 1935 to 1995 period, the consumer price index rose 12-fold. The annual cost of care at Facility ST, however, rose far faster (182-fold, or 15 times faster than the consumer price index). In the 1955 to 1995 period, the consumer price index rose nearly six times, whereas the cost of care at Facility ST rose approximately 50-fold, more than eight times the consumer price index. The cost of care at Facility D rose much more modestly but still rose 26-fold between 1955 and 1995. Of course, this means that certain categories of expenses increased at rates significantly higher than the inflation rate. In particular, salaries and utilities at both facilities and food, medical care, repairs and maintenance, and supplies at Facility ST increased at rates that far exceeded the inflation rate.

We obtained data from internal and external sources during our study. The data were mainly obtained through financial statements prepared by outside certified public accounting firms, from reports prepared by the staff at the facilities for one of the foundations in their area (which has provided funding for both institutions), and from the current executive directors and other reference materials. The data include the costs by type and category and the number of children and staff at the facilities. We extracted various revenues and expenditures from the previously mentioned data sources and adjusted them for inflation to determine the real cost per child per year using 1995 as the base year. Accordingly, all cost figures are in 1995 dollars and are shown in Table 15.1 (Facility ST) and Table 15.2 (Facility D). Also, all cost calculations are exclusive of depreciation on plant and equipment, which could not be estimated precisely (but could easily add more than 20% to the annual figures for the per child cost of care).[2]

### Cost of Care at Facility ST

Facility ST began operating as a home for disadvantaged children (or orphanage) in 1891 but had two major changes in the direction of care during the past three decades, each of which caused a dramatic hike in the real annual cost of care per child. As can be seen in Table 15.1, Facility ST cared for an average of 294 children in 1935 and 313 children in 1940. As clearly evident in Table 15.1 and Figure 15.1 (which depicts the data in Table 15.1 for selected years), however, from 1940 onward there was a substantial decline in the

**TABLE 15.1**  Annual Cost of Care per Child at Facility ST by Expenditure Category for Selected Years (1935-1995) in 1995 Dollars

| Expense Category (Cost per Child per Year; Inflation Adjusted) | $ per Year | | | | | | | | | | | | |
| --- | --- | --- | --- | --- | --- | --- | --- | --- | --- | --- | --- | --- | --- |
| | 1935 | 1940 | 1945 | 1950 | 1955 | 1960 | 1965 | 1970 | 1975 | 1980 | 1985 | 1990 | 1995 |
| Program expense | | | | | | | | | | | | | |
| Salaries | 881.85 | 1,113.70 | 1,331.58 | 2,176.81 | 2,371.62 | 3,098.85 | 4,202.67 | 6,487.42 | 10,914.00 | 28,184.36 | 19,422.14 | 29,736.08 | 36,693.11 |
| Food | 301.88 | 361.23 | 267.88 | 1,720.31 | 1,516.66 | 1,543.99 | 1,725.07 | 2,308.29 | 2,209.94 | 3,946.81 | 2,551.51 | 2,322.31 | 1,341.14 |
| Medical | 47.37 | 29.85 | 27.14 | 22.40 | 65.89 | 108.71 | 56.13 | 170.53 | 2,660.49 | 4,194.50 | 952.50 | 872.62 | 1,315.25 |
| Clothing | 151.46 | 187.37 | 274.97 | 249.10 | 268.64 | 452.24 | 478.63 | 677.67 | 711.20 | 505.36 | 267.79 | 62.24 | — |
| Supplies | 136.17 | 128.70 | 178.39 | 251.25 | 232.90 | 319.21 | 440.95 | 503.87 | 738.19 | 1,029.49 | 1,022.57 | 874.76 | 2,262.24 |
| Recreation | — | — | 53.13 | 73.60 | 84.09 | 71.83 | 82.21 | 62.97 | 152.72 | 251.74 | 139.58 | 349.99 | — |
| Utilities | 230.14 | 235.34 | 318.52 | 478.00 | 546.10 | 706.80 | 1,005.36 | 1,594.58 | 3,132.99 | 11,279.94 | 2,521.04 | 2,790.46 | 3,249.09 |
| Repairs and maintenance | 135.50 | 26.67 | 612.94 | 379.90 | 151.19 | 158.07 | 224.92 | 1,519.44 | 1,541.25 | 8,821.07 | 2,569.67 | 1,412.89 | 2,412.10 |
| Other program expenses | 181.61 | 440.77 | 168.93 | 263.20 | 117.91 | 154.62 | 4,491.51 | 1,939.06 | 2,400.88 | 5,482.19 | 2,010.68 | 2,468.21 | 3,043.21 |
| Total program expenses | 2,065.98 | 2,523.63 | 3,233.48 | 5,614.57 | 5,355.00 | 6,614.32 | 12,707.45 | 15,263.83 | 24,461.66 | 63,695.46 | 31,457.48 | 40,889.56 | 50,316.14 |
| Administrative expenses | 749.96 | 526.93 | 491.46 | 665.44 | 1,024.06 | 1,508.60 | 2,455.23 | 3,757.18 | 5,480.65 | 6,363.47 | 3,448.65 | 4,652.14 | 6,846.87 |
| Fund-raising expense | — | — | — | — | — | — | — | 148.22 | 2,315.82 | 5,729.83 | 3,532.90 | 3,078.30 | 6,347.14 |
| Productive enterprise expense | 1,154.03 | 817.18 | 792.37 | 840.73 | 885.47 | 1,322.79 | 2,052.24 | 1,048.03 | 916.73 | 1,118.07 | — | — | — |
| Total expense per child per year | 3,969.97 | 3,867.74 | 4,517.31 | 7,120.74 | 7,264.53 | 9,445.71 | 17,214.92 | 20,217.26 | 33,174.86 | 76,906.83 | 38,439.03 | 48,620.00 | 63,510.15 |
| Average number of children | 294.40 | 313.90 | 287.00 | 283.00 | 216.00 | 161.50 | 108.30 | 109.10 | 73.50 | 27.50 | 78.60 | 72.30 | 48.20 |
| Program staff level | 43.00 | 39.00 | 45.00 | 61.00 | 64.00 | 44.00 | 36.00 | 31.00 | 48.50 | 52.00 | 65.30 | 71.00 | 57.80 |
| Average children per program staff | 6.85 | 8.05 | 6.38 | 4.64 | 3.38 | 3.67 | 3.01 | 3.52 | 1.52 | 0.53 | 1.20 | 1.02 | 0.83 |
| Total staff level | 56.00 | 58.00 | 68.00 | 82.00 | 80.00 | 57.00 | 47.00 | 43.00 | 60.50 | 60.00 | 83.50 | 82.00 | 75.50 |
| Average children per total staff | 5.26 | 5.41 | 4.22 | 3.45 | 2.70 | 2.83 | 2.30 | 2.54 | 1.21 | 0.46 | 0.94 | 0.88 | 0.64 |

**TABLE 15.2** Annual Cost of Care per Child at Facility D by Expenditure Category for Selected Years (1950-1995) in 1995 Dollars

*$ per Year*

| Expense Category (Cost per Child per Year; Inflation Adjusted) | 1935 | 1940 | 1945 | 1955 | 1960 | 1965 | 1970 | 1975 | 1980 | 1985 | 1990 | 1995 |
|---|---|---|---|---|---|---|---|---|---|---|---|---|
| Program expense | Not available | Not available | Not available | | | | | | | | | |
| Salaries | | | | 1,650.84 | 2,035.45 | 2,721.88 | 4,248.19 | 7,702.12 | 8,463.46 | 10,347.67 | 13,134.78 | 17,140.37 |
| Food | | | | 1,516.66 | 1,544.03 | 1,725.06 | 2,308.27 | 2,139.12 | 1,817.85 | 1,959.76 | 1,498.43 | 1,278.81 |
| Medical | | | | 142.87 | 127.82 | 286.65 | 304.65 | 359.92 | 340.58 | 428.51 | 450.59 | 405.20 |
| Clothing | | | | 306.04 | 275.36 | 330.65 | 479.18 | 633.68 | 400.05 | 493.46 | 394.58 | 380.38 |
| Supplies | | | | 160.64 | 566.81 | 560.04 | 653.52 | 647.81 | 625.43 | 663.61 | 614.05 | 733.46 |
| Recreation | | | | 34.39 | 197.39 | 153.27 | 232.12 | 340.53 | 283.18 | 642.32 | 621.66 | 635.70 |
| Utilities | | | | 252.12 | 394.57 | 367.22 | 580.44 | 942.98 | 1,147.49 | 1,483.63 | 1,473.24 | 1,581.21 |
| Repairs and maintenance | | | | 344.69 | 157.79 | 201.70 | 388.98 | 687.40 | 668.43 | 735.71 | 901.98 | 716.31 |
| Other program expenses | | | | 1,034.41 | 1,113.82 | 1,079.74 | 1,361.26 | 2,392.45 | 1,682.21 | 1,435.85 | 1,589.08 | 1,365.55 |
| Total program expenses | | | | 5,442.66 | 6,413.04 | 7,426.21 | 10,556.61 | 15,846.01 | 15,428.68 | 18,190.52 | 20,678.39 | 24,236.99 |
| Administrative expenses | | | | 720.81 | 704.09 | 918.60 | 1,614.89 | 4,659.93 | 4,595.58 | 3,312.78 | 4,414.49 | 4,112.63 |
| Fund-raising expense | | | | — | 218.81 | 262.39 | 699.36 | 1,130.63 | 1,190.78 | 1,744.68 | 3,037.88 | 3,028.28 |
| Productive enterprise expense | | | | 870.22 | 946.60 | 1,288.97 | 1,421.13 | 2,117.65 | 1,558.72 | 1,415.58 | 1,030.38 | 972.47 |
| Total expense per child per year | | | | 7,033.69 | 8,282.54 | 9,896.17 | 14,291.99 | 23,754.22 | 22,773.76 | 24,663.56 | 29,161.14 | 32,350.37 |
| Average number of children | | | | 356.90 | 327.80 | 308.80 | 247.40 | 152.00 | 143.75 | 135.50 | 126.70 | 117.90 |
| Program staff level | | | | 55.00 | 65.00 | 72.00 | 85.00 | 86.00 | 79.00 | 72.00 | 71.10 | 81.10 |
| Average children per program staff | | | | 6.49 | 5.04 | 4.29 | 2.91 | 1.77 | 1.82 | 1.88 | 1.78 | 1.45 |
| Total staff level | | | | 73.00 | 82.00 | 88.00 | 100.00 | 107.00 | 104.00 | 99.50 | 89.10 | 96.70 |
| Average children per total staff | | | | 4.89 | 4.00 | 3.51 | 2.47 | 1.42 | 1.38 | 1.36 | 1.42 | 1.22 |

273

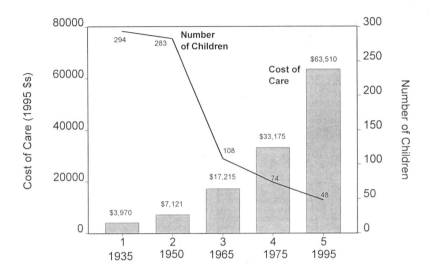

**Figure 15.1.** Annual Cost of Care per Child and Number of Children at Facility ST

number of children in care. The count of children in care decreased from 283 in 1950 to 162 in 1960, 109 in 1970, and 28 in 1980, after which there was a modest increase. There were 72 children in care in 1990 and 48 in care in 1995.

Facility ST's downward enrollment trend reflects the following forces: (a) the decline in the number of children available for institutional care (partially because of the general growth in real family incomes that reduced the need for outside, institutional care, and partly because of the rise in government programs—most notably, Aid to Families with Dependent Children and foster care); (b) attempts by the staff at Facility ST to reduce the children-to-staff ratio to increase the attention received by each child; and (c) two significant changes in Facility ST's mission that resulted in the admission of substantially more troubled children that, in turn, increased the required child care services that had to be provided by a larger number of staff members per child.

Because of the decline in enrollment in the 1940s, 1950s, and early 1960s, the real annual cost of care per child at Facility ST, excluding housing costs, rose from just under $4,000 (in 1995 dollars) in 1935 and 1940 to almost $9,500 in 1960 (a real increase of 144%, or 7% a year, for the 1940-1960 period) and to $17,215 in 1965 (an additional increase of 82%, or 16% per year, for the 1960-1965 period).

The first major shift in Facility ST's mission began in the late 1960s, at which time it began moving from providing care for disadvantaged children as an "orphanage" to providing care for children and their dysfunctional families as a "family service agency." As Table 15.1 reveals, this shift in philosophy caused another substantial jump in the average cost of care. The real annual cost of care per child rose to over $33,000 in 1975 (an increase of 93%, or more than 9% a year, for the 1965-1975 period).

The second change in direction occurred in 1976, after which the facility began the care of more seriously troubled youth, which again caused a dramatic increase in cost per child per year. With this shift and the drop in enrollment by two thirds to only 28 children, the real cost of care per child skyrocketed to nearly $77,000 in 1980. With the expansion of enrollment to 79 children in 1990, the average cost of care declined to under $49,000. Obviously, the average cost of care is sensitive to enrollment, as would be expected. In 1995, when enrollment was 48 children, the real annual cost of care was just under $64,000 per child (an increase of 91% for the 1975-1995 period).[3] Again, these cost data do not include use of plant and equipment that could add more than 20% to the cost of care (as will be discussed later).[4]

The changes in program staffing over time were another source of the cost changes. When the number of children in residence decreased by nearly half between 1940 (294) and 1960 (162), the number of staff involved in the delivery of the "program" (as opposed to support services) did not decrease. Indeed, the program staff size increased from 39 to 44, which meant that the average number of children per program staff person decreased by almost half, from 8.05 in 1940 to 3.67 in 1960. The average number of program-related staff decreased again by more than half during the next 15 years. Recently, the actual number of program-related staff decreased even further from 1.52 in 1975 to 1.02 in 1990 and 0.83 in 1995. Thus, for each child in care, 1.20 staff members were needed in 1995 as opposed to 0.12 program staff members in 1940—a 10-fold increase. As a consequence of the increase in the staff per child and the general increase in real wages of each staff person (which occurred because of tightening labor markets and the use of more highly trained staff people), the real salaries for program staff members per child went from $882 in 1935 to nearly $37,000 in 1995—a 41-fold increase.[5]

The changes over time in various categories of program expenses—food, medical care, clothing, supplies, recreation, utilities, repairs and maintenance, and other program-related expenses—appear to be highly variable. Some of the increases in expenses, however, no doubt relate to the fact that until the late 1960s the children provided significant labor on the farm and in the campus shops. During the 1950s, the amount of time the children in residence spent working in so-called "productive enterprises" (such as farm work, the print shop, and timber cutting) was estimated at 44 hours a week during the summer and 20 hours a week during the school year. Thus, with the loss of the child labor supply due to government regulations and mission changes, the home closed down all its farm and shop operations. The home began to purchase its food and maintenance and other services from outside sources.

Clearly, the increase in repairs and maintenance appears to be linked to the age of many of the buildings. Many of the buildings at Facility ST are several decades old, thus requiring significant repair and maintenance expenses to keep them operational. The repair and maintenance expenditures in recent years at Facility ST, however, have increased because, with rising program costs, maintenance on the buildings was deferred. Now, major costs are being incurred to renovate the buildings.

Education at Facility ST has gone through two major changes from 1935 to 1995. Facility ST maintained an on-campus school from 1933 to 1956, after which the 9th- through 12th-grade students began attending the local county public high school. By 1962, the 5th- through 8th-grade students were attending the county schools. Due to the disruptive nature of the children that the home admitted in its troubled youth program, however, in 1980 the on-campus school was reopened, thereby forcing the facility to hire teachers. Currently, there is a ratio of approximately 1 teacher for every 4 students at Facility ST.

### Cost of Care at Facility D

Facility D has kept the focus of its care on disadvantaged children, although the emotional problems of the children have become gradually more serious over time. As shown in Table 15.2, Facility D's real annual cost of care in 1950 was $7,500 per child (just $380, or 5%, more per year than Facility ST's cost of care per child). By 1960, however, the real annual cost of care at Facility D had increased to $8,283 per child, only 10% higher than the cost of care in 1950 (but 12% below the cost of care at Facility ST). As can be seen in Table 15.2 and Figure 15.2 (which depicts the data in Table 15.2 for selected

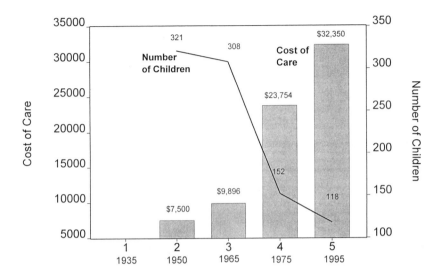

**Figure 15.2.** Annual Cost of Care per Child and Number of Children at Facility D

years), by 1970, the cost of care per child at Facility D had increased to $14,292, 72% higher than the 1960 cost of care. Costs continued to increase until, in 1995, the cost of care was $32,350 per child, more than four times the real cost of care in 1950.

At Facility D, the increase in program-related staff members per child was also substantial, although not nearly as dramatic as that at Facility ST. In 1950, at Facility D there were 7.38 children per program-related staff member. This ratio decreased to 2.91 in 1970 and 1.45 in 1995. Thus, for each child in care, 0.69 program-related staff members were needed in 1995 compared to 0.14 program-related staff members per child in 1950—a 5-fold increase in staffing per child from 1950 to 1995. Salaries for program staff members per child increased in constant 1995 dollar terms from $1,651 in 1950 to $17,140 in 1995—an increase of more than 12-fold.

Costs for Facility D have increased more slowly in recent decades than those of Facility ST due mainly to the fact that Facility D has maintained its focus on disadvantaged children. Its overall costs have also been much lower because it has served a larger number of children, over which it could spread many of its fixed costs. In 1950, Facility D had 357 children in residence (21%

more than Facility ST). Facility D had 328 children in 1960, 247 children in 1970, and 118 children in 1995 (twice or more than the number at Facility ST for each of these years).[6] In addition, it should be noted that for many years Facility D obviously placed more emphasis on regular maintenance and upkeep than did Facility ST (suggesting that Facility ST's costs may be more understated during recent decades than Facility D's costs).

Facility D has also controlled its costs by relying totally on off-campus schooling for most of the past three decades. In 1928, it began the practice of sending its children to public school for their last 3 years of education. Between 1948 and 1958, all but the first through third grades began attending public schools. In 1967, the remaining children began attending public schools—a tradition that continues to this day.

## ▪ Cost of Institutional Versus Family Care

The cost of institutional care appears to be "high," but the relevant question is "Compared to what?" Clearly, the cost of troubled children should be expected to be higher than the cost of care within normal families. This requires only that we ask the following: Is the cost of institutional care of disadvantaged children at, for example, Facility D out of line with the cost of care in "normal" families? To address this question, we report in Table 15.3 the expenditures per child in a family of four (two parents and two children) as estimated for 1995 by researchers at the U.S. Department of Agriculture.[7] Because child care expenditures vary with family income, we report the average child care expenditures for the following income groups: "low-income" families with annual incomes of less than $32,800, "moderate-income" families with annual incomes between $32,800 and $55,500, and "high-income" families with annual incomes of more than $55,500.[8]

Table 15.3 reveals that if only out-of-pocket expenditures—on food, transportation, clothing, health care, child care and education, and miscellaneous items (mainly entertainment)—on child care are considered, the cost of rearing a child in a family of four might be viewed as quite modest: $3,955 per child per year for a family that has an annual income of less than $32,800, $5,282 per child per year for a family that has an annual income of between $32,800 and $55,500, and $7,247 per child per year for a family that has an annual income of more than $55,500. Such data, however, exclude the cost of housing and, more important, the value of the parents' time applied to child care.

**Table 15.3** Estimated Cost of Rearing a Child in a Family, 1995

| Expenditures and Parental Time | Annual Family Income ($) | | |
|---|---|---|---|
| | (A) Less than $32,800 | (B) $32,800-$55,500 | (C) More than $55,500 |
| Expenditure | | | |
| Food | 1,150 | 1,386a | 1,768 |
| Transportation | 979 | 1,369a | 1,642a |
| Clothing | 535 | 619a | 822a |
| Health care | 415 | 512a | 608a |
| Child care and education | 350 | 595a | 1,001a |
| Miscellaneous | 528 | 801a | 1,406a |
| (1) Total expenditures per child without housing | 3,955 | 5,282a | 7,247a |
| (2) Value of parental child care time per child | 16,390[a] | 22,747[b] | 32,794[c] |
| (3) Total [1 + 2] | 20,345 | 28,029 | 40,041a |
| (4) Housing | 1,794 | 2,532a | 4,102 |
| Total of all expenditures and parental time [3 + 4] | 22,139 | 30,561a | 44,143 |

a. The value of parental time was computed on the assumption that the two parents have a combined income of $32,800 a year,, or a wage for each parent of $7.88 per hour. The calculation for the value of parental time also assumes that both parents spend a total of 60 hours a week caring for their two children, and that the parents spend a total of 56 hours a week sleeping and the sleep time is one tenth the hourly wage rate.
b. The value of parental time was computed on the assumption that the two parents have a combined income of $55,500 a year, or a wage for each parent of $13.34 per hour. The calculation for the value of parental time also assumes that both parents spend a total of 60 hours a week caring for their two children, and that the parents spend a total of 56 hours a week sleeping and the sleep time is one tenth the hourly wage rate.
c. The value of parental time was computed on the assumption that the two parents have a combined income of $80,000 a year, or a wage for each parent of $19.23 per hour. The calculation for the value of parental time also assumes that both parents spend a total of 60 hours a week caring for their two children, and that the parents spend a total of 56 hours a week sleeping and the sleep time is one tenth the hourly wage rate.

The expenditures on various categories of amenities—food, transportation, clothing, health care, child care and education, miscellaneous, supplies, and recreation—may not be strictly comparable for the institutions and for moderate-income families. We note, however, that, as evident in Table 15.4, when only those categories are summed, the institutional cost totals per child compare favorably with the cost for a family of four (with an annual income of $32,800 to $55,500). The annual cost for the moderate-income family per child is $5,282, whereas the annual cost per child in Facility ST is $4,918 and the annual cost per child in Facility D is $3,432. When housing, utilities, repairs and maintenance, and other program expenses are added, the annual cost per child increases to $7,814 for the family, $13,622 for Facility ST, and

**Table 15.4**  Cost of Basic Amenities of Rearing a Child in a Family and in
Two Institutions, 1995

| | Cost of Care per Child ($) | | |
|---|---|---|---|
| Amenity | Families With Annual Incomes of $32,800-55,500 | Facility ST | Facility D |
| Expense | | | |
| Food | 1,386 | 1,341 | 1,278 |
| Transportation | 1,369 | | |
| Clothing | 619 | | 380 |
| Health care | 512 | 1,315 | 405 |
| Child care and education | 595 | | |
| Miscellaneous[a] | 801 | | |
| Supplies | | 2,262 | 733 |
| Recreation | | | 636 |
| Total of costs per child without housing | 5,282 | 4,918 | 3,432 |
| Housing | 2,532 | | |
| Utilities | | 3,249 | 1,581 |
| Repairs and maintenance | | 2,412 | 716 |
| Other program expenses | | 3,043 | 1,366 |
| Total of costs per child with housing or related expenses | 7,814 | 13,622 | 7,095 |

a. Miscellaneous expenses include personal care items, entertainment, and reading material.

$7,095 for Facility D. We interpret this to mean that the basic institutional cost of care for disadvantaged children (Facility D) is approximately equal to or lower than the cost of care of children within a family. The basic cost of care for severely troubled children, however, is almost twice as high as the cost of care within a family.

The most important expenditure within institutions is the salary and fringe benefits for staff, as evident in Tables 15.1 and 15.2. Parents, however, also incur a time cost in the care of their children. The value of parental child care time can only be approximately estimated by considering the parents' foregone market wages. Of course, the calculated parental time value will depend on the assumptions relating to the wage rate and the number of hours spent on child care. The best we can do is report the cost under clearly identified assumptions.

We estimated the value of parental time for the three income categories in Table 15.3, assuming a combined family income for the low-income family (column A) of $32,800, for the moderate-income family (column B) of $55,500, and for the high-income family (column C) of $80,000. Assuming the families' income was earned equally by each parent in each family, the hourly wage rates were determined by assuming that each parent worked 40 hours a week for 52 weeks a year. This means that the hourly wage rates for the low-, moderate-, and high-income families were assumed to be, respectively, $7.88 (column A), $13.34 (column B), and $19.23 (column C). The annual dollar values of the parental time per child for each income category were computed by assuming that the two parents in each family spent a total of 60 hours a week in the care of their two children and by multiplying 60 hours times the category's respective wage rate.[9]

Some value must be given to the time the parents spend sleeping, given that they do provide supervision and security benefits for their children during the sleeping hours.[10] We arbitrarily assumed that the sleeping hours would be valued at one tenth the parents' hourly wage rate, and that the parents spend 8 hours a night sleeping. We consider these assumptions to be conservative, probably understating the value of parental time.

These assumptions relating to the value of parental time and the amount of time parents spend in child care lead to the following estimates of the annual value of parental child care time per child by income category represented in Table 15.3: $16,390 for the low-income family (column A), $22,747 for the moderate-income family (column B), and $32,794 for the high-income family (column C). This means that the total annual cost of child care per child (combining the out-of-pocket expenditures for items identified in Table 15.3 with the value of the parental time) is $20,345 for the low-income family, $28,029 for the moderate-income family, and $40,041 for the high-income family.

These last cost data can be used to evaluate the annual cost of care of disadvantaged children at Facility D, which was $32,350 per child (not including the cost of housing and grounds) and includes pay for the staff. The per child cost at Facility D is 59% higher than the total cost of care per child in the low-income family (Table 15.3, column A) but only 15% higher than the total cost of care per child in the moderate-income family (Table 15.3, column B). The per child cost at Facility D, however, is 19% lower than the per child cost of care in the high-income family (Table 15.3, column C).

One of the functions of a home for children is to increase the benefits the children might receive to more than what they would receive if they stayed with their (generally low-income) families. We would not normally expect the children in institutional care to receive benefits on par with children in high-income families. As a consequence, we consider the more appropriate comparison would be between the cost of care at Facility D with the cost of care in the moderate-income family. We conclude that the cost at Facility D is higher than the cost of family care, but it is not as far out of line as might be expected if the out-of-pocket cost of institutional care is compared with out-of-pocket expenditures of families.


## ▒ Sources of Support

Table 15.5 shows the sources of support and related percentages of support for both Facilities ST and D for 1950 and 1995. As can be seen, in 1950, Facility ST's revenues totaled approximately $254,000. It received approximately 60% of its support in 1950 from the church, more than 11% from the government, approximately 7% from the investment income on its endowments, and nearly 19% from individuals. These support categories accounted for approximately 97% of total revenues at that time.

By 1995, its revenues had grown to nearly $5 million, a 19-fold increase compared to revenues in 1950. Its church support increased in real terms from $151,225 in 1950 to $1.3 million in 1995. The church support, however, had by 1995 fallen to 26% of total revenues from nearly 60% in 1950. Individual support had almost totally evaporated by 1995. The compensating factor for these decreases was the 155-fold increase in real revenues from Facility ST's investment fund and the 32-fold increase in support from state and local governments. As a consequence, support from the investment fund increased to 53% of total revenues and governmental support increased to approximately 19%.

Facility D had real revenues of slightly more than $336,000 in 1950 and $3.9 million in 1995, an 11- or 12-fold increase. In 1950, Facility D's support from the church was $268,000, which amounted to approximately 80% of all revenues. By 1995, the church support increased in real dollar terms by 7-fold to more than $1.8 million, which constituted 48% of all revenues. In 1950, 6% of Facility D's revenues came from individual support and 7% from its investment fund. No moneys were obtained from the government in 1950. By 1995, the income from its endowments had increased to 31%, and individual support had increased to 13%. Less than 4% of revenues in 1995 came from the government.

From the data in Table 15.5, it appears that if a significant decrease in investment income on endowments occurred, Facilities ST and D would have

**Table 15.5** Sources of Financial Support for Facilities ST and D by Revenue Source for 1950 and 1995, in 1995 Dollars

|  | *Facility ST* | | *Facility D* | |
| --- | --- | --- | --- | --- |
| *Support Category* | $ | % | $ | % |
| 1950 | | | | |
| Church contributions | 151,225 | 59.64 | 268,232 | 79.72 |
| Duke endowment contributions | 9,999 | 3.94 | 8,056 | 2.39 |
| State and federal government fees | 28,203 | 11.12 | — | 0.00 |
| Investment income | 16,876 | 6.66 | 23,500 | 6.98 |
| Productive enterprises | — | 0.00 | 15,980 | 4.75 |
| Individual support | 47,246 | 18.63 | 20,501 | 6.09 |
| Miscellaneous income | — | 0.00 | 203 | 0.06 |
| Total | 253,549 | 100.00 | 336,472 | 100.00 |
| 1995 | | | | |
| Church contributions | 1,275,721 | 25.85 | 1,843,739 | 47.56 |
| Duke endowment contributions | 39,705 | 0.80 | 87,870 | 2.27 |
| State and federal government fees | 918,003 | 18.60 | 138,470 | 3.57 |
| Investment income | 2,616,928 | 53.03 | 1,213,551 | 31.30 |
| Productive enterprises | — | 0.00 | 60,650 | 1.56 |
| Individual support | — | 0.00 | 510,426 | 13.17 |
| Miscellaneous income | 84,269 | 1.71 | 21,988 | 0.57 |
| Total | 4,934,626 | 100.00 | 3,876,694 | 100.00 |

to reorganize their budgets drastically to cover expenses. This could be more of a problem at Facility ST, which relies more heavily on investment income, than at Facility D. Moreover, Facility ST would have a more difficult adjustment problem with any cutback in public funding for the care of children.

## ▨ Conclusion

As can be seen by our analysis, the cost of care of a disadvantaged child may be close to, if not more than, the cost of attending Harvard University for a year. It should be noted, however, this could also be said of the cost of care in moderate-income families—if the value of parental time is considered.[11] The cost of care for severely troubled children may be approximately twice the cost of care for disadvantaged children.

The relatively higher costs at Facility ST may be attributable to a number of factors that could not be assessed in this study, but the following are surely key factors: (a) a smaller number of children, (b) the additional educational expenditures (including the exceptionally low number of children per teacher), and (c) the additional counseling and monitoring services needed for severely troubled children.

From our review of the available but limited cost data, the following appear to be important ways that children's homes might be able to moderate the cost of care:

1. Increase the number of children in care.
2. Curb the number of program staff members.
3. Reduce staff salaries and fringe benefits, which may require a change in the credentials of the staff.
4. Expand the use of the children in the upkeep of the facilities and in provision of basic amenities.
5. In general, eliminate or modify many of the regulations relating to institutional child care that have been implemented during the past three or four decades, thus freeing up the institutions to make more cost-effective use of their limited resources.

The first two options imply increasing the children-to-staff ratio. The third option might require a change in the credentials of the staff, whereas the fourth option might require a liberalization of laws relating to child labor in institutions. Evidence in this chapter, however, suggests that the two homes provided more than adequate care when they had far higher children-to-staff ratios and were operated with staff with fewer credentials than currently exist in Facilities ST and D.

Clearly, deregulation of institutional child care, although potentially beneficial in terms of cost savings, represents a course of action that can only be addressed by policymakers outside of the institutions. Also, our comparison of the cost structures of the two institutions reveals that there might be substantial cost from reorienting child welfare policies of state and federal governments toward providing care in homes for disadvantaged children before the children need additional treatment for more serious emotional, physical, and psychological problems.

## ▓ Notes

1. The cost of extending the study to more institutions, which would have been desirable, was simply prohibitive and unrealistic. Many homes are unwilling to provide accounting records for the type of analysis we wanted to perform.

2. To estimate the real full cost of maintaining a home for disadvantaged children, including the cost of the buildings and other major assets, we can consider the following hypothetical facility model for an institution that would care for 143 children. We assume that such a home would require 100 acres of land that would cost (in South Carolina, where the two accounting authors work) $4,000 per acre and 64,000 square feet of living, recreational, and office space that would cost an average of $70 per square foot. The total required investment would be $4.9 million. Assuming an interest rate of 5%, the added interest cost alone would increase the real cost of care per child in 1995 by nearly $2,500 over the cost of care at Facility D, or $34,840 (this cost figure does not include depreciation expense, given that the depreciation expense should be recoverable through the sale of the real estate at the end of usage of the facility). Thus, we conclude that the cost of care at Facility D (excluding the cost of plant and equipment) is probably understated by no more than 8%. The total cost of care for a disadvantaged child appears to be much higher—possibly twice—than the cost of housing and accommodating youth under the South Carolina Department of Juvenile Justice. (In 1995, the cost of care per year per youth under the South Carolina Juvenile Justice System was $15,512, and the cost of care per year per prisoner in the South Carolina Corrections facility was $13,198.)

3. The increase in the cost of care in the 1975 to 1995 period may be partially explained by the fact that toward the end of this period, the home had a major change in administration, which may have temporarily increased the cost of care. The new head of the home reports that in 1997, the annual cost of care was decreased to $47,500 per child.

4. We checked the cost structure at another home for severely troubled youth. In 1995, the cost per child at this home was slightly more than $61,000, just 4% less than the cost at Facility ST. It is notable that Facility ST has three times the number of children in care than this other home for severely troubled children, which means it is not achieving the expected economies of scale.

5. It should be noted that we also found in our review of the Duke Endowment reports that Facility ST has substantially reduced its capacity to handle children during the past four decades. In 1950, Facility ST could accommodate 295 disadvantaged children, whereas in 1995 it could handle at most 68 troubled children.

6. Facility D's estimated capacity in 1950 was 295 disadvantaged children. By 1995, its capacity was decreased to 143.

7. See U.S. Department of Agriculture, Center for Nutrition Policy and Promotion (1995), as summarized in the *Statistical Abstract* (U.S. Department of Commerce, 1996, p. 456), with calculations added by the authors of this chapter. The cost estimates were made for 1990 and adjusted by the authors by consumer price index for the expenditure categories to put the estimates in 1995 dollars.

8.The 1993 median income for all families in 1995 dollars was $38,980. The 1993 median income for families with two income-earners in 1995 dollars was $50,016 (U.S. Department of Commerce, 1996, p. 468). Also, the estimated expenditures per child by category represent the average for the expenditures per child for various age groups.

9. We derived 60 hours of parental time each week by assuming that the parents spent a total of 8 hours each weekday and 10 hours each weekend day in the care of both their children. This means that each parent spent 30 hours a week on the children.

10. We note that assigning a minor value to the time parents spend sleeping can be justified because in some states, child care institutions must pay house parents for the time they spend sleeping.

11. We acknowledge that parents usually receive offsetting benefits for the care they give their children. This fact, however, does not alter the fact that they forgo income while caring for their children.

## ▓ References

Ford, M., & Kroll, J. (1995, April). *There is a better way: Family-based alternatives to institutional care*. St. Paul, MN: North American Council on Adoptable Children.

U.S. Department of Agriculture, Center for Nutrition Policy and Promotion. (1995). *Expenditures on children by families, 1994 annual report*. Washington, DC: U.S. Government Printing Office.

U.S. Department of Commerce, Bureau of the Census. (1996). *Statistical abstract of the United States*. Washington, DC: U.S. Government Printing Office.

# PART IV

## THE PATH TO REFORM

# Rethinking Orphanages for the 21st Century

*A Search for Reform of the Nation's Child Welfare System*[1]

RICHARD B. McKENZIE

F ew question the proposition that children need a good start in life. Far too many American children, however, fail to get the "good starts" that they need. It is widely acknowledged that there is a large number of children who are growing up without the supervision and guidance of one or both parents for much of the time while they are out of school. The statistics on child abuse and neglect are horrific.[2] More than 1 million cases of significant child abuse and neglect are substantiated every year. Five children in the country die each day from abuse and neglect. Approximately 22,000 babies are abandoned annually in the hospitals in which they were born. The incidence of child abuse and neglect of all forms more than doubled between 1980 and 1993.[3]

Adoptions have eased the troubles of many children, as have various forms of substitute public care, not the least of which has been foster parent care.[4] Only 6% of the babies abandoned each year in hospital nurseries are adopted. The foster care system is approaching a crisis state, given the speed with which the number of children in care is expanding while the number of available foster parents is contracting, the increase in the time children are staying in the system, the decline in the percentage of foster care children who are adopted out of the system, and the growth in the number of different foster care placements many children must endure.[5]

The foster care system had more than 600,000 children in care in 1992—an increase of more than 50% since 1986. At the same time, tens of thousands of children throughout the United States were waiting to be placed in the foster care system. The percentage of children in foster care who had been in the system for 2 or 3 years increased by almost 50% in just 7 years—from less than 11% in 1983 to nearly 16% in 1990. The percentage of children in foster care for 3 to 5 years increased from less than 12% in 1983 to almost 17% in 1990. Concurrently, the percentage of children adopted out of foster care declined by one third—from 12% in 1983 to less than 8% in 1990.[6]

Foster care was intended to be temporary care. One of every 10 children—more than 60,000 of all current foster care children—can expect foster care to be, in effect, permanent care, however, given that they will spend more than 7 years in the system. For too many children, foster care will also be unstable care, especially because siblings are often sent to different foster homes. Moreover, 23% of foster care children will have two placements, an additional 20% will experience three to five placements, and 7% will have more than seven placements, which means that more than one fourth of the children who enter the foster care system can expect to be shifted among more than three foster parents (SOS Children's Villages, USA, 1997) (and many can expect to experience dozens of placements).[7]

No doubt, many foster children have done well because their foster parents contributed much for very little payment. Signs of strain with the foster care system abound, however. Currently, children in foster care consti-tute less than 0.003% of the nation's population. Seventeen percent of state prisoners, however, are former foster care children, 40% of foster children leave the system to go on the nation's welfare roles, and 39% of the homeless youth in Los Angeles County are former foster care children (SOS Children's Villages, USA, 1997, p. 3).

Judges and child care workers throughout the United States openly decry the fact that many abused and neglected children will be sent home from the foster care system only to be abused again and returned to the system for another round of foster placements. Heads of group homes, which provide temporary care for troubled children, readily admit that many of their charges should never be sent home, but all too often abusive homes or additional foster care placements are the only options available.[8]

To state that the nation's child care system needs new options for care is an understatement of major proportion. One of the "new" options for a growing number of children will likely be an "old" option—the private "orphanage" (or children's home). This chapter reviews the policy obstacles that impede the return of private children's homes and offers suggested policy reforms devised at a symposium of researchers and practitioners.

## ▓ The Children's Home Option

In late 1994 and early 1995, policymakers and commentators furiously debated the issues of whether private orphanages (or long-term residential and educational care centers for disadvantaged children) should be brought back as a care option (see Chapter 6). Contrary to the way this debate ended— abruptly, without any apparent resolution of the central issue—the issue today is no longer whether private orphanages (or a modern variant of them) will return. Private orphanages never completely disappeared, as might be be- lieved. Not all children's homes folded or changed their missions to care for severely troubled youth. The Milton Hershey School in Pennsylvania, the Connie Maxwell Home for Children in South Carolina, the Masonic Home for Children in North Carolina, and the Palmer House in Mississippi are examples of children's homes that have continued to provide long-term care for disadvantaged children for much, if not all, of this century.[9]

New private orphanages (or children's homes) are springing up. SOS Children's Villages, USA, Incorporated, which has children's homes in 125 countries, has established a child care beachhead in the United States, with a new model for children's homes that has been tested and proven effective in Florida and Illinois and that will likely be duplicated throughout the country.[10] Moreover, some religious and civic groups have concluded that the disadvan- taged children who are now being tossed from one foster placement to another, and between foster placements and their own dysfunctional families, need the sense of security that comes from having a permanent home. The Lutheran Church of California is currently operating a program dubbed "20/20/20"—20 children's homes in 20 cities in 20 years. Children's homes that two and three decades ago became short-term treatment centers are reconsidering their mission, with an eye toward reintroducing long-term residential care for children who would otherwise not be able to return home or who would likely continue to move from one foster placement to the next.

Clearly, the nation's growing problems with family stability, child abuse and neglect, welfare reform, and foster care ensure that a modern form of private orphanage care will return. The relevant question is at what pace private orphanages (or whatever they are called) will spread, and this issue is critically related to the cost of care, which is high and increasing.[11]

## ■ Children's Need for a Good Start

To say that children need a good start is instructive but not sufficient. One child care expert, whose authority is grounded in his professional work and his background as an orphanage alumnus, suggests that a good start for a child almost always encompasses four attributes: connectedness, continuity, dignity, and opportunity (Seita, Mitchell, & Tobin, 1996):

> 1. By connectedness, it is meant that "children need to feel that someone is there for them, and that they are a part of someone else's life" (Seita et al., 1996, p. 93).
> 2. Continuity is "a sense of continuous belonging with another person or persons. The young person needs to feel a part of a greater whole and has an important position to play within it" (Seita et al., 1996, p. 96).
> 3. "To have dignity is to feel worthy. All children are worthy of respect, caring, love, thought, and courtesy" (Seita et al., 1996, p. 98).
> 4. Children need an opportunity to grow and develop, which means that "young people must be able to explore and express their capabilities without undue external barriers. Children must have access to quality education, recreation, and leisure, all at an appropriate developmental level" (Seita et al., 1996, p. 100).

The list is short and subject to quibbles. Seita et al. (1996) would be the first to acknowledge that the list of four attributes is not necessarily all-inclusive of children's needs. For example, children need to feel safe (which the authors would include under dignity), and they need some form of spiritual or moral nurturing or both (which the authors would include under continuity). The point is that children's needs are fairly basic and relatively easy to identify and categorize. The tough task is ensuring that children receive all the basics.

Most children will receive the good start they need from their biological families. Others will get a good start from adoptive families, and still others will benefit from some form of short-term and long-term foster care as the children's families reconstitute themselves. Work on improving the care children receive from their biological, adoptive, and foster families must continue for an obvious reason: These forms of care will always be the dominant means by which children get their starts in life. For a growing number of children, however, the various forms of family-based care available to them have been inadequate, if not destructive. Many disadvantaged children will never be adopted. This does not mean that adoption should not be encouraged and more widely used, with the legal and cost impediments to adoption reduced, as has been recommended (Bevan, 1996, Chapter 5).

. The unadulterated fact remains that many children should never be returned to their abusive and neglectful biological parents, and far too many children will spend years of their childhoods in what can only be called "permanent temporary care," year by year going from one temporary foster care placement to another. Could not these children find better childhood experiences in care centers that offer long-term, permanent substitute care that might not match the ideal of family life but would be significantly better than the next best alternative?

## ■ Reconsideration of Past Assessments of Orphanages

Past assessments of institutional care for children have been far too harsh. Admittedly, many child care experts have concluded, after reviewing a number of studies relating to the efficacy of institutional care, that private orphanages "damaged" the children in their care.[12] Although many orphanages may not have provided their charges with good experiences, a critical review of the child care literature relating to orphanages suggests that the studies themselves are defective in a number of regards, leaving open the question of whether the broad sweep of private orphanages throughout the United States during the first half of this century were as "bad" as has been suggested.[13]

Although all homes for disadvantaged children probably harmed some of the children in their care (as do some families), there is strong evidence that homes for disadvantaged children helped a substantial majority of their charges. The general conclusion drawn from the first and only large-scale survey of orphanage alumni (involving 1,600 respondents from nine orphanages in the South and Midwest) stands in sharp contrast to conventional wisdom and expert conclusion on orphanage life: As a group, the alumni have outpaced their counterparts in the general population by significant margins on practically all measures, not the least of which are education, income, and attitude toward life (see Chapter 7). The survey respondents seem to be saying that they received from their orphanage experience the required "connectedness, continuity, dignity, and opportunity" that constituted a good start and served them well later in life.[14]

The record of many homes of the past should be reassessed with an eye toward considering their "batting averages" relative to the batting averages of alternative systems of substitute care, most notably foster parent care. These assessments of the programs of past and current children homes should be remade with the goal of identifying "best practices" and avoiding many of the mistakes that were made in the past.

The case for temporary institutional care of seriously troubled children has been made and is widely accepted. The case for permanent care of disadvantaged children who have not yet become seriously troubled has not been widely accepted and needs to be restated with greater force. This case needs to be made with reference to the problems and deficiencies in the current substitute-care systems. What is needed, however, is not a contraction in the number of children who receive substitute care but an expansion in the array of care options so that children can be placed in environments that best serve their particular needs.

It must be acknowledged that many children will never prosper in an institutional setting. At the same time, experience has shown that many children can do well in such a setting, and they can surely do better in such a setting than they might do in a sequence of temporary placements. Private homes for children can provide a form of long-term, permanent care, from which a sense a security can develop. They can also provide much more, including improved educational opportunity, a sense of work ethic, religious and moral nurturing, and camaraderie and sense of community—attributes that the alumni of homes had in their childhoods and that are clearly evident at homes such as the Milton Hershey School in Hershey, Pennsylvania, and SOS Children's Villages that, as noted, are scattered across more than 100 countries worldwide.[15]

### ▓ Policy Impediments to Permanent Institutional Care

Greater use of the private orphanage (or permanent children's home) option, however, is currently inhibited by a variety of state and federal laws and regulations that encourage judges and child welfare workers to keep children with their biological but abusive and neglectful parents and to shun the use of long-term, institutional care. Many of these laws and regulations also have the effect of increasing the cost of long-term child care in institutional settings, which means that fewer children than otherwise will receive the type of permanent care they need.

Under current federal law (namely, the Adoption Assistance and Child Welfare Act of 1980), states must prove that they have made "reasonable efforts" to prevent the removal of children from their biological parents and to return children to their biological parents, a seemingly innocuous requirement. The policy intent of this federal law is understandable—to reverse the sharp rise in foster placements that occurred in the 1970s (which did, in fact, occur for a time)[16]—and few would question making reasonable efforts to keep families together. The problem, however, is that the term *reasonable efforts* has been unreasonably interpreted by practitioners in the child welfare system to mean that virtually every possible effort must be made to rehabilitate the parents and to reunite the children with their parents when the children have been removed.

The termination of parental rights is often delayed for years because the parents make little or no effort to change their abusive and neglectful ways. Abusive and neglectful parents can also slow down the termination process by, at times, making only marginal improvements in their behavior or by claiming that they have not been provided with ample state resources (through, for example, drug rehabilitation programs) to correct their behavior.

The accumulation of delays can mean that children are forced to remain with their parents long after parental abuse and neglect has been substantiated as extensive efforts continue to rehabilitate the parents and to stop the abuse. It has also meant that children have been repeatedly returned to abusive and neglectful parents to be abused and neglected again, and that, during this process, children have been forced to endure repeated cycles of multiple foster care placements (see Chapter 2).

The termination of parental rights of biological parents has become progressively more difficult and time-consuming, even for abusive parents who have committed repeated felonies against one or more of their children. Often, children who have not been abused (sexually, emotionally, or physically) cannot be removed from their abusing parent(s) even though one or more of their siblings has been abused.[17]

No one questions the importance of good family nurturing to children, and clearly state and federal law should not obstruct the continuance of family life when it supports the welfare of children in the families. As a result of extended state efforts to rehabilitate and reunite otherwise abusive and neglectful parents and parental rights not being denied, however, children age through repeated cycles of foster care placements and become progressively more troubled. Children's growing troubles should be expected with the buildup of insecurity as they are passed from one set of foster parents to another in the so-called "foster care drift." Understandably, children become less adoptable, eventually often requiring psychological care in institutional settings.

Indeed, researchers have found that the substitution of the foster care system for the institutional and orphanage care system in the 1950s and 1960s has (after adjusting for a number of other forces at work) lowered the adoption rate of disadvantaged children (see Chapter 9). Unfortunately, growing evidence indicates that the family rehabilitation and reunification programs have been ineffective, and children have not received the care they need or, worse, have literally been abused, albeit inadvertently, by the child welfare system that was designed to help them (Gelles, 1996; see also Chapter 4).

The child welfare system may have been predisposed to interpret reasonable efforts very generously because many experts and practitioners are convinced that any form of family care is to be preferred, even over the best form of institutional care, and also because the scope of care provided by state agencies can be expanded with a generous interpretation of what constitutes reasonable efforts. Regrettably, within the child aid system, there are built-in budget biases in favor of placing children in foster care and not moving them to institutional care.[18]

The system, however, has another, perhaps stronger economic incentive to make far more than reasonable efforts to rehabilitate parents and to reunify children with families that may or may not have been rehabilitated: The cost of institutional care, which might have to be paid for by state budgets, is very high—easily exceeding $30,000 per year per child—and the cost has grown substantially during recent decades (see Chapter 15). At one home for disadvantaged children, the annual cost of care per child in 1995 was more than four times the real (inflation-adjusted) cost of care per child in the early 1950s (see Chapter 15).

The growth in the cost of institutional care during the past five decades has been the result of many factors, including the rise in real wages of institutional caregivers and the intentional reduction the institutions have made in their children-to-staff ratios so that additional higher-quality and more personal child care services could be provided. The cost increases have also been partially self-inflicted by states, however, because of the increase in the detailed regulations that institutions must follow.

Currently, institutions must adhere to volumes of regulations and accreditation requirements that in printed form weigh several pounds. For example, in many states institutional children's homes must meet construction requirements that exceed the specifications in building codes for single-family homes, and regulations specify how many square feet of living space and toilets the homes must have for each child in care. Regulations also specify how many children are allowed in each bedroom and how many staff people with various credentials must be hired for each child in care. In addition, homes are required to pay house parents when they are asleep (see Chapter 13). Then, the institutions are limited in the work they can require their children to perform. They are further limited in the work they can ask of children in their care because of the liability they may incur in case of accidents (see Chapter 12). The financial problems of institutions have been compounded by the fact that, when the institutions accept public funding, they are told how long they can care for and treat children, and they are restricted in the extent of the required religious component of their programs—restrictions, no doubt, that have undercut the willingness of various denominations and civic groups to financially support institutional care (see Chapter 6).

## ▓ The Path to Policy Reforms

Ways must be found to ensure that private charitable, religious, and civic groups can develop creative and improved alternative institutional care opportunities that meet the local needs of identified populations of children. To develop these care options, the following changes in conditions appear self-evident:

1. Private homes, and their supporting religious, civic, and charitable organizations, must be given greater freedom to devise methods of care that are more cost-effective.
2. More children must be allowed to enter permanent institutional care before they have been repeatedly abused, experienced prolonged stays in the foster care system, and become troubled by the lack of permanency in their lives.[19]

Members of Congress and their staff have recognized the need for substantial reform in the country's basic child welfare laws. Also, there is reason to hope that laudable policy changes will be forthcoming because of the passage of the Adoption Promotion Act of 1997 (H.R. 867) by the House of Representatives in the spring of 1997, which is understandably intended to encourage adoption. Currently, this legislation is awaiting Senate action.[20] Broader changes are badly needed, however, because adoption will not be suitable for all disadvantaged children in need of a permanent place to call home.

To afford homes for children greater flexibility in their programs, the following very general policy recommendations need to be considered:

> *Lessen the regulatory burden on child care institutions:* There must be a broad liberalization of state licensure statutes and regulations applicable to residential educational institutions, the goals of which are to lower the costs of care facing current and would-be operators of such facilities and to promote innovation and entrepreneurial efforts.[21] We suggest that states license particular providers of residential child care, including churches and other civic and philanthropic organizations, and leave the management details of residential facilities staffing and programming to the licensed provider. In general, the states should be assigned responsibility for setting the standards of care, especially when public funding is involved, whereas the facilities should be in the business of determining how best in terms of quality and cost the standards can be met. Thus, we suggest the following:
>
> > 1. States adopt a statute that provides for a less regulated status of "registered" child care institution as an alternative to the traditional, more regulated "licensed" status (versions of which have been adopted in Florida and Mississippi).
> >
> > 2. States take steps to eliminate the statutes and regulations that currently discourage the use of volunteers and resident labor, to the extent allowed by applicable federal law.
> >
> > 3. State regulatory bodies recognize the role of the law in contributing to the high cost of starting up and operating residential facilities for children and engage in ongoing discussions with the providers of these facilities to find additional ways by which statutes and regulations can be relaxed or eliminated and thus reduce the start-up costs of new care facilities and the cost of continuing care.
>
> *Expand work opportunities in child care institutions:* Many state laws allow parents to assign their children a broad range of work responsibilities in the home, on family farms, and in businesses. Child care institutions should be afforded the same rights to assign work responsibilities to the children in their care.
>
> *Convert public child welfare funds to block grants:* A portion, if not all, of federal child welfare funds that are now allocated to foster care should be distributed to states as block grants, allowing states maximum flexibility in the placement of disadvantaged children in existing permanent institutional settings (e.g., SOS

Children's Villages, USA) and in the development, monitoring, and evaluation of new options for the permanent institutional placement of children.

To reduce the time children spend in foster care and to increase the chances for children to have a measure of permanency in their lives, the following policy recommendations must be considered:

*Elevate the importance of "permanence" in the development of child welfare policies:* Preserving families and reunifying children with their biological parents are worthy welfare goals, but they are hardly the only guiding goals that should direct child welfare policies, given the number of children who continue to be harmed by their parents. North Carolina legislators have taken the lead in having child safety take precedence over family preservation and reunification in directing that state's child welfare policies (Batten, 1997, p. C1). Policymakers must realize, however, that children can be "safe" as they are bounced among multiple foster care placements. Policymakers must take an additional step, making the establishment of a permanent residence for the child a higher public policy priority. This means that the time allotted for permanency planning for children in some jurisdictions, which, as noted, can stretch to a number of years or until the child grows to adulthood, must be shortened. We must impose an enforced time limit on the process of family rehabilitation and reunification before parental rights are ultimately terminated. Clearly, we must make subjecting the child to the fewest possible substitute-care placements a top priority.

*Narrow the range of cases in which reasonable efforts must be made to reunify children with their abusive and neglectful families:* The Adoption Act of 1997 (H.R. 867) proposes the type of change in federal child welfare law that is needed. Under this bill, states would not be required to make reasonable efforts to reunify a family in "aggravated circumstances" as defined in state law and in which a court has confirmed that a child has been subjected to such aggravated circumstances. Examples of aggravated circumstances are cases of abandonment, torture, chronic abuse, or sexual abuse. Reasonable efforts would also not be required when parents' rights to a sibling have been involuntarily terminated or when parents have murdered or committed manslaughter of another child. In determining the reasonable efforts to be made, the child's health and safety must be the paramount concern.

*Assign the initial investigation of cases of substantial abuse and neglect to the police and the criminal justice system:* Charges of child abuse and neglect, even in severe cases, are handled in many states by social workers. Shifting the assignment of investigative duties to the police and criminal justice system would eliminate the inherent conflict of interest of the child welfare system that currently frequently investigates and, at the same time, apportions resources for children who are found to be victims of abuse or neglect. (The police and the criminal justice system are also more likely to follow proper criminal investigative procedures and requirements, such as notifying suspects of their rights at appropriate stages of an investigation. In many instances, procedural errors alone cause substantial delays in the termination of parental rights.)

*Establish a rebuttable presumption of unfitness in the child welfare law:* This means, for example, that the intentional infliction of serious injury or the killing of a child or spouse must be presumptive grounds for the termination of parental rights for all surviving children.

*Shorten the timetable for the initial hearings on the termination of parental rights:* Instead of delays that can last for years, the timetable for initial hearings for children removed from their homes should be shortened to 12 months (as recommended by H.R. 867). Such hearings would be strengthened by requiring that the expected permanency outcomes—including whether and when the child would be returned home, placed for adoption, or placed in a home for children— be a part of the child's written plan.

*Speed up the notification of judicial authorities of cases of parental rights termination:* Delays in the termination of parental rights occur simply because judges have not been notified until after all avenues of parental rehabilitation have been exhausted. We must notify judicial authorities at earlier stages of potential cases involving the termination of parental rights—particularly when a parent commits a felony against his or her child.

*Establish guidelines for the permanent placement of children:* We must establish enforceable timelines for the permanent placement of children after the termination of parental rights. These guidelines should include guidance for the pursuit of adoption and institutional placement options.[22]

*Place responsibility for rehabilitation on parents:* Where parental rehabilitation is an issue in termination of parental rights cases, we must place the responsibility for rehabilitation entirely on the parent. We must eliminate the objection to termination of parental rights based on services not having been provided to the parent by the government or some other service provider (e.g., drug treatment programs for addicted parents). Such objections currently delay many cases of parental rights terminations.

*What is best for the children should be made the central issue in cases of termination of parental rights:* Parental rights are, no doubt, important. In trying to protect the rights of parents, however, the care of the parents' children can suffer. In far too many cases, the rule of "what are the rights of the parents" takes precedence over "what is best for the children."

*Require concurrent case planning for both reunification and termination of parental rights:* Often, attempts to terminate parental rights are initiated only after repeated efforts to rehabilitate parents have failed, resulting in prolonged stays for the children in the foster care system. If termination proceedings are initiated at the same time that efforts to rehabilitate are begun, and if reunification of a child with his or her parents is not possible, the termination of parental rights can proceed expeditiously.

*Evaluate parents' fitness to be parents at the beginning of child abuse and neglect cases:* The most fervently contested parental rights termination cases are usually those of neglect (rather than abuse). Often, the termination of parental rights is delayed because psychological and substance abuse evaluations of parents are not conducted until rehabilitation efforts have failed. These cases could be processed more quickly and soundly by initiating parental evaluations at the beginning of the investigations.

*Use public funds to encourage child care innovations:* In restructuring current federal law (specifically, Title IV), Congress should allow states maximum flexibility in the use of those funds among various care options, including institutional care. The purpose is to encourage new care options by more groups.

## ■ Concluding Comments

The child welfare system in the United States is helping hundreds of thousands of children. There are obvious problems within the system, however, including the lack of permanent care being received by many children. Private children's homes have never been a dominant form of care for children in need nor will they be a dominant form in the future. Nevertheless, many of today's disadvantaged children could benefit from the type of permanent care that children's homes have demonstrated they can provide. The evidence is mounting that children's homes have worked well in the past, are working well now, and can work even better in the future.

Institutional care has always been and will continue to be an imperfect substitute for loving biological, adoptive, or other substitute parents. It can, however, be an improvement in the care provided to many hard-to-place children compared to what they would otherwise receive. When loving and responsible parental care is not possible, children need, at the very least, the basic amenities of life. They also need permanency and security. The recommendations tendered here are intended to provide disadvantaged children with more opportunities to find that permanence and security in their lives.

# Appendix

# Rethinking Orphanages
for the 21st Century

*A Symposium in Search of Reforms
for the Nation's Child Welfare System*

Newport Beach, California
June 6 through 8, 1997

## List of Symposium Attendees and Observers

Ms. Melissa Beall
Office of Congressman Todd Tiahrt
428 Cannon House Office Building
Washington, D.C. 20515
(202) 225-6216; Fax: 225-3489
*mbeall@hr.house.gov*

Dr. Cassie Bevan
Ways and Means Committee
B317 Rayburn House Office Building
U.S. House of Representatives
Washington, D.C. 20515
(202) 225-1025; Fax: 225-9480
*cassie.bevan@mail.house.gov*

Mr. Dennis Braziel, Director
Group and Residential Care
Child Welfare League of America
440 1st Street, NW
Washington, D.C. 20001-2028
(202) 942-0314; Fax: 638-4004
*dbraziel@cwla.org*

Mr. Robert Chitister
Idea Channel
10539 Edinboro Rd.
McKean, PA 16426
(814) 476-7721; Fax: 476-1283
*ccabob@erie.net*

Ms. Conna Craig, President
Institute for Children, Inc.
18 Brattle Street
Cambridge, MA 02138
(617) 491-4614; Fax: 491-4673
*ccraig@ifcinc.org*

Professor Michael DeBow
Cumberland Law School
Samford University
Birmingham, AL 35229
(205) 870-2434; Fax: 970-2587
*medebow@samford.edu*

Dr. Glenn Ellmers, Research Fellow
The Claremont Institute for the Study of
Statesmanship and Political Philosophy
250 First Street, Suite 330
Claremont, CA 91711
(909) 621-6825; Fax: 626-8724
*ellmers@msn.com*

Professor Richard Gelles
Family Violence Research Program
University of Rhode Island
509A Chafee Social Science Center
Kingston, RI 02881
Phone/Fax: (401) 792-4138
*Gelles@uriacc.uri.edu*

Ms. Heidi Goldsmith, Executive Director
International Center for Residential
   Education
3726 Connecticut Avenue, NW, # 109
Washington, D.C. 20008
(202) 966-4304; Fax: 244-0820
*irehg@aol.com*

Mr. Derek Herbert
Institute for Children
18 Brattle Street
Cambridge, MA 02138
(617) 491-4691; Fax: 491-4673
*dherbert@ifcinc.org*

Ms. Carolyn Hicks
Legislative Director
Office of Congressman Dan Burton
2185 Rayburn House Office Building
U.S. House of Representatives
Washington, D.C. 20515
(202) 225-2276; Fax: 225-0016
*carolyn@burton.house.gov*

Mr. James Jones
Milton Hershey School
Founders Hall—Box 830
Hershey, PA 17033
(717) 520-2445; Fax: 520-2444
*sloaner@hershey.pvt.k12.pa.us*

The Honorable Kathleen Kearney
Circuit Judge, 17th Circuit of Florida
Broward County Courthouse
201 SE 6th Street
Fort Lauderdale, FL 33301
(954) 831-7093; Fax: 831-5572
*kkear1386@aol.com*

Professor Dwight Lee
Department of Economics
University of Georgia
Athens, GA 30602
(706) 542-3970; Fax: 542-4144
*lee@rigel.econ.uga.edu*

Dr. Allen Leland
20/20/20 Project, Lutheran Church
90 Faculty Street
Thousand Oaks, CA 91360
(805) 492-1121

Professor Douglas Magnuson
College of Saint Catherine
Project on Vocation, Work, and Youth
   Development
Box 4165
2004 Randolph Avenue
St. Paul, MN 55105
(612) 690-8718; Fax: 690-6024
*douglas_magnuson@pandora.stkate.edu*

Mr. Justine Matlick, Senior Researcher
Pacific Research Institute
755 Sansome Street, Suite 450
San Francisco, CA 94111
(415) 989-0833; Fax: 989-2411
*pripp@aol.com*

Ms. Karen McKenzie
3 Owen court
Irvine, CA 92612
(714) 854-7156
*kaminirvine@worldnet.att.net*

Professor Richard McKenzie
Symposium Organizer
Graduate School of Management
University of California, Irvine
Irvine, CA 92717-3125
O: (714) 824-2604; H: 854-7156;
Fax: 824-8469
*mckenzie@uci.edu*

Dr. Richard Pierce
Dean of Community Life
Milton Hershey School
Hershey, PA 17033
(717) 520-2061; Fax: 520-2068
*lepleyw@hershey.pvt.k12.pa.us*

Mr. Robert Stansel, President
Barium Springs Home for Children
P.O. Box 1
Barium Springs, NC 28010-0001
(704) 872-4257; Fax: 838-1541

Mr. Bernie Stumbras, President
SOS Villages, USA
1906 Capital Avenue
Madison, WI 53705
(608) 238-4584; Fax: 238-4611
*stumbras@midplains.net*

Mr. Donald Verleur, CEO
Olive Crest
2130 E. Fourth Street, Suite 200
Santa Ana, CA 92705
(714) 543-5437 ext. 115; Fax: 543-5463
*dverleur@aol.com*

Mr. David Villiotti
Executive Director
Nashua Children's Association
125 Amherst Street
Nashua, NH 03060-2043
(603) 883-3851; Fax: 883-5925

Mr. John Walters, President
Philanthropy Roundtable
1150 17th Street, NW, Suite 503
Washington, D.C. 20036
(202) 822-8333; Fax: 822-8325
*philtable@aol.com*

Dr. Delores Wardell
Licensed Clinical Psychologist
540 N. Golden Circle Drive, Suite 114
Santa Ana, CA 92705
(714) 558-0971; Fax: 550-0166
*wardell@pacbell.net*

Ms. Margaret MacFarlane Wright,
    Attorney
MARGARET MACFARLANE WRIGHT
A Professional Corporation
2472 Chambers Road, Suite 150
Tustin, CA 92780
(714) 832-9440; Fax: 832-9545
*mmwright@aol.com*

## ▓ Notes

1. The reform agenda presented at the end of this chapter was worked out at a 3-day symposium that was held in Newport Beach, California, and was sponsored by the Lynde and Harry Bradley Foundation. The symposium attendees, who generally support the proposed reforms, are listed in the appendix.

2. For details on the extent of the nation's problems of abuse and neglect, see Sedlak and Broadhurst (1996).

3. For a summary of statistics on child abuse and neglect, see Fagan and Hanks (1997).

4. For a review of the problems that potential adoptive parents face in their efforts to adopt children, see Craig (1995).

5. For a review of one state's child welfare system, see Matlick (1997).

6. For more details of the problems of the foster care system, see Bevan (1996).

7. No one knows how many children go through placements that reach into the dozens. Donald Veuleur, an officer in the Olive Crest home for children in Orange County, California, and Robert Stansel, president of Barium Springs Home for Children in Iredell County, North Carolina, attest to frequently working with children who may have been through three or four dozen foster placements.

8. For an example of how judges assess their options, see Chapter 3.

9. For reviews of beneficial residential children's programs in Israel, Africa, and Europe, see Beker and Magnuson (1996). For a review of the potential benefits of residential programs in the United States, see Goldsmith (1995).

10. For more information on SOS Villages-International, see the organization's home page: *www.sos.or.at/sos*. There are currently 361 SOS Children's Villages worldwide caring for approximately 30,000 children and supported by more than 6 million "friends" of the organization. All the world's major religions are represented in the villages, and each child is brought up in his or her own religion.

11. For an analysis of the cost of care at two child care institutions, see Chapter 15. Briefly, the authors of this chapter found that the annual cost of care at one home for severely troubled children was more than $64,000 per child in 1995, the annual cost of care in a home for disadvantaged children was more than $32,000 per child, and the annual cost of care per child at both institutions in 1950 (when they cared for disadvantaged children) was less than $7,500 per child in 1995 dollars.

12. For a summary of the criticisms, see Ford and Kroll (1995).

13. For a brief history of the orphanage movement in this country, see Chapter 5 and Seita et al. (1996). For histories of individual homes that appeared to have served a substantial majority of their children well, see Cmiel (1995), Goldstein (1996), and Zmora (1994). For a review of the scholarly child care literature as it relates to orphanage care, see Chapter 8 and Children's Bureau (1995).

14. The overwhelming majority of the respondents indicated that they maintain favorable assessments of their orphanage experience (see Chapter 7).

15. See Chapter 7 and Goldsmith (1995). For more information on SOS Children's Villages-International, use the following web site: *http://www.netwing.at/sos/*.

16. Foster care placements fell from one half million in the late 1970s to 300,000 by the mid-1980s. As noted, however, placements increased to more than 600,000 by the early 1990s. See Pelton (1989), Tatara (n.d.), and U.S. Advisory Board on Child Abuse and Neglect (1993).

17. For discussions of the problems children must face because of family rehabilitation and reunification efforts, see Chapters 3 and 4 and Gelles (1996).

18. For a political assessment of the growth of the child welfare system, see Chapters 10 and 11. Bordeaux and Bordeaux (Chapter 10) write, "Such a program creates clear incentives to place

children in foster care families. In addition to the open-endedness of these funds, the fact that under the AFDC program "administrative costs" of social services agencies were shared on a 50/50 basis with the federal government, further encouraged the bureaucratic tendency to grow like kudzu. That is, social services agencies were receiving unlimited funds from federal coffers for AFDC payments, which, as of 1961, included some foster children, and agencies were splitting administrative costs with the federal government. The greater the number of children placed with foster care families, the larger the child welfare agency budget" (pp. 182). The authors quote the *Encyclopedia of Social Work* (1987, p. 642), which concludes that "[s]tates that were heavily dependent on [AFDC foster care] funds had no incentives to move children out of foster care because funding was lost each time a child was discharged from placement."

19. For a set of policy recommendations designed specifically to curb child abuse, see Fagan and Hanks (1997).

20. Under H.R. 867, as amended by a bipartisan proposal accepted by voice vote, the current child welfare system would be reformed in numerous ways that are endorsed in this chapter: Certain aggravated circumstances involving children would be identified in which states can bypass or discontinue efforts to reunite abused or neglected children with their family; financial incentives would be provided to the states to move more children out of foster care and into adoptive families; and, for children under the age of 10 who have spent a substantial portion of their lives in foster care, states would be required to move expeditiously toward freeing these children for adoption—the timetable for the hearing that determines the child's future placement would be shortened from 18 months to 1 year; and states would be required to provide foster parents and relatives notice of all hearings and reviews. Additional minor and technical amendments are also included in the bill.

21. For an analysis of the extent and impact of institutional child care regulations in six states, see Chapter 13.

22. As recommended by H.R. 867, states would have to document steps taken to find and finalize an adoptive or other permanent home for the child, including placement in the custody of another fit and willing relative or home for children. Of course, biological and foster parents and relatives providing child care would be notified of reviews and permanency hearings regarding child placement and would be given the opportunity to be heard at these proceedings.

## ▓ References

Adoption Promotion Act of 1997, H.R. 867, 105th Cong., 1st Sess. 105 77 (April 28, 1997) (*http://thomas.loc.gov/cgi-bin/query/z?c105:h.r.867*).

Batten, T. (1997, July 30). Child safety tops family in senate vote. *Charlotte Observer,* p. C1.

Beker, J., & Magnuson, D. (1996). *Residential education as an option for at-risk youth.* New York: Haworth.

Bevan, C. S. (1996). *Foster care: Too much, too little, too early, too late.* Washington, DC: National Council for Adoption.

Children's Bureau. (1995, May). *Orphanage background materials.* Washington, DC: U.S. Department of Health and Human Services.

Cmiel, K. (1995). *A home of a different kind: One Chicago orphanage and the tangle of child welfare.* Chicago: University of Chicago Press.

Craig, C. (1995, Summer). What I need is a mom. *Policy Review,* 41-49.

*Encyclopedia of social work.* (18th ed.). (1987). Silver Spring, MD: National Association of Social Workers.

Fagan, P., & Hanks, D. B. (1997, May 15). The child abuse crisis: The disintegration of marriage, family, and the American community. In *Backgrounder.* Washington, DC: Heritage Foundation.

Ford, M., & Kroll, J. (1995, March). *There is a better way: Family-based alternatives to institutional care* (Research Brief No. 3). Washington, DC: North American Council on Adoptable Children.

Gelles, R. (1996). *The book of David: How preserving children can cost children's lives.* New York: Basic Books.

Goldsmith, H. (1995). *Residential education: An option for America's youth.* Hershey, PA: Milton Hershey School.

Goldstein, H. (1996). *The home on Gorham Street and the voices of its children.* Tuscaloosa: University of Alabama Press.

Matlick, J. (1997, March). *Fifteen years of failure: An assessment of California's child welfare system.* San Francisco: Pacific Research Institute.

Pelton, S. L. (1989). *For reasons of poverty: A critical analysis of the public child welfare system in the United States.* New York: Praeger.

Sedlak, A. J., & Broadhurst, D. D. (1996, September). *The third national incidence study of child abuse and neglect: Final report.* Washington, DC: U.S. Department of Health and Human Services, National Center on Child Abuse and Neglect.

Seita, J., Mitchell, M., & Tobin, C. (1996). *In whose best interest: One child's odyssey, a nation's responsibility.* Elizabethtown, PA: Continental.

SOS Children's Villages, USA. (1997, February 6). *A challenge to the nation: Safe and permanent homes for children* (Report to President William Clinton on adoption reform, p. 3). Alexandria, VA: Author.

Tatara, T. (n.d.). *Characteristics of children in substitute and adoptive care.* Washington, DC: American Public Welfare Association, Voluntary Cooperative Information System.

U.S. Advisory Board on Child Abuse and Neglect. (1993). *Child abuse and neglect: First steps in response to a national emergency: 1990.* Washington, DC: U.S. Department of Health and Human Services.

Zmora, N. (1994). *Orphanages reconsidered: Child care institutions in Progressive Era Baltimore.* Philadelphia: Temple University Press.

# Index

# About the Authors

**David J. Boudreaux** is President of the Foundation for Economic Education. He is author of "A Modest Proposal to Deregulate Infant Adoptions" (*Cato Journal*).

**Karol C. Boudreaux** is a research associate at the Center for Policy Research at Clemson University. She received a JD from the University of Virginia and is a PhD candidate at the University of Georgia.

**Del Bradshaw** is a certified public accountant and a founding partner of the accounting firm of Bradshaw, Gordon, and Clinkscale, P.A., in Greenville, South Carolina.

**William F. Chappell** is Associate Professor of Economics in the Department of Economics and Finance at the University of Mississippi.

**Conna Craig** is President and a trustee of the Institute for Children in Cambridge, Massachusetts. She advises governors, members of Congress, and other opinion leaders on restructuring foster care and adoption so that every child has the chance to grow up in a permanent family. She is author of "What I Need Is a Mom: The Welfare State Denies Homes to Thousands of Foster Children" (*Policy Review*, 1995, summer).

**Michael DeBow** is a professor in the Law School at Samford University in Birmingham, Alabama.

**Richard J. Gelles** is the Joanne and Raymond Welsh Chair of Child Welfare and Family Violence, School of Social Work, University of Pennsylvania. He is author of *The Book of David: How Preserving Families Can Cost Children's Lives* (1996).

**Heidi Goldsmith** is Executive Director of the International Center for Residential Education in Washington, D.C. She is author of *Residential Education: An Option for America's Youth* (Milton Hershey School, 1995).

**Derek Herbert** is Associate Director of the Institute for Children in Cambridge, Massachusetts. He directed the institute's 2-year study of public child welfare programs in all 50 states, which resulted in the publication of *The State of the Children: An Examination of Government-Run Foster Care* (National Center for Policy Analysis, 1997).

**Dwight R. Lee** is the Ramsey Professor of Economics at the University of Georgia at Athens. His many publications are in the area of public-choice economics, or the application of economic theory to political decision making.

**Ross D. London** is Juvenile Court Referee with the Superior Court of New Jersey and PhD candidate at Rutgers University School of Criminal Justice. He is a consultant on delinquency issues to the U.S. Department of Justice and is author of many articles, including "Early Childhood Intervention: A New Vision for Inner-City Education" in *Task Force Report of the American Society of Criminology* (1995).

**Joseph L. Maxwell III** is Field Representative for the Palmer Home for Children in Mississippi and editor of *Regeneration Quarterly*.

**John N. McCall** is Emeritus Professor of Psychology at Southern Illinois University-Edwardsville. He received a PhD in psychology from the University of Minnesota. He was raised at Barium Springs Home for Children in North Carolina during the 1930s and 1940s.

**Richard B. McKenzie** is the Walter B. Gerken Professor of Enterprise and Society in the Graduate School of Management at the University of California, Irvine. In addition to many other books and articles on economics and management, he is author of *The Home: A Memoir of Growing Up in an*

*Orphanage* (Basic Books, 1996). He was raised at Barium Springs Home for Children in North Carolina during the 1950s.

**Estella May Moriarty** is a circuit court judge in Fort Lauderdale, Florida. She has served on the board of directors of SOS Children's Village of Florida, CHARLEE Family Homes for Broward County, and Covenant House, Florida.

**Marvin Olasky** is a professor at the University of Texas and editor of *World,* a Christian weekly news magazine. He is author of 14 books, including *The Tragedy of American Compassion* and *Abortion Rites.*

**William F. Shughart II** is Professor of Economics in the Department of Economics and Finance at the University of Mississippi. He has published widely in public choice and policy economics.

**Margaret MacFarlane Wright** is a practicing attorney, specializing in labor law, in Irvine, California. She has also lectured in the Cornell University Law School.

**Donald Wyant** is a certified public accountant with the accounting firm of Bradshaw, Gordon, and Clinksdale, P.A., in Greenville, South Carolina.